Comparative Politics

Starting from the principal–agent perspective, this book offers a new analysis of government. It interprets political institutions as devices designed to solve the omnipresent principal–agent game in politics. In other words how to select, instruct, monitor and evaluate political agents or elites so that they deliver in accordance with the needs and preferences of their principal: the population.

This book explores whether there are any evolutionary mechanisms in politics which guide mankind towards the rule of law regime, domestically and globally. It combines a cross-sectional approach with a longitudinal one.

Comparing the extent of the rule of law among states, using a set of data from 150 countries concerning political and social variables, the author seeks to understand why there is such a marked difference among states. Taking a state-centred perspective and looking at countries with a population larger than one million people during the post-Second World War period, the book examines:

- the stability and performance of states;
- the conditions for the rule of law regime: economic, social, cultural and institutional;
- the evolution of governments towards rule of law.

Comparative Politics: The principle–agent perspective will be of interest to students and scholars of comparative politics, government, political theory and law.

Jan-Erik Lane is professor of comparative politics at the University of Geneva and he also teaches at the University of the South Pacific.

Routledge research in comparative politics

Comparative Politics

The principal–agent perspective

Jan-Erik Lane

Routledge
Taylor & Francis Group

LONDON AND NEW YORK

First published 2008
by Routledge
2 Park Square, Milton Park, Abingdon, Oxon OX14 4RN

Simultaneously published in the USA and Canada
by Routledge
270 Madison Ave, New York, NY 10016

Routledge is an imprint of the Taylor & Francis Group, an informa business

© 2008 Jan-Erik Lane

Typeset in Garamond by Wearset Ltd, Boldon, Tyne and Wear
Printed and bound in Great Britain by TJI Digital, Padstow,
Cornwall

British Library Cataloguing in Publication Data
A catalogue record for this book is available from the British Library

Library of Congress Cataloging in Publication Data
A catalog record for this book has been requested

ISBN10: 0-415-43206-5 (hbk)
ISBN10: 0-203-93554-3 (ebk)

ISBN13: 978-0-415-43206-1 (hbk)
ISBN13: 978-0-203-93554-5 (ebk)

Contents

Illustrations

Figures

Tables

Appendices

Foreword

The key problem in comparative politics being how to account for the variation in macro-political institutions, this book starts from the assumption that political regimes involve in one way or another a resolution to principal–agent problems in politics. They concern: How does one select, instruct and monitor rulers or politicians so that they govern a country in the interests of the principal of the political body, namely the population? This assumption sets the book off from other approaches to comparative politics and links this subdiscipline of political science with recent advances in game theory and the economics of information. The structure of the book in three parts follows from my ambition to offer a concise presentation of one of the main themes in comparative politics, namely *rule of law*, in terms of principal–agent theory.

Part I derives the core problems of political stability and democracy from a micro foundation in the principal–agent approach. According to this approach, the principal would search for institutions that *constrain* the agents, leading them to exercise political power in a predictable and accountable manner. Chapter 1 makes a survey of the states of the world as they may be counted today, looking at various properties of statehood, in particular state persistence, with state stability in general and regime longevity in particular discussed at length. In Chapter 2, state performance is analysed, including the record of states in terms of rule of law as well as key policy outputs and social outcomes.

Part II probes into the general conditions for rule of law. Chapter 3 focuses on the set of structural conditions and their consequences for rule of law. Employing various typologies for the presentation of institutions, Chapter 4 discusses the impact of salient institutions. In Chapter 5 the problem of regime transition is brought up, namely how states have recently tried to introduce economic and political regimes that restrain elites. Chapter 6 explores the implications of principal–agent theory for understanding electoral volatility in democracies.

Part III outlines an evolutionary theory explaining how systems of political authority develop. Chapter 7 identifies the key political selection mechanisms. Chapter 8 examines city states and ancient empires. Chapter 9 explores ancient empires, and Chapter 10 analyses feudalism: ancient and modern, while Chapter 11 deals with the modern state and colonialism. Chapter 12 examines the regionalisation of the state, and the concluding chapter states the case for the evolutionary superiority of the rule of law regime.

This study is based on a selected set of some 150 countries, all with a population larger than one million, for which Svante Ersson (in Parts I and II) managed to gather a set of data concerning political, economic and social variables. To come to grips with the immense variation in data about state and country characteristics around the world, I will use a country classification with 11 categories. The country categories in this classification include: (1) Arab, (2) Western Europe, (3) Eastern Europe, (4) other occidentals: North America and Australia plus New Zealand as well as Israel, (5) South Asia, (6) Sub-Saharan Africa, (7) Muslim non-Arab, (8) Latin America, (9) Turkish: Turkey and Central Asia, (10) Asean plus 3 and (11) The Pacific (The Philippines and Papua New Guinea). This classification takes a number of factors into account such as religion, ethnicity and historical legacy. It is based upon the recently surging interest in culture in general and civilisations in particular (Huntington, 1997; Lane and Ersson, 2005).

The level of exposition has been kept elementary, as my hope is that the volume could be used in graduate courses in comparative politics. Applying the principal–agent approach to comparative government, it looks upon the rulers or the politicians as the agents of the population, raising crucial questions about motivation, remuneration, monitoring and information as well as especially the rules that channel this interaction. I have drawn upon the Lane and Rohner article "Institution Building and Spillovers" in *Swiss Political Science Review* (2004), Vol. 10 (1): 77–90, as well as the Lane and Ersson article "Party System Instability in Europe: Persistent Differences in Volatility between West and East?" in *Democratization* (2007), Vol. 14 (1): 92–110. I could not have written this book without all the data assistance of Svante Ersson (Umea university) and the correctional skills of Sylvia Dumons (University of Geneva). The basic ideas in this volume were presented at seminars in the Political Science Department at the Hebrew University in Jerusalem and the University of South Pacific in Suva. I wish to acknowledge the assistance provided by a Hebrew University Forchheimer Visiting Professorship in the Department of Political Science in the spring of 2006.

Introduction

Micro foundations of comparative politics

Comparative politics has known a number of approaches, from the so-called traditional framework (classical institutionalism) over functionalism and systems analysis and the dependency approach to rational choice and neo-institutionalism or new institutionalism (Almond *et al.*, 2003; Newton and van Deth, 2005). The principal–agent framework for analysing how one group of actors – the principal – contracts with another set of actors – the agents – to get things done, has received increasing attention in economics and business administration (Laffont, 2003). The time has come to explore what this model offers when interpreting politics, either in micro studies such as elections or in macro studies such as with comparative politics. Polities are social systems that certain actors operate for specific purposes. Political systems are supported by certain groups of people and sometimes opposed by other groups. Polities give rise to benefits and costs for the human beings involved, which can best be stated in terms of the principal–agent model.

The basic motive in politics with the population is, I surmise, safety. Human beings set up and support political regimes because they wish to live in safety against foreign intruders or domestic violence. Thus a political community arises from the need for protection. Economies of scale explain why the community would turn to a set of agents to handle this protection, namely the rulers or the politicians (Olson, 2001; Barzel, 2002). Yet, how can the population contract with agents who take on this task concerning concrete objectives, tools of governance, remuneration of agents and so on? First and foremost, the principal would be interested in having influence over the agent as to selection, monitoring, dismissal, renewal and so on.

Thus, a political community in this model would have two kinds of interests: (1) peace and security; (2) control over the agents and decent remuneration of them. Political communities tend to regard foreign intrusion as especially threatening. Thus, they search for some mechanism that can offer protection against invasion. Similarly, internal political stability is high in esteem, since the population would wish to stay away from the Hobbesian predicament: war of all against all (*bellum omnium contra omnes*). The political community may be protected by a set of agents, the rulers, but who protects the community against the rulers if they wish to engage in oppression of their own community, or if they turn greedy, searching for huge resources in order to pay for pharaonic enterprises or their own lavish consumption? Juvenal, satirical poet of the late first and early second century AD, stated the rhetorical question *"Quis custodiet ipsos custodes?"* ("Who shall guard the guards themselves?") in *On Women*, discussing the usefulness of having eunuchs guard one's women. Thus, the rule of law perspective upon government arises as one solution to Juvenal's question.

Primarily, a polity provides protection of the life of the members of the community. The regime would need to keep out potential intruders as well as make sure that the internal order is not threatened by insurgency. When there are no outside threats from other political communities, then regime survival hinges upon internal matters. When a country has external and internal stability, then there results a total value, V, to society, covering economic and non-economic benefits from peace and prosperity. The size of V will vary with the type of society and its degree of economic advancedness.

Crucial here is the nature of the contract between the population and its guardian agents. Although the agents and the political community have similar interests in fending off foreign intruders and domestic anarchy or anomie, they differ in their opinions about the rights and privileges of the agents vis-à-vis the political community. Assuming that agents attempt to maximise their share of the community resources, they would be inclined or tend to loot, meaning amassing as much of the resources as they can for themselves unless constrained. Again assuming an ambition to maximise utility, the political community would prefer a modest remuneration for its agents, just enough to elicit a large effort. This sets up a game where the outcome will depend upon the capacity of the agents to drive the community to pay remuneration for the services of the agents out of the total value of society, V.

Both the community and the agents wish to safeguard the value V for themselves, keeping out intruders. This constitutes the basis of collaboration between the political community and the agents. Conflict arises concerning the division of V between the agents on the one hand, securing V(A), and the community on the other hand, to be given V(C) = V − V(A). The agents may, theoretically, be prepared to invest resources into the effort of maximising V(A) up to the limit where all of V(A) is dissipated. The political community would first and foremost look for a share of V that enables them to survive. When they are confronted by such predatory capture of V by the agents that their survival level is threatened, then uproar would be a rational strategy to pursue in order to push back the share V(A) of V. The principal may wish to limit the time that agents can enjoy the full value of government, opening up these tasks to competition. The principal will attempt to institutionalise the remuneration V(A).

One may conceive of alternative outcomes of the interaction between the political community and its guardian agents that become enshrined in the regime, as it were:

1 *Subjugation or oppression*: The agents conquer a community and treat all its value as belonging to them, or the agents install themselves as masters, treating the population as slaves or serfs. Agents force the population to deliver a huge chunk of the value V to them through, for instance, harsh taxation or abusive tax farming. Agents will loot whenever feasible.
2 *Mixed citizenship*: Part of the population is singled out for better treatment by the agents than the others, rendering to them the rights of citizenship (*Apartheid*). A large share of V will end up with the agents and the favoured part of the population (*nomenklatura*).
3 *Full citizenship*: The entire population is recognised as citizens with certain rights, also in relation to the agents. The compensation of agents is limited, leaving a considerable share of V to the political community (VC), although agents will demand compensation for their work.
4 *Rule of law*: The agents are bound by the law to respect institutions that guarantee against arbitrariness and secure a large number of rights for the citizens. Since agents will no longer be secure in power positions, they will want to be paid a decent remuneration.

A number of factors impact upon the outcomes (1)–(4), to be discussed below. These include the nature of the economy: commercial, agrarian or industrial; the culture: religion and ethnicity; as well as the geographical environment: intruders or not. Agents may pursue two kinds of strategies in relation to total value V in society. Either they take their stake after they have tried to maximise V, or they try to maximise their stake at the cost of a lower total value in society. When agents turn greedy, they often claim a huge part of the total value, which as a result dwindles. At the extreme, the rulers grab what they can and then more or less destroy the remaining value. The outcome of the principal–agent games in politics will depend upon the institutions handed down by the polity.

Institutions are the rules that constrain behaviour. In a principal–agent perspective upon government, the rules that structure authority and deliver competences and rights are crucial for structuring and restraining the political elites, the agents. They would tend to develop over time in a direction that favours the position of the principal, at least in a long-run perspective upon the evolution of regimes. Governance in general and government in particular involves a resolution to two major difficulties that arise when the population hires a set of agents to provide them with public policies that could in general be desirable to the people. They stem from various kinds of opportunistic behaviour on the part of the agent:

- *Pretending*, or the difficulty to spot the nature of the agent and his/her promises when making up a contract with him/her.

- *Reneging*, meaning that the agent says one thing but does another once the contract has been signed or closed.

Political institutions help resolve these major difficulties, called "adverse selection" and "moral hasard" in game theory (Rasmusen, 2006). Thus, rules may limit the time-span of political agency, and they may call for competition, meaning the disclosure of information about the hidden nature of agents as well as their hidden actions. Political institutions may invite some agents to check other agents, or allow certain agents to undo what other agents have decided. In my view, only the institutions of the rule of law offer sufficient protection against the opportunism of the agents, either *ex ante* or *ex post* the governance contract.

Thus, politics may be approached as an interaction between political elites and the population that lasts for a substantial period of time. In a democracy, this time frame is set by the rules for elections. Following this line of thought, one may look upon the state budget as a contract under which the people of a country put up resources to the government, which employs these to supply goods and services. In this interaction, it is the political elite that has the upper hand, since it tends to be much better informed about state matters. The government as a set of political agents may perform more or less adequately, but it would still claim remuneration from the resources of the state.

Given these stylised facts about government and political elites, one would wish to venture a model of politics as principal–agent games. The principal–agent model, originating in game theory with asymmetric information, has afforded interesting insights into contracting in the private sector. Just as insurance, litigation, farming and health care may be seen as contracting between principals and agents, so politics may be interpreted as a contract between people and politicians. It is not a one-shot contract but a relationship that unfolds through time where the politicians are evaluated on the basis of their promises and the outcomes. The question then arises: If politics is a principal–agent game, then what institutions strengthen the principal in relation to the agents restraining them?

Politics as a series of principal–agent games

Politics, as stated above, unfolds in the interaction among people. Max Weber's classical theory of authority identified schematically three key groups: (1) the power holders, (2) their servants (e.g. bureaucracy) and (3) the population (Weber, 1978). Politics is restrained in the interaction between these three main groups through explicit or implicit contracts that vary enormously in content, scope and enforcement. The models of asymmetric information have been used to understand contracting in the private sector, but they also offer insights into contracting in the public sector. Thus, the problem of bureaucracy (efficiency, size, budget expansion) appears to be the outcome of an asymmetric information game: principal–agent contracting. The time has come to consider also whether the Weberian relationship between the power holders (1) and the population (3) can be modelled as principal–agent games.

When the interaction between the power holders (1) and their servants (2) is modelled as an asymmetric information game, then these models unravel the risks involved for the principal when contracting with agents or agencies about the implementation of policies. It is true that the power holders, whatever their titles may be, cannot execute or implement their own policies without a large body of assisting organisations ("servants"), but the implementers of policy will not constitute a machine to be commended in a top-down fashion.

The problem, called the politics/administration separation, is endemic whatever form of administration is chosen. The administrative arm of government is not a simple machinery of people to turn to, operating always at maximum efficiency. Instead, the lessons from the discipline of public administration are that policy implementation moves along a road of many pitfalls and aberrations – *the science of muddling through*. The economic theory of information would summarise these difficulties, perhaps insurmountable, under two categories: moral hazard – *ex post* opportunism; and adverse selection – *ex ante* opportunism.

In public administration, there is always the danger that bureaux deviate from the pursuit of the objectives decided by their political masters, or that the bureaux engage in the maximisation of slack. Weber was, of course, well aware of this danger, speaking of "*Beamtenherrschaft*", where the bureaux take over the role of the government or Parliament, and "*Satrapenherrschaft*", where the bureaux start capturing turfs (Weber, 1978).

Yet Weber favoured bureaucracy, because he evaluated other principal–agent relationships from an historical point of view, rejecting traditional authority and charismatic domination due to their administrative inefficiency: arbitrariness or incompetence. He failed to see the relevance of market relationships to the conduct of government operations, which is what NPM has launched a theory about: tendering/bidding, contracting out or in, and the buying and selling of public services provision.

Moral hazard occurs when one contracting partner changes his/her behaviour following the conclusion of the contract – typically called "shirking", which however captures only one type of post-contractual opportunism. Adverse selection would not be difficult to exemplify from the history of political regimes where the servants of the ruler display their true nature by capturing the throne for themselves: the Mamluks in Egypt, the Carolingian *Major Domus* in France as well as the overturning of a king by one of his vassals (e.g. Simon de Montfort removing the English King).

If public administration and public management fit the principal–agent models, what to say about politics itself? This refers to the relationship between the population (3) and the power holders (1), as Weber called the political leaders. Before addressing this question, it may be worthwhile to pin down what the principal–agent model, and asymmetric information in contracting, is really all about.

Social interaction may target the production of an output with economic value, to be shared between a principal (owner of last resort) and an agent, working for the principal according to a contract with a long duration. Such contracts may be made between two persons (client – lawyer) or between one person and a group of people (landlord – sharecroppers), or finally among a large group of people and a small set of power holders (shareholders – managers, electorate – politicians). Assuming well-operating labour markets with perfect information, the principal would be able to contract with his preferred agent and pay a remuneration that maximises his profit, given that the contract offered is incentive compatible.

Enter asymmetric information and the principal is uncertain about whom he/she contracts with (adverse selection) and the probability of lacunae between the effort promised ex ante and the effort delivered ex post. If worse comes to worse, the principal may end up with a hefty loss when contracting high for big effort but receiving the meagre outcome of poor effort. There are three remedies against so-called opportunism on the part of the agent:

1   *Monitoring or surveillance*: It is costly and runs the risk of collusion between monitors and agents;
2   *Risk-sharing contracts*: The principal invites the agent to become a partner in sharing the final output, which is sometimes feasible;
3   *Retaliation*: The principal gets rid of the agent and may even try to spoil his/her reputation, if agent failure depends upon his/her negligence.

If a replay is allowed and the game extends over a long period involving several plays and replays, the outcome of the principal–agent interaction will reflect complexity. In general, it holds for several private sector market situations that the principal would favour to pay for low effort when he/she cannot observe effort or perhaps even verify it ex post. The same is true of bureaucracy. What, then, about high-profile public sector games, especially politics, i.e. the contract between the population and politicians?

Politics as principal–agent contracting

In a modern polity, it is the population at large that is considered to be the principal. It would need a state in order to provide for itself internal stability and foreign protection, following the classical public finance theory of government. Thus, politicians or rulers would be the agents of the people. This sets up the principal–agent game, in which the politicians will provide the population with policies that – presumably – promote the welfare of the country, while at the same time receiving remuneration in the form of a salary, fringe benefits, power and prestige.

There are two extreme solutions to this game, which may not be very probable and are certainly not desirable. They should however be stated as ideal-types between which real-life solutions are to be found:

1 *Looting*: The politicians monopolise the advantages for themselves, treating the population as a means to their own enrichment.
2 *Imperative mandate*: The politicians can only enact policies in accordance with concretely transmitted preferences by their electors.

Interestingly, whereas looting sometimes occurs today (e.g. Zimbabwe, North Korea, Myanmar), the institution of imperative mandates has rarely been applied. One may wish to refer to Burke's eloquent defence of the institution of free mandates, but it suffices to observe that the imperative mandate fails on transaction costs. Rousseau argued for a similar restriction of the role of politicians, confining them to merely execute the referenda. But modern polities do not operate in this way, since it is typical of the modern state that politicians have considerable autonomy as agents of the body politic. What rules or mechanisms would have an impact upon whether the game ends closer to looting or closer to the imperative mandate?

A ruler cannot govern a modern state by him/herself. Government would need a team of politicians – ministers, under-secretaries and policy consultants. When these politicians are seen as agents of the people, one has begun the journey towards a constitutional monarchy or democratic presidency.

Time

It matters whether there are rules restricting the time period of holding office. In general, the longer a ruler is in place, the less likely it is that the population will have the upper hand when it comes to distributing the gains from the work of its agents. Stated somewhat differently, the longer the rulers last, the more probable it is that they use their power to enrich themselves, eliminating whatever opposition may be forthcoming from the population.

In traditional or tribal authority, there tend to be few time limits upon ruling. In principle, the ruler and his family have a legitimate claim upon the throne of a hereditary nature. This does not exclude that they may at the end of the day seek legitimacy from the people, claiming that they rule in the best interests of each and every one. Religion has been used to sanction absolutist notions of rulership that of course deny the very nature of reciprocity in the principal–agent interaction. Today, such an approach is used in only a few Muslim countries.

The time limit upon presidents is actually sometimes more demanding than that for the premier, despite the fact that premiers would have to resign as soon as there is a vote of no confidence. Some premiers have lasted much longer than the usual two-times-four-year periods with presidents, although several presidents have often been tempted to extend their time in office through special techniques.

Representation

The population may demand that the agents be their agents, i.e. elected somehow by the people. In politics, the existence of several agents reflects diversity with the principal. The population has different interests, as evidenced by ethnic, religious or economic cleavages. If one agent were to represent all these interests, such an agent would have considerable autonomy to decide on a course that benefits first and foremost him/her. One may interpret this fact about representation in cost terms. When there are considerable differences in preferences among social groups in the population, then the costs could rise for certain groups, which lack proper representation among the agents. Thus, a multiparty system would, all other things being equal, reduce the potential losses for social groups. In a one-party state, the risk is not only that one social group (majority/minority) prevails over another for a long time, but also that the agent pursues his/her own agenda, favouring first and foremost him/herself.

Competition among multiple agents

The interests of the principal may require several agents, but there is nothing in principle that prevents collusion among agents. Sometimes one observes in multiparty systems a drift in the direction of the protection of agents' interests, as if the various agents were working together on a selfish agenda. When there is a grand coalition, the problem is recurrent.

Perhaps, then, it is not so much multiple agents that matter but adversity. Only when agents fight among each other – contestation in predictable manner – can there be protection of the interests of the principal. There must be at least a two-party system so that the principal can shift from one agent to another, forcing them to compete with each other. One may identify two classical models in politics that capture this insight from the principal–agent perspective. According to Schumpeter's elite democracy, agents using this approach will always constitute an elite in relation to the people. But they can be made to serve the people through competition. The difference between a democracy and a dictatorship is that competition in the former system is institutionally constrained, so that the outcomes are predictable and non-violent. In Downs' proximity model, various principals will seek out the agents that are closest to their core preferences. In a two-party system with one dimension (left–right), the agents will compete for the support of the median voter. In the directional model of party choice, the voters will seek agents who give direction for future policy change, even if they place themselves at policy extremes (Merrill and Grofman, 2005).

The competitive mechanism, however important it may be, may not be enough when there is asymmetric information. Competition among agents is modelled with Schumpeter and Downs as a one-stage game with perfect information. Starting from other assumptions, one arrives at the predicament that an agent promises one set of policies but delivers another. Somehow competition among agents is not enough.

Checks and balances

Agents need not compete for the same offices. They could restrain each other by occupying different offices that counterbalance the others. Such countervailing forces would reduce the opportunism of agents and force them to promote the common good of the principal. The classical mechanism was identified already by Montesquieu: *trias politica*.

Within the stylised structure of offices – executive, legislative and judicial – agents may be motivated to monitor each other against a common set of criteria, linked with public goods for the principal. Presidential regimes would in theory score high on *trias politica*, but in practice may be different, as presidents engage in *decretismo* as well as judicial intervention. A parliamentary regime, although fusing the executive with the legislature, may develop compensatory mechanisms that enhance *trias politica*, such as oversight committees, an Ombudsman office and select commissions.

There are two views about the relative ratio of advantages and disadvantages of judicial review, whether it takes the form of the American system or the Austrian-German system. One position maintains that it is vital for enhancing checks and balances, while another view claims that it leads to unnecessary judicial politicisation.

The existence of countervailing forces may, however, lead to blockage. Such agents, when being able to block each other, may turn into so-called veto-players (Tsebelis, 2002). Although this would make dictatorship unlikely, it may also make democracy pusillanimous. Agents may fight each other to such an extent that political instability or inertia result. This kind of political instability where agents block each other should be distinguished from volatility in the principal itself.

Electoral volatility

It has often been argued that multiple voter switches destabilise a state. Thus, if the principal delivers constantly changing parties, that would disrupt Parliament. Excessive voter volatility could be interpreted as a sign that the principal consists of too many diverse groups with little in common in their preferences. The established view on electoral volatility is that it is potentially dangerous for political stability. However, from a principal–agent perspective voter volatility may enhance the power of the principal over the agent.

To switch from one agent to another in an election offers a venue for evaluation, calling for the agent to be responsible for his/her actions or non-actions. Agency switches also work on the basis of anticipation, as agents would fear a massive switch towards a competitor. Thus, electoral volatility may indicate an active principal, evaluating the agent with the threat of desertion.

It is difficult to conceive how *new politics* could be introduced without electoral volatility. This would be the case especially in parliamentary systems based upon party governance; i.e. power rests with highly disciplined political parties that control the access of individual politicians to government positions. When the principal cannot get rid of the agent, it may not matter much that the principal can monitor the agent.

Monitoring and surveillance

Politics in a modern state is complex, involving issues with lots of various specialised knowledge. It is the agents who have the information advantage. The general public is poorly informed about the technicalities involved in policies. Public policies are done by huge bureaucracies harbouring expertise, often at combined levels of government. When things go wrong, it is far from obvious who is to blame. All policies rely upon probabilities. As nature changes, policy failure may result, although no one has committed any particular errors. How, then, are political agents to be held accountable? The principal may rely upon two tools of monitoring:

1   Political agents monitoring each other: Ombudsmen, select committees, parliamentary investigations, senate hearings.
2   Mass media surveillance.

These two forms of monitoring are not independent of each other, because the external news media rely to a large extent upon internal information-gathering in the political system. The occurrence of so-called leaks shows how well aware agents are about mass media effects.

If the gathering and spread of information is controlled by the agent, then the principal is in a weak position, being extremely vulnerable to asymmetric information advantages. Reducing asymmetric information may be done through specialised information-gathering and analysing agents – audit bureaux, efficiency task forces, evaluation or assessment groups – that may be public or private. Making enquiries into the doings and non-doings of agents may be linked with judicial analysis of responsibility – the Ombudsman office. Or it may be linked with reporting to Parliament.

When one set of political agents investigates another set, or when a bureaucracy examines political agents, there are two dangers:

1   *Collusion*: The investigating team participates in a cover-up either by hiding information or merely not transmitting it fully.

2   *Exaggeration*: The enquiry is partisan, expecting to score self-seeking benefits from the spread of rumours or half-truths.

The mass media is often considered to be so important to the political system that it is designated as the public discourse or the *fourth estate*. As long as it merely reports upon true information, its operations support the principal. However, the mass media may turn into a separate state within the state, directing the principal and the agents by selectively reporting news and spreading values. In Western elections, for instance, the mass media sometimes play a major role in influencing the scoring of the winning agent in elections.

Institutional mechanism: rule of law

A number of persuasive arguments have been launched stating the positive role of government in society. Some of them assume that government is a set of *benevolent* actors who target the public interest. Others assume that the struggle for power among various agents leads them towards the achievement of the common good – *private vices* – *public benefits* (Mandeville). Yet, from a principal–agent perspective, the guardian question can always be raised: *Sed quis custodiet ipsos custos?*

The arguments that state a positive role for government are numerous, including:

1   *Lord protector*: government offers safety against anarchy.
2   *Defensor pacis*: government assures peace in the country.
3   *A just society*: government creates and passes on the institutions for a well-ordered society.
4   *Welfare state*: government secures a minimum standard of living for each and every citizen.
5   *Chief regulator*: government enforces the rules of the economy, making sure that violations are punished with a high probability.
6   *Public goods promoter*: government supplies goods and services to society which no other party would have the incentive to do.

Even if one endorses all these six arguments in favour of the state, there would still be the guardian question, as governments take possession of the immense resources of the modern state. The arguments for a restriction of the role of government in society are equally numerous:

1   There is no such thing as the public interest. All interests are personal.
2   Public goods have enormous distribution impact, favouring some at the expense of others.
3   Government consists of people who always pursue egoistic goals.
4   Even if government were altruistic, it gets caught up by special interests.

5   Rent-seeking is typical of all public regulation.
6   Politicians are in the game for personal reasons besides their call. They seek some form of remuneration for their services.

Whether one looks upon government as a set of altruistic agents or as a set of Machiavellian agents, it is still the case that the guardian question arises. Altruistic politicians may develop in the wrong direction, as agents who are given an easy ride may be tempted to defect towards the employment of more vicious practices.

The agency problem is perhaps even graver in the public sector than in the private sector. When managers destroy a company, there are usually warning signs indicating to the owners that things are going wrong. In the state, such signs may elicit more repressive actions on the part of politicians. The power resources of the state tend to be bigger than those of private enterprise, except for multinationals, and these resources may be used at great harm to the principal.

Only rule of law offers the institutions necessary for channelling the ambitions of politicians as agents to promote on a long-term basis the interests of the population as principal. "Rule of law" is a complex term referring to a number of restrictions upon the state. Together, they work fundamentally against the looting strategy of the agent, monopolising the state on the basis of the claim that only he/she has the correct information about how to further the public interest. Rule of law also endorses representative institutions such as Parliament and its competences (budgeting, legislation, oversight and inquiry), undoing the relevance of the other extreme solution to the principal–agent game, the imperative mandate. The rule of law regime introduces rights and competences, restraining political elites.

Political agents and incentives

One may argue that the established approaches to comparative politics lack adequate micro-theoretical foundations. Polities are analysed as if they were actors, having needs and moving towards some sort of equilibrium. This is *reification*, or the fallacy of misplaced concreteness. Polities are aggregates made up of individual actors interacting in terms of the principal–agent relationship. Politicians would assume the role of agents of the population willingly, given that there is something to be gained for them in this interaction. The population would need to remunerate its politicians for handling government. The question of "how much" arises naturally in democratic politics, as the politicians and other agents are to be paid out of the resources of the country, i.e. ultimately GDP. The pecuniary rewards of the political agents involve a number of things: salary, expenses, allowances, perquisites. The non-pecuniary rewards may also be important to the politicians: prestige, power and reputation. The quid pro quo question arises in all democratic politics: How much remuneration is enough to elicit a major effort from politicians? The question of incentives is crucial in all principal–agent types of games (Macho-Stadler *et al.*, 2001; Ricketts, 2003; Campbell, 2006).

The pecuniary rewards for political office would have to come from taxes, i.e. ultimately from GDP. Although the money allocated to political agents may constitute a tiny portion of GDP, the population would still be interested in knowing whether paying more means a higher probability of better policy outcomes. All other things being equal, the principal would wish to pay less, given that the results are the same. The remuneration of the agents will always come out of the pockets of the population, meaning in the last resort from GDP. As GDP grows, so will the claims on remuneration from the politicians. One may speculate about whether the total costs for the remuneration of the politicians grow proportionately to GDP, or whether it outpaces the expansion of total societal resources. Take as examples the growth of the costs of the entire White House complex in Washington DC, including all agents with contracts with the President, or the Élysée Palace in Paris where the French President handles a huge budget.

The politicians will always motivate their costs with the work that they have to do for their people. The crux of the matter is that politicians get paid even when they offer poor service or minimum effort that may bring misery to the principal. This is why it is so essential to devise some mechanisms according to which politicians in power may be held responsible during their period of tenure, as well as to ensure that such tenure has a fixed time period so that badly performing agents can be removed. Actually, in democratic politics reward tends to be linked not so much with different salaries but with the possibility of staying in power. Of the three kinds of agents that the population employs in a democratic regime – executive, legislative and judicial – the pay is always highest for the executive agents, be they presidents or premiers. Then comes the remuneration of the legislators and finally the pay for the judges. In some countries the differentials in remuneration among executive, legislative and judicial agents may be very large, as judges in particular are paid on a lower scale. It may not always be in the interest of the principal to keep the pay of its agents low, as, for instance, a low remuneration of judges may indicate that the rule of law is poorly protected.

Executive agents tend to run big intelligence operations, using the argument that the business of modern government is growing increasingly complex, requiring much intelligence-gathering and analysis. However, paying for huge overheads in ministries is no safe guarantee for wise decisions. The principal would probably be more interested in funding certain agents that work directly for it, such as the Ombudsman, who is linked with the legislature and not the executive.

The peculiar nature of the contract between people and politicians appears in a clear form when the remuneration question is raised. It is difficult for the electorate to condition remuneration upon performance.

The crux of the matter is exactly that the electoral contract has no incentive mechanism built into it. Whether politicians are high-effort or low-effort agents, their pay cannot be differentiated during their period of tenure. Rewards can only be withheld during the re-election process, meaning that re-election is the key mechanism for linking performance with rewards. Only termination of the elected politicians will normally bring an end to his/her remuneration, with the exception of the pension that tends to be set favourably in several countries, at least relatively speaking.

The value of politicians is their net contribution to the total value in society. It need not be positive, as some governments cost a lot and achieve little. The value of total economic output is only an inaccurate measure of total value in society. Politicians may enhance non-economic values such as national identity, peace among minorities and a sense of direction for the future. But in any case, what politicians are paid must somehow come out of GDP.

Politicians display different skills besides expressing different values. According to the basic tenet of principal–agent theory, the set of political agents can be divided into high performance on the one hand and low performance on the other. It only takes one example such as Robert Mugabe to illustrate how costly a politician may be to a country – in this case his own country, Zimbabwe.

The arena where politicians are chosen is the electorate. Can the voters differentiate between high-effort and low-effort agents? The ambiguity of the electoral contract does not help voters identify the nature of politicians, as talk is cheap and promises come up for fulfilment long after they have been made. Opportunism on the part of politicians may turn up a handsome gain in the short term, although it may eventually spell disaster in the long term.

If polities rest upon contracts between a principal and a set of agents, then the rules governing these contracts must be of crucial importance. Institutionalism in whatever form, or the study of rules and their enforcement, has always been a core enterprise in comparative politics. The principal–agent model offers a perspective upon the importance of rules, structuring the interaction between the principal and the agents.

There is a school of political thought which underlines the major role that individual actors play in politics, whether or not they possess charisma: elite theory, theorising the impact of political leaders, whether in a democratic or non-democratic regime. The theory of democratic elitism from Pareto to Schumpeter was so profoundly criticised that it almost died out. Yet, there are of course political elites, not only in monarchical (the royal family) or authoritarian (the party or the military) regimes but also in democratic systems. At the start of the twenty-first century the gulf between political leaders and the masses could hardly be more wide. Political leaders may conduct their business either in terms of highly disciplined political parties – party government – or they could operate freely as political entrepreneurs. In both European democracy – party government – and American democracy – congressional entrepreneurs – opportunism channels the interaction between leaders and citizens to a considerable extent.

Elite theoreticians

Systematic thinking about political elites is to be found with a series of European scholars, theorising the advent of mass politics in the wake of modernisation, urbanisation and industrialisation: Pareto, Mosca and Michels, although one could also mention Weber and Schumpeter. What unites the two Italians and the one German is that they not only described democratic elitism but also displayed favourable attitudes towards it, in two cases (Pareto and Michels) endorsing fascist values, at least to some extent, whereas Mosca remained opposed to both democracy and Italian fascism. Let us examine the theories of these almost forgotten political theorists to see what may be salvaged from elitism for the understanding of governance and political inequality in the twenty-first century.

Pareto

Mussolini attended Pareto's lectures at the University of Lausanne. "I looked forward to every one", Mussolini wrote later, as this was a teacher outlining the fundamental economic philosophy of destroying political liberalism. Yet Pareto never joined the Fascist Party, but due to heart disease lived isolated in his villa on Lac Léman. The new Italian government offered honours to Pareto: delegate to the Disarmament Conference at Geneva, Senator of the Kingdom, as well as listed as contributing to El Duce's periodical *Gerarchia*. Pareto (1848–1923) was born in Paris of mixed Italian–French ancestry. He received a high-quality education, completing his degree in engineering at Turin, and turned to political life, expressing strong views in favour of free enterprise economic theory and free trade. His public lectures were often controversial, and were sometimes terminated by the police. Pareto retired from active political life as Professor of Political Economy in 1893. He turned to sociology late in life with his *Treatise on General Sociology*, and two smaller volumes, one being *The Rise and Fall of the Elites*.

To Pareto, there are two types of elites within society: the governing elite and the non-governing elite, each having two distinct mentalities: the speculator and the rentier. The speculator is the progressive, filled with Class I residues, while the rentier is the conservative, with Class II residue type. A propensity in healthy societies for the two types to alternate in power takes place as follows. After speculators have made a mess of government, the conservative forces step in and replace them. The process is cyclical and more or less inevitable. Rulers become weaker and less capable of bearing the burden of governing. In the end, the ruling class falls from power. Thus, "history is a graveyard of aristocracies". A dominant group, in Pareto's opinion, survives only if it provides opportunities for the elite of other origins to join in its privileges and rewards. Thus, he favours the opportunity for all competent members of society to advance into the elite. It should not hesitate to use force to defend these privileges and rewards, but aristocracies of long standing tend towards self-defeating humanitarianism.

Published late in his life, *The Transformation of Democracy* comprises Pareto's theories that focus upon what he considers to be the consequences of allowing a money-elite to dominate society. Pareto's observation that European democracies in the 1920s were increasingly being transformed into plutocracies led him to favour the fascist regime, which, however, failed completely in replacing the rule of law regime. Pareto's theory amounts to an extreme version of a principal–agent model where the agents strive to dominate the principal by various methods.

Mosca

Gaetano Mosca (1858–1941) was born in Palermo, Sicily, and his Sicilian background surfaced in his hostility towards democratic ideology and the parliamentary system, evident already in his first major work, *On the Theory of Governments and Parliamentary Government* (1884). In 1887 Mosca accepted a position as editor of the proceedings of the Chamber of Deputies, from which he would develop an understanding of the realities of politics. Mosca's ideas were first systematically presented in *The Ruling Class* (1896). Here, a principal–agent theory is launched involving the concept of a weak principal. Whatever the form of government, power is always in the hands of an organised minority, the "ruling class", which has authority over the majority by virtue both of certain characteristics that vary according to the epoch and the situation and due to the power derived from organisation per se. The ruling class justifies its rule by a moral or legal principle, the *"political formula"*, which tends to be consonant with the conceptions of the community governed. After Mosca won the chair of constitutional law at the University of Turin, he went into active politics, elected to the Chamber of Deputies in 1908 among the conservatives. In 1912 he voted against extension of the suffrage. From 1914 to 1916 he was under-secretary for the colonies, and in 1919 he became a senator. Mosca moved from an initial position of benevolence to one of open opposition to Italian fascism. Young fascist intellectuals approved of Mosca's criticism of the majority principle and his anti-parliamentarianism. Mosca was called to the University of Rome in 1923, where from 1925 to 1933 he held Italy's first chair of the history of political institutions and doctrines.

Michels

A pupil of Weber, Michels' key idea is the so-called *Iron Law of Oligarchy*, which – he claims – holds for all mass organisations. Michels (1876–1936) studied in England, at the Sorbonne, and at German universities. He became a socialist while teaching at the University of Marburg. He was active with the radical wing of the Social Democratic Party of Germany, but he left the party in 1907. At the University of Turin he taught economics, political science and sociology, meeting Mosca. In 1914 he became Professor of Economics at the University of Basel, where he stayed until 1926. His last years were spent in Italy teaching economics and the history of doctrines at the University of Perugia, openly endorsing fascism. His major book *Political Parties* examined the dimensions of democracy as a functioning system, going beyond a mechanical view of political parties as a precisely ordered system of authority and influence. Michels offered a view of politics that is bottom-up and untidy, what Linz now calls a "reciprocal deference structure" (Linz, 2006). Michels was not simply the father of the iron law of oligarchy, but theorised politics as a network of responsiveness, responsibility and accountability.

Elitism theory: agents with too few principal–agent restrictions

Elite theory should not be discarded because of Pareto's, Mosca's and Michels' political preferences. Already the case of Mosca shows that elitism may be adhered to without fascism. The basic fallacy in classical elite theory is the belief that elites are compactly coherent groups that act with one predominant goal, namely to propagate themselves in power (Mills, 1999). This entails a theory of collusion or even treason among agents in relation to the population as their principal, which seems absurd given the logic of elite competition with Schumpeter. What remains relevant today is the focus upon the gap between ordinary citizens and economic and political elites. In addition, in democracies, the gulf between leaders and citizens has increased since around 2000, making political leaders and parties prevail over citizen groups and social movements. From a principal–agent perspective, the fascist regime was an evolutionary misstep, a faulty mutation as it were.

Political elites play a role in politics either organised into political parties or acting more or less independently as political entrepreneurs. Political parties may succeed in monopolising access to politics, acting as highly cohesive groups with a large degree of party discipline. Or political parties may co-exist with major personalities in politics, acting as entrepreneurs in economic life, sometimes setting up their own parties.

The Schumpeter theory of agents in politics rejects elitist theory that looks upon the principal of the body politic with disdain and bypasses the rules which restrain the political leaders. If it is true that political elites are superior to the ordinary population, will they then coalesce and attempt to disabuse them from the principal? Only rules restraining such opportunitic behaviour on the part of elites could undo such a drive. In several countries, the political elites are constrained by the party they adhere to – party government. Schumpeter's *Capitalism, Socialism and Democracy* from 1942 added the political market – elections – to the theory of political elites. It is a strong antidote to opportunistic behaviour on the part of agents when political entry is open.

Party government

In modern polities, political agents will be either political parties or political entrepreneurs, depending upon the discipline in the party system of the country. Political agents will also be forthcoming in civil society, where associations seak to influence political power, such as organised labour, producer pressure groups and NGOs. In many countries, political parties constitute mechanisms for the mobilisation of social opinions, offering candidates in the formation of governments. Sartori argued that when society becomes politicised, the traffic rules that plug society into the state are established by the party system. Parties become channelling agencies for the political canalisation of society (Sartori, 1976: 41). Sartori moved beyond the institutional analysis of party systems in terms of rules about the number of parties – one-party system, two-party system and multi-party system (Duverger, 1954) – to propose a typology underlining the ideological distance between the parties in the party system, i.e. polarisation. The left–right distinction is not the only relevant way to sort out political actors into various sets according to beliefs, but its universal applicability cannot be doubted. It crops up whenever political parties start to organise and engage in activities, both in advanced and Third World countries.

An enquiry into the rule of law has to recognise political parties as an important variable. Party systems, the national configuration of individual political parties, may be regarded as one of the main links between government and society. Political parties may be viewed as the formal organisations for expressing cleavages in the social structure, groups acting more or less as vehicles for social movements. Representative government would be inconceivable without the existence of party systems, but their influence is not confined to democratic states. The political party plays a crucial role in that it expresses the ideological continuum from the extreme right to the extreme left as in the form of a horseshoe where *"les extremes se touchent"*.

The Sartori typology focused upon both polarisation and fragmentation in the party system, questioning the chances of survival of polarised polities. A party system involving centrifugal drives, irresponsible opposition and unfair competition is not conducive to stable democracy (Sartori, 1976: 140). Sartori underlined the central role of so-called anti-system parties in shaping the party system. A party is anti-system when it undermines the legitimacy of the regime it opposes (Sartori, 1976: 133). Sartori recognised communist and fascist parties as anti-system parties, countries having strong communist and/or fascist parties being characterised by political instability. The model seems to be valid for classical examples of state instability such as the Weimar Republic (1918–1933), France during the Fourth Republic (1946–1958) and Italy in the 1970s. Polarisation is hardly as relevant today with the collapse of most communist parties and the hesitance of right-wing populist parties to endorse fascist opinions about, for example, the need for violence or war and anti-Semitism.

Political entrepreneurs

Schumpeter's (1989) concept of the driving force in the marketplace – the entrepreneurs – fits well with a principal–agent framework for analysing today's politics. In several countries, politicians rise to the position of wealthy power brokers, controlling elections, the executive and the legislature. No more obvious is the role of the political entrepreneur when he/she is capable of setting up a new party in order to further his/her election prospects. However, politicians may exercise a degree of independence also in party systems with long-established parties. The distinction between presidential and parliamentary regimes is relevant for the separation between entrepreneurial systems and systems characterised by party discipline. The politician as political entrepreneur has a larger space for action when he/she may decide whether to run for presidential office. In addition, senators may act as political entrepreneurs in some party systems.

Organised interests

Elites may have an influence on politics besides the electoral channel. When the concept of a political elite is broadened to include also the actors in civil society aiming at influencing policy-making and policy implementation, then one would wish to link the role of organised interests and the NGOs to supporting rule of law. There are two theories about the role of civil society in influencing politics and policies, one based upon narrow egoistic interests and another founded upon the spread of social preferences. Olson's self-interest-based collective action hypothesis claims that pressure groups will have an influence over politics to the extent that they can overcome the free-rider problem promoting narrow group interests. Pressure groups will mainly be producers who can handle collective action problems, such as employers' associations or crafts or guilds (Olson, 1965). Only when trade unions manage to overcome the free riding difficulty will they be able to exert pressure upon politicians or political parties. The third sector hypothesis, namely focusing upon the recent growth in NGOs, provides a wider role for social interests, as people support a civil society with not only narrow interests but also altruistic ones.

Two models for the interaction between civil society and government have emerged, reflecting different historical legacies, or path dependency (Olson, 1982): (1) *Corporatism*. Organised interests are strong in terms of membership coverage and they possess a direct institutionalised channel to politicians in terms of agenda power, legislative hearing and impact upon implementation. Corporatism can sometimes exhibit such institutionalised features as to remind us of state corporatism (e.g. when membership ceases to be voluntary). (2) *Lobbyism*. Organised interests use money in order to get leverage over politics. The contacts between pressure groups and politicians are less institutionalised than under corporatism and are more focused upon a quid pro quo between monetary support and policy or regulation. The interests of big business tend to be well organised in advanced countries, although ordinary people know little about the thick carpet of pressure groups for industry.

From the perspective of rule of law, it is the legal status of trade unions that matters most. The rights of association are basic, which is why any restriction upon the free operation of trade unions signals a democratic deficit. In addition, the status of trade unions also impacts upon political stability, as restrictions upon the free operation of the rights of associations tend to lead to protests, strikes and the occurrence of political violence. Several authoritarian states have tried to boost trade union membership in order to employ the unions as vehicles for regime goals. Thus we cannot expect that trade union density goes hand-in-hand with the freedom of collective action.

Institutionalism

Typical of the evolution of comparative politics has been the preoccupation with the analysis of one type of regime: constitutional democracy. Scholars have attempted to understand the economic, social and cultural conditions for the stability of a democracy as well as the internal mechanics of the demo-cratic regime, its institutions. In institutionalism or neo-institutionalism, the emphasis is on the impact of rules upon outcomes: democracy or dictatorship, rule of law or authoritarianism. Political institutions, when enforced, con-strain opportunism among the agents of the body politic, helping the prin-cipal to structure authority and its exercise. A regime that provides for rule of law offers a solution to the principal–agent problem in all macro politics, namely: How to devise rules that constrain the politicians to serve the inter-ests of their populations? There is, however, a large variety of political insti-tutions, and it is an open question which ones promote the rule of law best. Let me provide a short overview of how political institutions have been analysed in comparative politics.

James Bryce (1838–1922) argued that a democracy requires a moderating legislature like the British House of Commons. A legislature of the British type means that sharp and divisive conflict is avoided and that government expediency is emphasised to the exclusion of caucuses and opportunists. Moreover, he also underlined a political culture that fosters a consensus-orientated oligarchy governing a democracy: a small size of the polity, a homogeneous social structure, an agriculturally based economy, and a history of successful resolutions of conflicts in a democratic fashion. Bryce's strong preference for British democracy – adversarial democracy or Westminster-type democracy – has been challenged by scholars who argue that there are other models of democracy that are relevant to the interpretation of the stability of the democratic state. Yet Bryce initiated the search for models that deliver rules conducive to a viable democratic state, either Westminster institutions or – in the Lijphart tradition – consociationalism (Lijphart, 1975, 1977, 1999).

Friedrich saw democracies as species of constitutional government (1950, 1963), as it involves legality, division of power and civic rights. Friedrich underlined institutional properties, social conditions and cultural characteristics. The first category contains a responsible bureaucracy, an effective diplomatic service, an efficient and powerful judiciary, a deliberating legislature, separation of powers and a constitutional arbitration system. The second category contains economic affluence, informative media of communication and extensive political integration of various interests in society. Third, a viable political tradition feeds on consent between diverging groups and is harmed by animosity between major social interests. What is required is a sort of balanced heterogeneity in society and politics, democracy being threatened by the intensity of political and social conflict, particularly concerning fundamental procedures and ultimate objectives.

From the perspective of the principal–agent model, *rule of law* is truly relevant, especially when combined with popular elections exhibiting a high level of citizen participation. It is the outcome of the operation of numerous institutions: executive, legislative and judiciary. Besides, it also involves the respect of civil and political rights. Loewenstein, favouring the concept of power, claimed that the distinction between democracy and autocracy was essential to the understanding of modern political systems. The modern democratic-constitutional state tries to establish equilibrium between the various competitive and pluralistic forces within society. In modern autocracy, social control and political power are monopolised by a single power holder, subordinating the individual to the ideological requirements of the group dominating the state (Loewenstein, 1965: 7).

Institutions structure principal–agent interaction. H. Finer (1932) stated that two things are necessary for a "complete act of government": to resolve and to execute. The identification of both *politics* and *administration* as the targets for enquiry in comparative politics increased the scope of comparative analysis of the state (Peters, 1987; Rowat, 1988). Finer's model of the state comprised country institutions for the following: (1) the electorate; (2) the parties; (3) the legislature; (4) the Cabinet; (5) the presidency; (6) the administration; and (7) the courts of justice. To cover the variety of principal–agent institutions, Blondel made norms the crucial element in government. They pattern how government behaves and what it accomplishes. *Participation*: the extent to which there is a mass society, or a continuum from monarchy to democracy; *means of government*: monolithic or pluralistic society according to the freedom of the press, meetings and political parties; *ends of government*: the probability that citizens can move up the social ladder as well as the degree to which resources are owned privately. The combination of these dimensions gives a number of categories or five types of political regimes (Blondel, 1990: 25–32): (1) liberal-democratic regimes, (2) egalitarian-authoritarian regimes, (3) traditional egalitarian regimes, (4) populist regimes and (5) Authoritarian-egalitarian regimes. Whereas communist systems scored low on participation and high on radicalism, the developing countries are characterised by more participation but less radicalism. On the other hand, the rich Western countries offer high levels of participation while at the same time having liberal means of government without being either conservative or radical concerning the ends of government policies.

S.E. Finer divides the states of the world into five main kinds of systems: (1) the liberal-democratic state; (2) the totalitarian state; (3) the quasi-democratic regime; (4) the facade-democracy; and (5) the military regime. Such a state typology remains relevant to the understanding of comparative government in the early 2000s (Finer, 1970: 55). Public government stands for government of the "territorial state" (Finer, 1970: 38–53).

- *Participation versus exclusion*: All government is the exercise of power of an elite over the population in a country, but the involvement of the masses varies in government: the extreme form of direct democracy in the form of the referendum and the polar extreme type of popular submission. In between, the representational model provides the masses with a mechanism of popular control.
- *Coercion versus persuasion*: Some rulers rely on coercion and fear, whereas a less repressive form is manipulation and deference in traditional societies with tribal chiefs, religious leaders or noblemen. Among the developing countries the population is regimented by monopolistic groups as, for example, a one-party state relying on new nationalistic symbols. Finally, there is bargaining based on the cognition of interests among various social groups, the typical way of governing a liberal democracy.
- *Sub-group autonomy versus sub-group dependence*: The overall position of societal groups in relation to those in power may vary. Groups may constitute themselves freely, express their interests and viewpoints and intervene in the political process up to the point of criticising or even hindering the activities of the government. Or groups could express views and interests only to the extent that government allows.
- *Representativeness versus order*: Public government may enhance the maintenance of law and order, bringing about predictability. However, the notion of responsiveness means that government changes its operations to fit in with public opinion. What is necessary is a trade-off between these two demands, either emphasising order or underlining representativeness.
- *Present goals versus future goals*: When a government makes policies, it is under pressure to consider both present-day goals and future goals as they may impinge on policy-making today.

The new institutionalism, stating that "institutions matter", gained definitive momentum during the 1980s rejecting behaviouralism of the 1960s,
and suggesting that the importance of country-specific institutions had been
neglected. Rules are as important as behaviour, as the politics of a country is
constrained by its institutions. Of particular relevance is the state institutions, which frame what actors can and cannot do – we must "bring the state
back in", according to one institutionalist phrase (Skocpol, 1979). Two different brands of neo-institutionalism have emerged, one sociological in tone
and the other rational choice-inspired. The first focuses upon the growth of
institutions throughout time, on the basis of the claim that the history of
institutions matters – *path dependency*. The second deals with institutional
design, or how institutions may be framed such that they channel behaviour
in certain intended directions. In both *historical institutionalism* and *rational
choice institutionalism*, rules and their enforcement are given a major role in
shaping outcomes.

The neo-institutionalist research programme of the rational choice school
is a very ambitious one, trying to establish firm links between rules and outcomes (Tsebelis, 1991). Bates introduced rational choice institutionalism
into the analysis of Third World countries, explaining how short-term interests led leaders to choose policies or even institutions that were detrimental
in the long-term perspective (Bates, 1981, 1989). One major question in
rational choice analysis concerns the choice between two types of executives:
presidentialism or parliamentariarism. Writing or rewriting a constitution,
one could take into account which type of executive best enhances political
stability and democracy (Shugart and Carey, 1992). The same question may
be raised in relation to the structure of the national assembly: unicameralism
versus bicameralism (Tsebelis and Money, 1997). It is necessary to link the
findings from institutional evaluation with the principal–agent game.

An elaborate rational choice theory of political institutions is to be found
in Tsebelis (2002), where key political rules such as presidentialism and
bicameralism push the actors in certain policy directions, such as towards
outcomes based upon cooperation, bargaining or conflict. What is crucial in
the framing of the rules of the games is whether a group of political actors
achieve the position as a so-called "veto-player", i.e. they can impact upon
decisions through their capacity to block decision-making processes, such as
the Supreme Court or a Constitutional Court in Europe, or the president
with a suspensive veto in legislative matters. In politics, political actors tend
to behave rationally, meaning to maximise their interests, where the outcomes depend upon the prevailing institutions, shaping how much power
the political actors may exercise, especially enhancing their bargaining position. Veto-players have a paradoxical impact upon politics, as they first
promote policy stability in restricting the possible outcomes (*core* of the
game), but this may create political instability, as the status quo becomes
too protected. The existence of veto-players in a polity could enhance the
rule of law, as in such a polity most political groups of a reasonable size

would have a say in deciding policies, laws and budgets. In a sense the concept of veto-players is akin to the consociational or deliberative models of democracy. Yet, why would principals favour policy stability ahead of political stability?

Sociological neo-institutionalism is more longitudinal than cross-sectional in its perspective upon institutions (March and Olsen, 1989). Countries tend to be captured by their institutional legacies, meaning that institutions become political cultures and develop interests in their self-perpetuation. Thus, there exist several kinds of presidentialism – North American, South American, French – as well as many forms of parliamentarianism – British, German, Norwegian – and different institutional set-ups reflect the weight of the past upon the present and the future. In the sociological approach to institutions, rules become historical forces, if not myths, but the claims of the new institutionalism that institutions matter, whether cross-sectionally or longitudinally, have to be evaluated critically in order to draw the correct implications for the institutional design of the state (Goodin, 1996). The claim that institutions matter would not be difficult to integrate within a comparative methodology, had it not been for the thesis that the country-specific institutions are idiosyncratic and require some kind of hermeneutic approach. The institutional dimension cannot be overlooked when comparing states across the globe, but the logic of comparative methodology requires that institutions be comparable between countries and across time. A critical question in comparative politics is whether the same institutions in different countries have the same impact upon the state. This is a problem for comparative model-building, which requires some kind of generalisation about the variety of conditions for the state, its stability and performance.

Historical institutionalism emerged alongside sociological and rational choice institutionalism. It reacted against the common premise of functionalism and systems analysis that the environment impacts upon politics in the same way, independently of the institutional set of the state. It also rejected the assumption of behaviouralism that actors perform outcomes in a uniformly deterministic fashion. Instead, several historical analyses portrayed different outcomes depending upon the variety of preferences of the players as well as the alternative institutions in place at specific times. The resort to historical analyses of systems of political authority opened up a new dimension in comparative politics, which used to be focused upon most recent events and developments. Thus, historical institutionalism increased the awareness of the variety of political arrangements claiming that the present was to a great extent a function of the past – the theory of institutional legacies. However, historical institutionalism did not launch a theory about political evolution, which is perhaps somewhat surprising given the interest of neo-institutional economics in the evolution of institutions. What comes across in several major works in historical institutionalism is the extent to which institutions and preferences become conflated, meaning that institutions develop their own interests in survival (Steinmo *et al.*, 1992). Yet, institutions coming from the past may be undone, because they do not result in desirable outcomes. Historical institutionalism offers a wealth of information about polities mankind has set up to solve the basic principal–agent problem in governance. Its lessons should be incorporated into comparative politics, especially if one looks for an evolutionary theory of political systems (Mahoney and Rueschemeyer, 2003). Comparative historical analysis offers a new wealth of information about political institutions, their weaknesses and strengths from a survival point of view (see Part III). Comparative politics used to be almost exclusively cross-sectional in methodology, but with historical institutionalism it can also use longitudinal evidence.

Institutionalism underlines that rules "when enforced" matter greatly for outcomes. Although institutions tend to develop into legacies, they have a rationale in relation to the objectives or interests of human beings. The principal–agent framework offers a coherent perspective upon institutional choice, as the population would wish to have institutions that constrain political elites towards rule of law outputs.

Political agents: outputs and outcomes

The outcome perspective in comparative government has been much researched in the emerging field of comparative public policy. In the traditional approach, almost nothing was said about what governments in fact did, as the focus of interest was on the structure of the state. To look at policy outputs or governmental programmes as well as policy outcomes or social results in a comparative perspective added a new dimension. Public policy as a new interdisciplinary effort in the social sciences opened up important areas for research such as unemployment, health care, social security and education. Public policy examined not only how government was run (administration) but also what it accomplished in terms of its programmes (policy outputs) as well as in terms of social impact (policy outcomes) (Wildavsky, 1979). The orientation of comparative politics towards public policy was based on the attempt to understand what different states do (policy outputs) and actually accomplish (policy outcomes) (Heady, 1979; Heidenheimer *et al.*, 1990; Wildavsky, 1986, 2006). Granted the institutional differences between various states in terms of governmental structures, citizens' rights and political party or trade union operations, are these distinctions relevant to the understanding of allocative and redistributive differences (Castles, 1982; Lybeck and Henrekson, 1988; Pierson and Castles 2006)?

There is in the literature on the theory of democracy an interest in a host of hypotheses about the consequences of alternative *types* of democracy. Edeltraud Roller has examined the claims made on the part of these models by scholars such as Lijphart, Tsebelis, Colomer, Huber, Schmidt, Fuchs, Castles, Schnapp, Crepaz and Armingeon, employing a rich data set covering 21 OECD countries for the period 1974 to 1995. The basic idea in this literature is that alternative models of democracy are conducive to different social outcomes, since the dichotomy between majoritarian democracies and negotiation (consensus) democracies in particular has real-life implications in the form of different policy results (Roller, 2005). Although she interprets her mainly negative findings with care and caution, she cannot but falsify these hypotheses. One would thus be inclined to conclude that it is democracy in general that is most important for outcomes such as political stability, rule of law and human development (quality of life).

The problem with the models of democracy literature is: (1) *Referential opacity*: which countries belong when to one category and not another? (2) *Terminological ambiguity*: what is a negotiation (consensus) democracy? (3) *Conceptual drift*: how can there be veto-players when there are no explicit rules about absolute or suspensive veto? (4) *Addition of incommensurables*: federalism + first past the post = what? Unitarism + corporatism = what? Two-partyism + legal review with codified constitution = what? (5) *Enigmatic classification*: how can social democratic hegemony in Sweden and Norway be put under negotiation democracy?

Political systems, like any social system, will always be the outcome of rules, preferences and objective conditions. Institutions matter, but the correct methodology for uncovering institutional effects is to examine the operation of each and every institution one by one and not to add them up in arbitrary typologies. The great enigma in this literature on the variety of models of democracy and their differential outcomes is, of course, how to clarify the key types, conceptually and referentially. I know what presidential or semi-presidential democracy is, but I have no idea where it should be classified: majoritarian or negotiation democracy?

From a principal–agent perspective, outcomes are of crucial importance. It is the perception of outcomes that gives to the principal–agent game its dynamic character, as the principal would wish to establish whether the promises of the agents, assuming governmental power, have been fulfilled. In private sector contracting between a principal and his/her agents, optimal contracts for joint action may be found, given full information about outcomes, allowing the principal to set the remuneration of the agent equal to his/her marginal contribution to the value of the outcome. With asymmetric information, only second-best solutions can be derived, because the agent will receive an informational rent proportional to his/her information advantage, resulting in a corresponding efficiency loss. Public sector contracting between principals and their agents will not come close to optimal contracts as the consequences of asymmetric information are exorbitant, meaning that outcomes will most certainly differ widely from promises.

In the private sector, the principal can offer his/her agents a remuneration linked with the results achieved, thus solving the motivation question. In the public sector, incentives cannot be handled in this way, except for public enterprises. Since the value of the outcomes in the public sector is not forthcoming in the form of a market price, the remuneration of political agents will be in the form of a fixed salary plus various fringe benefits. Thus, the value of policy outcomes such as education or health care, however large they may be, cannot be employed for the purpose of remuneration or risk-sharing.

Political agents will tend to be paid a fixed remuneration, whether its size varies mainly with the general affluence of the country. Historical legacies may play a role, as the relative size of agency remuneration may be larger in traditional regimes than in legal-rational regimes – take the example of Saudi Arabia, Brunei or the United Arab Emirates. The implication of fixed remuneration is that the length of time of political agents must be limited. Thus, rules will be devised that restrain the time duration of governmental offices.

Whichever agent wields power, he or she has a contract with the principal. Government is a set of agents who deliver policy outputs to the principal, resulting in policy outcomes. In a democracy, the contract between principal and agent is explicit, made on election day, whereas in an autocracy it remains implicit. But even in an autocracy the implicit understanding of ruling is that the agents will promote certain objectives, such as the common good and citizen well-being, meaning that they can be evaluated with outcomes. All political contracts are incomplete, however, as the hiatus between contracts *ex ante* and contracts *ex post* is unbridgeable.

Since the agents produce social or macroscopic outcomes and contribute, positively or negatively, to the affluence of a country, their remuneration must be fixed and not dependent upon these macro outcomes. The risk would be unbearable otherwise. In a democracy, it is the principal who assumes almost all risk, whereas in a military *coup d'état* it is the agent who assumes part of the risk, making him/her extremely vulnerable to charges of mismanagement when the transition to democracy occurs.

Rules and preferences

If one asks what the social reality consists of, then it is not enough to answer: human beings. They also enter nature, as studied by several of the natural sciences. The social sciences would analyse a part of human beings, namely human behaviour that is orientated somehow towards other human beings. I would suggest that two entities frame human interaction: rules and preferences. But how are they related?

Rules state what is duty and right. Preferences state what people want to achieve. Thus, rules would frame preferences by impacting upon what can be done, i.e. the choice set of alternatives. However, alternative rules may emerge depending upon which preferences people adhere to, meaning that preferences impact upon rules. For instance, the rules of a market economy frame how incentives may work themselves out in concrete economic interaction. But it is also the case that certain preferences support a market regime more than other preferences.

Theorising rules and preferences brings one into much debated issues in economic, political and legal theory. Outcomes depend upon both rules and preferences. One view has it that rules are more important for outcomes, whereas another argues the other way around. Concerning the origins of rules, it has been argued that legal norms have a special status in that they can be clearly identified. On the other hand, it has been claimed that legal rules emerge from a broad consideration involving both economic and political principles. Let me elaborate somewhat upon some of the points that these antinomies raise.

The primacy of rules: institutionalism

Institutionalism, whether old or new, claims that rules not only influence the choice options but that they actually determine behaviour or interaction. There are several versions of this strong institutionalist thesis: (IT) Rules determine social interaction. One could argue for (IT) in two different ways, however: by means of the so-called analytical position or through empirical evidence. The neo-institutionalist theory developed by March and Olsen (1989) is the most extreme example of the analytical position. They arrive at their message that institutions matter simply by defining "institutions" as almost everything in the social world: rules, preferences, motives, interests, legacy. As every scholar is free to choose his own terminology, it is pointless to criticise March and Olsen. They offer many examples that illuminate the importance of institutions. Yet, from a methodological point of view, this is not the way forward. The concept of an institution should be defined without reference to what it is supposed to explain. I suggest an institution is a rule that is enforced. This definition stays away from the analytical position.

Institutional economics tends to argue in favour of (IT). Thus, against mainstream economics, it is stated that the framing of the rules and their proper enforcement explains major macro effects, such as the triumph of occidental capitalism. Only the rules of the Western market economy can bring about a major rise in the output of goods and services. "Modern capitalism" according to Weber is a highly institutionalised phenomenon, being driven by a set of transparent rules that set it apart from other kinds of capitalism.

The distinction between genesis and transplantation is crucial when discussing institutional economics. It may be true that modern capitalism was born in Western Europe, reflecting a set of conditions that were not present in other civilisations. But it also holds true that the institutions of capitalism may be exported elsewhere and operate effectively, as the economic ascension of East Asia shows.

Election system theory deals with path dependency. Different rules will score different winners from the same set of preferences – that is the core idea. The method of election has a large impact upon how candidates or choice alternatives are chosen, as the difference between majoritarian and proportional techniques shows. Yet the question then arises in relation to path dependency, namely: How do societies choose their preferred election technique? Anticipating path dependency, some societies prefer full positional methods such as the STV (single transferable vote), whereas others like truncated choices.

Just as evolutionary theory predicts that survival fitness will lead to better species, so one may ask whether the evolution of social systems results in better rules. Thus, economic institutionalism predicts that the most productive rules will emerge. Somehow economic actors will stimulate institutional development towards the most profitable economic arrangements.

The institutions of the market economy have been invented and enforced because they work, and they create more wealth than do alternative institutional arrangements. Economic actors will call upon the state to reform economic institutions so that they are conducive to maximum output. Somehow the rules find their optimum just as the struggle for survival leads to the most adaptive species. What, then, would be the end state of institutional development in politics?

The primacy of preferences

Against institutionalism, one may argue that human beings decide on the basis of their preferences. This is the core of so-called methodological individualism. Human behaviour, being intentional, is guided first and foremost by motivation, i.e. wants and beliefs. Rules come second, as they do not determine behaviour but only condition it. Methodological individualism claims: (MI) Human behaviour is determined by preferences. Thus economic actors seek profits and rents, avoiding losses, and political actors aim for power, prestige and economic gain. They would take institutions into account, but the rules only affect the choice options and not the picking of a special alternative. When confronted with too constraining rules, actors would simply cheat in order to have their preferences prevail. The thesis (MI) receives support from rational choice, where no institutional scheme is strategy proof.

Evolution of rules

Legal rules or institutions play a major role in social systems, because they are more constraining than moral rules or customs. Thus, it is important to theorise the nature of legal rules and their contribution to the evolution of human societies. Economists would focus upon contract law, especially tort law, and public regulation, whereas political scientists would research constitutions and human rights.

What has been much debated in jurisprudence is the firmness of legal institutions. Can they be easily identified? Legal rules would come high on a measure of degree of institutionalisation, as typical of law is the sanction. Whether or not rules are applied is a probability phenomenon, as perfect rule obedience hardly exists and a complete lack of rule respect would signify that the rule is obsolete.

The attempt to make legal rules sharply identifiable was launched by positivists in jurisprudence searching for some identification criteria that would make a clear demarcation between legal rules and moral norms. These attempts were rebuffed by scholars who either argue that key norms would always be moral ones or claim that legal rules stem from the behaviour that judges happen to engage in.

The most elaborated thesis about the evolution of rules is to be found in *Law and Economics*, stating that legal decision-making explicitly or implicitly fosters economic efficiency in the market. However the rules are framed, the judges would not wish to enforce rules that hinder the effective operation of the market economy. The reaction to the Calabresi–Posner theory of the long-run interpretation of legal rules has been on the whole negative, as it is stated that judges merely establish what is right, given the existence of the rules (Posner, 1993, 2004).

From a political science perspective, the contribution of legal rules must be searched for in the state. Thus, legal rules would impact upon the kind of state that is oriented towards the respect for rules on a grand scale, the *Rechtsstaat*. Rule of law requires a massive institutionalisation of the state. When judges and jurisprudence insist upon respect for the rules, they strengthen the *Rechtsstaat*. Actually, the *Sozialstaat* would also be unthinkable without rules and their enforcement.

Societies tend to institutionalise interaction among human beings. One theory says that institutionalisation comes from a need for predictability. Another theory suggests that there is an endogenous evolution towards rules that promote economic efficiency. A more promising approach is to look at the institutionalisation from the point of view of politics and power. Seen in this perspective, legal institutionalisation is linked with the rise of rule of law, constitutional monarchy or democracy.

Conclusion

A theory of the polity has to search for the determinants of regimes among the forces of human motivation. Polities are institutions set up and operated by human beings according to the logic of the principal–agent model. The environment of politics plays a major role in shaping the probability of regime survival, such as whether the setting is agrarian or industrial, urban or rural, poverty, affluence and so on. But the decisive stimuli for changing a regime come from the actors involved, i.e. human beings. Political regimes are social systems that human actors operate for specific purposes by setting up and running institutions. Below, I will concentrate on the implications of principal–agent theory for comparative politics – see Rasmusen (2001).

Time has come to apply the principal–agent approach to politics, given its success in economics and law – see Laffont (2003).

The principal–agent game is by now well known in the market setting, introducing the implications of asymmetric information into the neoclassical decision model – see Furubotn and Richter (2005). If the model can be used with many insights into insurance, litigation, farming and health care, then perhaps it can also be used to illuminate interaction in the state. Modern government is based upon the idea that the population as principal selects, hires, instructs, evaluates a set of politicians as agents. Actually, much of the institutional paraphernalia of the modern state can be interpreted as devices to minimise self-seeking behaviour on the part of government. In politics, it is government that has the upper hand and it may not reveal its true nature to its principal until it is too late. A principal–agent model of politics targets the relationship between the population as the principal of the state on the one hand and the set of politicians who contend for government on the other. This interaction results in contracts that are ambiguous and difficult to monitor. Thus, there arises the possibility of opportunistic behaviour on the part of the agent. Only the enforcement of institutions can reduce the consequences of opportunism with guile. Actually, comparative politics may be seen as the study of how alternative institutional arrangements constrain – more or less – politicians. I argue that the rule of law framework of institutions constrains the most.

The principal–agent model (PAM) offers a new perspective upon politics from two angles (Moe, 1984). First, it models the interaction between government and its bureaux and agencies (Calvert *et al.*, 1989). Second, it illuminates the interaction between government and its population, suggesting that politicians or rulers are the agents of the principal of the *body politic*, namely the people. The people of a politically organised nation or state considered as a group would always need a set of agents to handle governance matters. I suggest that the rule of law framework offers the best approach for structuring these principal–agent relationships that recur in all forms of political regimes, also historical ones (Anderson, 1979, 1996).

Part I

States

Stability and performance

I would suggest that two main goals surface when principal–agent interaction is to be structured. Drawing upon political theory developed in England during the seventeenth century, there is first the story of stable government from *Leviathan* (1651) in which book Thomas Hobbes identified the primal task of any government, namely internal social stability, law and order, and external peace. Second, there is the competing story of government saying it is a trust, designed first and foremost to enforce rule of law and human rights, as suggested by John Locke in his *Two Treatises on Government* (1690).

Both of these objectives – political stability and rule of law – define principal–agent interaction in government. Following these objectives of government, one may analyse the states of the world today according to the following two macro properties: the degree of political stability and the degree of rule of law. Thus, one may classify some 30 big countries in relation to the above framework in the following manner as for the early twenty-first century, allowing for the fact that countries change sometimes from one category to another:

- *Stable rule of law*: USA, Germany, France, UK, Italy, Japan, India, Brazil, Spain, South Africa, South Korea.
- *Unstable states*: Turkey, Bangladesh, Indonesia, Russia, Philippines, Nigeria, Egypt, Congo, Ethiopia, Ukraine, Colombia, Myanmar, Mexico.
- *Stable but no rule of law*: China, Vietnam, Thailand, Iran, Pakistan, Saudi Arabia.

By concentrating on the state in the early twenty-first century, I do not wish to nourish the image that the state is a compact sovereign organisation that can impose a unique and unambiguous will upon society. Instead, I share the view that the state is a multifaceted organisation sending often contradictory signals meeting with opposition from various levels of government or from society (Migdal, 1988, 2001). Besides analysing the distinction between rule of law and dictatorship, one should include state stability as a separate aspect of the state. States, whether democratic or authoritarian, may be more or less stable. In addition, there are some countries where a modern state does not work – anarchy or anomy, as it were.

Principal–agent contracting would in the long run result in the creation of the institution of the state, as it alone could offer security to the population and at the same time restrain the agents of the political body towards the respect of rights with the principal. However, there are many alternative institutions framing principal–agent interaction within legal rational authority with different outcomes. Chapter 1 surveys the occurrence of states in the world today and attempts to give some measure of their stability and longevity. Chapter 2 looks at the states from Locke's perspective, namely to what extent they promote the rule of law.

1 The states of the world

Introduction

The basic problem is to identify the typical properties of the set of states, huge in terms of population, such as China, India, the United States, Indonesia and Brazil as well as tiny states (e.g. Tuvalu, Kiribati, Iceland, Grenada and Swaziland). I focus on one well-known definition of the concept of the state that is also employed by the international community when identifying the present states of the world, albeit not entirely consistently, and I single out regime stability as one of the two basic points of reference for the understanding of comparative government. The concepts of political instability and state stability may be defined in several ways.

Much speculation has focused on the nature of the state. To say what is characteristic of the state is closely tied up with the difficult question about the state concept, its meaning or connotations. To constitutionalists, the state is a law-orientated organisation, creating rules as well as enforcing them. To power realists, the basic property of the state is the use of or threat of employment of physical force. For economists, the state allocates public goods: law and order, i.e. services to be paid for by means of taxation. Some definitions of the "state" underline legitimacy, whereas others emphasise might. Finally, one approach to the state suggests that there are reasons of state, whereas another approach links the state with the legal order.

Politics may be interpreted as a general phenomenon occurring in all kinds of social systems: primary groups, kinship, neighbourhood groups, large villages or small towns, towns and small cities, big cities and large interest organisations, small states, medium-sized states, large sub-states or metropolitan areas, giant nation-states and finally in the large international organisations such as the UN, WHO, ILO and FAO. Political systems may be identified in all kinds of social systems (Easton, 1965). A polity is a more specific phenomenon as it is tied to the following concepts: country, people and the political body as the set of citizens. Comparative politics analyses politics at the macro level, the polity or, as I prefer, "states". The concept of government is amorphous, as it can stand for central, regional or local government. In this chapter we enter into a preliminary discussion of which are the states of the world. The concept of the state is an essentially contested notion, as the theoretical debate around the meaning of the word "state" is large, to say the least (Jellinek, 1966; Held, 1991; Kelsen, 2005).

The search for a definition of the concept of the state has resulted in a number of state theories which are not in agreement upon the necessary and sufficient properties that would identify the state (Dunleavy and O'Leary, 1987; Vincent, 1987). Yet talking about the reference or denotation of "state" is not as puzzling as the discussion about the meaning or connotation of "state". As long as one only asks for what the word "state" stands for in reality, specifying a few necessary or sufficient criteria that allow us to apply the concept to the real world, then things are not that difficult or complicated. Standard reference books list the number of existing states in almost the same manner.

Whether a state is to be said to exist or not in a society is most of the time a clear-cut task to be decided by evidence, because there are standard indicators that give guidance. True, in marginal cases it may not be easy to tell whether there is a state in a society. A state may cease to exist, as in Lebanon in the early 1980s, or in Somalia in the early 1990s, resulting in anarchy. Or it may not be clear whether an organisation really could be called a "state". Is there a Vatican state, literally speaking? One state may be broken up into several states, as in former Yugoslavia, since different claims to territorial sovereignty constitute always a cause of severe conflict. Taiwan is no doubt a state, but it is not recognised internationally as such – an instance of statehood that is not recognised in public international law.

If the problem of the present-day reference of the concept is not a major one because it may be solved by means of standard identification criteria, then its historical application brings out far more conceptual difficulties. When did states first appear? Were there states in a similar sense of the concept among the Romans, in old China or Mughal India and in the Medieval Ages as after the Renaissance in Western Europe? When did a kind of *modern*-type state appear for the first time? The question of the origins of the state concept remains a topic for vivid discussion and disagreement, as some would deny that there have ever existed any other states than the modern ones (Poggi, 1978, 1990; Evans *et al.*, 1985; Meinecke, 1997).

Weber's concept of the state

Weber made a systematic presentation of "Basic Sociological Terms" (1978: 3–62), among which the concept of the state is included. After having introduced his concepts of authority and of a ruling organisation, starting from the elementary concept of a social action as intentional behaviour, Weber arrives at the following ideal-type definition:

A compulsory political organisation with continuous operations will be called a "state" insofar as it upholds the claim to the monopoly of the legitimate use of physical force in the enforcement of its order.

(Weber, 1978: 54)

There are here mentioned a few properties that can help us delimit a set of states: monopoly on physical force, legitimacy of a system of rules, continuous activity within a territory, and obligatory organisation membership of the population. This is the modern concept of the state, which Weber did not apply to traditional or charismatic regimes. But it remains an ideal-type, meaning that there are bound to be borderline cases when the probability that government really controls the use of physical violence is not so high (e.g. Ivory Coast). How many real states are there in Western Africa in the early twenty-first century? Does Afghanistan have a state?

A state may be characterised by its special mode of organisation: laws, resources by means of taxation, and civil servants and other employees (Rose, 1984). Below, we will employ Weber's concept of the state. Its strength is that it focuses on a single visible insignia of the state, namely the monopoly of the application of legitimate physical violence for a specific territory. It is well expressed in the international law criteria for the recognition of a state. We make no assumption about the compactness of the state, as it has been argued that Weber had a bias in favour of a strong state (Migdal, 2001). This is actually questionable, as Weber from his historical perspective was keenly aware that states vary tremendously in how each has institutionalised its essential elements: the legal order, the control of physical violence and the protection of the population in its territory. Just as he made no hidden assumption about state strength, so he refused to equate the modern state with a nation-state.

It should be pointed out that Weber's state concept makes no commitment as to any of the properties of a nation, thus not mingling the two concepts of a state and a nation into a "nation-state". It is often stated that the most powerful community today is the "modern nation-state". What, then, is such a state as the nation-state? A state is the organised machinery for the making and carrying out of political decisions and for the enforcing of the laws and rules of a government. The state includes not only officials and office buildings, but also soldiers, police officers and gaols. A state recognises no higher decision-making power outside itself – a "sovereign" state. Typical of a state is the tie to a country – a geographical area of "material, economic, physical, and psychological independence" (Deutsch, 1980: 117). Such geographical areas may be populated by what may be designated as a "people", i.e. a group of persons with a linguistic or cultural identity. Or such an area may host two or more people – a multi-ethnic state as it were. The occurrence of several ethnic or culturally distinct groups within a nation-state – social heterogeneity – may affect the strength of the state, as internal conflict is more probable in so-called divided societies.

Deutsch underlined the dynamic aspect of states: "their ability to steer themselves" – his cybernetic framework of government (Deutsch, 1963), emphasising goals, decision-making and implementation, information and feedback about policy performance, as well as memory and coordination. The process and machinery of government is orientated towards these elements in a so-called steering loop. And power is the central derivative property in political systems, its location determining the nature of the steering system (Deutsch, 1980: 150). Political systems like nation-states may be centrifugal (decentralised) or centripetal (centralised), and they may be associationist or dissociationist depending on the existence of autonomous, small self-governing groups such as local governments, labour unions, cooperatives and churches. However, if "nation-state" means a state where the citizens belong to one and the same ethnic community, then the so-called "modern" state is not necessarily a nation-state.

Do the above requirements of a modern state imply the existence of a nation? In political sociology, Rokkan's well-known theory of "nation-building" examines the process of state establishment in Western Europe (Rokkan *et al.*, 1970). The establishment of a modern state was a continuous process of institution-building in countries where also a high degree of social cohesion slowly emerged. But how much social consensus among various people in the state territory is enough to qualify a state as a nation-state? The process of nation-building resulting in a compact state would be much more difficult a task in societies where there is extensive social heterogeneity. Here, creating a nation-state may amount to the breakup of a state into several units.

The fuzzy nation concept is surrounded by myths about what constitutes a nation. Smith defines the crucial concept of "national identity" in the following way:

> As a named human population sharing an historic territory, common myths and historical memories, a mass, public culture, a common economy and common legal rights and duties for all members, the nation is a multidimensional concept.
>
> (Smith, 1993: 43)

Typical of a state is the exercise of public power over social groups in a predictable manner in a geographically tight space according to a legal order. These social groups, however, need not constitute a homogeneous society in any of the aspects that Smith lists. In fact, the concept of a nation is an essentially contested concept in the social sciences (Smith, 1998, 2004). Tracing the equation state = nation = people back to the rise of nationalism as a political doctrine in the nineteenth century, Hobsbawm underlines that the only stable component is the state:

> What is a (or the) nation? For the chief characteristic of this way of classifying groups of human beings is that ... no satisfactory criterion can

be discovered for deciding which of the many human collectivities should be labelled in this way.

(Hobsbawm, 1990: 5)

As a matter of fact, the relationship between the state and the various ethnic and religious groups in society is a complex one, which renders the concept of nation-state precarious. Against the nationalist principle of one nation, one state, it may be argued that its implementation may not be conducive to the foundation of compact states. Quite the contrary, nationalism may threaten minorities or it may lead to secession or irredentism. The basic principle about national self-determination may come into conflict with the principles of human rights (Donnelley, 1989; Brownlie, 2003). One crux of the problem of the nation-state is that when multicultural states are broken up into a set of smaller nation-states, there may exist no limit on how far the splitting up of the state should go. The nation-state may not only represent the liberation of subjugated people, but it may itself foster contempt for the rights of lingering minorities. The identification criteria on a nation are simply not clear, as both subjective and objective characteristics may be employed: a distinctive *ethnie*, a culture, a historical destiny or legacy, and so on (Anderson, 2006; Spencer and Woolman, 2002).

It is, I wish to emphasise, vital to keep the concepts of state and nation separate, because it is an open question how they are related to each other. It may well be the case that the stability of the state comes under pressure if the population within the state boundaries hosts groups with different cultures (e.g. national identities). However, it is also possible that social heterogeneity could stimulate state vitality operating as sources of multicultural diversity – multiculturalism challenging nationalism. In the early twenty-first century, state-building is more relevant than nation-building due to increasing multiculturalism. Fukuyama writes about governance in the twenty-first century:

> State-building is the creation of new government institutions and the strengthening of existing ones. In this book I will argue that state-building is one of the most important issues for the world community because weak and failed states are the sources of many of the world's most serious problems, from poverty to AIDs to drugs to terrorism.
>
> (Fukuyama, 2004: ix)

It is not clear what "*state-building*" involves. Fukuyama sometimes speaks about "*nation-building*" as if it is the same as state-building (Fukuyama, 2004: 38). State-building takes two forms for him: scope and strength of state activities. Whereas the first dimension covers the size of state operations measured in terms of public expenditures divided by GDP, the second dimension stands for institutional effectiveness, i.e. the degree to which the laws of the state, its legal order, are successfully enforced. The basic argument of Fukuyama is that a state is strongest when it has smaller scope but higher institutional efficiency. I would like to argue that what is critical in state evaluation is the extent to which states display regime stability as well as adhere to the rule of law. It is not enough that the legal order is enforced, but it should also comprise human rights and political competences. In addition, whether a state delivers few or many services is not always related to whether or not it is stable. One should leave questions about state scope and state strength open, not including them in the definition of the state, as well as keep nation and state analytically separate.

A nation is a people with a common identity, be it language, history or merely imagination. A state is a legal corporation with certain definitive characteristics. One cannot put up an equation: state = nation, because some states harbour several nations (Spain) and some nations do not have a state (Kurds). Moreover, immigration and globalisation lead inexorably to the multicultural society with *diasporas* and *ampersands* (Cohen, 1997; Ember *et al.*, 2004; Huntington, 2005; Sheffer, 2006). Governance of a multicultural society requires the politics of mutual respect among communities, as the time of the homogeneous nation building its own state is a thing of the past (Kymlicka, 1996, 2001).

The identification of present states

Standard reference books talk about "countries of the world", the "nations of the world" (*Encyclopaedia Britannica: Book of the year*, 1991: 746, 531) or the "states and territories of the world" (Taylor, 1983: 273). Sometimes there are references to the "political entities of the world" (*Encyclopaedia Britannica: Book of the year*, 1964: 533) or "national political units" (Russett *et al.*, 1968: 935). The variation in usage indicates that the identification of a state is not altogether a clear-cut task, as sometimes the states of a federal country are included. Besides formal recognition as a state by other states in the world, the recognition by the United Nations is the most important hallmark of statehood that an emerging state can receive. It may almost be described as a performative act, the granting of UN membership being conducive to state legitimacy.

The organisation of the United Nations was created in 1945. It has included an increasing number of states on the basis of a formal recognition of UN membership. But it should be pointed out that the United Nations also takes some kinds of size criteria into account, because some small states such as Nauru, Tonga and Tuvalu in Oceania were not accepted as member states until 2000. In addition, Switzerland waited until 2004 to apply for membership, and North and South Korea were not included in the UN until 1991, although for different reasons. Montenegro was accepted as a member in 2006. Table 1.1 shows the increase in the number of members of the UN.

During the 1950s and the 1960s a large number of new states were integrated into the UN framework, which reflects the breaking up of the colonial

Table 1.1 United Nations' member states

	1945	1950	1960	1970	1980	1990	2000	2006
Number of members	51	60	99	127	154	159	189	192

Source: Based on United Nations (2006) available at: www.un.org/members/growth.shtml.

empires – British, French, Spanish, Portuguese and Dutch – after the Second World War. One state to be accepted in the 1980s was the Sultanate of Brunei Darussalam in Far East Asia in 1984. The fall of the USSR had the consequence that the number of states that are members of the UN increased greatly. Thus, in the early 1990s a number of states from the Soviet empire were among the new member states entering the United Nations, including Namibia (1990), Estonia, Latvia, Lithuania, Korea Dem Peoples' Republic, Republic of Korea, Marshall Islands, Micronesia (all in 1991), San Marino, Armenia, Azerbaijan, Kazakhstan, Kirgizstan, Moldova, Tajikistan, Turkmenistan and Uzbekistan (all in March 1992), as well as Bosnia-Herzegovina, Croatia, Slovenia and Georgia (all in July 1992). At the same time Yugoslavia was excluded from the United Nations, and Serbia and Macedonia were not permitted to enter until 2000. In 1993 the Czech and Slovak republics entered the UN. A number of principalities are members of the UN such as San Marino, Monaco and Lichtenstein, and many of the tiny Pacific Island states are members.

Israel has been the only UN member to be excluded from a regional group. Geographically, the State of Israel would belong to the Asian Group, but that group has repeatedly denied Israel's admission. Israel has accepted an invitation to become a temporary member of the Western European and Others (WEOG) regional group. Israel's membership in the group is restricted: it has to reapply for membership every four years. For the first two years, Israeli representatives were not allowed to run for positions on the UN Council. Israel was not allowed to present candidacies for open seats in any UN body and it is not able to compete for major UN bodies, such as the Economic and Social Council, for a longer period. Israel is allowed to participate in WEOG activities only in the UN New York office, being excluded from the UN offices in Geneva, Nairobi, Rome and Vienna. Thus, the State of Israel is the only UN member not permitted to stand for election to the full range of UN bodies. A country may be excluded or suspended from the UN, but it has not occurred except when the Former Yugoslavia collapsed in 1992. It is mind-boggling to understand how war-torn Somalia can uphold its membership (since 1960). Iraq had actually entered the UN already in 1945. It was in 1971 that the General Assembly decided "to restore all its rights to the People's Republic of China and to recognise the representative of its Government as the only legitimate representative of China to the United Nations". China took the seat of

Taiwan in the Security Council, and Taiwan was excluded. There have been calls for the suspension of certain regimes accused of genocide, such as Kampuchea (Pol Pot regime) and Sudan.

The UN has recognised 192 countries as member states, but the World Bank (WB) speaks of more than 200 countries and territories in its global tables. Which countries are outside of the UN framework but inside the World Bank statistics? Answer: Besides Taiwan, some remaining colonies or dependent areas or old colonies such as Anguilla, Cayman Islands, French Guiana, Guam, Hong Kong, Macao, Netherlands Antilles, Puerto Rico, Reunion, Taiwan and the Virgin Islands. Besides, the WB also mentions the West Bank and Gaza, which points to the problem of specifying the boundary of Israel, formal or real. Outside of both the UN and World Bank classifications are only the Cook Islands (free association with New Zealand), and Nauru, which is the world's smallest island nation, covering just $21\,\mathrm{km}^2$, the smallest independent republic, and the only republican state in the world that does not officially have a capital.

There are a few internationally acknowledged reference books that may be consulted, as they list the states of the world at some point in time, based on various criteria. One such source is the *Encyclopaedia Britannica*, cited above. In the edition from 1911 there is a list in the index section, whereas later lists of states enter the various editions of *Book of the Year*. It should be pointed out that the 1911 list is far from entirely certain and that later *Britannica* makes no distinction between sovereign and non-sovereign states such as the United States of America on the one hand and California on the other.

Other often-used sources are the different editions of the *Statesman's Yearbook* as well as the *World Handbook of Political and Social Indicators* with its three editions. In the *Statesman's Yearbook* there is a table of contents which lists both states (e.g. USA) and territories of countries (e.g. Florida) such as India and Kerala, although this distinction is quite clear. In a similar way the *World Handbook* from 1972 and 1983 lists states and territories. Here we also enter the classification of states made by Russet *et al.* in 1968 where units with a population of more than 10,000 inhabitants were included. Again, both independent states and states that were included in a confederation were included.

Thus, there are in reality one *narrow* identification and one *broad* identification of the states of the world in these well-known reference books. *Encyclopaedia Britannica* starts in 1911 with 153 states, which had risen to 162 in 1965 and 175 in 1970 to reach a high of 217 in 1980 based on a broad identification. The number of 186 in 1990 is more in line with the narrow identification criterion. The *Statesman's Yearbook* offers the following series: 1925: 70/181; 1940: 71/194; 1956: 113/174, and 1991: 182/198. The *World Handbook of Political and Social Indicators* counts to 133 states in 1964, 137/199 states in 1972 and 154/231 states in 1983, giving both the narrow and the broad classification. Russet *et al.* (1968) present one count for the twentieth century, amounting to 154/267 states. The listing of two sets of states, on the one hand sovereign states and on the other all so-called states including member states that form part of a union, is bound to create confusion. It all depends on how formal constitutional matters are matched by real-life differences between territories that are described as regional governments and territories that are confederated states. We focus on the set of so-called sovereign states and discuss the nature of federal states as a separate issue.

For the early 1990s a list of states may be derived from the *World Development Report*, which includes states that are members of the World Bank and have more than one million inhabitants besides all the smaller states. In addition to *Fischer Welt Almanach* one may use two French sources: *L'etat du monde 1991* and *1990 Atlas Statistique: Encyclopedia Universalis*, which both count sovereign and dependent states. The *World Development Report* counts the number of states that are larger than one million inhabitants to 124 and the total number of states to 185. *L'etat du monde* counts sovereign states to 171 and all states to 195 whereas the count of *Encyclopedia Universalis* contains 165 sovereign states and 220 states all in all. The sudden process of creating new states comes out nicely when *Fischer Welt Almanach* identifies 171 states in 1991 but an astonishing 191 states in 1992. One may wish to employ the distinction between a narrow and a broad definition of "state" when conducting research about the states of the world. We focus chiefly upon so-called sovereign states according to public international law. It seems that there is enough agreement among various sources to count the number of states in the narrow sense of sovereign states as approximately 190 in 2000. We follow the World Bank in making a distinction between states with a population that is larger than one million inhabitants and tiny states with a smaller population. Thus this means that there are some 150 states that this study will analyse.

States as institutional probabilities

Weber underlines political organisation that is compulsory in his definition of the state. In states, membership is highly regulated with strict rules about residence, citizenship, visas, passports, tax liability and so on. This is one of the distinctive features of the modern states when compared with ancient despotism or the feudal polities. Given this institutional emphasis upon compulsory membership (*census*), one may draw an elementary picture of the states of the world, remembering that in reality the existence of a state depends upon the probability that its ideal-type properties are fulfilled.

The unit of analysis in comparative politics may be identified quite easily if one resorts to the concept of a Weberian state. Some scholars use the phrase "the modern state", but the use of the qualification "modern" is somewhat arbitrary. It has been claimed that the concept of a modern state entered the history of mankind around the Renaissance period and the seventeenth century (Tilly, 1975; Held *et al.*, 1983; Anderson, 1986; Hall, 1986;). However, to pin down more exactly what a modern state amounted to in Western Europe is a matter for historical research.

The Weber state is identified by its monopoly on the legitimate use of physical force within a specified territory, which is never 100 per cent. It thus combines both the power aspect and the legal or moral implication of the state concept. When we start searching for the unit of analysis in comparative politics, the plausibility of the Weberian state concept derives from two sources, making it a better choice in a strategy for the conduct of comparative work than other candidates such as polity, government, nation and political system.

First, the identification criteria are highly tangible or visible: territory, population, military and police forces, attitudes towards legitimacy. We have seen in this chapter that states may vary tremendously in terms of state area and people. Yet the state may be truly small or large in terms of territory or harbour gigantic or tiny populations, and still operate as a Weber state. There can be no talk about a proper size for a state, or some magic size where it functions optimally. Second, the Weber state concept is not only an abstract scientific notion, but it actually points to organisations that constitute a kind of reality of their own. Ongoing international politics identify the states of the world in action, meaning that the concept of the state as used by, for example, the UN constitutes a performative notion. What is a state is what a state does or what is called a "state". The practice of international politics involves that the major actors orientate towards each other within a state-centred subjective framework, which is given official sanction in various ways.

The crux of the matter is that these two criteria on the present-day states – the conceptual criteria in the Weber state definition and the actor-based subjective criteria in international relations – coincide to such an extent that they designate almost the same units of analysis as the so-called "states" (except for Taiwan). When there is disagreement about whether a state really exists, such as in Kampuchea or Somalia in the 1980s or Afghanistan in 2005, then the critical issue is whether there is a high enough likelihood that some organisations can manage to uphold a monopoly on the employment of physical force. This is exactly the core of the Weber definition, namely that a state is in reality a probabilistic phenomenon.

Size is often considered a fundamental property of states, as if it were a universal criterion for distinguishing between important and unimportant states. Different indicators may measure the size of a state. States vary tremendously whether measured by means of area of the territory or the population that constitutes the citizens or the inhabitants. The two size properties of area and population do not covary perfectly as there are states with a large population and a small territory, such as The Netherlands, as well as states with a huge territory and a medium-sized population, such as Australia. Yet size may be considered important, because one may argue that the variation in area or population matters for the entire fabric of the state and how it operates basically. There are a few models of the state that try to pin-point the effects of size on the state.

It must be emphasised that state size is one thing and state importance another. The two properties may be correlated, but they are not identical analytically speaking. The selection of states with more than one million inhabitants covers 77 per cent of all the states of the world, which contain within their borders 99.8 per cent of the world population. In the Wikipedia listing of the size of states, Fiji occupies slot 156 with a population below one million (839,000). Tuvalu is one of the smallest states with a rank number of 192 for a population of 11,000. Actually, there are no natural criteria that may be used for identifying any self-evident degree of proper state size. Nor is there, it seems, any absolute lower or higher limit on state area or population. Thus in 1990 a large number of states (or 63 out of 130, i.e. 49 per cent) had a population of more than one million but less than ten million. Polynesian Niue had only 2,000. Although self-governing, Niue is in free association with New Zealand. Yet very small states must find it burdensome to offer outside diplomatic representation.

Where are the really big states placed on the world map? And where do we locate the really tiny states? Remembering the distinction between two measures on size – area of the state territory and number of inhabitants in state citizenship – a rough picture may be drawn with a few broad strokes. Several populous states are to be found in Asia, as it contains some 59 per cent of the population. Asia is not that large in terms of area, but it certainly comprises much of the world's population. We have a few giant states with huge territories: China, India and Indonesia. Japan inhabits a far smaller territory. South Asia and Far East Asia comprise a number of populous states: Pakistan, Bangladesh, Vietnam, the Philippines, Thailand and South Korea. In Asia Minor there are two huge states with large territories: Turkey and Iran. The size of the territory of the states in Asia varies, although Asia comprises almost 60 per cent of the people of the world on some 20 per cent of the area of the Earth. In Oceania, the states do not have large populations, but there is one state that is big in terms of area: Australia. In the Pacific we find a large number of tiny states: Vanuatu, Samoa, Federated States of Micronesia, Tonga, Kiribati, Marshall Islands, and Palau.

Turning to Africa we would expect to find that population density is much lower than in Asia. The reverse relation between size of population and size of territory holds for Africa as it consists of 23 per cent of the area of the world but hosts 12 per cent of the world's people. This reflects a long-term developmental trend where for two centuries the population of Africa declined relatively speaking (Table 1.2). One cause was, of course, the transportation of a huge number of slaves across the Atlantic. The historical population trend for America is the opposite. At first the conquest of America resulted in a terrible reduction in the population, which was followed by a long trend of population growth. Actually, despite the immense

Table 1.2 Population of the continents (in percentages)

	1750	1850	1950	1750	1850	1950
Africa	13.0	8.5	8.0	13.0	8.1	8.2
America	1.9	5.1	13.3	1.6	5.8	13.7
Asia	65.2	63.4	54.9	65.8	63.9	54.2
Europe	19.6	22.8	23.2	19.2	8.1	8.2
Oceania	0.3	0.2	0.5	0.3	0.2	0.5

Sources: Adapted from Cipolla (1965: 99); Woytinsky and Woytinsky (1953: 34).

population growth in Asia, it is the case that the relative share of the world population for Asia has declined since 1750 (Cipolla, 2003).

Now, the sharp rise in population growth in Africa since the Second World War has reversed this trend, Africa now hosting some 700 million people. There are quite a few populous states in Africa, although Nigeria is the only really giant state on this continent: Egypt, Ethiopia, South Africa, Sudan, Zaire and Kenya as well as Tanzania. There are many states in Africa that are medium sized in terms of population, meaning they fall in between the range of larger than one million and smaller than 25 million. The very small states include: Cap Verde, Comoros, Equatorial Guinea, Sao Tomé, Swaziland and Principe.

On the American continent the USA scores high on both size of population and size of territory. America is the largest of all the continents and, besides the USA, it also includes Canada with its vast territory as well as Brazil with its huge population and immense land area. Here one should also mention populous Mexico. As a matter of fact, there are in addition many states with a population that is larger than ten million: Argentina, Colombia, Peru as well as Venezuela, Chile, Ecuador and Cuba. At the same time several states in the Caribbean are quite small: Antigua and Barbuda, Bahamas, Barbados, Belize, Dominica, Grenada, Guyana, St Kitts Nevis, St Vincent and Suriname.

It remains to look at Europe including Russia, although it has a very sizeable Asian part in Siberia. Typical of the European states is the high density of their population, reflecting that their territories are not that large, with the exception of Russia. The populous states are Germany, France, Italy and the United Kingdom. Spain, Poland and Romania also have large populations. Greece and Portugal are not as densely populated as the Netherlands or Belgium. Tiny states with a population of less than one million people may also be found in Europe: Andorra, Iceland, Liechtenstein, Luxembourg, Malta, Monaco and San Marino.

International indicators normally result in the Pacific Island countries being scored on the low side. Indeed, some are classified as "fragile states", to use the international development jargon, according to three of the governance indicators calculated by the World Bank: government effectiveness, rule of law and control of corruption. Samoa and Palau are the only two countries that come in the top half of the ranking on all three indicators. The others are below average on at least one indicator, and some on all three (http://info.worldbank.org/governance/wgi2007/).

It can be especially difficult for small countries to develop effective institutions. The alternative approach is to rely on the institutions of other countries. This can be done either by developing regional institutions, which is the approach of Pacific Regionalism, or by importing institutions from other countries. Both of these approaches have a lot to commend them. The Pacific Region harbours fragile states, but it has demonstrated that it can compete in global markets. The success stories included in the Pacific economies include copra and cocoa in Melanesia, coffee in Papua New Guinea and East Timor, squash in Tonga, horticultural products including root crops in Fiji and the Polynesian Islands, vanilla in Papua New Guinea and Tonga, tourism in Fiji, Vanuatu and the Cook Islands, and oceanic fisheries, especially tuna, across the region.

International migration should be seen as an opportunity for fragile states. The Philippines is a good example of a country that has consciously adopted a policy of promoting labour exports, as that country's experience suggests. While migration will not in itself make a country rich, it can be a very important income generator and stabiliser. Today over eight million Filipinos work overseas and send remittances home equal to 14 per cent of GDP. East Timor is currently planning a pilot Emigrants Worker Program. As these countries have done, other Pacific Island governments can also attempt to facilitate the movement of labour through bilateral negotiations and licensed migration schemes with richer countries.

An extensive variation in the size of the states in the world is to be found on all continents. For Europe, Africa, America, Asia and Oceania the within-continent variation is larger than the between-continent variation both with regard to area and population. It may be pointed out that these two dimensions – territorial size and population – do not go together to a high extent. The simple Pearsons' correlations between territorial size and size of population amount to $r = 0.50$ when the large number of tiny states are included (168 states), but it is smaller, $r = 0.48$, in a selection of states with more than one million inhabitants (129 states). Actually, there is a staggering variation in population density measures, combining population and area. The highly dense states include Singapore, Bangladesh, Taiwan, Mauritius, South Korea and the Netherlands. The sparsely populated states include Mongolia, Namibia, Mauritania, Australia, Botswana, Libya and finally Canada. The small sparsely populated states in the South Pacific and also PNG with just under six million inhabitants became independent rather recently, having British, German, Australian and New Zealand colonial legacies. France still holds sizeable territories in the Pacific (French Polynesia, New Caledonia) as is also true of the United States (e.g. Guam, American Samoa).

One may speculate if the tendency towards the establishment of new states will go on into the twenty-first century. The economic conditions for state creation have improved in the sense that small territories with a population of around one to three million people may become integrated into the world economy, making it possible to reach an acceptable standard of living although the state is not self-sufficient. This means that large territories may be broken into small compact states as a result of, for example, nationalism, at the same time as the new area is even more strongly integrated within the international economy, as in Slovenia or Croatia in former Yugoslavia.

In the classical doctrine of state sovereignty it was often stated that self-sufficiency is a necessary condition for state stability (Levy, 1952). The strong integration processes in the international economy have had the consequence that economic self-sufficiency guaranteed by some proper state size population-wise or in terms of territory no longer constitutes a *sine qua non*. A city-state like Singapore is almost totally non-self-sufficient, importing almost everything and exporting more than the GDP, but it strongly maintains its independence and stability. As a matter of fact, it was Malaysia that asked Singapore to leave the federation in 1965, which put Singapore in an awkward position being surrounded by Muslim countries, much improved though through Singapore's regional and global links.

As the discipline of comparative politics has emerged as one of the core sub-fields of political science and sociology, there is an inbuilt paradox that has never been fully resolved. It is the fact that all countries are counted as equals, although they are incredibly different in size. One may perhaps wish to reflect over the possibility of launching a different approach, which concentrates upon the big countries where most of mankind live. The 30 most populous countries in the world have a population of over 40 million, and this small set of the most populous countries covers almost three-quarters of mankind. Analysing how they are governed is a huge step towards understanding how most people live on the Earth from the political point of view. They exemplify all the major distinctions one has made in comparative politics, such as: federal–unitary, democracy–dictatorship, stable–unstable, majoritarian–proportional, modern–traditional, old–new, rich–poor, Muslim–non-Muslim, communist–non-communist and so on.

Here, a picture has been drawn of what entities are referred to as the unit of analysis for comparative politics, the set of internationally accepted states as it were. The finding in this chapter is the immense increase in the number of states since the Second World War. Whereas terms such as "political system", "nation-state" and "polity" remain abstract and difficult to pin down, Weber's state concept allows one to speak of truly important social systems acting and interacting with each other across the globe. The drive has evidently been towards more and more states, but there are limits to the creation of new compact states. It seems reasonable to focus on some proper subset of states, as it is difficult to gather information about each one. Such a sample could be drawn in various ways, but here I take the availability of data into account while at the same time selecting all the large populous countries. Actually only a handful of very tiny states have been left out.

It is vital to underline that comparative government could not possibly deal with the state in its entirety. There has to be a selected focus on a few state properties, because there are so many aspects of the state that are of potential interest. Focusing on stability may involve a conservative bias. However, this is not necessarily so, as one may enquire into various aspects about the stability of a state without committing oneself to the value of state stability. Actually, even though one may wish to understand the conditions for state stability, one could call for change asking for the creation of a new state, or the transformation of the regime as well as rapid changes in political leadership. Rule of law appears to me to be a more promising perspective upon the state than democracy. As it is far from clear or obvious how democracy is to be defined, whether or not it is an occidental conception, rule of law has a universal significance.

State longevity and regime stability

The basic tenet of the modern state as it evolved from the Renaissance to the twentieth century, identified in the Weberian state concept, is bureaucracy. The basic distinction is that between person and office or "*stato*", meaning that the modern state is a set of social mechanisms that separates as much as possible the roles from the individual persons or lifestyles of rulers. In Part III, I will discuss one hypothesis claiming that the superiority of the occidental state over other regimes (e.g. Oriental despotism) stems from its institutional traits, which to a greater or lesser extent can resist the personal aberrations of individuals.

States rise and fall as if they were creatures of their own making. There is a tradition of approaching states as biological phenomena, as if they had a life of their own, their special life processes determining their fate. The functionalist as well as the systems approaches came close to treating the state as if it belonged to some sort of specimen as being a kind of organism. This is called "reification" in the terminology of the philosophy of science or the fallacy of misplaced concreteness. In this chapter I discuss state age without any assumption that states are organisms. The purpose of this section is to enquire into the time-span of states.

It is true that there is often talk about states ceasing to persist, but when is a state to be declared dead; alternatively when can states be said to "persist"? There are bound to be changes in the state, but equating all kinds of change as a threat to state longevity will not do, as states may enhance their prospects of survival by flexible adaptation. Although states cannot be approached as some kind of organism, a few concepts relating to state age are relevant to the understanding of the nature of the state. Acknowledging that it is possible to lay down alternative criteria for how long a state has existed, it is difficult to do so without some concept of state age. But how is such a concept to be arrived at? For the purpose of conducting a comparative enquiry it would be interesting to examine the longevity of states, or more specifically whether state age varies considerably. But how to measure state age? When has a state ceased to exist?

Here, I will approach the concept of state age by focusing on a few of the Weber state properties. State longevity refers to how the basic institutions of states fare over time. Recalling the Weber definition of the state concept, states are distinguished by singling out the following properties: (1) territory; (2) a legal order or regime; and (3) monopoly on the use of physical violence. For the purpose of analysing state longevity, I focus on territory and the monopoly on the employment of physical force. A major change in two of these properties indicates that a state has perished, namely (1) and (3). A state is a probability phenomenon, as state survival increases as a function of the likelihood that (1) and (3) are maintained over time. It is undeniable though that it remains somewhat arbitrary how one labels a change in these two state properties as "major". I will refer to changes in (2) as regime instability.

The probability that a state perishes increases when its territory disintegrates, or when sustained and successful challenges to its legal order occur in the form of internal violence (protest, anarchy, anomy) or external subjugation to foreign powers. We know already that present-day states vary enormously in terms of territorial size and population, but states differ also in terms of age, i.e. state longevity.

To calculate the time-span of a state involves tricky measurement problems. Resolving the problem of determining the birth year of the states of today is to a considerable extent a matter of convention. Whether a state that has experienced profound changes, as, for instance, the United Kingdom with the fall of the British empire, is to be considered as of old age, remaining somehow the same, or is to be counted as a new young state, having lost much of its territory – there is no way to resolve this problem once and for all. In concept formation in the conduct of scientific enquiry, every decision about definitions has its pros and cons.

How different state age may be appears when one considers a few countries that are close to each other. Egypt appears to be the oldest existing state in the world, having had a number of regimes from the early Pharaohs to the present-day republic. But the newly founded states in neighbouring Chad, Uganda and Sudan almost ceased to exist during the 1980s due to anarchy.

The enquiry into the longevity of present states of the world is based upon the concept of "the modern state" in sociological theory. Being distinct from the medieval feudal state ("*stændestaat*"), a so-called modern state is distinguished by the employment of legal-rational authority. States are organisations with institutions:

> The modern state is perhaps best seen as a complex set of institutional arrangements for rule through the continuous and regulated activities of

individuals acting as occupants of offices. The state, as the sum total of such offices, reserves to itself the business of rule of a territorially bounded society.

(Poggi, 1978: 1)

The modern state originates in Western Europe during the Renaissance, but receives its typical configuration during the eighteenth and nineteenth centuries, when its claims to sovereignty were accepted both internally and externally (Part III). A modern state may have widely different regimes. The modern state is characterised by its monopoly on the legitimate employment of force, which implies that legal control is crucial. Kelsen's legal theory claims that the state and the legal order are the same phenomenon (Kelsen, 2005), which brings out how closely the survival of states is connected with the peaceful operation of law in societies with a specified territory. When there are difficulties in upholding the legal control over a territory, then state persistence is threatened.

States are fragile. Most of the states of the world are young. States are often created as the result of major social changes such as war, and some states succumb to the atrocities of anarchy or civil war. However, state death and state birth may occur in a peaceful manner. But, in general, state transformation tends to be a violent process, as it involves clashes between groups striving for power. Moreover, states may also collapse due to an invasion from another state – a violent process of change, to say the least. Several invasions of other countries in the twentieth century, undoing more or less their states, proved to be merely temporary, as with the Nazi-German and Japanese onslaughts.

There are old as well as young states. Some states persist for centuries whereas others come and go. A few states are highly compact ones where state identity has been nurtured by the experiences of several generations from belonging to one and the same state. Many states have been founded so recently that the process of nation-building is precarious. There are even states that lack an identity to such an extent that their very survival is at stake. Thus, states have different time-spans. Many new states have been created and old states are being dissolved. States may persist over centuries or they may perish after only a couple of decades. Yet, this may sound as if states had lives of their own, but states are not biological units as the organic theory of the state claimed. States are complex manmade organisations that have artificially created structures, which may be abolished by fiat. As it is true that states may be founded by intention or dissolved by decision, we must also underline that states may have a longevity that lasts over many generations.

The concept of the identity of a state may be defined to involve several things such as the maintenance of a set of structures of authority regulating the use of force within a territory of roughly the same boundaries. The fundamental problem here is that there is no natural criterion that we can use to decide when a state has changed so much that its earlier identity has been lost. Since both territorial boundaries and authority structures change over time, states can be identified differently.

What is taken as the starting point of a state is a matter of convention, but it is not arbitrary. Although there are different criteria that may be used, one has to be consistent once one criterion has been selected. Thus, the origin of the French state may be dated to 1944 after the Nazi occupation, or 1815 after the Napoleonic wars or even further back in time to 1775, 843 or 741, but then the same time perspective must be employed for other states. In order to display alternative ways of identifying the time-span of present-day states, three standard source books are consulted in Table 1.3.

First, Table 1.3 shows that the identity of states may be pinned down in time in slightly different ways, depending upon what countries are involved and what is to count as "independence". Western Europe has had a large number of independent states for a long period of time. On the American continent the average year of foundation dates back to the 1820s, whereas modern independent states in Oceania emerged in around 1900. Africa, Asia and the Muslim and Turkish civilisations have by far the largest number of young modern states. The European state has been around for a longer time than the states on the other continent, reflecting, as underlined, the diffusion of the modern state model from Western Europe.

Table 1.3 indicates that state age is very short in relation to the length of time of human existence on Earth. Many states are not yet 100 years old. Old states die and young states were being instituted in the early 1990s. Thus, the persistence of a state cannot be taken for granted. Look, for

Table 1.3 Year of state independence (median scores)

CIV	Derbyshire/ Derbyshire	CIA World Factbook	Britannica World Data
Arab	1951	1951	1951
Western Europe	1839	1701	1845
Eastern Europe	1955	1991	1991
Other occidentals	1867	1901	1901
South Asia	1947	1948	1928
Africa Sub-Sahara	1960	1960	1960
Muslim non-Arab	1947	1947	1945
Latin America	1830	1821	1822
Turkish	1991	1991	1991
Asean	1948	1945	1948
Pacific	1960	1936	1960
Eta squared	0.18	0.17	0.11

Sources: Based on Derbyshire and Derbyshire (1999); *Encyclopaedia Britannica* (2000); *CIA World Factbook* (2007).

example, at the tremendous changes of the scope of the territory of the German state during only the twentieth century. Although the word "state" may be used in a variety of meanings, we focus here on what is called the "modern" state. Sometimes it is also called "nation-state", but this expression is more confusing than clarifying. Using the concept of a Weber state, it is widely recognised that a few examples of this form of state emerged fully blown in the seventeenth century in Europe after the end of the great religious wars. What is decisive in our conceptualisation is the *probability* to which an organisation has implemented the population properties of the state concept: (1) direct relation of authority between the rulers and ruled with (2) clear territorial specification of boundaries and (3) monopoly on the legitimate use of physical force in that territory.

The modern state is not necessarily a nation-state, but it may be said to be a European state, as the concept of a "*stato*" dates back to around 1500 in Western Europe. There are consistently sharp differences in state age geographically. The fact that the European state was capable of subjugating large parts of the world, creating various types of domination structures in America, Asia, Oceania and Africa – colonies, dominions, protectorates – implies that there would be a geographical pattern. The indicators on state age reflect this process of exporting the European state to other continents, first to America, then to Oceania and Asia and finally to Africa.

State longevity is not the same as state stability. States that persist over time may be very different in terms of stability. A state may harbour different regimes and they may change their constitutions more or less often. Regime changes tend to be the outcome of challenges of the established state and constitutional revisions may be the formal expression of system changes. The notion of stability has a prominent place in comparative politics, although it is an inherently ambiguous term that has to be handled with great care. States may display longevity, yet they may have been unstable for some time. We wish to use a concept of state stability that is independent of the concept of state longevity. Thus, although the French state may be said to be very old, one cannot claim even that it has been stable during the entire post-Second World War period. A state may appear to be stable for decades only to suddenly collapse, as did the Soviet Union. Or a state may remain stable, persisting, as it were, indefinitely, such as the United States. How can we employ indicators that allow the measurement of not state age but state stability? I will use the third property of the Weber state concept – the legal order or regime – in order to describe state stability. A new state may tend either towards stability or instability, which may also be true of an old state for certain time periods. Thus, state age or longevity is one thing and short-term political instability another, although it is quite possible that a country suffers from instability over long periods of time. It is true that some present-day states have endured for a long period of time. Several states have, however, been recently founded. As states that persist over long periods of time may also experience instability, it is necessary to move to an analysis of state stability. And newly founded states cannot take their existence for granted, as their *raison d'être* or legitimacy may be questioned, i.e. resulting in regime instability.

Political instability may be either of a short-term or a long-term nature. What starts as dissatisfaction with policies and leaders could spill over into questioning the legitimacy of the regime. If no workable solution can be found about a new regime, then the entire state may crumble. Thus, political instability may be the starting point of long-term system transformation. Thus, one basic aspect of state instability is the lack of regime continuity (Eckstein and Gurr, 1975; Sanders, 1981). Political regimes may topple in a country while the state territory remains intact. This has often happened in European countries such as France, Spain and Italy as well as outside Europe in Latin American or Asian countries (e.g. Argentina and Iran).

Recognising that the concept of state stability is ambiguous, it is vital to find at least one or perhaps two aspects of this concept that allow measurement. I suggest a few ways to measure regime stability as well as portray a picture of its variation among various kinds of state, authoritarian as well as democratic.

Institutional foundations of states

The Weber state properties imply that states have a legal order or some system of political rule that it maintains within a territory by means of the special political instruments that are conducive to a monopoly on the employment of physical force. Speaking of state stability, we have to take into consideration the occurrence of fundamental revisions of the *order* or so-called regime changes.

The concept of a political regime is difficult to pin down more concretely, but it refers to the fundamental elements of public law, such as constitutional law. It would consist of the basic laws of the state that regulate the state organs, their powers and competences. These rules constrain the powers of various state bodies, channelling their activities into various functions, creating mechanisms for power sharing. Such rules may be collected and given a formally rational structure in written constitutions (Bogdanor, 1988: 4).

It should be pointed out that countries may have constitutions that are orientated towards power diffusion or checks and balances but at the same time the ongoing practice of these states is straightforwardly authoritarian. After all, the USSR was given a constitution in 1936, the "Stalin constitution" that spoke of "Fundamental Rights and Duties of Citizens" (Chapter 10). A state that moves towards dictatorships from democracy may either dispel explicitly its constitution or simply go on implicitly as if nothing had happened. It is always the *enforcement* of the rules which creates institutions.

Moreover, some states have had oppressing constitutions (e.g. South Africa with the apartheid system). The harsh racist regime introduced in 1948 following the electoral victory of the Nationalist Party was based on a legal framework including a constitution that severely restricted voting rights and an intricate system of pass laws that restricted the movement of the black population (Worger and Clark, 2003). One may speak of a fascist constitution when a corporatist-autocratic structure is introduced by means of formally written documents, such as was the case in Italy and Spain.

The regime constituting the institutional bedrock of the state cannot be identified with the written constitution. In order to describe the institutional web of a state one must look at ongoing practices and their orientation towards formally stated and actually employed rules. It is not enough to focus exclusively on some specific set of formal documents called a "constitution". As a matter of fact, the concept of a constitution is an ambiguous one.

The concept of a constitution is of help to the study of state regimes if it is employed with care. A few distinctions have been emphasised in the literature (Bogdanor, 1988), which are relevant when the concept of a constitution is used for the analysis of regimes.

First, there is the separation between a written constitution and an unwritten one. However, this distinction is not really that important. Since very few countries have unwritten constitutions (e.g. the United Kingdom, Israel and New Zealand) it is not a very informative conceptual pair. In addition, since "unwritten constitution" means only that there is no *codified* constitution, i.e. no formally existing, concretely specified set of documents that are designated "the constitution", it is not only a theoretical possibility that countries that lack a constitution also have basic institutional rules. This is very much the case in the United Kingdom, where some special documents have a type of constitutional status – Magna Carta (1215) and Habeas Corpus (1679) among others – and there is agreement as to which practices have the status as binding conventions (Jennings, 1951, 1961). To quote Bogdanor:

> If by "constitution" we mean simply the rules, whether statutory or not, regulating the powers of government and the rights and duties of citizens, then Britain, like other civilised states, has always possessed a constitution; but clearly this was not what Tocqueville had in mind when he made his famous declaration that Britain had no constitution.
>
> (Bogdanor, 1988: 53)

When there is talk about states not having a constitution one usually has in mind not only that there is no compact document comprising fundamental state laws, but also that the regime does not fall back upon the existence of a set of fundamental laws that are different from ordinary positive law. In this meaning there is no constitution in the United Kingdom, although it has what Dicey called a "historic constitution" (Dicey, 1982).

Second, there is a distinction between the "formal" constitution and the "real" constitution in use. Constitutional documents, even if so designated, are not safe indicators or true descriptions of the basic institutions of the state, because the rules outlined may be obsolete to some extent or simply outright misleading. The constitution in use is a set of rules that are actually followed, meaning obeyed, sanctioned or enforced in state activities and which are regarded as legitimate by if not a majority of the population in the state at least so by the key groups of power holders. Thus, Edmund Burke referred in his speeches and writings to the "British Constitution", although it has never been codified (O'Brien, 2002; Stanlis, 2006). Here, we come close to the regime concept and its important place in the state, but which rules belong to the real constitution may not be easy to specify. It is sometimes possible to use the formal written constitution as an approxima-tion of the real regime realities. Several countries have established or rewrit-ten constitutions recently, which could minimise the distance between constitutional formalia and constitutional realia.

Third, constitutional documents tend to have a special legal status. The so-called constitutional status places the fundamental laws on a higher level than positive law or the main legal order. Sometimes such a constitutional status is protected by means of a constitutional court. Constitutional law may be designated a special status by means of the requirement of separate decision procedures for constitutional change or revision – constitutional inertia. A constitution implies not only well-designed documents but may also involve a special legal status. One may differentiate between a *thin* and a *thick* interpretation of the constitutional concept. In the thin connotation a "constitution" would be any implicitly understood and accepted conventions directing fundamental state activities. In the thick connotation, a constitu-tion is a set of formal documents having a special status above the ordinary legal order, safeguarded by special mechanisms such as a constitutional court, or outlining very special decision rules concerning a change in the constitution.

The complex nature of the constitutional concept means that it is not an easy task to identify the actually operating principles or the true normative order of the state. In addition, constitutional documents have an ideological flavour, revealed in the shifting popularity of various constitutional ideas from one time period to another. Some constitutions are short but efficient, such as the US constitution, whereas other constitutions may be extremely long but not always enforced (India, Portugal).

Constitutional diffusion

Constitutions are not made from scratch, but stem from both international constitutional theory and the history of the individual country. Constitu-tions emerged with the American and French revolutions. One may see the effects of constitutional diffusion by looking at the date of origin of key state constitutions. Thus, several of the constitutions enacted at the end of the eighteenth century or the beginning of the nineteenth century expressed the principles of the division of powers according to the Locke doctrine or the Montesquieu model, expounded in *The Spirit of the Laws* (1748). The constitutional state became politically relevant at the end of the eighteenth century. Constitutionalism was launched as a political theory about good government to be implemented by the introduction of a written constitution. The theory of *liberal constitutionalism* of the eighteenth century in the Benjamin Constant synthesis in *On the spirit of conquest and on usurpation* from 1815 (Constant, 1988) involved:

> The doctrine which, in the secular age of the autonomy of politics inherent in the principles of "national sovereignty" and "sovereignty of the people", demanded that this kind of state should have a written Law which would set out the rights and obligations of citizens and institutions established to make them work, with all the checks and balances required to watch over the proper functioning of state and society on behalf of people.
>
> (Ionescu, 1988: 35–36)

The two model constitutions at that time were the 1787 American constitution – a constitutional republic – and the 1791 French one – a constitutional monarchy. They inspired the making of several constitutions all over the world. Constitutional monarchy was institutionalised in Spain in 1812, Norway 1814 and Belgium 1831. The American presidential system was adopted in Latin America with the exception of Brazil up until 1891, which copied the 1822 Portuguese constitution, which followed the 1812 Spanish constitution.

Actually, the French and American constitutional principles were the chief contenders, because the British Westminster model was not fully developed until the mid-1850s. Then, the English constitutional tradition and its peculiar contribution – parliamentarianism (Bagehot, 1969) – spread to the dominions of the emerging empire as opposed to the Crown Colonies, which were governed from Westminster. Not only were several European states with their orientation towards constitutional monarchy given a constitution, but the constitutional diffusion also reached Turkey (1876), Japan (1889), Persia (1906) and China (1912).

The doctrine of separation of powers in combination with the prevalent notion of a "*Rechtsstaat*" or rule of law was embodied in the constitutional codifications around 1800. The state was looked upon as a set of branches of government: executive, legislature and judiciary; they were to be assigned separate power functions: rule application, rule-making and rule adjudication; and they were to be staffed by different actors: kings with ministers or presidents, parliamentarians and judges. By such separations it was hoped that a kind of power balance would be established. Adding the unitary – federal dimension of the state a large number of hybrid types were established during the nineteenth century. Strong presidential powers resulted in the Latin American context, whereas the English system gravitated towards the doctrine of constitutional monarchy with parliamentary sovereignty, with the German and Austro-Hungarian constitutions placed somewhere in between, underlining royal prerogatives and a strong state bureaucracy. A constitutional monarchy recognised the negative rights of citizens, but failed to endorse democracy.

In the twentieth century there have been three waves of constitutional diffusion. The end of the First World War was followed by the introduction of new democratic constitutions which emphasised human rights (e.g. the Weimar Republic constitution in 1919, Yugoslavia and Poland in 1921 and Romania in 1922). A second wave occurred after the end of the Second World War when the term *"Sozialstaat"* became as valid as *"Rechtsstaat"*. Many constitutions enacted after the end of the Second World War emphasised several kinds of human rights including positive liberties such as the right to employment (e.g. the 1949 Basic Law of the Federal Republic of Germany and the Italian constitution from 1948).

This rephrased or anticipated the international declarations concerning human rights, negative as well as positive, from 1948 by the United Nations and from 1950 by the European Council. Freedom of speech and association are negative liberties, whereas the rights to social support and employment enter positive liberties. The recent emphasis on positive freedom is not only apparent in new constitutions in the so-called rich world such as Spain (1978) and Portugal (1976/1982) but also in the Indian constitution of 1949, adding to "Fundamental rights" so-called "Directive principles of state policy" (Finer, 1988: 30).

The major declarations of human rights in the eighteenth century were almost exclusively orientated towards the concept of negative freedom, underlining what governments could not do to their citizens: the Declaration of Independence in the United States in 1776, the French Declaration of Human Rights in 1789 and the American Bill of Rights of 1791.

A third wave of constitutionalism was set in motion by the collapse of communist regimes in Eastern Europe as well as the drive towards democracy in the Third World. Actually, the many recent regime changes may be seen as a test in constitutionalism and institutional design, i.e. its power to suggest proper political institutions that would enhance state stability. Constitutional rules whether in the thin or thick sense (above) may contribute towards predictability in state activities and operations, but they may also fail to become institutionalised.

Regimes

The difficulties besetting the concept of constitution cause us to return to the concept of the regime. It does not display the ambiguities typical of the constitutional concept, which make it hard to tell which if any normative order really exists: the written versus the unwritten one, the formal or the real one and so on. There is hardly a general definition of the concept of a political regime available in the literature, but the words "regime" and "regimen" are tied together with institutions.

Whereas the so-called *ancien regime* in France denoted a concrete regime in space and time analysed by, among others, Tocqueville (1988), it remains somewhat of an arbitrary task to identify each and every institution in each country, especially stating their life-span. It would make things easier if one had recourse to a set of clear type concepts, which would allow us to classify country regimes. Easton made a distinction between three basic political objects: the authorities, regime and political community (Easton, 1965: 172). "Political community" would be the territorial dimension of state referring to the state members seen as a group of persons bound together by a political division of labour (Easton, 1965: 177). "Regime" would cover properties such as values, norms and structure of authority. Regime norms specify the procedures to be used in making and implementing public decisions. "Authorities" would refer to people in ruling positions. Evidently, a crisis in the regime would hit the very institutional foundation of the state, whereas a rejection of the authorities could be resolved by appointing new leaders with or without major changes in the regime.

The problem is the connection in the regime concept between its value and norm component on the one hand and the behaviour component on the other. How to handle the concept when there is a smaller or larger amount of inconsistency between first – the normative content of a regime – and the second – the actually prevailing rule? Was there a sharp regime change in India when Indira Gandhi ruled in a dictatorial manner from 1976 to 1977? Operational criteria that measure the occurrence of regime changes would be helpful in comparative enquiry. One may distinguish between a few major typologies of political regimes.

A political regime is a set of rules that structure the interaction between the principal and his/her agents in politics. The institutions of a polity may more or less restrain the rulers or politicians. When a country changes the basic rules of the political game from monarchical or authoritarian practices towards rule of law, then a major regime change has occurred. And vice versa, as when the military declares emergency law, dispelling a constitution with rule of law. The institutional variety of rule of law regimes is large, which is also true of authoritarian regimes. Several typologies over the variety of political regimes have been constructed in comparative politics, a few of which will be mentioned below, as they may be employed to tap regime changes empirically.

Traditional regimes

Weber had more to say about the major kinds of historical regimes than about present-day democracy. To Weber, political legitimacy results from a special feeling or mode of looking upon government where the population considers the legal order or the regime morally binding. Yet he underestimated how extensive physical force may be employed for political purposes. Naked power rulerships may last for quite some time, as post-Second World War events testify: Khmer Rouge rule in Cambodia, Chinese domination in Tibet, Saddam Hussein in Iraq, the Shah Pahlavi regimen in Iran, Pinochet in Chile, Trujillo in the Dominican Republic, Papa Doc Duvalier in Haiti, Idi Amin in Uganda and Mengistu in Ethiopia, as well as a few periods with large-scale repression in East European communism. Authority involves that those ruled follow the directives – commands or laws – of the rulers. A regime or a system of prescriptions may be accepted as legitimate either because it has always been accepted – traditional authority – or because the leaders are obeyed out of a special relationship of venerability – charismatic authority. Finally, there is modern authority or the legally rational type (Weber, 1978: 215).

Weber made a number of distinctions between traditional authority systems that are applicable mainly in historical analysis. Here, we note the following types: gerontocracy, patriarchalism, patrimonialism, sultanism, estate-type domination, feudalism, medieval corporatism and absolutism (Weber, 1978: 217–301). Traditional authority systems tend to be changed by the power of charismatic leaders: "It Is Written, but I say onto You", in the words of the Bible. However, charismatic authority is fundamentally unstable, as it cannot solve the successor problem. The only viable option to democracy as plebiscitary leadership, according to Weber, is the introduction of the rational legal authority type, where politicians employ bureaucratic rule, i.e. exercise power in terms of rules. Legal-rational authority is rule *by* law, if not rule *of* law.

When we turn to the regime experiences of the twentieth century, it is impossible not to place democracy at the forefront. There exist now only a few cases of Weberian traditional authority systems. The *sheikh* or *emir* (*amir*) and *sultanate* regimes in the Middle East and Borneo could be classified in this way, as is also true of the few remaining *real* monarchies such as those in Jordan, Morocco and Thailand. The current number of traditional regimes is not large, as Table 1.4 shows.

Some of these absolutist regimes have taken steps to introduce constitutions or representative institutions that confer an aura of constitutional monarchy upon the rulers. Nepal even had democratic elections in 1991. This is a kingdom in deep trouble, facing armed resistance from the only left-over Maoist guerrilla in the world. Yet a few of them lack a constitution entirely, for example, large Saudi Arabia referring only to Sharia. Several traditional regimes are located in quite small states. One may note that several of the traditional regimes feed upon oil resources and the rent involved in petrol production. Kuwait introduced the female vote in 2006.

There have occurred a few cases of sultanic rule in the other pejorative sense of tyrannical or completely arbitrary political leadership. One could mention, for instance: Bokassa (Central African Republic), Nguema (Equatorial Guinea), Mobutu (Zaire), Mugabe (Zimbabwe) and Eyadema (Togo) in

Table 1.4 States with traditional rule 2006

Country	Population	Rulership	Year of foundation
Bahrain	0.7	Reigning Emir	1971
Bhutan	2.3	Monarchy (Maharaja)	1947
Brunei	0.4	Sultanate	1984
Jordan	6.0	Kingdom	1946
Kuwait	2.5	Sheikhdom	1961
Nepal	28.3	Monarchy (Maharaja)	1846
Oman	3.1	Sultanate	1744
Qatar	0.9	Sheikhdom	1971
Morocco	33.2	Kingdom	1956
Saudi Arabia	27.0	Monarchy	1932
Swaziland	1.1	Monarchy	1967
Thailand	64.6	Monarchy	1350
Tonga	0.1	Monarchy	1970
Tuvalu	0.01	Monarchy	1978
United Arab Emirates	2.6	Federation of Sheikhs	1971

Source: Adapted from Derbyshire and Derbyshire (1999); *The Statesman's Yearbook* (2007).

Africa, although these leaders were presidents by title. Or one could mention some Carribean states such as Haiti (Duvaliers) and the Dominican Republic (Trujillo) (Chehabi and Linz, 1998). Much of traditional rule remains in the internal structures of many states, such as kinship and primary political groupings in several African states and also in the Pacific Ocean. Local chiefs or kinship structures are sometimes publicly accepted as part of the state structure in order to increase the legitimacy of the rulers (South Africa, Fiji). Traditional authorities may be organised in houses of chiefs operating as intermediaries or brokers between central power and the localities and receive government sanction as well as salaries (e.g. Botswana). Clientelism in Africa is often legitimised on the basis of tradition as with the spread of neo-patrimonialism following independence (Chazan *et al.*, 1999).

Legal rational regimes

Weber's classification from the early twentieth century was not equally detailed and comprehensive when he looked at modern states. He clearly identified the key difference between parliamentary and presidential regimes in addition to the communist regimes (Weber, 1978: 1000–1200). Considering the victory of the democratic regime since the Second World War, an institutional typology that distinguishes between different democratic regimes is helpful. At the same time it should be emphasised that many states are not democracies. Thus, in addition, we need to distinguish between various kinds of dictatorship (Linz, 1975; Ferdinand, 1991). There is thus a variety of democratic and authoritarian regimes.

Democracies

It is readily seen that parliamentary states are not the only rule of law regimes. Presidential institutions may also achieve rule of law, although it must be recognised that many presidential regimes are non-democratic. This brings us to the classical distinction between English parliamentarism and American presidentialism. Bagehot has already stated in *The English Constitution* from 1867 that countries need to make a choice between two kinds of executives:

> This fusion of the legislative and executive functions may, to those who have not much considered it, seem but a dry and small matter to be the latent essence and effectual secret of the English constitution; that competitor is the presidential system. The characteristic of it is that the president is elected from the people by one process, and the House of Representatives by another. The independence of the legislative and executive powers is the specific quality of the presidential government, just as their fusion and combination is the precise principle of cabinet government.
>
> (Bagehot, 1993: 66)

Bagehot, writing after the American Civil War, focused upon the distinction between two constitutional principles, on the one hand the principle of balance of powers and on the other the idea of parliamentarianism as power fusion. Bagehot argued that the parliamentary mode of government was superior to the presidential regime in terms of state performance. One needs to qualify the notion of presidentialism by making a distinction between strong presidentialism and weak presidentialism. In the former regime the president exercises true executive powers independently of Parliament, whereas in the latter there is parliamentarianism, the president acting only symbolically.

The distinction between parliamentarianism and true presidentialism may be combined with the separation between majoritarian and proportional election systems (Taagepera and Shugart, 1991). The election system is a set of central institutions for structuring principal–agent interaction in government. In a rule of law regime, the two major alternatives are the majoritarian methods on the one hand and the proportional methods on the other. Switzerland would exemplify *collegiado*, i.e. presidentialism due to its special executive where the presidential post rotates in a type of government of the French type from 1794: "*le directoire*". Parliamentary systems may comprise states with weak monarchs or weak presidential heads of states, but also states with strong presidents such as Finland and France – semi-presidentialism – that have both premier and president with prerogatives.

Authoritarian regimes

One may wish to distinguish between alternative forms of dictatorship, from totalitarian regimes to tutelage or benevolent authoritarianism (Linz, 2000).

How does one identify various types of dictatorships, some of which are rationally instituted while others tend towards traditional authority or arbitrary rule, based merely upon the threat of naked power? Linz has dealt with the problem of sorting out the basic categories of non-democratic types (Linz, 1975, 2000; Chehabi and Linz, 1998). One may wish to distinguish between right-wing authoritarianism, inspired by fascist ideology (economic nationalism), and left-wing authoritarianism, following the communist model of the state and the economy (command economy).

There are a variety of non-democratic polities, one of which is the authoritarian type. Temporary military regimes may result in an authoritarian regime or they may return to democracy. The practical relevance of the Leninist type of regime has been drastically reduced in the world of today with the exception of China, because it was hardly conducive to state stability or a good state performance record. However, there are other kinds of authoritarian regimes.

An authoritarian political system is not simply a dictatorship in the sense of one-man rule; dictatorships are transitory polities, which may develop into an authoritarian regime when the exercise of power is institutionalised. Nor is authoritarianism the same as totalitarianism; a totalitarian regime is one in which: (1) power is monistic and monolithic; (2) there is an elaborate ideology which provides for the legitimisation of the regime and a *Weltanschauung* for cultural life; and (3) citizens are highly mobilised in terms of the ideology of the single ruling party.

An authoritarian regime may be a stable system of rule according to Linz. It is a mixture of democracy and totalitarianism. In terms of performance the authoritarian polity stands between the pluralism of democracies and the monism of totalitarian rule, in between the moderate multi-ideological belief system of the former and the ideological penetration of the latter, and without the intensive political participation of the masses in totalitarian systems and the openness of power elite groups in democracies. Authoritarianism is different from the contestation and participation typical of a democratic polity, yet not identical to the one-dimensional nature of the power systems in totalitarian regimes with its heavy mobilisation of the masses. Modern authoritarianism is more rational in the conduct of state operations than so-called sultanistic regimes (Chehabi and Linz, 1998). Authoritarian regimes differ along three basic dimensions: the extent of limited pluralism, the degree and type of participation, and the extent of ideological penetration of one single belief system. They are easily separated from democratic regimes, but the borderline to totalitarian regimes is less strict (O'Donnell, 1988).

Bureaucratic authoritarianism, according to O'Donnell's concept, occurred in Latin-American countries during various periods of time, alternating sometimes in a peculiar circular fashion with democracy or semi-democracy. Bureaucratic authoritarian regimes may be created by military coups as in Brazil in 1964 and in Argentina in 1966, or they may emerge out of earlier fascist experiences as in Spain and Portugal. Typically such regimes involve limited channelled participation and they are set up as a reaction to radical movements threatening both the established order and the future of a democratic polity. Such regimes may develop a more comprehensive supporting ideology such as organic statism or what Schmitter (1983) called "state corporatism".

Regime longevity and constitutional changes

If a regime is of such basic importance to the state, then it is important to ask how stable regimes tend to be. One way to tap regime longevity is to measure when the current constitution of a state was introduced. If done recently, it implies that the regime has been changed more or less due to most probably a transition from dictatorship to democracy or the introduction of Sharia law into the Basic law. There are two opposing views on constitutional reform. One view claims that the constitution should be left unchanged as far as possible, enhancing state stability. Another view argues that constitutional policy-making is adequate, using constitutional reform to mirror basic changes in society. Table 1.5 shows the average age of the current constitution for ten groups of countries.

Constitutional longevity is only true of the so-called occidental world in a narrow sense, meaning Western Europe and North America and Australia and New Zealand. In all other categories of countries, constitutions have been changed recently, also in Eastern Europe. Table 1.5 indicates again fundamental political instability in many parts of the world, as the age of the current constitution is young. The eta scores indicate that longevity of

Table 1.5 Current constitution (median years)

	Britannica 2000	n	CIA World Factbook 2005	n
Arab	1975	14	1972	15
Western Europe	1953	17	1948	17
Eastern Europe	1992	20	1993	20
Other occidentals	1900	5	1941	4
South Asia	1978	3	1978	3
Africa Sub-Sahara	1992	36	1992	36
Muslim non-Arab	1972	6	1979	7
Latin America	1982	22	1981	22
Turkish	1993	7	1993	7
Asean	1989	14	1978	14
Pacific	1981	2	1981	2
Total	1990	146	1987	147

Source: Based on Derbyshire and Derbyshire (1999); *Encyclopaedia Britannica* (2000); *CIA World Factbook* (2007).

constititution differs systematically from one civilisation to another (eta = 0.644, eta squared = 0.415 for Britannica scores, and 0.594 and 0.353 for CIA scores).

The current constitution of a state is less old than the state itself, meaning that regime changes tend to take place frequently. Even in Europe with some of its old states there have occurred numerous constitutional changes. Most interestingly, states differ in constitutional stability within each of the continents. Most regime changes have occurred in the states in Africa, America and Asia, but the average age of the current constitution is not very different between the new world and the old European world contrary to the finding with regard to state age. Most constitutions in the world are of a rather young age, which means that constitutional changes are frequent. Political life is hazardous in many countries, to say the least. The current constitutions among the states of the world have on average been adopted or changed after 1945. This applies in particular to Africa and Asia where colonial rule received its final blow after the Second World War.

Countries where there has been no major constitutional revision for a long time include Australia, Canada, Ireland, Mexico, the Netherlands, New Zealand, Norway, Saudi Arabia, and the United States. However, this does not guarantee that the current regime is universally accepted as legitimate, which, for example, the problem of national identity in Canada shows. Regime stability, as measured by length of time of the current constitution and the number of constitutional changes, occurs *inter alia* among the democracies in the affluent world, but not all affluent countries are characterised by regime stability. A few liberal welfare states have experienced major constitutional or institutional change such as Belgium, France, Spain and the UK.

In several Third World countries there have been major constitutional changes recently: Ethiopia, Yemen, Algeria, Chad, Cambodia, South Korea, Iran, Afghanistan, Nicaragua, the Philippines, Central African Republic and Sudan. Not many Third World countries are characterised by constitutional stability. However, traditional rule in patrimonial systems such as Saudi Arabia, Oman, Qatar, the United Arab Emirates and Morocco appears stable. How much longer will communist rule prevail in countries such as China, North Korea, Vietnam, Laos and Cuba? In countries afflicted by the horrors of civil war or anti-colonial fighting new regimes have been introduced: Angola, Mozambique and Namibia. The surge in the late 1980s and early 1990s in the foundation of new states implies by necessity the introduction of new regimes, as is the case in the former Soviet Union, Eastern Europe and Former Yugoslavia.

Constitutional longevity tends to be short, although states may persist for centuries. Had we recognised the Nazi occupation of Europe as a constitutional change – it certainly was so in one sense – then the countries with the same regime for longer than 50 years would be very small in number. At the same time, constitutions matter, for example, in a few countries with a firm belief in the legitimacy of their political regime where the old constitution is considered almost sacred: the United States and Norway.

Yet formal constitutional change and regime instability are not the same. Another way to measure regime stability is to focus directly on the transitions between the two major types of regime in this century, i.e. democracy versus dictatorship. It would involve a number of more valid indicators, as each and every constitutional change does not signal regime instability. Thus Denmark in 1953, Sweden in 1974 and Switzerland in 2000 introduced new constitutions, but they merely codified what was long accepted as legitimate through implicit practices, making the written constitution less obsolete.

As things now stand it appears that the relevant constitutional choice or the basic regime alternatives would be a democratic regime versus dictatorship. The stability of these two regime types – democracy and dictatorships – may be singled out for special analysis. Although the number of stable democracies did not count for more than one-sixth of the total number of states, the variation over time in the stability of democratic and non-democratic regimes may be mapped. By looking at the indices for the degree of democracy, covering all kinds of regimes scoring high or low on democratic properties over time, one may gain insights into the state variation in regimes. There is a constant risk of the collapse of democratic institutions in some parts of the world where democracy is sought but never firmly institutionalised. Similarly, dictatorships are not stable everywhere. Table 1.6 indicates the fluctuation in democracy and dictatorship for various periods between 1945 and 2005 as well as estimating the average length of the lifetime of a regime.

The finding is here that regime reshuffling, moving back and forth between democracy and dictatorship, has occurred since the end of the war on all the continents with the exception of the very stable Oceania. It is particularly pronounced in Latin America and Africa but it also occurs in several Asian states. It is not the very same states that score high on regime instability all the time, as a short examination of a few spectacular transitions from democracy to dictatorship (or vice versa) shows. Low regime change scores belong to the set of states which are either stable democracies or stable dictatorships. Regime instability has been pronounced in Latin America and Africa, where a number of transitions have occurred from civil rule to military rule or even back again in cases such as Argentina, Bangladesh, Burkina Faso, Ecuador, Honduras, Bolivia, Thailand, Peru, Paraguay as well as Iran. At the same time the score for Europe has risen sharply, which captures the fall of the communist regime systems and the introduction of new regimes into Eastern Europe.

One overall finding here is that regime instability has been strongest first and foremost in Latin America. In Africa there is also a general regime instability, but it refers more to the competition between more or less authoritarian civil rule on the one hand and military government on the other. Part

Table 1.6 Long-term instability post-Second World War (means)

CIV_GRP	Variation in democracy (1975–2005)		Variation in democracy (1975–2005)		Regime durability		Regime changes	
	(CV)	n	(St. Dev.)	n	(2003)	n	(1950–2003)	n
Arab	0.30	15	0.80	15	27.3	15	7.4	15
Western Europe	0.034	18	0.31	18	60.8	16	1.3	18
Eastern Europe	0.29	20	1.62	20	8.0	20	4.5	20
Other Occidentals	0.007	5	0.061	5	118.4	5	0.4	5
South Asia	0.24	4	1.17	4	51.3	4	4.8	4
Africa Sub-Sahara	0.38	36	1.41	36	8.8	36	7.5	36
Muslim non-Arab	0.39	7	1.22067	7	4.57	7	10.00	7
Latin America	0.24	22	1.40	22	22.2	22	8.00	22
Turkish	0.32	7	0.89	7	11.6	7	4.1	7
Asean	0.29	14	1.05	14	30.8	13	7.8	14
Pacific	0.16	2	1.10	2	22.00	2	5.5	2
Eta squared	0.34		0.28		0.6		0.3	

Sources: Based on Marshall et al. (2005); Freedom House (2006).

of the regime instability in Asia stands for the difficulties in introducing and consolidating democracy.

State stability and political unrest

Could there be political instability even though the political regime remains firm? The concept of stability in politics is ambiguous. On the one hand, there are concepts referring to long-term stability such as regime persistence and constitutional longevity. On the other hand, short-term stability concepts stand for leadership crisis or government duration. Government stability is a tricky concept. When governments come and go frequently or when the leadership of a state is replaced within short time intervals, then there could be talk of political instability. However, it must be remembered that political leadership that lasts too long may also indicate political instability.

The concept of political stability or instability is a complex notion, meaning that it is difficult to apply in a straightforward manner in comparative politics. It comprises several kinds of phenomena, such as protest, death from domestic violence, civil war, anarchy, rapid governmental turnover, state financial crises and regime change. Here, I will target only the latter form of political instability, namely a major change in the *real constitution* of the country.

The pattern of long-term instability is not the same as that of short-term instability. Take the case of Saudi Arabia, for instance (Abukhalil, 2004). Although there have occurred numerous manifestations of political instability in this regime since its inception in 1932, including both the killing of one king (Faysal in 1975) and one *coup d'état* (Faysal in 1964), Saudi Arabia cannot be considered an unstable political regime. It has only a minimal constitution (Basic law of government from 1992), but the same framework of rules and ideas has been consistently applied for almost a century, namely political Wahabism.

Generally speaking, regimes last longer in Europe and Oceania than on the other three continents. Particularly in Latin America, Asia and Africa regimes do not last for long. Here, we have the shift back and forth between various regimes, especially between democracy and dictatorship but also between right-wing and left-wing authoritarianism. Countries that have fallen into anarchy such as Liberia, Sierra Leone, the Ivory Coast and Somalia as well as Afghanistan and Colombia are to be considered as fundamentally unstable politically, as they lack any form of constitution or constitutional continuity. Actually, these countries do not even have dictatorships, as they are ruled partially by warlords.

Political instability is a multidimensional concept. Political instability includes short-term events such as protests, strikes and mass demonstrations as well as long-term trends like the change of the basic frontiers of the country (Migdal, 2001: 135–169). It is possible to argue that, for example,

Table 1.7 Short-term political stability (1996–2004) (means)

civ_grp	n	pse 1996	pse 1998	pse 2000	pse 2002	pse 2004
Arab	15	−0.70	−0.48	−0.28	−0.44	−0.59
Western Europe	18	1.19	1.30	1.35	1.21	1.10
Eastern Europe	20	0.23	0.19	0.11	0.23	0.02
Other occidentals	5	0.83	0.95	0.94	0.48	0.63
South Asia	4	−0.46	−0.51	−0.66	−0.68	−0.69
Africa Sub-Sahara	36	−0.43	−0.57	−0.62	−0.65	−0.69
Muslim non-Arab	7	−0.90	−1.05	−1.09	−1.27	−1.50
Latin America	22	−0.10	−0.13	−0.02	−0.16	−0.34
Turkish	7	−0.45	−0.32	−0.55	−0.70	−0.95
Asean	14	0.30	0.29	0.32	0.44	0.17
Pacific	2	−0.65	−0.19	−0.43	−0.66	−0.98
Total	150	−0.04	−0.05	−0.04	−0.11	−0.25

Source: Based on Kaufmann *et al.* (2005).

Table 1.8 Analysis of variance of short-term political stability rankings

	Eta	Eta squared
pse 1996 * civ_grp	0.59	0.34
pse 1998 * civ_grp	0.63	0.40
pse 2000 * civ_grp	0.65	0.43
pse 2002 * civ_grp	0.64	0.41
pse 2004 * civ_grp	0.66	0.44

Source: Author.

the Russian state has remained intact since the foundation of the Moscow principality in the twelfth century, yet it has experienced traditional, authoritarian and democratic regimes – regime changes coupled with revolutions, both violent and peaceful. Table 1.7 presents scores for short-term political stability around the world according to a composite measure by the World Bank.

In these country rankings, one notes that Western Europe and other occidental countries come out as politically stable, whereas the opposite is true of the Muslim groups, the Turkish group and Sub-Saharan Africa. In between these groups one finds South Asia, Asean and Latin America. Table 1.8 confirms that the country classification chosen captures a considerable part of the country variation in political stability/instability.

Table 1.7 demonstrates roughly the same picture as indicated in Table 1.6 (long term), namely that political stability is firm in Western Europe, North America and Oceania, medium in Latin America and Far East Asia but low in the Muslim civilisations, Africa and Turkestan, as well as in the Pacific. I will employ the long-term political instability measures below when enquiring into how rule of law and political stability are inter-related.

Conclusion

The concept of state stability identifies an essential aspect of the state, although it may be interpreted in various ways, as it is a multidimensional concept like political stability. Here, I target the longevity of the regime, or what Weber called the "real constitution". The number and gravity of constitutional changes may be singled out as a measure of state instability, but the application of this measure is not straightforward, due to the problems that beset the concept of a constitution. I focus upon the average duration of regimes or the number of regimes since the end of the Second World War.

State instability is not the same as either democracy or dictatorship. This concept refers more to the pendulum in between these two regime types that have dominated the state since the decrease in the number of traditional regimes. But it also covers the fundamental lack of a state when civil war or anarchy prevails. It is essential to examine the extent of state stability, although it must be admitted that it is a multifaceted concept also covering short-term political instability such as protests, strikes, government turnover and financial turmoil. Here, I focus upon regime instability or regime longevity.

The main finding is, then, that state stability is precarious. The average length of time for a political regime is hardly more than 15 to 20 years. Yet there is an interesting pattern of country variation, which warrants a search for an explanation of why state instability is endemic in several countries. Many countries have changed their regimes during the post-war period, but some of these have experienced a cyclical fashion moving to and fro between alternative regimes, in particular from democracy to dictatorship and vice versa. Again, several countries have not achieved regime stability today, as the country is ruled by means of an emergency law or merely on the basis of a military regime, or by means of an opaque constitution that is not really enforced. When the state fails, anarchy, civil war, anomie and warlordism surface – with terrible consequences for the principal of the political body, the population (Kalyvas, 2006) (see Appendix below).

Appendix 1.1 Occurrence of civil and ethnic wars (1946–2004)

Continent	Country	Begin	End	Type of war
Africa	Algeria	1991	2004	Civil war (Islamic militants)
Africa	Angola	1975	2002	Civil war (UNITA)
Africa	Burundi	1972	1973	Repression of Hutus
Africa	Burundi	1993	2004	Ethnic war (Tutsis against Hutus)
Africa	Chad	1965	1994	Civil war
Africa	Congo-Brazzaville	1997	1999	Civil war
Africa	Djibouti	1991	1994	FRUD rebellion
Africa	Ethiopia	1974	1991	Ethnic war (Eritreans and others)
Africa	Ethiopia	1977	1979	Ogaden war ethnic violence (Somalis)
Africa	Ethiopia	1999	2000	Ethnic war (Oromo separatists)
Africa	Guinea-Bissau	1998	1999	Civil war (coup attempt)
Africa	Ivory Coast	2000	2004	Civil war (north, south and west divisions)
Africa	Liberia	1985	–	Repression of dissidents (failed coup)
Africa	Liberia	1990	1997	Civil war
Africa	Mauritania (1979)	1975	1989	Colonial war (Western Sahara)
Africa	Mozambique	1981	1992	Civil war (RENAMO)
Africa	Nigeria	1966	–	Repression of Ibo
Africa	Nigeria	1966	1970	Ethnic war (Biafra separatism)
Africa	Rwanda	1956	1965	Repression of Tutsis
Africa	Rwanda	1990	1994	Ethnic war (Tutsis vs. Hutu regime)
Africa	Rwanda	1994	–	Ethnic violence (Hutus target Tutsis)
Africa	Rwanda	1994	1998	Ethnic war (Hutus vs. Tutsi regime)
Africa	Rwanda	2001	–	Ethnic war (attacks by Hutu guerrillas)
Africa	Sierra Leone	1991	2001	Civil/ethnic war (RUF/Mende)
Africa	Somalia	1988	2004	Civil war
Africa	South Africa	1983	1996	Ethnic/civil war
Africa	Sudan	1956	1972	Ethnic war (Islamic vs. African)
Africa	Sudan	1983	2002	Ethnic war (Islamic vs. African)

(Continued)

Appendix 1.1 Continued

Continent	Country	Begin	End	Type of war
Africa	Uganda	1971	1978	Ethnic war (Idi Amin regime)
Africa	Uganda	1981	1986	Repression of dissidents
Africa	Zaire	1960	1965	Katanga civil war
Africa	Zaire	1977	1983	Repression of dissidents
Africa	Zaire	1996	2004	Civil war (ouster of Mobutu and aftermath)
America	Argentina	1976	1980	The Dirty War repression of dissidents
America	Chile	1974	1976	Repression of dissidents ("disappeared")
America	Colombia	1949	1962	La Violencia civil war (Liberals)
America	Cuba	1957	1959	Civil war (Castro ousts Batista)
America	El Salvador	1979	1992	Civil war (FMLN)
America	Guatemala	1966	1996	Repression of indigenous peoples
America	Nicaragua	1978	1979	Civil war (Sandinistas)
America	Nicaragua	1981	1990	Civil war (Contras)
Asia	Afghanistan	1978	2002	Civil war
Asia	Azerbaijan	1990	1997	Ethnic war (Nagorno-Karabakh)
Asia	Bangladesh	1971	–	Ethnic war (Bengali independence)
Asia	Bangladesh	1975	1992	Ethnic war (Chittagong Hills)
Asia	Cambodia	1970	1975	Civil war
Asia	Cambodia	1975	1978	Khmer Rouge repression of dissidents
Asia	Cambodia	1990	1997	Civil war (Khmer Rouge)
Asia	China	1946	1950	Chinese civil war
Asia	China	1947	–	Repression of Taiwan dissidents
Asia	China	1959	–	Repression of counter-revolutionaries
Asia	China	1966	1975	Cultural Revolution
Asia	China	1990	–	Repression of dissidents
Asia	China	1956	1967	Ethnic war (Tibetans)
Asia	India	1946	1948	Partition (Muslims vs. Hindus/Sikhs)
Asia	India	1952	2004	Ethnic war (northeast tribals; Assam separatists)

(Continued)

Appendix 1.1 Continued

Continent	Country	Begin	End	Type of war
Asia	India	1983	1993	Ethnic war (Sikhs)
Asia	India	1990	2004	Ethnic war (Kashmiris)
Asia	Indonesia	1963	1993	Ethnic war (Papuan–West Irian)
Asia	Indonesia	1965	1966	Repression of Chinese/communists
Asia	Indonesia	1976	1992	Colonial war (East Timor)
Asia	Iran	1978	1993	Civil war (Islamic state)
Asia	Iran	1979	1985	Ethnic war (Kurds)
Asia	Iraq	1961	1993	Ethnic war (Kurds)
Asia	Iraq	1996	1998	Ethnic war (Kurds)
Asia	Israel	1965	2004	Ethnic war (Arab Palestinians/PLO)
Asia	Laos	1960	1973	Civil war
Asia	Lebanon	1975	1991	Ethnic war (various sects)
Asia	Malaysia	1948	1956	Repression of Chinese by Malay militia
Asia	Myanmar (Burma)	1948	2004	Ethnic war (Karen, Shan and others)
Asia	Nepal	1996	2004	Civil war (UPF "People's War")
Asia	North Korea	1950	1953	Korean War (civil war)
Asia	North Vietnam	1958	1975	Vietnam War (civil war)
Asia	Pakistan	1973	1977	Ethnic war (Baluch separatism)
Asia	Philippines	1972	1997	Civil war (New Peoples Army)
Asia	Philippines	1972	2004	Ethnic war (Moros)
Asia	Sri Lanka	1983	2002	Ethnic war (Tamils)
Asia	Sri Lanka	1987	1990	Civil war (JVP–Sinhalese extremists)
Asia	Syria	1981	1982	Repression of dissidents (Muslim)
Asia	Yemen	1994	–	Ethnic war (south Yemenis)
Asia	Yemen AR	1962	1970	Civil war (following coup)
Asia	Yemen PDR	1986	1987	Civil war
Europe	Bosnia	1992	1995	Ethnic war (Serbs, Croats, Muslims)
Europe	Croatia	1991	–	Civil war (Croatian independence)
Europe	Croatia	1991	1995	Ethnic war (Serbs)

(*Continued*)

Appendix 1.1 Continued

Continent	Country	Begin	End	Type of war
Europe	Georgia	1991	1993	Civil war
Europe	Georgia	1991	1993	Ethnic war (Abkhazians–Ossetians)
Europe	Georgia	1998	–	Ethnic war (Abkhazia)
Europe	Greece	1945	1949	Greek civil war
Europe	Russia	1994	1996	Civil war (Chechnya secession)
Europe	Russia	1999	2004	Ethnic war (Chechen separatists)
Europe	Tajikistan	1992	1998	Civil war
Europe	Turkey	1984	1999	Ethnic war (Kurds)
Europe	Yugoslavia	1998	1999	Ethnic war (Kosovar Albanians)
Oceania	Papua New Guinea	1988	1997	Ethnic war (Bougainville)

Source: Marshall (2005).

2 Rule of law

Introduction

States are made up of constructed organisations that are supposed to deliver services to their populations, especially their citizens. The population hires and instructs agents – political elites – to provide them with goods and services they badly need. Besides safety, the principal may want his/her agents to deliver rights, especially human rights. Polities differ in terms of how their institutions restrain the political elites to respect the requirements of rule of law. The modern state is highly active in terms of its many programmes or policies. Although government constrains people's activities in many ways, it is hardly defensible to speak of the state as if it had a life of its own. The organism model treats the state as a coherent unit with independent life and its own purpose(s). This is *reification* or the fallacy of misplaced concreteness, treating the state as if it were an entity besides the citizens of the state. The state comprises many organisations at various levels of government that operate a huge variety of services. Basically, there is a principal–agent problem in the relationship between the citizens and their state, because government, although proclaiming that it enhances the public interest, may pursue a variety of objectives corresponding more or less to citizen preferences. The famous slogan from the French revolution – *Liberté, égalité* and *fraternité* – may be interpreted as an attempt to define this principal–agent game in politics.

A government pursues a variety of objectives in order to exercise its legitimacy over the population. State evaluation is a method for monitoring the activities of the political elites holding them accountable to the population. What, more precisely, could count as state performance with regard to the basic objectives of liberty and equality? I will discuss present-day data from the states of the world, evaluating state records about liberty and equality. The analysis of state performance is a large field of research, especially within public policy or policy analysis (Parsons, 1995; Hill, 2004). Protecting rule of law is a key aspect of regime performance, as this type of regime offers both freedom in the form of human rights and a certain level of equality to its citizens. Fraternity or brotherhood is linked with the notion of a nation or nation-state. I will argue that its relevance will not be the same for the twenty-first century as it was for the twentieth century due to the emergence of multicultural societies (Kymlicka and Norman, 2000).

Performance analysis

The two basic political ideals from the French Revolution could constitute the starting point for systematic state performance evaluation: *liberté* and *égalité*. The findings here indicate that states perform very differently with regard to these two basic values in a democracy according to Tocqueville's concept (1990). In the public policy approach, one makes a separation between policy *outputs* or state decisions and activities on the one hand and policy *outcomes*, or the social results of such decisions and activities, on the other. It is conceivable that a state may engage in a number of activities which do not reach their social goals for two entirely different reasons: (1) the decisions and actions of the state have the correct causal direction in terms of a set of publicly stated legitimate goals such as freedom and equality, but their impact is as a matter of fact not sufficient to implement the goals; and (2) the state operates a number of programmes which could not possibly result in the achievement of these legitimate social purposes. It makes a difference if (1) or (2) holds. Thus, we shall look at not only the overt activities of the state, but also at a set of crucial economic and social outcomes in order to see what impacts the state may have covertly.

There is fundamentally no limit to the various outputs or outcomes to be included in a state evaluation enquiry. Policy analysis and outcome evaluation could cover any governmental programme, from health care to education to criminal policies. Economic policy-making covers a number of outcomes that are relevant for the analysis of political stability, such as unemployment, inflation and economic growth. What matters here is the system importance of state performance. I will look at a few macro-evaluation criteria that may be justified from a normative point of view concerning what constitutes a good or a bad state in terms of a principal–agent framework, especially when the normative criteria selected are considered the legitimate ones to employ, by the state inhabitants themselves, their elites or the international community. Thus, the emphasis here is here upon civil and political rights. Among the set of performance outcomes, I will examine the following macro objectives: (1) quality of life, and (2) income distribution, remembering that social outcomes are a function of many conditions besides politics.

Rule of law measure

Democratic vitality involves both the institutionalisation of human rights of various kinds and a true probability that the power position of the ruling elite may be contested. When indices constructed in order to measure the occurrence of democracy are examined, the central place of human rights becomes evident. In particular some human rights are *sine qua non* for any democracy: freedom of thought, speech, association and the freedom of the press. Other human rights such as *habeas corpus* principles are relevant for democracy in an indirect way. Finally, there is the right to vote in free and fair elections. Dahl made a distinction between democracy and *polyarchy* in the following way:

> Polyarchies, then, may be thought of as relatively (but incompletely) democratised regimes, or, to put it in another way, polyarchies are regimes that have been substantially popularised and liberalised, that is, highly inclusive and extensively open to public contestation.
>
> (Dahl, 1971: 8)

Dahl distinguished two fundamental institutional dimensions of states: degree of public contestation and degree of participation. When both dimensions are low, there are closed hegemonies; a low degree of public contestation and a high degree of participation implies inclusive hegemonies; a high degree of public contestation and a low degree of participation characterise competitive oligarchies, whereas a high degree of public contestation and a high degree of participation would be typical of democracies. To Dahl, democracy is the ideal-type of regime (Dahl, 1956, 1989), but it is not strictly feasible in real life today. The closest one could get, realistically speaking, is what he called "polyarchy", although I will speak of "rule of law" regimes.

A number of indices have been constructed in order to measure the country variation in the institutionalisation of the rights and duties that substantiate the abstract concept of rule of law. The core of these indicators is the occurrence of civil and political rights making these indices indicators of the spread of rule of law around the world. In order to qualify as government of and by the people, a specific set of institutions has to be introduced and maintained in a country. Rule of law institutions would be of two types. First, there are the participation rules that lay down the presuppositions for the activation of the electorate in relation to referendums and national elections. Second, there are the power and competency rules that specify the procedures for how the political elites may compete for and exercise power.

The concept of constitutional democracy is intimately connected with the concept of rule of law as well as liberty as a set of civil and political rights. Table 2.1 presents one standard indication on democratic performance in the form of state respect for civil and political rights for various periods ranging from 1970 to 2004 where civil or political liberty is handled as a quantitative variable, allowing one to rank states of the world according to their degree of rule of law.

Rule of law is much less visible on the two continents of Africa and Asia in contrast to Europe and Oceania. Listing a few countries there that have had a liberal or semi-liberal regime, though not fully institutionalised

Table 2.1 Rule of law (average scores)

Civilisations	Frind 72		Frind 80		Frind 90		Frind 100		Frind 104	
Arab	3.04	14	3.41	14	2.90	15	2.85	15	2.90	15
Western Europe	8.50	17	9.51	17	9.79	18	9.67	18	9.96	18
Eastern Europe	2.05	5	2.65	5	6.25	5	7.23	20	7.64	20
Other occidentals	9.55	5	9.70	5	9.70	5	9.70	5	9.70	5
South Asia	6.06	4	6.44	4	5.31	4	5.50	4	5.50	4
Africa Sub-Sahara	3.14	33	3.16	35	3.52	36	5.04	36	5.48	36
Muslim non-Arab	3.89	7	2.93	7	2.82	7	3.68	7	4.21	7
Latin America	5.77	22	5.67	22	7.27	22	7.17	22	7.17	22
Turkish	6.25	1	4.00	1	7.00	1	2.82	7	3.25	7
Asean	3.56	12	3.25	13	4.23	13	4.70	14	5.07	14
Pacific	4.00	1	6.25	2	7.38	2	7.75	2	7.38	2
Total	4.79	121	4.89	125	5.50	128	5.99	150	6.26	150

Source: Based on Freedom House (2006).

during the entire post-war period, I could point to the following: India, Sri Lanka, Malaysia and Singapore. There is not much rule of law in Africa; yet tiny Mauritius and fairly rich Botswana constitute interesting exceptions. The new strong demands for democratisation in Africa have not met with an institutionalisation of civil and political rights. The situation is different on the American continent. Here, we have not only the US and Canada with their long democratic experiences, but also a number of countries where their states have protected civil and political rights but only for specific periods of time – *Latin Americanisation.* Perhaps the risk for Latin Americanisation would now exist mainly in the new democracies in the Khanates or Central Asia, as rule of law in Latin America has consolidated considerably since this huge wave of democratisation initiated in 1990. Table 2.2 links the rule of law score with the civilisation categories.

In Europe, the iron curtain separated the democracies in Western Europe from the so-called people's democracies in Eastern Europe from 1945 up until 1989. One could find traces of a Latin American pattern in Southern Europe. In Greece, civil and political rights were fragile up until the introduction of the new regime in 1974, following the collapse of the military regime installed in 1967. Portugal (1926–1974) and Spain (1939–1975) have had long experiences of authoritarian rule. In both Portugal and Spain, political coercion proved to be both strong and long-lived. The Franco regime was installed after the civil war of 1936 to 1939 and the Salazar regime was formed in 1932. The Franco regime remained intact up until the death of the *Caudillo* in 1975, when typically the successor problem proved impossible to solve. The Portuguese dictatorship foundered in 1974 following defeat in the independence wars in the Portuguese colonies in Africa.

Waves of democratisation

The number of rule of law regimes have grown substantially since 1990. Not only the former East European countries and several new states in the former giant Soviet Empire have or have attempted to establish rule of law, but so also has Latin America. Constitutional democracy may increase also in Africa (e.g. in South Africa). Since 1990 a new and truly strong wave

Table 2.2 Analysis of variance of rule of law scores

Measures of association	Eta	Eta squared
FRIND 72 * CIV	0.71	0.51
FRIND 80 * CIV	0.79	0.62
FRIND 90 * CIV	0.81	0.65
FRIND 100 * CIV	0.74	0.55
FRIND 104 * CIV	0.72	0.52

Source: Author.

of democratisation has spread civil and political rights all over the world, although Huntington identified the following three long-term waves: (1) 1828–1926; (2) 1943–1962; and (3) 1974–1990 (Huntington, 1991: 16). If the hopes for a strong movement towards liberty come true, then almost 50 per cent of the states of the world would institutionalise rule of law.

Yet, one may wish to issue a warning that there could occur reversels in the trend towards increased democracy (e.g. Thailand, Fiji), but there are actually reasons to be more concerned about growing political instability (anarchy, civil war, anomy) than outright dictatorship in several of our groups of countries (Ivory Coast, Congo, Iraq, Lebanon, Nepal, Sri Lanka, East Timor, Ecuador).

In early 2000, there were, in addition to the countries in Table 2.3, a set of about 40 potential candidates for the title of "democracy". Some have recently introduced new rule of law-orientated constitutions safeguarding civil and political rights. Yet constitutional formalia is one thing and political practice another. In some of these countries such as Malaysia and Singapore a long-nurtured hope for democracy has failed to materialise. In Central Asia the problem of consolidating rule of law is a major concern in several countries.

The concept of *Latin Americanisation* is resorted to in order to pin down a swing back and forth between liberty and coercion, i.e. in most cases military rule, characteristic of several states in Central and Latin America in the twentieth century (O'Donnell and Schmitter, 1986; Linz and Stepan, 1996). It implies not only that civil and political rights were fragile in Argentina, Brazil, Chile and Peru, but also that civil administration was not easily maintained for longer periods of time in these countries. The modern state concept was introduced in Latin America in the early nineteenth century in rebellion against European colonial powers. After independence there followed a period of constitutional rule during which certain steps towards rule of law were taken. Thus, by the First World War, several of the states in South and Central America could be designated as democracies having universal male suffrage and competitive party systems (Table 2.4). However, the twentieth century has been marked by political instability, i.e. a succession of *coups d'états* and periodic dictatorships, especially prior to 1990.

Around 2000, most dictatorships had been demolished in South and Central America. It is possible to render Latin Americanisation as a concept a wider field of application than only Central and South America. There are now several states whose attempts at moving towards rule of law may be reversed, either bringing dictatorship back in again (Przeworski, 1991) or ending up in an outcome where there is some degree of democratic legitimation of government, but it fails to achieve full consolidation of rule of law, such as in Russia, Central Asia or Sub-Saharan Africa where anarchy occurs in one country after another. Several presidential regimes are semi-dictatorships or fully authoritarian, such as Turkmenistan and Zimbabwe.

Table 2.3 Stable rule of law 1960–1987

	Rustow (1967)	Dahl (1971)	Wesson (1987)
USA	x	x	x
Canada	x	x	x
Jamaica		x	
Trinidad		x	x
Barbados			x
Mexico	x		
Costa Rica	x	x	x
Columbia	x		x
Venezuela			x
Chile	x	x	
Uruguay	x	x	
United Kingdom	x	x	x
Ireland	x	x	x
Netherlands	x	x	x
Belgium	x	x	x
Luxemburg	x	x	x
France	x	x	x
Switzerland	x	x	x
Spain			x
Portugal			x
Germany FR	x	x	x
Austria	x	x	x
Italy	x	x	x
Greece	x		
Finland	x	x	x
Sweden	x	x	x
Norway	x	x	x
Denmark	x	x	x
Iceland	x	x	x
Lebanon	x	x	
Israel	x	x	x
Japan	x	x	x
India	x	x	
Sri Lanka	x		
Philippines	x	x	
Australia	x	x	x
NewZealand	x	x	x
N	31	30	28

Source: Adapted from Rustow (1967); Dahl (1971); Wesson (1987).

A rule of law regime may be considered to be the best type of polity, as judged by state evaluation criteria such as human rights, but one may wish to distinguish between alternative rule of law regimes, as within democracy theory. Coming from the consociational tradition, Lijphart (1984) introduced two ideal-types. Whereas Lijphart had argued that both of these sets of

Table 2.4 Rule of law in Latin America (1945–1986)

	Introduction of female suffrage[a]	Years of democracy[b]	Years of dictatorship[c]
Argentina	1947	7	35
Bolivia	1952	1	41
Brazil	1932	30	12
Chile	1949	18	24
Colombia	1957	33	9
Costa Rica	1949	42	0
Cuba	1934	7	35
Dominican Republic	1942	9	33
Ecuador	1929	25	17
El Salvador	1939	18	24
Guatemala	1965	22	20
Haiti	1950	0	42
Honduras	1955	0	42
Jamaica	1944	28	0
Nicaragua	1955	0	42
Panama	1946	11	31
Paraguay	1961	0	42
Peru	1955	30	12
Trinidad/Tobago	1946	25	0
Uruguay	1932	29	13
Venezuela	1947	29	13

Sources: a Adapted from Skidmore and Smith (1984: 66); Derbyshire and Derbyshire (1999: 123–128); b–c Gurr (1990).

Notes
b States are classified as rule of law if their score is 4 or higher on the Gurr scale.
c States are classified as non-democracies if their score is 3 or lower on the Gurr democracy scale.

institutions were conducive to state stability, it now seems that he claims that the consensus model could be superior to the Westminster model, judged by performance criteria (Lijphart, 1991a, 1991b). The Lijphart model is a very general one, covering not only state format and government institutional conditions but also properties referring to the party system. It raises the question: Do the concepts of Westminster democracy and of consensus democracy have empirical reality, i.e. is there a strong tendency towards the patterns in these two models? Consider the following facts with regard to the distinction between Westminster and consensus democracy:

- *State format and executive structure*: Federal as well as unitary states may be either presidential or parliamentary. Presidential regimes are based upon the separation of powers, but they do not endorse multi-party system or PR.
- *State format and legislature*: It is not the case that unitary states tend towards one kind of legislative chamber format such as mono-camer-

alism or asymmetric bi-cameralism, as the examples of France, the Netherlands, Italy and Spain show to varying extents.

- *Election system, state format and executive structure*: The Nordic countries, Spain, Portugal and Greece fall outside of the prediction that PR and multi-dimensional issues promote the creation of grand coalitions. It is not difficult to find states that are federal in nature but which are run by majoritarian election methods (e.g. Canada, Australia and India). And several countries that have practised grand coalitions are unitary states such as the Netherlands, Belgium (up until 1990) and Lebanon.

One must remember that the Lijphart model, like Weber's, is a so-called ideal-type, i.e. as extreme theoretical constructs they are more tools of analysis than minute empirical descriptions. The Lijphart model serves as a corrective to the prevailing image that the Westminster model is the true or effective model for parliamentary democracy. Yet Lijphart's argument does not really cover presidentialism, which in its pure form may be seen as a type of adversarial democracy but also as a mechanism for power separation. Presidents are elected by a majoritarian technique, but as both the head of state and the leader of government, they cannot be fired by Parliament, except by impeachment. It is true that power-sharing institutions along the consensus model could make democracy more stable in many Third World countries. Yet, when Swiss-type institutions have been tried in a few countries with deep-seated cleavages – Lebanon, Sri Lanka, Nigeria – they have not succeeded in stabilising the state. As a matter of fact, there are several models of democracy, as many institutional set-ups may achieve a high degree of rule of law.

The public sector

Looking at government from the principal–agent perspective, there is always the hope that government will be for the common good of its people. Thus, besides anarchy the worst that could happen is that a state becomes a warrior state, either conducting war with its neighbourhood states or engaging in genocide towards one of its minorities. Positively, a government could attempt to increase the general level of affluence in the country by underlining the importance of economic growth, bringing about sustained economic development. The principal of the body politic may wish government as its agents to promote not only equality under the law but also equal results as outcomes of egalitarian policies. Thus, welfare may be as important as rule of law as a key political objective in principal–agent interaction.

Government in societies where the economy delivers a surplus that may be divided among the population may either support a welfare state (Western Europe) or promote a welfare society (Australia, USA). When governments set up and fund welfare states, equality is a major concern. State performance may be measured by looking at policy outputs or outcomes in order to find out how much they contribute towards the achievement of equality. Equality may be fostered by means of the tax state as well as through specific redistributive programmes that target services or cash benefits for lower income people.

Allocative programmes

Equality may be enhanced by government activity reflected in the overall size of the public sector or in the composition of the public sector. States vary in the size of their public sectors as well as in the main orientation of these towards equality-promoting policies, such as health and education expenditure as well as transfer payments in social security. In order to understand the size of government, one must look at both the allocative part, comprising services, and the distributive part, comprising transfer payments. Generally speaking, transfer payments are low, as a percentage of GDP, in welfare societies and almost non-existent in poor and medium-income Third World countries. Table 2.5 presents an overview of government size measuring public resource allocation with the exclusion of transfer payments. The allocative state does not vary much in size as a percentage of GDP. It is GDP that differs enormously.

Distributive programmes

A welfare state not only provides a number of services virtually without cost to its citizens; the allocation of education of various kinds includes obligatory primary education and a variety of opportunities with regard to secondary and higher education. Health care comprises both open and closed somatic care involving a large number of medical specialities. The allocation of social services consists of both old-age care and services to a number of clientele. In addition, a welfare state operates transfer programmes – cash payments or money checks, the size of which is indicated in Table 2.7 when compared with the data in Table 2.6.

In reality, a large redistributive state can only be found in Western Europe. Economic poverty is a definitive barrier to cash payments, as the low score for Africa indicates. But there exist some patterns of public resource allocation in Third World countries that are welfare state orientated (MacPherson and Midgley, 1987). Although the limits set by financial constraints cannot be bypassed in an analysis of the Third World state (Wilensky, 1975), social policies do have a history dating back to colonial times in the developing countries, although they tend to be directed towards urban elites.

Although the number of countries covered in Table 2.6 is not large, it is true that states differ considerably in their efforts to run equality-enhancing programmes. However, while transfer programmes are almost

Table 2.5 Size of the public sector: general government consumption in percentage of GDP (means)

CIV_GRP	G 1975	G 1980	G 1985	G 1990	G 1995	G 2000	G 2001	G 2002	G 2003
Arab	30.6	27.6	28.4	27.5	25.0	23.5	23.6	23.8	24.2
Western Europe	21.9	23.1	23.3	23.6	24.7	26.6	26.6	27.4	27.7
Eastern Europe	20.7	16.3	17.0	22.8	24.8	23.9	23.9	23.5	22.1
Other occidentals	27.2	27.8	26.7	25.2	23.8	24.5	24.6	24.8	24.7
South Asia	10.0	9.6	12.1	12.2	13.1	13.5	13.4	13.1	12.4
Africa Sub-Sahara	17.6	18.3	18.0	17.1	16.5	16.2	16.4	16.5	16.5
Muslim non-Arab	15.6	15.2	13.5	14.8	12.6	12.3	12.2	11.8	11.6
Latin America	14.9	16.0	16.4	15.1	14.0	15.2	15.0	15.1	15.2
Turkish	15.7	15.9	11.4	13.8	13.3	16.4	16.5	17.5	17.0
Asean	16.0	17.6	18.6	17.2	17.8	19.0	19.7	19.4	18.3
Pacific	26.6	20.2	17.7	21.0	16.5	18.3	16.3	15.7	15.0
n	99	105	106	111	113	113	113	113	117
Eta squared	0.3	0.3	0.3	0.3	0.4	0.4	0.4	0.4	0.4

Source: Based on Gwartney and Lawson (2006).

Table 2.6 Size of the public sector: general government consumption and transfers in percentage of GDP (means)

CIV_GRP	PUB 75	PUB 80	PUB 85	PUB 90	PUB 95	PUB 200	PUB 201	PUB 202	PUB 203
Arab	39.6	34.0	32.8	35.1	31.6	30.5	30.2	30.1	31.8
Western Europe	40.1	41.9	44.6	44.6	47.2	46.4	46.6	47.5	48.6
Eastern Europe	61.5	40.9	38.6	49.1	42.8	42.2	41.7	41.1	38.6
Other occidentals	40.5	43.4	42.9	41.8	39.1	39.0	39.0	36.9	36.5
South Asia	16.7	17.5	18.5	19.8	19.9	19.7	19.4	18.7	18.2
Africa Sub-Sahara	21.0	21.1	23.8	21.4	20.3	22.0	22.9	23.5	23.7
Muslim non-Arab	24.2	22.8	18.4	26.1	18.0	18.6	16.5	16.1	16.6
Latin America	19.5	20.8	22.1	20.5	20.3	21.9	20.9	20.8	20.9
Turkish	21.7	21.9	21.8	17.7	21.7	19.2	19.3	20.2	19.7
Asean	18.6	19.7	21.3	20.1	22.1	23.1	24.4	23.9	24.8
Pacific	15.5	13.5	19.0	23.4	14.0	20.4	18.4	17.9	18.6
n	75	78	83	88	96	92	94	95	96
Eta square	0.5	0.6	0.5	0.6	0.6	0.6	0.6	0.6	0.6

Source: Based on Gwartney and Lawson (2006).

non existent in the Third World, the redistributive state is huge in certain OECD countries, such as the Netherlands with 28 per cent, Belgium with 23 per cent and France with 22 per cent of the GDP in 1990, which means a higher level of state commitment than in the Scandinavian welfare states, which, however, are larger in terms of public resource allocation.

Economic affluence is a necessary but not sufficient condition for extensive transfer payments. Some welfare states in Western Europe concentrate more on transfer payments, whereas others are more active in public consumption. Thus, in 2000 Italy's allocative branch of government was slightly smaller than its redistributive branch. However, the opposite holds for Sweden, Denmark and the GFR. In welfare societies such as the United States, Japan and Australia, public consumption is much greater than redistribution. In a few super-rich oil-exporting countries there are considerable public sector expenditures such as in Saudi Arabia, Qatar and the Arab Emirates, offering several public services free to their populations.

Growth of government

Public sector growth is a universal phenomenon. The expansion of government during the post-war period is to be found in states on all the continents. This is called Wagner's Law. When data are added up for the entire public sector – public consumption and redistribution (social security, transfer payments) – the expansion of the tax state in Western Europe becomes even more evident (Rose, 1984, 1989).

The public sector consists of the activities of governments on various levels and with various functions. On the one hand, there are the functions of the guardian state: internal and external order. On the other hand, there is the set of welfare state functions. According to Table 2.8, the share of military expenditure would belong to the guardian state concept whereas the share of educational and health expenditure would constitute part of the welfare state, promoting equality. Both types of state expenditure have risen sharply since the 1960s. Among Asian states the increase in military spending is very pronounced, which to some extent is also true of African states. In Europe the main trend is the relative expansion of the welfare state and the relative decline in the military budgets.

Some states allocate a considerable part of the resources of the country to military effort. In recently available data, the really big military spenders in terms of expenditures/GDP include: Iran, Israel, Oman, Saudi Arabia, Syria, North Korea, the United Arab Emirates and the United States. The concentration on military spending in the states situated in the Middle East and the Persian Gulf is enormous. The fall of the Soviet empire meant a real opportunity to engage in mutual arms reduction, at least among the superpowers. Thus the global demand for and supply of arms went down in the 1990s, but developments after 9/11 have pushed military spending upwards. In addition, the states around the Taiwan Straits engage in heavy military spending. The US takes on two-fifths of all military expenditure, absolutely speaking, but, since American GDP is so huge, the relative size of military spending is higher in several other countries.

Other states focus heavily on equality-enhancing welfare state expenditures (i.e. on programmes within health care and education), meaning around 15 per cent of GDP: Austria, Belgium, Canada, Denmark, Finland, France, FRG, Ireland, the Netherlands, New Zealand, Norway, Sweden and Switzerland. Welfare societies (i.e. countries with a high standard of living that are strongly market orientated) tend to trust voluntary exchange mechanisms more than budget allocation in the provision of welfare-enhancing services to their populations. The welfare states are, on the contrary, those countries that to a considerable degree trust public budget-making with extensive tasks – allocative and redistributive – in order to guarantee their citizens a decent level of welfare. The welfare societies are those countries that rely heavily on well-functioning markets to provide their consumers or citizens with a high standard of living. Both the welfare states and the welfare societies belong to the so-called set of rich countries, mainly the OECD countries. While both kinds of states are very well-off in terms of economic affluence with a high GDP, they have different philosophies about the welfare state, one favouring broad-based generous programmes and the other clinging to narrowly focused client needs-defined programmes (Castles, 2004).

The public sector in the OECD countries has grown from a level of about 20 to 25 per cent of GDP at the end of the Second World War to roughly 45 to 55 per cent in some European welfare states in 2000, when the exceptional growth process was brought to a halt. In addition, welfare societies have experienced the growth of government. Two questions arise: Why has this general growth in *the tax state* (as Schumpeter called it) in the rich advanced capitalist countries? Why has the public sector grown in such a *different* manner in various countries? There is general agreement about the impact of affluence upon the size of the state, government expenditures being positively related to GDP growth (Wagner's Law). But much more is involved, as democracies tend to have larger governments than do authoritarian regimes. From a principal–agent perspective, it seems crystal clear that economic growth allows the population to demand more from its agents, the politicians or political parties. In addition, some political parties have offered exceptional public sector growth to the electorate, gaining support in many West European countries.

To understand the substantial variation in the size of the state, measured by means of taxes and expenditures, one needs to make the distinction between a welfare state ideology (continental European model) and a welfare society ideology (Anglo-Saxon model). It has been debated whether the emergence of the welfare state has its sources in the growth of an egalitarian culture (Thompson *et al.*, 1990; Kuhnle and Kildal, 2005), or has its roots in a revisionist socialist ideology, together with Christian democracy and social liberalism (Esping Andersen, 1985, 1999). In any case, the welfare state is still expanding in the less affluent of the OECD countries, whereas public sector expansion in the very affluent countries in the OECD came to a halt around 2000. Portions of the electorate may send signals to the politicians that they wish to have policies with an egalitarian emphasis, but equality of results is hard to achieve.

Social outcomes

Although standard economic measures such as the GDP and GNP indicators tap much about country living conditions, they do need to be complemented by a set of social indicators that describe quality of life or the level of human development as well as the distribution of welfare in a society. What matters is how economic affluence translates into general conditions of living among the population. The economic capacity of a state may be employed for various purposes, only one of which could be the reduction of mass poverty. A description of the country variation by the human development index complemented by an income distribution index would inform us about the social environment of states, which after all is affected by government policy performance.

Quality of life

Quality of life is the crucial aspect of the human condition. It denotes a variety of things such as health and sanitary conditions, education, birth rates and life expectations. One indicator on quality of life is the human development index, which focuses on people's life expectancy, literacy and income for a decent standard of living (United Nations Development Programme, 2003). Another relevant composite index is Morris' physical quality of life index (Morris, 1979). The HDI index portrays a picture of the differences in the human predicament, which, however, tend to be smaller than the immense variation in GDP or PPP (Table 2.7).

The human predicament in Africa is on the whole grim. Although conditions have hardly improved, at the same time there are exceptions which should be noted. The tragedy of Africa is that the average values for the African continent are far below those of Oceania and Europe. Angola, Benin, Bhutan, Ethiopia, Guinea, Liberia, Niger, Sierra Leone, Somalia and Zaire are the unfortunate ones, whereas conditions are brighter in Morocco and Tunisia in the North, Gabon in Central Africa, and for South Africa. In Asia there is immense mass poverty but it tends to be not as bad as in Africa with the exception of Bangladesh and Myanmar. Thus, India, Pakistan and Indonesia score low on the indicators but not as low as the highly unfortunate countries in Africa where anarchy or civil war bring disaster for the civilian population. Table 2.8 strongly links the variation in human development with civilisations.

Table 2.7 Quality of life: human development index (1975–2003) (means)

Civilisations	HD 75	n	HD 80	n	HD 85	n	HD 90	n	HD 95	n	HD 00	n	HD 03	n
Arab	0.537	10	0.59	11	0.62	11	0.62	12	0.67	13	0.69	10	0.72	14
Western Europe	0.85	17	0.86	18	0.87	18	0.89	18	0.91	18	0.93	18	0.94	18
Eastern Europe	0.779	1	0.79	3	0.80	3	0.79	13	0.78	15	0.80	14	0.81	19
Other occidentals	0.845	5	0.86	5	0.88	5	0.89	5	0.92	5	0.93	4	0.94	5
South Asia	0.438	3	0.47	3	0.51	3	0.55	3	0.58	3	0.54	2	0.60	4
Africa Sub-Sahara	0.38	25	0.42	27	0.44	29	0.45	30	0.45	31	0.47	25	0.46	35
Muslim non-Arab	0.44	4	0.46	4	0.54	5	0.57	5	0.60	5	0.66	4	0.65	5
Latin America	0.66	20	0.67	21	0.69	21	0.70	21	0.72	21	0.76	16	0.76	22
Turkish	0.59	1	0.61	1	0.67	2	0.71	3	0.68	4	0.68	2	0.72	7
Asean	0.69	7	0.72	7	0.70	7	0.72	9	0.73	10	0.72	7	0.76	12
Pacific	0.539	2	0.57	2	0.58	2	0.60	2	0.63	2	0.53	1	0.64	2
Total	0.600	95	0.63	102	0.64	108	0.67	122	0.68	128	0.71	103	0.70	143

Source: Based on UNDP (2006).

Table 2.8 Analysis of variance of HDI scores

Measures of association	Eta	Eta squared
HD_75 * CIV	0.89	0.80
HD_80 * CIV	0.87	0.76
HD_85 * CIV	0.85	0.73
HD_90 * CIV	0.86	0.73
HD_95 * CIV	0.85	0.72
HD_00 * CIV	0.89	0.78
HD_03 * CIV	0.88	0.77

Source: Author.

The spread between miserable states and well-to-do states on the American continent is quite substantial, but is not yet as huge as that between the poor states in Asia on the one hand and Japan, Singapore and South Korea on the other. What matters are life opportunities, and they tend to be low in countries such as Bolivia, Peru, Ecuador, Haiti and Honduras. The United States and Canada outdistance the other states by far, but in terms of general conditions of life Chile, Brazil and Uruguay are better off than Ecuador and Central America.

Yet the major finding comparing economic indicators with general social ones is that in Europe the vast differences in economic affluence between the West and the East do not translate into sharply separated life conditions. There is an interesting curvilinear connection between economic affluence and general quality of life. Very low levels of affluence result in truly miserable social conditions, but as the GDP indicator ascends towards higher levels, the quality of life indicator at first rises proportionately but then evens out. There is an *asymptotic* nature to the relationship between levels of affluence (GDP per capita) and the human condition (human development index).

The distribution of income is another vital addition to be made when analysing the human predicament. The use of income distribution scores warns against any simple conclusion that increases in total economic output must result in more affluence for the entire population. At the same time rapid processes of economic growth could be beneficial for the broad masses in the population, even if the income distribution remains skewed to the advantage of the rich.

How income inequality is to be measured is a controversial issue in itself. Table 2.9 contains the scores of a number of indices, where the higher the scores the more unequal the distribution of income. The common finding for all indices is that inequalities of income are larger in poor countries than in rich ones, whatever measure of income differentials one may employ. Actually, income equality was larger in the West European welfare states than in the former communist states. Generally speaking, the amount of equality in the

Table 2.9 Income inequality (1990–2000) (Gini indices: means)

CIV	GI 90	n	RGI 90	n	GI 00	n	RGI 00	n	GINI AVE	n
Arab	37.1	6	36.9	6	39.2	2	38.8	2	43.3	9
Western Europe	30.8	17	30.8	17	30.6	17	30.8	17	32.2	17
Eastern Europe	32.3	20	32.3	20	34.6	20	34.6	20	30.3	20
Other occidentals	37.3	5	37.3	5	37.4	4	37.4	4	38.1	5
South Asia	39.5	3	38.2	3	45.3	1	43.7	1	40.8	3
Africa Sub-Sahara	51.4	26	50.3	26	41.3	6	40.9	6	48.8	33
Muslim non-Arab	35.1	5	34.4	5	31.3	3	31.4	3	35.0	5
Latin America	51.2	20	50.9	20	52.7	16	52.5	16	49.9	21
Turkish	38.6	7	38.4	7	41.0	5	40.6	5	35.8	7
Asean	38.3	12	37.9	12	39.9	4	39.8	4	38.0	13
Pacific	48.7	2	48.2	2	49.5	2	48.2	1	48.5	2
Total	41.1	123	40.7	123	39.0	79	39.0	79	41.0	135

Source: Based on WIDER (2005).

Table 2.10 Analysis of variance of GINI scores

Measures of association	Eta	Eta squared
GI_90 * CIV	0.81	0.65
RGI_90 * CIV	0.80	0.64
GI_00 * CIV	0.84	0.70
RGI_00 * CIV	0.83	0.68
GINI_AVE * CIV	0.75	0.57

Source: Author.

distribution of income is related to the level of economic affluence by means of the so-called Kuznets' curve (Lane and Ersson, 2001). It predicts that income inequality will rise in a process of rapid economic development only to decline once a substantially higher level of economic affluence has been reached. There are still traces of the operation of the Kuznets' mechanism among states following a long process of economic growth in the world economy since the end of the Second World War, meaning a negative interaction between the GINI index and GDP. However, the amount of income inequality is also affected by public policies. Some countries (e.g. the Nordic ones) pursue income equality more vigorously than other countries, such as the USA. Yet the Kuznets' effect is today not as strong as it was when he suggested this theory in the 1950s. In any case, income inequalities tend to be very high in medium-income rapidly developing countries such as Brazil, South Africa, Egypt and Pakistan. They are also increasing sharply in China and India.

It must be admitted that income distribution data are beset by problems of reliability as well as validity when employed across such a large set of countries. Yet it stands out clearly that states with an advanced economy have more of income equality than do poor states. The implication would then be that income inequalities could be accepted much more easily in rapidly growing economies than in stagnating ones, because over time economic prosperity would increase income equality. The finding is that one of the major human values of the French Revolution – equality – has its best chances in states with an advanced economy (Table 2.9).

Income inequality, as measured by various Gini indices in 1990 and 2000, varies strongly with civilisations (Table 2.10). It is endemic in Latin America, Sub-Saharan Africa, South Asia and Asean. There is more income equality in the occidental groups, especially Western Europe, where both affluence and egalitarian preferences in the political elites play a role. There is thus double poverty: the poverty of countries and the poverty within countries.

Inflation

It is possible in performance perspective upon the state to broaden the outcome analysis, bringing in other factors besides affluence, income distribution and quality of life. Here I raise the issue of inflation, as governments have a duty to contain it. One must recognise that the connection between state performance and social outcomes may be tenuous, in particular in countries hit by strong external sudden shocks to their economies. Governments may try hard to counteract social maladies such as hyperinflation and massive unemployment, but the resources of government may be too small and the resilience of society too weak. There could be poor state performance because of two reasons: either government doing the right things but without sufficient strength, or simply doing the wrong things.

Yet, bringing in inflation data widens the economic and social performance analysis of governments. In admitting that there are considerable problems in arriving at reliable comparable data on country differences in inflation rates I merely indicate below how states differ with regard to this key economic outcome. Hyperinflation means severe economic hardships for the broad population. It occurred first and foremost in Latin America, but also in some African countries. Historically unique examples of hyperinflation include: 1922 Germany 5,000 per cent; 1985 Bolivia >10,000 per cent; 1989 Argentina 3,100 per cent; 1990 Peru 7,500 per cent; 1993 Brazil 2,100 per cent; and 1993 Ukraine 5,000 per cent. Inflation rates have recently climbed over 100 per cent in the following countries: Argentina, Bolivia, Zimbabwe, Angola, Mozambique, the Ivory Coast and Afghanistan.

Massive unemployment in particular but also hyperinflation enters any description of a dismal human predicament if one takes equality as the starting point. Massive levels of unemployment occur in some Third World countries, but may also occur in Eastern Europe. As high a figure as 40 per cent and more has been reported for South Africa, which is probably not unique for Third World countries. The welfare reduction implications of high unemployment figures are not automatic. There are informal economies everywhere, which provide alternative employment opportunities. Whereas hyperinflation occurs almost exclusively in Third World countries with weak economies, high levels of unemployment may also show up in medium-income or even rich countries. Even in some OECD countries unemployment has reached a level of over 10 per cent, which means hardship for a substantial proportion of the population. There is a clear long-term trend towards an increase in unemployment in the states with an advanced economy.

A "misery index" has been proposed that equates economic unhappiness as a weighted sum of inflation and unemployment. This formula – misery = inflation per cent + unemployment per cent – implies that the general population would be as unhappy about a 1 per cent rise in monetary inflation as they would by a 1 per cent increase in unemployment, which is debatable. Unemployment is perhaps more painful than inflation for the individual person, but hyperinflation is certainly cause for more misery for a country than even the substantial unemployment typical of, for example, France and Germany in the early 2000s. Governments have some degree of freedom in

Table 2.11 Inflation

civ_fin	Infl 6173	n	Infl 7390	n	Infl 9098	n	Infl 9598	n
Arab	3.6	4	13.0	8	16.1	8	11.8	10
Western Europe	5.2	18	10.7	18	3.6	18	2.2	18
Eastern Europe			35.4	2	161.7	4	55.1	17
Other occidentals	4.5	5	25.0	5	4.4	5	3.4	5
South Asia	5.3	2	10.0	3	10.6	3	9.4	3
Africa Sub-Sahara	4.0	6	17.5	20	15.6	22	145.5	24
Muslim non-Arab	57.8	3	13.7	3	13.5	4	16.9	5
Latin America	11.1	19	188.7	20	124.2	20	16.2	20
Turkish	6.4	1	42.9	1	78.6	1	72.3	2
Asean	3.9	5	7.8	6	10.1	8	13.1	11
Pacific	7.9	1	10.9	2	8.9	2	9.9	2
Total	9.1	64	54.5	88	41.6	95	45.7	117

Source: Based on World Bank (2000).

Table 2.12 Analysis of variance of inflation rates

Measures of association	Eta	Eta squared	Sig.
Infl 6173 * civ_fin	0.52	0.27	0.06
Infl 7390 * civ_fin	0.40	0.16	0.18
Infl 9098 * civ_fin	0.38	0.15	0.17
Infl 9598 * civ_fin	0.18	0.03	1.0

Source: Author.

relation to the alternative performance criteria. For the human development index as well as inflation, general economic factors play the major role. However, it remains the case that governments may take actions that seriously impair the predicament of their population including the release of hyperinflation and unemployment, such as in Zimbabwe during Mugabe's rule (Table 2.11). Inflation rates do not vary in accordance with civilisational categories (Table 2.12).

Conclusion

From the principal–agent perspective upon government, one would focus especially upon rule of law, i.e. the enforcement of civil and political rights as well as the separation of powers. The occurrence of constitutional democracy varies considerably from one continent to another, indicating the extent to which the population has been successful in restraining its political elites. To explain the country variation in rule of law is a major task in comparative politics. States also differ in terms of public policies as well as policy outcomes. The welfare states constitute a special case, given their high commitment to equality, accomplished to a considerable degree by means of public expenditures. The human development index informs about the general quality of life in societies. Quality of life depends upon affluence, but the relationship takes the shape of an asymptotic curve, meaning that the quality of life is greatly enhanced by increases in GDP among poor and medium-rich countries. Among the rich countries, the human development index is hardly affected by increases in GDP.

I turn now to the question of understanding or explaining the variation in rule of law among countries: Which factors are relevant when accounting for the country variation today? There is a whole body of literature in comparative politics which suggests that we take into account the economy, the social structure, culture and political institutions. Let me pin down some of the most discussed models and test them empirically, whether they can be found in the history of political thought or in recent comparative politics. Comparative politics is replete with questions about: WHY? The states of the world differ in terms of important aspects of the state, such as political stability and rule of law. Let me now formulate a number of hypotheses about the condition for rule of law, and test them by means of models. The model is an equation which links one (correlation) or several (regression) independent variables (*explanans*) with the dependent variable (*explanandum*). I will cast the net widely, meaning that I will examine several models in political science, economics, sociology as well as political thought about the conditions that increase or decrease the probability of a state having a regime with a rule of law. Testing a model involves not only looking at the empirical evidence but also accounting for the interaction between variables by means of mechanisms. However plausible from a theoretical point of view a model may be, it still needs empirical support.

Part II

Conditions that support rule of law

The principal of the political body would, I assume, be interested in contracting with a set of agents about how a country could be governed resulting in stable rule of law. The extent to which that may succeed depends upon both exogenous and endogenous factors. In order to explain the probability of rule of law, one needs to pay attention to the social systems that surround the political regime as well as to the nature of the political institutions in the country in question. Certain economic, cultural and social conditions increase the probability of rule of law, whereas other conditions decrease these probabilities. Although no environment of politics, strictly speaking, excludes the introduction of rule of law, there is a set of factors that impact positively upon the probability or stability of a rule of law regime. One may wish to speak of physical, economic, social and cultural factors, promoting or demoting the probability of rule of law.

Although principal–agent interaction would be primarily dependent upon the institutions of a country, the social, cultural and economic systems that co-exist with the political system cannot be bypassed. They condition, favourably or negatively, the possibility of arriving at rule of law as the political regime. In the social sciences, these exogenous conditions have been extensively researched in democracy theory. I will here restate some of the main results using new data. The strength of these correlations between background factors and the occurrence of rule of law should be compared with the links between political institutions and rule of law reported on in Chapter 4.

3   Environmental factors

Introduction

Social determinism is a perspective that loomed large in the study of comparative politics. It was argued that stability and performance are the result of major factors in the environment of the state: social structure in general and economic factors in particular. A number of models have been suggested on the assumption that politics at the macro level is a function of or greatly influenced by large-scale social forces. The crucial question is: How much?

Stating that social forces are causally relevant to the understanding of states is very different from the claims of, for example, economic determinism within the modernisation approach, which models state properties as almost a strict function of the development of capitalism or as totally shaped by the structural transformation from *agraria* to *industria*. In this chapter the purpose is to discuss the open-ended question of how much impact social structure has upon rule of law. Although I examine here the empirical relationships in the form of simple correlations, I will return to the problem of how they can be interpreted in terms of a regression model in Chapter 5.

Size and climate

Very different structural conditions have been suggested in order to understand the viability of the state as well as its performance records. With regard to physical conditions, there are two contradictory theories about the effects of size, one favouring small and the other large scale. The climate model argues that basic climatic conditions such as a tropical climate are relevant, as closeness to the equator would be conducive to institutional feableness and political instability.

The idea that regime viability is related to the size of the state has had many adherents in the history of political thought. Plato in *The Republic* and Aristotle in *Politics* regarded the city-state as the superior type of state formation. Although the Romans showed that a city-state might be transformed into a giant empire, the prevailing line of argument in republican theory was to favour smallness, as virtue with human beings as political animals (*zoon politicon*) was achieved more easily in the small city-state. Republicanism, or the "Machiavellian Moment" to set up a viable civic republic, recurred in Old England and New England during their revolutions (Pocock, 1975). Montesquieu, focusing on a republic, and Rousseau, dealing with popular participation, claimed in 1748 that democracy could only materialise in a small state:

> In a large republic, the common good is sacrificed to a thousand considerations; it is subordinate to various exceptions; it depends on accidents. In a small republic, the public good is more strongly felt, better known, and closer to each citizen; abuses are less extensive, and consequently less protected.
>
> (Montesquieu, 1989: 124)

Montesquieu differentiated between three basic types of rule or political regimes: republican, monarchical and despotic government. In a republic the people as a body have sovereign power, as in a democracy (Montesquieu, 1989: 10). Now, democracies as republics may take action to secure stability. Montesquieu qualifies his argument by opening up the possibility of a medium-sized federal republic as a compromise (Montesquieu, 1989: 131). What is necessary and viable is a constitution that has the advantages of a republic and the external force of a monarchy, states Montesquieu, pointing to the republic of Holland as an example. Rousseau favoured the small state, not only in *The Social Contract* (1762) but also in his study on rural Corse, *Constitutional Project for Corsica*.

One may point to Singapore, Hong Kong and Bermuda as successful examples today of the polis model, at least from an economic point of view. Yet, these city-states are not representative of states or cities in general. Super-rich Bermuda remains an Overseas Territory of the United Kingdom with a tiny population. The fate of Hong Kong (SAR = special administrative region) with its seven million population and high standard of living is difficult to predict when it changed from British administration to communist China rule in 1998. Singapore is an independent and economically viable city-state, but it has yet to fulfil all the requirements of rule of law. In fact, the trend is towards giant cities in which millions of people live, although as only parts of states (Dogan and Kasarda, 1988b). Table 3.1 renders two different estimates of the size of these metropolis areas, which actually seldom coincide with the legally defined city borders.

The coming of the metropolis instead of the ancient polis means that local government will increase in importance at the expense of national politics. How are such mega-cities to be run, several of which are larger than many states? After all, several states do not reach a population that is larger than ten million, whereas many cities in the Third World have passed this limit. Thus, cities like Bangkok, Lima, Kinshasa, Lagos, Madras and

Table 3.1 The growth of mega-cities (1950–2005) (million inhabitants)

	1950	1985	2000	2005
Baghdad	–	7	13	–
Beijing	7	9	11	10
Bombay	3	10	16	20
Buenos Aires	5	11	13	13.5
Cairo	3	9	13	15
Calcutta	4	11	17	15.5
Chicago	5	7	7	9.5
Dacca	–	5	11	13
Dehli	–	7	13	19
Istanbul	–	7	12	11.5
Jakarta	2	8	13	17
Karachi	–	7	12	14
London	10	10	9	12
Los Angeles	4	10	11	18
Manila	–	7	11	15
Mexico City	3	18	26	23
Milan	4	7	8	–
Moscow	5	9	10	13.5
New York	12	15	16	21
Paris	6	9	9	10
Rio de Janeiro	4	10	13	12
Sao Paulo	3	16	24	20
Seoul	–	10	14	22
Shanghai	10	12	14	18
Teheran	–	7	13	12
Tokyo/Yokohama	7	17	17	12

Source: Based on 1950–2000: Dogan and Kasarda (1988b: 15); 2005: The Principal Agglomerations of the World www.citypopulation.de/World.html).

Bangalore now constitute social systems of the size of many states (e.g. the Nordic countries, Ireland, the Baltic and the Balkan states).

The polis model was rejected by those who argued that state size would bring more advantages than disadvantages. When the United States was to be formed, there was a lengthy debate about the pros and cons of small and large republics. Whereas Thomas Jefferson repeated the standard argument in favour of small government, Alexander Hamilton and in particular James Madison stated a case for large government. In the *Federalist Papers* appearing between 1787 and 1788, Madison published his well-known article about size, factions and democracy, containing the following argument for a large state:

> Hence, it clearly appears, that the same advantages which a representative republic has over a direct democracy, in controlling the effects of faction, is enjoyed by a large over a small representative republic – is enjoyed by the Union over the states composing it.
>
> (Madison *et al.*, 1961: 47)

What could threaten a democracy, or a republic as it was often called, was the domination of special interest groups seeking favours from public legislation and budget-making – "rent-seeking" in modern public choice terminology (Olson, 1963, 1982). Madison saw a large state as the self-correcting force against factionalism. Where there would be many factions due to large-scale politics, the invisible hand of competition would see to it that they would cancel each other out, especially if the choice of basic institutions favoured the competition between interests (Ostrom, 1987). By implication the size of the state or a democratic state would enhance both stability and performance.

Dahl and Tufte (1973) unpacked the size model into a set of hypotheses that in one form or another have been propounded in the history of political thought. If size in its various aspects such as territory or population would have an impact upon stable rule of law, then how could we account for such an impact in terms of a theory about the mechanisms which translate size into state properties? The Dahl and Tufte model identifies two dimensions that are related to size: system capacity and citizen effectiveness (Dahl and Tufte, 1973: 24–25). State size would be positively related to system capacity. Citizen effectiveness would be negatively related to state size. Thus, there are two opposite forces involved: the viability of a state would be increased by system capacity but decreased by citizen ineffectiveness.

The mere fact that today there are about 30 states that have a population of less than a million people as well as 30 states with a population larger than 40 million constitutes a warning against any strong hypotheses about the implications of size on stability and rule of law. There is a clear divergence between political nationalism and economic international integration after the Second World War, meaning that tiny states could be economically viable as long as they find a place in the world economy. However, a few economists have argued that small state size comes with inefficiency in terms of how the costs of effective management and good governance can be shared among the people concerned (Alesina and Spolaore, 2003). Other economists underline the fact that small states are often remotely located island states, such as the Pacific Rim, where other conditions impact negatively upon a stable rule of law (Hughes and Gosarevski, 2004).

Montesquieu is well known for his theory that climatic conditions have an impact on the state and society:

> If it is true that the character of the spirit and the passions of the heart are extremely different in the various climates, laws should be relative to the differences in these passions and to the differences in these characters.
> (Montesquieu, 1989: 231)

What Montesquieu hinted at on the basis of hypotheses about the impact of frost and heat upon the human spirit was that there would be North–South differences in the form of industry versus laziness, equality versus slavery or

Table 3.2 Distribution of states by climate and distance from the Equator

Civilisation	Tropical	Dry	Temperate	Cool	Total	Distance from the Equator (mean)
Arab	0	15	0	0	15	0.2719
Western Europe	0	0	14	4	18	0.5113
Eastern Europe	0	0	5	15	20	0.4847
Other occidentals	0	1	3	1	5	0.3946
South Asia	2	0	2	0	4	0.2058
Africa Sub-Sahara	27	6	3	0	36	0.1171
Muslim non-Arab	2	4	1	0	7	0.2500
Latin America	18	1	3	0	22	0.1628
Turkish	0	6	1	0	7	0.4119
Asean	7	1	5	1	14	0.2336
Pacific	2	0	0	0	2	0.0950
Total	58	34	37	21	150	0.2777
Eta squared					0.674	0.7600

Source: Based on EIU (1965); CIA (2007).

freedom versus servitude (Montesquieu, 1989: Part III). The hypothesis that climate affects society profoundly reappears in the theory of Oriental despotism (Part III, this volume). In any case, classifying states according to a simple climatic scheme allows us to derive a distribution that could be used for testing Montesquieu's idea (Table 3.2).

The climatic model suffers from the same weakness as the size model, namely the lack of mechanism that could explain why climate would make a difference to state stability and rule of law. Among the countries along the equator, we have the industrious and well-managed Singapore, brutally authoritarian Myanmar, civil war-torn Sri Lanka as well as anarchical Congo (Zaire), poor and unstable Madagascar, anarchical Papua New Guinea and the Solomon Islands as well as the largest stable democracy in the world, India.

Social structure

There are several models that emphasise general social conditions. The modernisation theme argued that state transformation was induced from society through major structural changes such as the Industrial Revolution or the urbanisation process. One may also distinguish the fragmentation models stating the impact of social heterogeneity, i.e. ethnicity or religion.

Modernisation

Grand-scale transformation of the social structure and its political consequences were modelled in the *modernisation* theme, emerging from the

1960s. It was argued first that a major transition from *agraria* towards *industria* in the rich countries but also among the poor countries has transformed or will change society profoundly. Second, it was believed that this major social structure change would have tremendous political consequences (Lerner, 1958; Deutsch, 1963). Not underestimating the importance of the modernisation theme, it remains the case that there is a risk of reductionism involved here. The general modernisation theme generated several models about the consequences of major social transformation for the state (see Diamond, 1999). Thus an often used agricultural model claimed that the transition from an agrarian society to an industrial one, measured by the reduction in the relative size of agricultural employment, would be accompanied by state instability and rising expectations about democracy.

Evidently, many countries in Africa and Asia still have a large part of their populations employed in agriculture, or roughly 50 per cent. Yet, among Third World countries the reduction in agricultural employment is an ongoing process of social change, and it has been pronounced in, for example, Latin America. When the population is to be found in agricultural employment, one may expect to find dictatorship, all other things being equal. Democracy feeds upon mass mobilisation, which is more easily forthcoming in an urban and industrial setting.

Table 3.3 shows a considerable variation in the size of agriculture as a percentage of GDP. It is very small in the post-industrial societies but still considerably large in several groups of states, or contributing 25 per cent to GDP.

Backward countries generate some 30 per cent of their GDP from agriculture. This variation in agriculture's contribution to GDP follows civilisational categories (Table 3.4).

One interesting agricultural model emphasises the ownership structure where institutions that make the subjugation or exploitation of the peasantry relatively easy result in less stability and democracy. Thus, the role of the Spanish *Latifundia* system lingers on in Central and South America, creating immense inequality and a huge landless proletariat. In several Asian countries there is widespread use of sharecropping, which tends to lead to severe indebtness and thus dependency among farm labour towards the landlord. An independent peasantry has a stronger position in the rich world than in the developing countries. Peasants and farm labourers seek landownership, which enhances political stability according to basic theory in neo-institutional economics, focusing on the importance of secure and transparent property rights (Bardhan, 1991).

Sharecropping is still used in many rural poor areas today, notably in India (Byres, 1983). Much of the recent economic literature on sharecropping has been devoted to a debate as to whether and under what conditions the institution is more, less or equally efficient to two other forms of cultivation relationship, namely fixed rent systems and wage labour. The landowner would allow a sharecropper to use the land in return for a share of

Table 3.3 Size of agriculture in terms of GDP (means)

Civilisations	Agva 80	n	Agva 90	n	Agva 95	n	Agva 00	n
Arab	10.7	12	13.1	11	11.3	9	14.9	10
Western Europe	5.9	12	4.9	16	3.8	16	3.2	17
Eastern Europe	14.3	6	17.8	15	14.9	18	11.5	20
Other occidentals	5.7	4	3.7	4	2.5	2	4.2	4
South Asia	46.0	4	38.0	4	33.4	4	30.4	4
Africa Sub-Sahara	31.0	32	30.1	35	29.1	34	29.1	35
Muslim non-Arab	35.3	6	33.3	6	30.0	5	28.3	6
Latin America	15.4	19	14.8	21	13.8	21	11.1	22
Turkish	26.4	1	28.9	5	23.2	7	23.8	7
Asean	17.7	8	24.7	12	23.8	12	20.6	12
Pacific	29.1	2	25.4	2	24.2	2	21.2	2
Total	20.9	106	20.7	131	19.2	130	17.7	139

Source: Based on World Bank (2000, 2005).

Table 3.4 Analysis of variance

Measures of association	Eta	Eta squared
agva80 * civ_fin	0.673	0.453
agva90 * civ_fin	0.636	0.405
agva95 * civ_fin	0.601	0.361
agva00 * civ_fin	0.632	0.400

Source: Author.

the crop produced on the land. Legal contract systems such as *métayage* (French origin) and *aparcería* (Spanish) occur widely, and Islamic law has a traditional *"musaqat"* (sharecropping) agreement for the cultivation of orchards. The typical form of sharecropping is generally seen as exploitative and a cause of rural instability, particularly with large holdings of land where there is inequality between the parties. Sharecropping agreements can, however, be made as a form of tenant farming or share-farming that has a variable rental payment, paid in arrears. The advantages of sharecropping in other situations include enabling access for women to arable land where ownership rights are traditionally vested only in men (Ludden, 2005). The system occurred extensively in China and India, colonial Africa, Scotland and Ireland, but also in the United States during the Reconstruction era (1865–1876). Sharecropping is one of the peculiar institutions of the agrarian economy. Like the *Latifundia system*, it fuels social unrest (Moore, 1968), although the exploitation of peasants and farm labourers may take worse forms, such as slavery in the New World and serfdom in Eastern Europe, especially Russia (Blum, 1966).

An urbanisation model may supplement the agricultural model, which views the state as significantly influenced by the transformation of a society from a sparsely populated structure to a densely populated one (Table 3.5).

Industrialisation and urbanisation are modelled in the modernisation approach as creating the conditions for so-called *mass politics*, i.e. popular participation with a probable demand for democracy (Allardt and Rokkan, 1970). By bringing the population together in large urban concentrations it may be mobilised in political action. Traditional rule would be seriously weakened, as mass politics involves the demand that civil and political rights be introduced as well as participation augmented. The modernisation models predict that states with a large part of the population within the agricultural sector or in the countryside would probably not reach a stable rule of law.

Fragmentation: ethnicity and religion

When the importance of social conditions for politics is emphasised, then often so-called *cleavages* are focused upon. The concept of a cleavage refers to the alignment of the population around social dimensions which are conducive to conflict, manifestly or in a latent fashion (Rae and Taylor, 1970). Social or cultural fragmentations occur when strong social groups are organised against each other. Typical cleavage bases include religion, ethnicity and class, and the fragmentation models claim that the extension and intensity of cleavages have a strong impact upon the state, in particular stability. The fragmentation model claims that a stable state could not possibly occur where there is strong dissent among major social groups about the direction of the political community. Social heterogeneity along cleavages could topple rule of law and lead to political instability in a political body. Among various social cleavages such as ethnicity, religion and class the fragmentation models underline especially ethnic but also religious fragmentation. State stability and state performance will be low in countries where there is both extensive and intensive religious and ethnic dissension, whether openly or tacitly.

The level of fractionalisation varies from one country to another according to the two cleavages of ethnicity and religion. Table 3.6 presents data on the occurrence of fractionalisation in a state in terms of ethnicity and religion. The ethnicity fragmentation index and the linguistic fragmentation index captures the size of the *ethnies* in a country as well as of the dominant language. One may assume that the fragmentation scores would hardly have changed rapidly over the past decades. The ethnic fragmentation index is scaled the other way around to the ethnic domination index, which measures how large the share of the population that belongs to the dominating language group is. The religious fragmentation index – R1 – is scaled as the ELF index, meaning that higher scores imply more fragmentation.

On average, ethnic fragmentation tends to be high in Africa, somewhat lower in America and Asia, whereas it is generally low in Europe and in

Table 3.5 Urbanisation (means)

Civilisation	Urban 70	n	Urban 80	n	Urban 90	n	Urban 98	n
Arab	42.680	15	52.887	15	61.687	15	66.760	15
Western Europe	68.278	18	72.022	18	74.472	18	76.996	18
Eastern Europe	47.725	20	56.465	20	60.715	20	62.224	20
Other occidentals	79.960	5	81.420	5	82.380	5	83.000	5
South Asia	12.175	4	13.775	4	15.225	4	17.170	4
Africa Sub-Sahara	18.003	36	23.694	36	29.794	36	34.889	36
Muslim non-Arab	22.100	7	26.557	7	30.943	7	35.280	7
Latin America	50.773	22	56.082	22	61.182	22	64.816	22
Turkish	42.486	7	44.443	7	46.700	7	47.083	7
Asean	40.423	13	44.708	13	49.108	13	51.789	13
Pacific	21.400	2	25.250	2	31.900	2	36.800	2
Total	40.656	149	46.287	149	51.122	149	54.502	149

Source: Based on World Bank (2000).

Oceania. Religious fragmentation is calculated on the basis of the relative size of Protestants, Roman Catholics, Muslims and the other world religions. High religious fragmentation scores are to be found mainly in Africa but also in Europe and Oceania.

Since the within-group differences are larger than the between-group differences, it is worthwhile to identify countries that score very high on these two fragmentation indices meaning that their fraternity may face severe challenges (Table 3.6). Ethnic cleavages have an in-built tendency towards political violence according to Horowitz (1985).

A few countries score very high on the ethnic fragmentation index – Uganda, Tanzania, India, Kenya, Nigeria. The pattern of ethnic fragmentation in a country would certainly have political implications. Thus, there is a risk that when ethnically distinct populations are mixed in territories, it could result in an explosive predicament, as in Former Yugoslavia where the Serbs, Croats and Muslims constituted considerable minorities within Croatia and Bosnia and Herzegovina, or as in Rwanda or Burundi with their two peoples, the Hutus and the Tutsis. A number of countries score high on the religious fragmentation index, but they are generally not the same ones that score high on the ethnicity index. Religious fragmentation in countries such as Togo, Malawi, Kenya, Ethiopia and Tanzania is high. The Pacific Island states suffer from political instability derived from ethnic cleavages, either within the same nation (PNG) or between natives and Indians (Fiji).

A few very large states have had to accommodate both ethnic and religious fragmentation: Indonesia, the former USSR, Nigeria, Sudan, South Africa and Malaysia. The fact that some of these countries have had difficulties in maintaining some sort of state shows that stability may be very difficult to arrive at in countries with extensive and intensive ethnic or religious fragmentation.

Is ethnic and religious fragmentation – mutually reinforcing cleavages *the* major challenge to political unity? Actually, all the major types of cleavages – ethnicity, religion and class – could cause civil war, but ethnic or religious fragmentation tends to be more divisive. A fragmented society, especially along ethnic or religious lines, tends to evolve into two or more principals. How can they be brought to work in government where it is urgent that there is one principal for the body politic? The consociational school of comparative politics came up with the answer a grand coalition, bringing all major groups on board. This is an institutional response to a divided society. One may only reflect on the omission of this solution in African politics and its reasons for it with the basic motives of the chief players in the many civil wars that have plagued Sub-Saharan Africa so much.

Religion

Among the cultural models of politics a few deal with the role of religion. What is at stake here are a few hypotheses that single out Protestantism,

Table 3.6 Ethnic and religious fragmentation

Civilisation	ELF 10	n	ELF 11	n	RELFR 10	n
Arab	0.43	14	0.25	15	0.27	15
Western Europe	0.19	18	0.22	18	0.34	18
Eastern Europe	0.39	20	0.35	20	0.51	20
Other occidentals	0.41	5	0.44	5	0.70	5
South Asia	0.53	4	0.65	4	0.33	4
Africa Sub-Sahara	0.70	36	0.70	35	0.59	36
Muslim non-Arab	0.57	7	0.43	7	0.24	7
Latin America	0.43	22	0.17	19	0.34	22
Turkish	0.45	7	0.43	7	0.33	7
Asean	0.29	14	0.32	14	0.45	14
Pacific	0.26	2	0.59	2	0.43	2
Total	0.40	14	0.40	14	0.43	150
Eta squared	0.43	–	0.48	–	0.32	

Sources: Adapted from Alesina *et al.* (2003).

Notes
Ethnic fragmentation (ELF 10), Linguistic fragmentation (ELF 11), Religious Fragmentation (RLF 10).

Buddhism as well as an Islamic culture as of crucial importance (Huntington, 1993; Weber, 1993). As a matter of fact, it has been claimed that the religious systems of the world have opposite political consequences: whereas the Protestant ethic would be supportive of democracy, the Islamic ethos would be negative to democracy. The same applies to Buddhism. Our question is: How important are these two major religious belief systems for regime stability and rule of law? Let us first look at how these world religions show up in the world today (Table 3.7).

If Protestantism implies thrift for Weber (2003), then we may expect that affluence is higher in Oceania and Europe than elsewhere. If an Islamic culture involves a degree of religious submission, then we may expect less of secularisation in general in Asia and Africa. Politically, the Protestant model could be interpreted to entail that its Calvinist spirit is conducive to respect for human rights, whereas the Islamic model could imply that Islamic fundamentalism presents a formidable threat not only to the institutionalisation of liberty and political rights but also to state stability.

Charismatic leadership occurs to a considerable degree in Muslim societies, the recent ascendance of Osama bin Laden as a global leader of terrorism being perhaps the most spectacular example. The major cleavage in Muslim societies between two religious traditions, Sunni and Shi'a, may be linked to the concept of charismatic leadership, which has, after all, a religious basis with Weber. Shi'ism is the charismatic version of Islam, underlining that leadership of the community rests with *Imams* or *Maddhis*, who benefit from divine grace, being the legitimate successors of Ali, the cousin

Table 3.7 Protestantism, Buddhism, Islam and Hinduism (percentages; means)

Civilisation	Prot 2000	n	Budd 2000	n	Musl 2000	n	Hind 2000	n
Arab	0.373	15	0.233	15	86.967	15	1.200	15
Western Europe	30.483	18	0.267	18	2.056	18	0.111	18
Eastern Europe	5.280	20	0.020	20	7.935	20	0.025	20
Other occidentals	15.760	5	0.840	5	3.180	5	0.460	5
South Asia	0.625	4	37.850	4	6.500	4	45.750	4
Africa Sub-Sahara	13.450	36	0.053	36	25.147	36	1.397	36
Muslim non-Arab	1.086	7	0.429	7	84.171	7	2.500	7
Latin America	8.045	22	0.218	22	0.636	22	1.114	22
Turkish	0.214	7	0.129	7	75.914	7	0.000	7
Asean	2.785	13	50.938	13	6.592	13	1.169	13
Pacific	30.800	2	0.250	2	3.100	2	0.000	2
Total	10.130	149	5.621	149	24.657	149	2.103	149
Eta squared	0.297	–	0.715	–	0.717	–	0.558	–

Source: Adapted from Barrett et al. (2001).

of the prophet Muhammed. Sunni stands for tradition and entrusts leadership of the community with a caliph, who may inherit the office or be somehow elected. Sunni is the institutionalised version of Islam, placing the backbone of religious adherence in the obeisance of the precepts of Muslim jurisprudence, the historical four schools (*fiqh*).

Political leadership of a Muslim country is no longer exercised by caliphs or a maddhi. Muslim countries are either kingdoms or sultanates (traditional authority) or presidential republics (legal-rational authority). Yet, the split between Sunnis and Shi'ites lingers on with huge political consequences (Lapidus, 1989). Adherents of Shi'ism are found around the world. Some countries have a higher concentration of followers, such as Iran, Iraq, Pakistan, India, Afghanistan, Lebanon, Azerbaijan and Bahrain. The usual rough estimate is that some 15 to 20 per cent of all Muslims follow Shi'a Islam.

In some countries religious sects within Sunni as well as Shi'a play a major political role: the Alawites in Syria, the Druzes in Lebanon, the Kahrijites in Oman and the Wahhabites in Saudia Arabia as well as the Talibans in Afghanistan. The existence of these sects has had a strong influence upon state stability. Only the Kahrijites have had a political philosophy that contains seeds of democractic thought, as they favour election as the method of appointing the leaders of the community.

The political implications of Islam are closely connected with the struggle between sects. In a sense, the origin of sects in Islam is the solution to the successor problem of replacing the prophet, the so-called Shi'ites only accepting descendants of Ali. Yet conflict arose early also among the Shi'ites whether to follow the so-called Ismailis (Seveners) or the mainstream Shi'ites (Twelvers). The Nusayris or the Alawis in Syria belong to the Ismailis, as do the Druzes in Lebanon, athough they display several differences between each other. Another sect of Mustalian Ismailis – called the *Assassins* – are mainly to be found in the Indian province of Gujarat, but there are also such communities in Arabia, the Persian Gulf, East Africa and Burma. Altogether, they number several hundred thousands. The tensions between these sects as well as between Sunnis and the sects have always had political repercussions for Islamic societies, as no formal doctrine of tolerance has been forthcoming as widely accepted within Islam. Yet, the most pressing political impact does not come from the various ideas about the legitimate *"commendeurs des croyants"*, as King Muhammed VI designates himself, claiming he is a descendant of the prophet. Whether one believes in a caliph (Sunni), or five, seven or twelve Imans (Shi'a), descending from Ali, the community must still be governed by priests and the *ulemas*, i.e. the religious scholars with the power to issue so-called *fatwas* to the *umma*. And the state will be very interested in somehow controlling the selection of the leaders of the community, the *umma*.

Three alternative relationships between state and religion tend to surface within the Muslim civilisation (Enayat, 2005):

- Mainstream Sunni model (*routinisation*): The state has control over the religious community, which is on the whole moderate, accepting social and economic modernisation. Religion has become pinned down to certain routines within the community (*umma*) (e.g. faithful respect for the five duties or pillars of faith). Religious leadership is not charismatic. The state pays for the mosques including the salaries of the sheiks.
- Iranian Shi'a model (*theocracy*): The state is in the hands of the religious community, which however accepts a certain amount of autonomy of the state. The religious community (*Ayatollah*) imposes fundamentalist constraints upon society and state. Religious leadership involves charisma, at least during certain times when a so-called religious leader (*madhi*) emerges (Cole, 2002). The insistence upon the Imamat conception of leadership of the religious community favours charismatic authority to an extent that is neither accepted in moderate Sunni nor in radical Sunni fundamentalism.
- Islamic fundamentalism (*salafism*): Religious leadership is both charismatic and encompassing, meaning aims covering both state and society. Only Saudi Arabia is organised according to a fundamentalist state ideology: Wahhabism. Muhammad ibn Abd al-Wahhab (d. 1792) could be considered the first modern Islamic fundamentalist. He employed his charisma to impose the doctrine that absolutely every idea added to Islam after the third century of the Muslim era (about CE 950) was false and should be eliminated. In addition, Afghanistan experienced Islamic fundamentalism when the so-called Talibans ruled the country for a few years around 2000. As Bin Laden comes from Saudi Arabia and is Wahhabi himself, Wahhabi extremism has become a global movement. Yet the most powerful source of Islamic fundamentalism is the Muslim Brotherhood, initiated in 1928 in Egypt but today present all over the Muslim world, not least in Pakistan's many *madrassas*, inspired partly by Mawdudi's charismatic leadership (Musallam, 2005). Besides religion one should include the family in the analysis of exogenous conditions for rule of law.

Family values: individualism versus collectivism

It remains for me to say something about the spread of individualist as against collectivist values in general in society. The family structure model (Todd, 1983) helps one to tap the spread of cultural values in a society (Thompson *et al.*, 1990). The family model tries to classify a country variation in family structure according to two conceptual pairs: liberty versus authority and equality versus inequality. Here, I employ a scale that ranks the various family patterns after how much freedom there is to leave the family and how unequally the family inheritance is divided (Table 3.8). Each state is identified as having one major predominating family structure.

Table 3.8 Family systems (frequencies)

Civilisation	African family systems	Endogamous community family	Anomic family	Exogamous community family	Egalitarian nuclear family	Authoritarian family	Absolute nuclear family	Total
Arab	0	15	0	0	0	0	0	15
Western Europe	0	0	0	1	5	9	3	18
Eastern Europe	0	0	0	15	3	2	0	20
Other occidentals	0	0	0	0	0	1	4	5
South Asia	0	0	1	3	0	0	0	4
Africa Sub-Sahara	33	1	1	0	1	0	0	36
Muslim non-Arab	1	4	1	1	0	0	0	7
Latin America	0	0	0	1	21	0	0	22
Turkish	0	5	0	2	0	0	0	7
Asean	0	0	6	5	0	3	0	14
Pacific	0	0	2	0	0	0	0	2
Total	34	25	11	28	30	15	7	150

Source: Adapted from Todd (1985).

The classification scheme in Table 3.8 targets the occurrence of freedom and inequality in the family. It may be transformed into a scale of family collectivism and individualism, where higher scores indicate autonomy as well as that one child inherits all, which would favour mobility and economic development, whereas low scores indicate the opposite, namely authority in family obedience but equality in inheritance. There are clear differences between the continents (e.g. the African family structure and that in Oceania). One would expect that different family structures constitute a country pattern of cultural variations, which would have an indirect impact on politics. The family structure would express different kinds of fundamental political orientations – individualism versus collectivism which could mould political attitudes having an impact on the state (Eckstein, 1966).

Economic conditions

A basic distinction may be made between two kinds of economic models of rule of law: the economic systems model and the general affluence model. One may argue that state properties are related to a particular type of economic system. On the other hand, one may claim that it is not the system itself but the level of affluence or rate of growth of affluence that conditions state performance. In institutional economics, the emphasis is upon the link between the institutions of the market economy and those of rule of law. But the affluence model underlines the general productive capacity of the country, i.e. its GDP, and its consequences for rule of law.

Affluence

Following a theme in *Political Man* by Lipset (1960), Cutright argued as early as 1963 that democracy is linked to GDP or GNP, as measured by standard indicators. Adelman and Morris argued in 1967 for a close link between affluence and democracy. Wilensky claimed in 1975 that economic factors (affluence) are of crucial importance for politics, in particular state performance meaning public policies. A higher level of affluence results in more public spending, as the supply of as well as the demand for public policies increases with abundant resources. Wilensky's model is a modern version of Wagner's law (Borcherding, 1977), which implies that societies that are more affluent will engage in welfare spending, which societies that are poor cannot afford. But how much of state performance could be accounted for with economic factors? Which economic factors are relevant as well for regime stability?

The level of economic affluence may be measured in various ways. Table 3.9 presents both gross domestic product and gross national product on a per capita basis from 1980 to 2005 as well as purchasing power parities.

Table 3.9 Level of affluence: purchasing power parities and gross domestic product (US$) (means)

Civilisation	PPP 80	n	PPP 90	n	PPP 00	n	PPP 05	n	GDPC 99	n	GDPC 01	n	GDPC 02	n
Arab	5,201	14	5,461	14	7,334	14	7,943	14	6,452	15	6,661	15	6,866	15
Western Europe	9,242	18	17,487	18	27,281	18	31,620	18	22,322	18	23,783	18	27,827	18
Eastern Europe	4,014	19	6,856	19	7,429	20	10,015	20	5,023	20	6,737	20	8,180	20
Other occidentals	9,302	5	16,984	5	25,511	5	29,333	5	23,020	5	24,160	5	26,420	5
South Asia	608	4	1,310	4	2,315	4	2,948	4	1,640	4	1,977	4	2,250	4
Africa Sub-Sahara	1,096	35	1,632	35	2,112	35	2,496	35	1,946	36	2,043	36	2,191	36
Muslim non-Arab	1,253	5	2,050	5	3,107	5	4,036	5	2,088	7	2,452	7	2,771	7
Latin America	2,935	21	3,981	21	5,940	21	6,497	21	5,535	22	5,604	22	5,609	22
Turkish	1,981	7	3,411	7	3,148	7	4,339	7	2,684	7	3,620	7	4,528	7
Asean	2,484	13	6,027	13	10,646	13	12,555	13	9,498	14	10,009	14	10,678	14
Pacific	1,626	2	2,295	2	3,123	2	3,431	2	3,050	2	3,150	2	3,350	2
Total	3,637	143	6,080	143	8,750	144	10,302	144	7,233	150	7,848	150	8,788	150

Source: Based on IMF (2006) and CIA (various years).

Notes
Purchasing power parities (PPP) and Gross domestic product per capita (GDPC).

Affluence varies from high levels in the so-called OECD countries over medium levels in Asean, Eastern Europe and Arabia to low levels in Sub-Saharan Africa, South Asia and the Pacific and Turkish civilisations. The enlargement of the EU will bring about economic convergence all over Europe, despite the fact that the economic separation between Southern West Europe and Southern East Europe is a sharp one. Yugoslavia, Romania and Bulgaria cannot expect to catch up with Portugal, Spain, Italy and Greece any time soon. Counting the former USSR as part of Europe, the same observation applies to it. An unresolved question is how much the real affluence level was reduced in the process of economic system transformation until the economies of Russia and some of Khanates began to pick up in 2000.

On the American continent there is the clear-cut economic north–south divide. The United States and Canada have a standard of living which is several times as high as that in the Latin American states: Uruguay, Brazil, Argentina, Venezuela and Chile among the better-off countries, and Peru, Colombia, Paraguay and Bolivia among the less well-off. In Central America there are states doing fairly well such as Mexico and Costa Rica but also states that are not doing so well such as Honduras, Cuba and Haiti.

Characteristic of the states on the Sub-Saharan continent is extreme poverty. Actually, only a few countries in North Africa have moved out of the poor predicament of African states where Gabon, Botswana and South Africa also constitute exceptions. Thus Egypt, Algeria, Morocco and Tunisia differ from Nigeria, Kenya, Tanzania, Malawi, Zambia and Zaïre as well as Madagascar. In several states economic conditions must be characterised as extremely harsh, in particular in countries that have experienced long civil wars. In Zimbabwe, Mugabe as the agent of the population appears to have reversed the basic relationship in government, making him the principal of the population as agent to him.

The variation in affluence on the huge Asian continent differs from that of the African continent, as there are, besides the poor Third World states, also some very rich countries. On the one hand the oil-exporting countries are affluent, some of them more than others. Saudi Arabia, Oman and the United Arab Emirates have standards of living comparable to the OECD countries, whereas Iran and Iraq are closer to the conditions in several Third World countries, in particular the latter after the two devastating Gulf Wars, which have destroyed much of Iraq's infrastructure. Iran suffers economically from its isolation in the Gulf.

In Southeast Asia besides Japan the so-called Baby Tigers have shown that the gap between rich and poor countries may be closed in a relatively short time period (Balassa, 1991). The level of affluence in Japan as well as in the newly industrialising countries – Singapore, Taiwan, South Korea and Hong Kong (SAR in China) – may be compared with several West European states. The contrast to the predicament in the populous Asian states – China, India, Pakistan, Bangladesh, Indonesia and Myanmar – is stark, but

Asian poverty is not quite as bad as African poverty. Yet China is developing extremely rapidly, moving towards the medium-income countries such as Thailand and Malaysia. In Oceania, Australia and New Zealand belong to the rich set of OECD countries, whereas Papua New Guinea belongs to the Third World, which is also true of the many small Pacific Island states.

According to another economic model, dynamism in the economy matters for politics. Acknowledging that the rate of growth may hover in a random fashion from one year to another, it is maintained that the long-term differences in average growth rates are of crucial importance for politics. Slow processes of economic decline may result in state instability. The relative deprivation model would imply that political change would be most intense during periods of social change, for example, during rapid increases or decreases in affluence. Thus the prospects of a move towards rule of law would be substantially higher in periods of economic growth, stimulating new political demands. It is true that yearly growth rates in national economies fluctuate considerably as a response to short-term conditions (business cycle), but economic growth rate measures averaged out for a number of years are telling indicators of sustainable dynamic processes in a country. The substantial long-term growth rates for Asia are all the more impressive, as they cover an immense country variation between truly dynamic economies and states where the economy displays long-term sluggish growth. The dismal development on the African continent is apparent in the growth data, whereas the American data hides both strong economic expansion as well as economic retardation. In general, the variation in GDP follows civilisational categories (Table 3.10).

It is difficult to narrow down the consequences of a long-term economic growth process, but it sets the tone for the conduct of life within a country that affects all spheres of life, also politics. The level of affluence may be more important than the rate of change in the economy, but a sustainable real growth rate at about 3 to 5 per cent per year means a lot for the standard of living within a decade. Just as countries with strong economic growth can climb upward from the set of poor states towards the rich countries, so can rich countries tumble downward. The developments in South East Asia and their counter-examples in Latin America testify to the fuzzy borderline between rich and poor countries. The level of affluence as well as the rate of change in the economy would be of interest for understanding state properties. It is not difficult to model state performance with regard to the level of affluence or rate of change in affluence. However, other relevant economic factors may be identified.

Openness of the economy

Emphasising the implications of economics, the openness of the economy may be underlined. The Impex model claims that the economic interaction between nations matters politically, i.e. trade (Cameron, 1978). The openness

Table 3.10 Analysis of variance: purchasing power parities and gross domestic product

Measures of association	Eta	Eta squared
ppp_80 * civ_fin	0.772	0.595
ppp_90 * civ_fin	0.855	0.731
ppp_00 * civ_fin	0.849	0.721
ppp_05 * civ_fin	0.852	0.727
gdpc_99 * civ_fin	0.848	0.719
gdpc_01 * civ_fin	0.851	0.724
gdpc_02 * civ_fin	0.859	0.737

Source: Author.

of the economy could influence the state in several ways. The original Cameron model argued that the higher the Impex measure, the more there would be of welfare policies, the state compensating for the uncertainty stemming from the world economy. It seems that the extent of openness in an economy depends on how large a nation is in terms of population. The larger the nation the less openness there is, indicating that we may expect to find openness among the smaller European democracies (Table 3.11).

Overall openness has greatly increased during the past 40 years, Asean scores being highest and Muslim non-Arab lowest. Interestingly, the scores on the openness of the economy do not vary at all with the civilisation category (see Table 3.12).

The countries of Eastern Europe score unexpectedly high in early 2000, despite their heritage as former command economies. The high figure for Asia brings out the existence of a number of so-called NICs and NECs that score very high on the Impex index. The extent to which an economy is characterised by openness may have an impact on rule of law in either of two ways. It could mean more resources, which would enhance state stability, or it could signify more foreign influence (e.g. a push for a stronger role for ideas about human rights).

Indebtedness

Any discussion of economic conditions and the impact of the economy upon the polity must include the dependency model (Cardoso and Faletto, 1979; Frank, 1967) employed in particular by Latin American economists and sociologists under the inspiration of Prebisch to explain slow economic development and authoritarian reversals (Prebisch, 1971). Let us finally look at the indebtedness of a country (see Table 3.13).

Total debt/GNP tends to be high for Sub-Saharan Africa, the Pacific and the Turkish civilisations. Surprisingly, the various measures of country indebtedness do not vary systematically with civilisation category. This is a negative

Table 3.11 Openness of the economy: IMPEX

Civ_ fin	Open 70	n	Open 80	n	Open 100	n	Open 103	n
Arab	59.6	10	83.4	12	71.5	11	72.1	13
Western Europe	63.9	17	75.0	17	91.7	18	92.5	18
Eastern Europe	62.6	1	70.3	4	110.4	18	106.2	19
Other occidentals	42.0	5	55.0	5	60.6	5	57.8	5
South Asia	24.9	3	45.5	4	67.0	4	54.8	4
Africa Sub-Sahara	55.3	29	69.6	32	69.7	34	68.76	35
Muslim non-Arab	23.6	5	51.4	6	50.6	5	48.0	5
Latin America	41.1	20	53.5	21	62.1	22	66.2	21
Turkish	10.3	1	17.1	1	100.4	7	90.3	7
Asean	68.5	9	115.9	8	146.3	10	128.4	10
Pacific	57.5	2	74.3	2	96.5	2	99.0	1
Total	52.1	102	69.4	112	83.4	136	81.0	138

Source: Based on World Bank (2000, 2005).

Table 3.12 Analysis of variance: IMPEX

Measures of Association	Eta	Eta squared	Sig.
Open 70 * civ_fin	0.372	0.139	0.166
Open 80 * civ_fin	0.360	0.129	0.150
Open 100 * civ_fin	0.516	0.266	0.000
Open 103 * civ_fin	0.477	0.228	0.000

Source: Author.

finding for the *Dependistas*, who tend to argue that debt payments and overall indebtness vary according to the core-periphery division (Table 3.14).

Only Sub-Saharan Africa displays consistenly high indebtedness among the groups of states in Table 3.13, but there are heavily indebted countries in all categories, as indicated by the low eta scores. Thus, indebtedness can hardly be a major factor behind the varation in affluence, which tends to follow civilisation categories, although it may be the cause of state failure in a few specific cases. Actually, most countries have a considerable debt, but only a few countries are drowning under the burden of debt service. Some countries are capable of handling huge debts without political instability.

Economic institutions

Predicting that the economic system of capitalism comprises its own seeds of destruction, Karl Marx formulated an economic model about state instability or revolution that has played a major role in social science theory (Bell, 1996). Admitting that there are problems of interpreting what the exact shape of the Marx model would be like, it does warrant a

Table 3.13 External debt: various measures

Civilisation	EDT XGS	n	PVPRXGS	n	EDT PRGNI	n	PVPRGNI	n	DEBPRXGS	n	INTPTXGS	n
Arab	204.7	10	199.5	10	70.6	10	67.7	10	18.9	10	6.4	10
Eastern Europe	146.5	19	143.8	19	67.2	19	65.5	19	22.0	19	3.9	19
Other occidentals	131.0	1	85.0	1	45.0	1	29.0	1	11.0	1	1.0	1
South Asia	181.0	4	149.8	4	55.0	4	45.5	4	10.5	4	2.8	4
Africa Sub-Sahara	512.5	35	340.0	35	123.9	35	88.9	35	11.8	35	3.7	35
Muslim non-Arab	174.3	4	143.5	4	46.3	4	42.0	4	14.0	4	3.5	4
Latin America	171.1	20	152.0	20	59.0	20	51.6	20	21.0	20	7.0	20
Turkish	173.5	6	158.0	6	78.2	6	70.2	6	25.0	6	4.5	6
Asean	175.0	8	126.1	8	74.3	8	58.1	7	11.4	7	1.6	8
Pacific	127.0	2	125.5	2	82.0	2	80.0	2	18.5	2	4.5	2
Total	279.2	109	212.2	109	84.3	109	68.8	108	16.8	108	4.4	109

Source: Based on World Bank (2005).

Notes
EDTGS:Total external depts (EDT) to exports of goods and services (XGS); PVPRXGS; Present value (PV) of EDT as % of XGS; EDTPRGNI: EDT as % of gross national income (GNI); PVPRGNI: PV as % of GNI; DEBPRXGS: Total debt service as % of XGS; INTPTXGS: Interest service as % of XGS.

Table 3.14 Analysis of variance of external debt measures

Measures of association	Eta	Eta squared
edtxgs * civ_fin	0.445	0.198
pvprxgs * civ_fin	0.312	0.097
edtprgni * civ_fin	0.413	0.171
pvprgni * civ_fin	0.228	0.052
debprxgs * civ_fin	0.324	0.105
intptxgs * civ_fin	0.355	0.126

Source: Author.

search for the economic system sources of state instability. Is capitalism conducive to state instability? Or are the major forms of economic systems systematically related to rule of law? Perhaps Marx was wrong, meaning that stable rule of law is to be found in so-called capitalist systems, or the market economies?

In institutional economics, an economic system has a structure in which the market, private property institutions and public systems for budget allocation and redistribution are mixed. The analysis of economic systems thus recognises: (1) the organisation of decision-making: centralisation and decentralisation; (2) the provision of information and coordination: market or plan; (3) property rights: private, cooperative and public; and (4) the incentive system: moral or material (Monthias, 1976; Gregory and Stuart, 1989). Various distinctions are often made between types of capitalism, market socialism and the planned economy, where China would constitute the only actually existing market socialist regime. Gastil's (1987) framework was a refined one, including: (1) *Capitalist*: a high degree of economic freedom and relatively little market intervention by the state; (2) *Capitalist-statist*: substantial state intervention in markets and large public sectors, although the state remains committed to the institutions of private property; (3) *Mixed capitalist*: an activist state with income redistribution, market intervention and regulation, although the size of direct budget allocation of resources is not that large; (4) *Mixed socialist*: some economic freedom, private property and individual initiative within the framework of a socialist economy; and (5) *Socialist systems*: basically command economies with little economic freedom, private property and individual initiative. All classifications systems are open-ended and Gastil's placement of some countries may be discussed. Gastil portrayed a complicated country variation in economic institutions, but one would wish to consult a simple measure of the amount of economic freedom in various countries around the world, covering almost a hundred cases, allowing for change "over time" in economic institutions. Table 3.15 contains the market economy scores for three different time periods, constructed by the Fraser Institute (Gwartney *et al.*, 2006).

Table 3.15 Economic freedom index scores (1975–2003) (means)

civ_fm	EF 1970	EF1975	EF 1980	EF 1985	EF 1990	EF 1995	EF 2000	EF 2001	EF 2002	EF 2003
Arab	4.9	4.7	4.8	5.4	5.1	5.8	6.3	6.4	6.3	6.4
Western Europe	6.4	5.7	6.1	6.3	6.9	7.3	7.5	7.4	7.4	7.5
Eastern Europe	–	–	4.2	4.4	4.0	4.7	5.8	6.1	6.3	6.4
Other occidentals	6.4	5.8	6.1	6.3	7.0	7.7	7.9	7.8	7.8	7.8
South Asia	4.9	4.1	5.0	4.8	4.9	5.6	5.9	6.0	6.0	6.0
Africa Sub-Sahara	4.7	4.4	4.4	4.5	4.7	5.0	5.6	5.7	5.7	5.7
Muslim non-Arab	4.9	4.4	4.0	4.6	4.6	5.1	5.5	5.8	5.8	5.9
Latin America	5.1	4.8	4.9	4.5	5.1	6.1	6.5	6.5	6.4	6.4
Turkish	3.6	3.8	3.5	4.7	4.8	5.8	5.8	5.3	5.5	5.9
Asean	6.5	6.3	6.2	6.3	6.5	6.9	6.8	6.7	6.7	6.8
Pacific	5.2	4.8	4.9	5.4	5.9	6.8	6.5	6.3	6.2	6.2
Total	5.7	5.2	5.1	5.2	5.4	5.9	6.4	6.4	6.4	6.5
n	53	66	95	102	105	114	114	114	114	114
Eta square	0.5	0.4	0.5	0.4	0.5	0.5	0.5	0.4	0.4	0.4

Source: Based on Gwartney and Lawson (2006).

The scores for the 1990s are, on average, higher than the scores for the 1970s and 1980s. The 1989-initiated regime transitions had profound implications all around the world, affecting not only the command economies but also countries adhering to economic nationalism, as well as to a lesser extent the mixed economies. The profound process of globalisation has involved not only a dramatic increase in trade, foreign direct investments and financial transactions, but also a spread of regime changes, modelled first and foremost upon the basis of market economics notions.

The questions about the economic system conditions for the state come readily to mind. Is decentralised capitalism a necessary or sufficient condition for state stability or state performance? Why did the communist state collapse – was it due to its inefficient planned economy or its general lack of political legitimacy? Hayek stated a clear case for decentralised capitalism (1944, 1996), when he argued that any kind of state planning would threaten freedom in a democracy. One difficulty with Hayek's libertarian position is that it bypasses the large differences between forms of capitalism, the decentralised market economies and the welfare states. It is vital that one notes the gulf between decentralised capitalism on the one hand and state capitalism (economic nationalism) on the other.

The opposite argument to libertarianism has been stated by Lindblom (2002), who claims that state interference in the economy in the form of planning and welfare spending increases democracy. Favouring not only the welfare state with its large public sector but also idealist schemes for market socialism, Lindblom launched an attack on decentralised capitalism as biased in favour of the so-called capitalist firms and multinationals. Whereas Hayek and Lindblom tried to establish a relationship between economic system and state performance, Myrdal linked state stability with a planned economy. He claimed that economic development can only be forthcoming where the state is strong, bolstered by a socialist economy of some sort (Myrdal, 1968). The difference between the "soft state" in India and the "strong state" in China, claimed Myrdal, conditions the strategy of economic development, especially the use of planning, which Myrdal strongly favoured. Yet today both China and India have turned to the market economy, replacing the plan entirely. Besides, India harbours rule of law.

Relevance of social, cultural and economic conditions

A number of models which claim that social conditions are important for understanding the state have been identified. Could they offer insights into why rule of law differ from one country to another? Modelling the sources of stability and rule of law with regard to social conditions is a challenge to knowledge about the complexity of politics. Political outcomes depend upon many factors, which entails that states could hardly be a simple function of their physical and social environments.

One way to check if these social conditions are relevant for explaining these aspects of the state is to look at simple correlations (see Table 3.16). What one might realistically hope for is to find a few significant relationships that one can employ for further theory-building. The insights from testing general models need to be combined with case study findings. Yet it is a great help to know what holds on average when it comes to the social conditions which impact upon rule of law.

Several findings may be noted in Table 3.16. First, the relevance of economic factors for the state is strongly confirmed by the data. What matters most obviously for rule of law is the level of affluence and the size of agriculture. One needs to enquire into whether indebtness is conducive to regime instability or dictatorship in some countries. Economic freedom goes together with rule of law.

Second, there is the finding that Islamic domination tends to be combined with lack of democracy. It confirms the theory that the weak institutionalisation of a separation between state and church, secular and sacred in

Table 3.16 Relevance of social, economic and cultural conditions

	Corr.	*Sig.*	n
lnPop	−0.110	0.179	150
Climate	0.395**	0.000	150
AGVA 00	−0.566**	0.000	139
AGVA 04	−0.453**	0.000	981
ELF 10	−0.319**	0.000	149
ELF 11	−0.230**	0.005	146
Relfr 10	0.044	0.592	150
GDPC_02	0.590**	0.000	150
PPP_02	0.583**	0.000	144
EDTXGS	−0.217*	0.023	109
DEBPRXGS	0.196*	0.041	109
PVPRXGS	−0.212*	0.027	109
EF 2000	0.607**	0.000	114
EF 2003	0.651**	0.000	114
Prot 2000	0.333**	0.000	149
Musl 2000	−0.507**	0.000	149
Budd 2000	−0.107	0.193	149
Urban 98	0.396**	0.000	149
FAK 11	0.570**	0.000	150

Notes
** Correlation significant at the 0.01 level (2-tailed).
* Correlation significant at the 0.01 level (2-tailed).
Rule of law (Table 2.1); Pop-population: US Census Bureau (2006); climate (Table 3.2); AGVA-agricultural added value (Table 3.4/3); ELF-ethnic and religious fragmentation (Table 3.8/6); level of affluence (Table 3.11/9); external debt (Table 3.13/15); EF-economic freedom (Table 3.18/15); religion (Table 3.9/7); urbanisation (Table 3.5); FAK-family system (Table 3.10/8).

typically Islamic states makes a transition to democracy a difficult process. Third, there is confirmation for the family structure model.

Fourth, the fragmentation models display weak correlations. If there is indeed such a weak interaction between ethnic or religious heterogeneity and rule of law, then this is an important finding in relation to widely accepted beliefs about state performance. The hypothesis that ethnic fragmentation leads to state instability predicts a negative correlation between the variables. The finding is that the relationship is negative, but it is too weak to support the hypothesis. There are too many countries that are unstable and ethnically homogeneous. Not all states that are ethnically fragmented are unstable or authoritarian. Ethnic homogeneity is not a sufficient condition for rule of law, nor is it a necessary condition. There is a negative correlation between ethnic fragmentation and rule of law, but it is not as strong as is claimed in the fragmentation models. There are simply too many countries that score low on rule of law that are not strongly heterogeneous ethnically.

Conclusion

Principal–agent contracting, aiming at rule of law, is promoted by certain economic, social and cultural conditions. Social determinism involves a strong model about the environmental impact upon politics. What could be done to ameliorate state behaviour if physical, social, economic or cultural factors were of decisive importance? One major finding here is the absence of social determinism in all the correlations reported on in Table 3.16, which implies that hopes for better state outcomes are not altogether in vain. At the same time, rule of law does not occur in a social or economic vacuum. Clearly, several cultural conditions are contributory, whether positive or negative. The other major finding is that, in particular, economic factors in a wide sense must be taken into account when modelling rule of law.

4   Impact of political institutions

Introduction

Comparative government would benefit from looking at institutions within a principal–agent framework. Thus seen, political institutions would be erected and supported for their contribution in structuring the interaction between politicians and the population. Those institutions that promote the rule of law would be especially interesting to the principal, as they would allow him/her to restrain the agents, while at the same time sending clear signals about what they would want the agent to accomplish.

The new institutionalism argues correctly that the country-specific configurations of political institutions lie at the heart of the state. Neo-institutionalists could also be correct when it is affirmed that each state has its own very special set of institutions that determine much of its political life – *path dependency*. It may even be true that some interpretive methodology like hermeneutics may be an adequate research strategy when approaching the state with the aim of capturing all its institutional details (Powell and Dimaggio, 1991; Newton and van Deth, 2005).

Yet whatever emphasis is placed upon the unique institutional context for state outputs and outcomes, in the last resort comparative government has to rely upon some type of nomothetical methodology if it wishes to state how much various institutions matter. Political institutions have to be compared in order to identify which states have similar or dissimilar institutions and similar or different outcomes (Almond *et al.*, 2003). Which institutional concepts are the most valid in a comparative research strategy?

Institutions, principals and agents

To find institutional concepts that are comparative or truly cross-cultural presents a difficulty when looking at the institutional conditions of rule of law. The other equally hard problem is to find indicators that allow us to enter institutional conditions alongside other kinds of conditions for the state (e.g. the economic factors that were found to be relevant (Chapter 3) for the explanation of state properties). These two requirements for an institutional analysis of the state cross-culturally, derived from the logic of comparative methodology, entail that the complex institutional web in each single country must be traded for a few general concepts that may be employed in comparative modelling (Bebler and Seroka, 1990).

Political institutions may be interesting due to their intrinsic value or their effects on outcomes. The focus here is upon the latter instrumental aspect for the analysis of which a few general categories need to be introduced. The analysis of institutional patterns could not possibly be as rich in nuances in comparative analysis, as is required if one were to look at political institutions for their intrinsic value. What, then, does the overall picture about the impact of institutions upon the rule of law look like? The principal–agent framework offers a theory in terms of which the impact of institutions may be interpreted in a meaningful way. Which institutions would a principal wish to design, given that he/she is driven by the motive to maximise both safety and human rights? Principal–agent theory has analysed many forms of contracts – client–laywer, shareholders–CEOs, landlords–tenants. What are the insights to be gained from looking upon politics as principal–agent gaming?

The history of political thought contains numerous suggestions to the effect that institutional properties of various kinds have an impact – a set of models that form much of the heart of political science. As the basic institutions of the state may vary considerably, a number of relevant institutional models may be recognised. Let me introduce a few distinctions between political institutions in a stepwise fashion, starting from the most general ones and moving towards more specific ones, seen from the principal–agent perspective. The rules that define the most basic conditions for politics regulate the relationship between citizens and their political elites. Who may participate in elections? How are the candidates selected? And what are the institutions for the interaction between various elites, for instance, in terms of various forms of decision-making: executive, legislative and judicial? Moreover, one may ask whether federalism matters.

Participation

The vitality of the democratic regime comes from competition, although it must be constrained by the rules of constitutional democracy, based upon a consensus on fundamental values shared among the competing groups. One may well argue that competition is more important than participation. From the principal–agent perspective, the most crucial feature of democracy is that the principal has a real possibility to change from one agent to another, meaning contestation among politicians or political parties. Elections and party systems are structured by institutional rules. Contestation is manifested in the shape of the party system as well as in the size of the largest party.

Yet, crucial for the extent to which rule of law has been institutionalised is a large degree of contestation. The nature of the party system is the clue to the level of contestation in the political life of a country (Tingsten, 1965). The extent to which contestation is permitted in the public institutions of a country is crucial for the logic of politics in that country, competition being as important in politics as in markets. In, for instance, Schumpeter's model of democracy, the *open entry conditions* among elites for opposition are considered as more important than actual levels of participation (1944). The crucial distinction is that between one-party states and states where the rules acknowledge the independent existence of more than one party.

One may differentiate between two kinds of one-party system based on their relations to the state. One type of one-party system is characterised by the domination of the state over the party, whereas in the other type the party is on top, controlling the state. Looking for examples of the first kind – the state on top of the party – one should turn to Latin America and Africa, whereas the other type was practised in communist states, in Eastern Europe as well as in communist regimes in the Third World. The existence of a one-party system, institutionalised by severe punishment for any attempt to organise independent parties that could contest the position of the hegemonic party, indicates much about the spirit of government. In the state-dominated one-party system, the party is typically only an appendix to the state and its rulers, resulting in clientelism or corruption. In the Leninist model, the party dominates the state, meaning that its hierarchy first decides and then the government hierarchy implements ("*parallelism*") (Table 4.1).

Multi-party systems operated in Africa towards the end of colonial rule and during the first stage of independence. But African political parties have been in decline since independence, as in most states they have been run

Table 4.1 Electoral participation in the early 1990s (voters in percentage of VAP)

Civilisation	Vote 1990s	n
Arab	53.2	9
Western Europe	74.6	18
Eastern Europe	67.0	20
Other occidentals	70.3	5
South Asia	68.2	3
Africa Sub-Sahara	54.7	29
Muslim non-Arab	67.7	5
Latin America	61.1	21
Turkish	72.7	6
Asean	67.0	9
Pacific	78.0	2
Total	63.9	127
Eta squared	0.2	

Source: Adapted from IDEA (1997).

down in favour of the burgeoning state machine. In Latin America, there has been the dominance of the state over the parties. Many of them were founded as ruling parties *ex post* the regime creation. And parties founded *ex ante* have faced difficulties in maintaining their freedom when the regime swings from one kind to another. The Mexican Institutional Revolutionary Party (PRI) and the Peronists in Argentina are examples of large and long-lived state-dominated political parties in Latin America, as is true of the Colorado Party in Paraguay (Randall, 1987). The Kuomintang Party in Taiwan would also be a good example of a hegemonic party, at least for several decades after Chiang Kai-shek established his regime there in 1949.

The new wave of democratisation in Africa has implied that political parties again are looked upon with enthusiasm and not suspicion. Constitutions in a number of countries have been revised, undoing the one-party regime. However, party government has hardly become the typical mode of day-to-day politics in the Third World due to a close identification of one hegemonic political party with the state. When politics has a strong charismatic tone, dominant personalities tend to surface, often legitimating their personal grip upon power by means of the introduction of a loyal party, as, for instance, in Kazakstan or Turkmenistan.

Adversarial, concurrent and consociational democracy

The theory that democratic instutions if adequately institutionalised enhance rule of law may be found among several scholars (Held, 1987; Sartori, 1987). John Stuart Mill formulated a classical argument in 1862: the notion of democracy as popular participation was non-implementable in large states, but party government by means of representative institutions offered a realistic approximation to democracy. Decision-making in a system of representative institutions based upon majoritarian election techniques would enhance political stability if the internal and external environment in society were favourable. But are the institutions of adversarial democracy always conducive to stability?

Besides majoritararian democracy, democracy based upon proportional rule should be taken into consideration. Two different frameworks of institutions for democracy – adversarial and concurrent – may be identified. A richer institutional description of states is necessary, as there are other kinds of institutions than majoritarian representative ones that are also conducive to regime stability and rule of law. Actually, a persistent critique of Mill's representative and majoritarian model claims that other kinds of institutions are to be preferred (Pateman, 1970; Lively, 1975; Mansbridge, 1983; Elster, 1998). Scholars who favour participatory democracy or deliberative democracy are sceptical towards the model of adversarial democracy. Against the Schumpeter emphasis on elite competition, they underline widespread participation. As opposed to the Downsian focus on the decisive placement of the median voter (Downs, 1957), they underline the significance of bargaining among substantial groups in order to find a solution by discussion. Finally, the Riker prediction that minimum-sized government would constitute the backbone of stable government (Riker, 1962, 1982) has been criticised in favour of oversized coalitions including grand coalitions or the capacity of minority coalitions to function normally during an election period.

Thus, there is a long-standing tradition of democratic thought that requires more than a majoritarian interpretation based on the virtues of plurality voting in different bodies. "Real" democracy, it is stated, requires more than plurality or simple majority. South Carolina senator Calhoun elaborated a succinct argument about the necessity of so-called *concomitant majority* in *A Disquisition on Government* (1851). Calhoun's argument was set forth in a particular situation where he stubbornly defended the vested interests of the South in the USA, including slavery by means of a confederatist interpretation of the constitution involving the right of nullification and secession. Calhoun saw the operation of the concurrent majority institution in the capacity of the Roman tribunes of the plebs to veto a proposal under discussion in the Senate, in the infamous principle of *liberum veto* in the Polish *Diet* during the seventeenth and eighteenth centuries as well as in the strategic power game between the three estates in English government before the firm establishment of parliamentarianism: the King, Lords and Commons. However, Calhoun was first and foremost interested in the application of his principle to the basic problem of defining the state in a federal or confederal context. Just as the six nations in the *Iroquois Confederacy* – Mohawks, Oneidas, Cayugas, Senecas, Onandagas and Tuscororas – were sovereign, only acting together on the basis of unanimity opinion, Calhoun claimed the Southern states had the same legal status within the Union. He saw basically two types of government: constitutional government versus absolute government, the two having different guiding principles: compromise and force (Calhoun, 1953: 29). Yet democracy models may emphasise institutions that guarantee the rights of minorities and offer them institutionalised access to policy influence. Calhoun stated:

> It is this negative power, the power of preventing or arresting the action of government, be it called by what term it may – veto, interposition, nullification, check, or balance of power – which, in fact, forms the negative power. In all its forms, and under all its names, it results from the concurrent majority.
>
> (Calhoun, 1953: 28)

A modern statement of the advantages of concurrent majorities is to be found in Tsebelis and his idea of so-called *veto players*. Looking at the presidential regime when it obeys the logic of rule of law, Tsebelis finds that a system of counterweighting powers between executive, legislative and judicial agents fosters stability in that the institutions of separation of powers force the agents to engage in bargaining. This in turn leads to a definition of politics as negotiation, and not imposition.

The idea of stable government as dependent upon institutions that enhance compromise government was developed already in the 1960s by Lijphart, who launched the word "consociationalism" as a theoretical term for a set of mechanisms that are conducive to state stability (Lijphart, 1974). The key term dates back to Althusius' *"consociatio"* or the association as the explicit form for creating state institutions. Althusius argued in *Systematic Politics* (1603) that a state is made up of various groups in society that give their consent to government. The various associations constitute the political body, reinforced continuously by consensus-building. Whereas majoritarian scholars emphasise a concept of stable government as a zero-sum game where the plurality winner takes all in a competitive setting where cross-cutting cleavages have a centripetal force (Lipset, 1960; Riker, 1982), their critics claim that stable government required an entirely different institutional framework, at least in so-called divided societies (McRae, 1974).

Consociational democracy underlines the occurrence of so-called segmented pluralism, meaning that society is characterised by strong cleavages in a plural society with ethnic or religious groups, in combination with the employment of so-called concordant democracy, i.e. special institutions that enhance compromise and consensus (Lijphart, 1977). Lijphart meant by *"consociational democracy"* government by elite cartels, designed to turn a democracy with a fragmented political culture into a stable democracy (Lijphart, 1974: 79). The concept of concordant democracy was developed by Lehmbruch to denote a strategy of conflict management by cooperation and agreement among the different elites instead of democracy by competition and majority decision (1979), similar to the way corporatist institutions may function. Lijphart modelled state stability and performance as dependent on grand coalitions, mutual veto, proportionality in the translation of votes into seats as well as federalism (Lijphart, 1977: 25–52). The consociational model was later generalised by Lijphart into the consensus model (Chapter 3). One key indicator of majoritarian or proportional democracy is the election system employed for legislative assemblies (Duverger, 1992: Shugart and Wattenberg, 2003 (Table 4.2)).

In relation to the important institution of electoral formulas, they may be said to be either majoritarian, proportional or both (mixed systems). In order to summarise the direct consequences of election formulas which cover several technicalities such as size of electoral district, threshold, number of seats to allocate and so on, one may employ the disproportionality index. This measures the extent to which the mandates a party receives in an election deviate from the number of votes received, relatively speaking (Taagepera and Shugart, 1991; Lijphart, 1994; Colomer, 2004).

In elections, the electorate picks its political agents who will represent them, conducting the business of legislatures for a period of generally four to five years. In order to avoid the agents' temptation to steer clear of the

Table 4.2 Election systems

Civilisation	PR	Semi-PR	Plurality	Majority	Total
Arab	1	2	6	2	11
Western Europe	16	0	1	1	18
Eastern Europe	11	5	0	4	20
Other occidentals	2	0	2	1	5
South Asia	1	0	3	0	4
Africa Sub-Sahara	10	4	15	7	36
Muslim non-Arab	1	1	3	1	6
Latin America	16	2	2	2	22
Turkish	1	1	1	4	7
Asean	1	3	7	1	12
Pacific	0	0	2	0	2
Total	60	18	42	23	143
Eta squared					0.251

Source: Based on IDEA (2002).

monitoring and evaluation of the principal, the electorate needs several agents working for the principal under a scheme of competition. Thus, the principal is well served by agents checking and balancing eath other. Yet, the electorate may have conflicting ideas about who the agents should be. Thus, there may be several principals as well as many agents. This situation is probably the one Lijphart had in mind when he argued for the institutions of *Konkordanz* democracy: PR, oversized coalition governments and consociational behaviour among the elites representing the various parts of the electorate.

Federations and confederations

Federalism is the institutional theory which claims that a federal state format is a guarantee of stability and rule of law (Elazar, 1968, 1987, 1991; Riker, 1975). However, the facts about federations do not support such a positive evaluation. Federal states like the Soviet Union with its 15 union republics, former Yugoslavia with six republics and two autonomous regions, and former Czechoslovakia with its two republics did succumb. A look at the examples of federal states in the world indicates that rule of law is hardly an omnipresent characteristic with governments that call themselves "federal" (Table 4.3).

Moreover, Table 4.3 indicates that the federal framework for a state is not used as frequently as the adherents of the federal model would like. The number of federal states is quite small, considering the total number of states. It is true though that the set of federal states hosts a large proportion

Table 4.3 Federal states

Country	Number of states/provinces	Court of Appeal
Argentina	23 P, 1 FD	Supreme Court
Australia	6 S, 1 FD, 1 T	High Court
Austria	9 *Länder*	Constitutional Court
Belgium	10 P	Supreme Court
Brazil	26 S, 1 FD	Supreme Court
Canada	10 P, 3 T	Supreme Federal Court
Ethiopia	9 S, 2 T	Supreme Court
Germany	16 *Länder*	Constitutional Court
India	28 S, 7UT	Supreme Court
Malaysia	13 S, 1 FD	High Court
Mexico	31 S, 1 FD	Supreme Court
Nigeria	36 S, 1 T	Supreme Court
Pakistan	4 P, 2 T	Supreme Court
Russia	21 R, 2 FD	Constitutional Court
Sudan	25 S	Constitutional Court
Switzerland	26 Cantons	Federal Tribunal
United Arab Emirates	7 Sheikdoms	Ruler's Court*
United States	50 S, 1 FD, 14 T	Supreme Court
Venezuela	23 S, 2 FD	Supreme Court

Source: Adapted from *Statesman's Yearbook*, (1989–2006).

Notes
* The United Arab Emirates include the former so-called *trucial* states from the colonial period: Abu Dhabi, Dubai, Sharjah, Ajman, Umm al Qaiwain, Ras al Khaimah and Fujairah.

of the population of the world, but it holds equally true that not all states that are large have the federal framework. The unitary state framework is used in China, Indonesia, Japan and most of the large European countries. Population-wise, there are small federal states like the United Arab Emirates, Austria and Switzerland. There is an ambiguity as to the identification of the set of federal states. It has been argued that unitary states may develop in the direction of a federation, or semi-federalism: Spain and Italy with their historical autonomous provinces as well as even the UK under recent devolution to Scotland and Wales. On the other hand, it has also been claimed that only federal countries that respect the rule of law may be considered "true federations".

Looking at territorial size, huge states employ the federal framework such as Russia, Canada, the USA, Brazil, Mexico, Nigeria, Australia, India, Pakistan as well as Argentina. Several of these countries cannot be characterised as stable rule of law countries during the post-war period. However, federalism is not only appropriate as a framework to be employed in states with vast territories, because it is employed in states with extremely small territory such as the marginal cases of the Comoros – 400,000 people on

2,000 km^2 – and St Kitts-Nevis with a few thousand inhabitants on 200 km^3 or among some of the islands in the Pacific Ocean. On the contrary, the unitary framework is used in a few territorially huge states like China, Bangladesh, France and the Republic of South Africa. At the same time, it should be pointed out that a formally federalist framework is not the same as real power decentralisation. Some federal systems are quite centralised (e.g. Austria and Mexico). Unitary states may display decentralisation as well, in particular if the local or regional governments possess considerable discretion (Page, 1991).

Actually, it is not easy to pin down what federalism stands for except in a formal constitutional sense. First and foremost, federal states are those states that call themselves so. Characteristic of federalism is the existence of government elected from below at the regional level, but such devolution of state power may occur not only in formally unitary states like Spain and Italy but also in traditionally centralist France, where the process of devolution in the 1980s has changed the Napoleonic state. Second, one often-used indicator on state decentralisation is the division of the allocation of funds within the public sector between central government and lower levels of government. Measuring the proportion of central government's final consumption in relation to general government's final consumption, federal states tend to have lower proportions than unitary governments. In federal states there tend to occur both national and provincial legislation, symmetrical bicameralism and a constitutional court with legal review.

What matters is the underlying idea of the state, i.e. whether it derives somehow from a confederatist notion of the state as consisting of member states such as in former Czechoslovakia with its two parts: the Czech lands and Slovakia. The member states of a federal union are considered the constituent parts of the state that have rights against the federal government, to be protected within a constitutional framework, often including a special court of appeal. The dividing line between federal states and confederal states is related to the rights of the member states to relinquish the obligations of the union contract. Actually, one of the most conspicuous examples of this mode of organising the state is what replaced the Union of Soviet Republics in 1990: the Confederation of Independent States (CIS). Perhaps one may also call the British Commonwealth a confederation, but it is a borderline case.

The increase in the visibility of international organisations that has taken place during the post-second World War period may be interpreted as a new form of confederalism, particularly with regard to the UN, WTO and especially the European Community, the Council of Europe and the European Security Council. The growth of international regimes is characteristic of the post-Second World War developments, challenging the sovereignty of the national state (Krasner, 1982; Keohane, 1984). One cannot neglect the international regimes when one tries to account for state stability and performance. The international system has a formal impact upon the state in the form of membership criteria. Thus not all kinds of states are accepted to enter international communities. The requirement of human rights has grown stronger in the 1980s and 1990s. This applies to the Council of Europe, the European Union and the Organization of Economic Cooperation and Development (OECD). Membership of international regimes also opens up the possibility of receiving a number of benefits such as economic aid and military protection.

Regionalisation also results in confederations. Thus, a considerable number of regional regimes have been created in order to improve upon *inter alia* free trade: the EU, Asean, NAFTA and Mercosur, for instance, as well as the former COMECON in Eastern Europe. The distinction between a trade agreement and a confederation is not always crystal clear (Chapter 12). The rapidly growing number of international and regional organisations in the world since 1945 has made confederations the most relevant form of political organisation. NATO would be the classic example of a military confederation.

Presidentialism

A basic institution of states is the type of executive it employs for immediate government purposes, or administration. The basic separation is between parliamentary executives and presidential systems, although various subtypes of presidential and parliamentary regimes may be identified. At the same time, this separation is not exhaustive. Other kinds of executives exist such as real monarchical rule, military juntas and communist politburos. Several of the states with a formal monarchy have parliamentary executives. Military as well as communist regimes often employ the presidential regime, at least symbolically or as a façade.

The classification of presidential systems cannot be entirely based on constitutional formulas, because parliamentarianism may be practised within a state where the head of state is a president, such as in South Africa. Presidentialism, if it implies a real type of rulership, must be defined in such a way that it does not overlap with the occurrence of parliamentary executives. Semi-presidentialism is the mix of a powerful president and premier. The executive in Switzerlands *collegiado* is the Federal Council, consisting of seven members elected from various cantons for four years of office by both chambers of the Swiss Parliament, the Council of States and the National Council. The Federal Council cannot dissolve Parliament and it cannot be removed by means of a vote of non-confidence. The seven members of the Federal Council act as ministers heading each one of the seven administrative departments of the Swiss republic. The Swiss Parliament also elects one of the members of the Council as the President of the Confederation for only one calendar year. There are also countries with symbolic presidentialism, i.e. the president is the head of state, merely representing the country.

Whereas presidentialism implies a republic, parliamentary executives could exist in both republics and monarchies as long as the latter does not amount to personal rule by the monarch. Listing the countries with real presidentialism, a classification of limited and unlimited presidential executives may be employed (Derbyshire and Derbyshire, 1999). The distinction between limited and unlimited presidentialism refers to roughly constitutional against unconstitutional presidential states (Table 4.4). In this classification, the semi-federal states have been categorised as examples of real federalism (Table 4.4).

The above identification of presidential executives is not quite complete, because communist states have also employed presidentialism. Actually, the earlier communist regimes in Eastern Europe had presidents just as remains true of China today. Moreover, the dividing line between presidential states and military regimes is often blurred, as sometimes the leader of a *coup d'état* attempts to legitimise his rule through a presidential plebiscitary, for instance, Pinochet.

The distinction between constitutional and unconstitutional presidentialism indicates what is often stated about the nature of presidential regimes, namely that they engender the possibility of authoritarian drift. There are two opposing views in the literature evaluating the outcomes of presidentialism. The negative hypothesis states that it is conducive to democratic instability or even dictatorship (Linz and Valenzuela, 1994), whereas the positive evaluation argues that this is not necessarily so, presidential democracy sometimes operating stably (Shugart and Carey, 1992; Mainwaring and Shugart, 1997; Hagopian and Mainwaring, 2005). One test of whether presidentialism leads to deviations from the rule of law occurs when the incumbent president faces the end of his/her second period: Will the president accept the most usual constitutional restriction of only one re-election period? Or will there be an attempt at a constitutional revision opening the way towards presidential domination, as e.g. *decretismo*?

Table 4.4 States with presidential rule

Civilisation	Mixed	Limited presidential	Unlimited presidential	Total
Arab	2	3	4	15
Western Europe	3	1	0	18
Eastern Europe	7	7	2	20
Other occidentals	0	1	0	5
South Asia	1	0	0	4
Africa Sub-Sahara	1	24	5	36
Muslim non-Arab	1	1	2	7
Latin America	1	18	0	22
Turkish	0	1	5	7
Asean	1	3	0	13
Pacific	0	1	0	2
Total	17	60	18	149

Source: Adapted from Derbyshire and Derbyshire (1999).

Parliamentarianism and bicameralism

Under the rules of parliamentarianism, the premier governs the country, given that he/she has the confidence of Parliament, with the possibility to dissolve Parliament if there is a vote of no confidence. In some countries, the prime minister will be formally invested in his/her office by a vote in Parliament. These three basic principles – investiture, right to dissolve and vote of no confidence – admit of certain variations from one country to another. For instance, the German Parliament cannot remove one *Kanzler* without designating a new one, and the Norwegian *Stortinget* cannot be dissolved at all. In some countries, the president has certain prerogatives in relation to the election and removal of the premier. Yet, the variation in parliamentarianism between the continents is closely tied up with rule of law (see Table 4.5).

In Africa we find few functioning parliamentary systems, as it is not in conformity with the African way of ruling, namely presidentialism often combined with one-party states, whether in a leftist or rightist orientation. Asia knows little of parliamentarianism except for South Asia and Singapore – the legacy of the British Empire. Oceania with its three states all have Westminster-type regimes with strongly institutionalised parliamentarianism. After the fall of the communist regimes, most European countries adhere to parliamentarianism but quite a few practise semi-presidentialism. There is a rich institutional variation in how parliamentarianism is practised in Europe, as the simple classical British model is only used at Westminster. As emphasised above in case studies, the variety of institutional characteristics becomes more detailed.

The choice between unicameralism versus bicameralism has been singled out as having a strong impact upon outcomes (Tsebelis and Money, 1997). Bicameralism enhances policy stability, meaning that several groups can

Table 4.5 States with parliamentary rule

Civilisation	Parliamentary	Total
Arab	0	15
Western Europe	14	18
Eastern Europe	4	20
Other occidentals	4	5
South Asia	2	4
Africa Sub-Sahara	3	36
Muslim non-Arab	2	7
Latin America	2	22
Turkish	1	7
Asean	4	13
Pacific	1	2
Total	37	149

Source: Adapted from Derbyshire and Derbyshire (1999).

Table 4.6 Legislative institutions

Civilisation	Unicameral	Bicameral	Total
Arab	14	1	15
Western Europe	8	10	18
Eastern Europe	12	8	20
Other occidentals	2	3	5
South Asia	2	2	4
Africa Sub-Sahara	29	7	36
Muslim non-Arab	4	1	5
Latin America	9	13	22
Turkish	5	2	7
Asean	10	4	14
Pacific	1	1	2
Total	96	52	148

Source: Based on *Encyclopaedia Britannica* (2000).

bargain about laws and budgets, which leads to power sharing among so-called veto-players. On the other hand, when the president and the legislative assembly go into a stalemate, both being veto-players, political stability may be harmed (Tsebelis, 2002). Now, one would wish to know whether the chamber system – one chamber, two chambers symmetrical or asymmetrical – really matters for the rule of law, looking at a large number of countries. It is true that legislative assemblies tend to exhibit special institutional features in one country compared to another. Here, one can mention the alternative rules of the *navette* between the two chambers, when a bill is accepted in one chamber but rejected in another. Parliaments employ different methods of voting in order to churn out a final bill from all amendments proposed to the original bill. Yet, here the focus is upon whether bicameralism is conducive towards rule of law. Table 4.6 indicates the variation in legislative institutions.

Whether a country practises parliamentarianism or not, it will still need a national assembly. Parliament will be responsible for legislation, taxation and budgeting, even if it does not select or remove the Cabinet. The national assembly would be the prime representation of the principal (i.e. the electorate), and the agents in Parliament would exercise the sovereignty inherent in the people. Thus, parliamentary institutions matter both under presidentialism and parliamentarianism. Under symmetrical bicameralism, the principal would be represented by two different sets of agents, which theoretically should improve the lot of the principal.

Authoritarian institutions

Authoritarianism comes in several forms, from benevolent tutelage to rascist nationalism. Dictatorships exist around the world in many forms, the more authoritarian the harsher, and the more totalitarian the more encompassing. One may argue that authoritarianism was at its peak in communist states or in unconstitutional systems with a fascist orientation, especially in Nazi Germany. At the same time though such states attempted to legitimise their power domination by invoking the so-called true interests of the people, their populist orientation contrasting with the exclusiveness typical of military or traditional regimes. The occurrence of authoritarian institutions on the continents is mapped by two indices in Table 4.7.

Whereas the military junta model is hardly a European phenomenon with the exception of Greece between 1967 and 1973, right-wing dictatorship is certainly not unknown on the European continent, although its legitimacy is nil after the regime changes in Spain and Portugal. Left-wing authoritarianism faces the same problem of legitimacy, few people believing the international proletariat and its dictatorship. Several regimes in Africa, Asia and Central and South America have been military ones, which has led to state instability being high on these continents. In Asia dictatorships, right-wing or left-wing, have been a prevailing regime type, reflecting the historical legacy of Oriental despotism.

Military regimes

Military juntas have been able to usurp power for periods of time, most often in South Korea, Pakistan, Indonesia, and Myanmar and in the Middle East. Military regimes are transient regimes; the crux of the matter is the successor problem. A part of the military establishment would seize the state for the accomplishment of some specific purpose that is only relevant for a certain period, linked with so-called national interests. After a few years, the

Table 4.7 Some authoritarian institutions

Civilisation	Communist	Military	Absolutist	Total
Arab	0	1	5	15
Western Europe	0	0	0	18
Eastern Europe	0	0	0	20
Other occidentals	0	0	0	5
South Asia	0	0	1	4
Africa Sub-Sahara	0	3	0	36
Muslim non-Arab	0	1	0	7
Latin America	1	0	0	22
Turkish	0	0	0	7
Asean	4	1	0	13
Pacific	0	0	0	2
Total	5	6	6	149

Source: Adapted from Derbyshire and Derbyshire (1999).

usurpation of power has to find a renewed cause or the military regime has to be dismantled. The logic of a military government is thus that it must falter sooner or later, as there can be no legitimate successor but a non-military regime.

Thus, military regimes do not last for long. With the notable exception of the Stroessner dictatorship in Paraguay, no military junta has survived for more than ten years. However, often the rule of military juntas is not dismantled in favour of democratic rule. Instead, some military rulers attempt to prolong their *de facto* rule by introducing presidential rule, which could confer *de jure* status on their dictatorship. Events in Nigeria, Uganda and Pakistan have exemplified this logic of *de facto* military rule with attempts to legitimise dictatorship through the introduction of presidential plebiscite. Latin America has been freed from the coups during the past decade, but many African countries have experienced military intervention lately, thereby increasing political instability.

The distinction between the military junta and the one-party model as the instrument for repression is related to the separation between right-wing and left-wing dictatorships, albeit not to 100 per cent. What distinguished left-wing non-democratic rule was the combination of a one-party state with socialist ambitions towards some kind of planned economy. Right-wing dictatorship could also use the one-party model, but it will almost certainly be based on a military regime (e.g. in Asia where there have been right-wing coups in a few countries such as Thailand). There have been examples of left-wing military dictatorships, such as Myanmar, where military coups in 1962 and 1988 paved the way for the brutal "Burmese Way to Socialism". The *coup d'état* was typical of Latin American politics in the twentieth century.

A military coup in 1952 in Bolivia triggered a popular uprising, which led Paz Estenssoro to assume the presidency although he had failed to achieve a majority in the 1951 election. In 1964 the Barrientos coup overthrew the Paz government. A coup in 1971 brought Banzer to power and in 1980 there was a new one among the some 190 military coups during the 154 years of independence in Bolivia. Regime instability in Peru is similar to that of Bolivia. A number of coups have taken place, introducing, for example, the Velasco military junta between 1968 and 1975. However, there have also been attempts at democratic rule, challenged in the 1980s and early 1990s by "Sendoro Luminoso", a Maoist guerrilla. Both Bolivia and Peru after Fujimori returned to the rule of law in 2000.

The events in the Dominican Republic are well known from the perspective adopted here. Dictator Trujillo was assassinated in 1961 having ruled since 1930 following a coup. In 1962 Juan Bosch was elected president in free elections only to be ousted by a coup the following year as well as in 1965. Most attention on any coup in Latin America was no doubt given to Pinochet's overthrow of socialist president Alliende in Santiago de Chile in 1973, establishing a dictatorship that lasted up until 1989. In Cuba, Batista came to power by means of a coup in 1952 only to be ousted in 1959, defeated by the Fidel Castro insurrection, which had been initiated already in 1953 but failed then as well as in 1956, when Castro returned from exile only to flee to the hills. In addition in Latin America, there was the resignation of Juan Peron in 1955, with the restoration of civilian government, which Peron had smashed with his 1945 military coup, as well as the Rojas' regime in Colombia, introduced by a coup in 1953 and abolished in 1957 by a coup during the ten-year period '*La Violencia*' when a quarter of a million people are said to have died. Today, Colombia is cut in two through a long civil war with a Maoist guerrilla. Moreover, there were coups in Guatemala (Arbentz's fall in 1954), in Honduras (Diaz's fall in 1956) and Venezuela (short-lived military regime in 1958 under Larrazábal).

In addition, the Muslim world has witnessed numerous *coup d'états*. In 1952 a group of young army officers led by Gamal Nasser overthrew King Farouk in Egypt by means of a military junta. In 1953 Egypt became a republic, but not until 1954 did Nasser assume a leading position as prime minister. In Pakistan in 1958, General Ayub Khan seised power and in 1977 General Zia ul-Haq overthrew Ali Bhutto's democratic rule, following which Bhutto was hanged. Likewise the strong military involvement in Turkish politics, since the charismatic Ataturk regime was established in 1923, has been displayed in several coups. The 1960 coup led to the execution of Prime Minister Menderes and the 1980 coup resulted in martial law, suspending all democratic political activity up until 1983. The 1965 Indonesian military coup established a long-lived period of domination for the army, but the acting president – Sukarno – was not formally removed from office until 1967, only to die under house arrest in 1971. Suharto moved to legitimise military supremacy by presidential authoritarian rule, involving the wiping out of opposition groups such as the Communist Party in atrocious persecutions between 1965 and 1967. Suharto was removed in 1998, when Indonesia introduced democracy in a fragile state.

Shortly after the collapse of colonial rule, Africa started to experience political instability with many coups. Thus in the Central African Republic Bokassa introduced military rule in 1962, which initiated a period that became more and more idiosyncratic until Bokassa was ousted in 1979. A few military coups in Nigeria in 1966 gave power to Gowon, but his rule, which involved civil war with the Ibos between 1967 and 1970, only lasted up until 1975. During the 1980s there occurred a whole series of coups. Nigeria returned to civilian rule after dictator Abudja's death in 2000. Actually, there have been straightforward coups in most African countries (e.g. Togo (1963), Zaire (1965), Gabon (1967), Somalia (1969), Benin (1972), Rwanda (1973), Sudan (1985), Burkina Faso (1969, 1980), Burundi (1966, 1987), Niger (1974), Chad (1975), Ethiopia (1977), Ghana (1966, 1972, 1978) and Liberia (1980)). The military forces in the newly independent states gained the upper hand early on in political developments, as in Zaire where they helped Mobutu to power in 1965 and in Uganda where Idi Amin overthrew Obote in 1971, who returned shortly to power after Amin's strange regimen was crushed in 1978, only to be overthrown again by Museweni. Yet, a few strong, if not charismatic, leaders such as Kaunda in Zambia, Mugabe in Zimbabwe, Kenyatta in Kenya, Nyerere in Tanzania and Banda in Malawi as well as Houphouët-Boigny on the Ivory Coast, established dictatorships based on the one-party model as the mechanism for control.

In the early twenty-first century, military intervention in politics is down in Latin America. The number of coups is still high in Sub-Saharan Africa. One may analyse the coups from different angles: (1) degree of success, (2) negative or positive results and (3) recurrent or one-shot event. Military coups are not always bad in the sense of overthrowing democracy and causing economic havoc. A military coup may target dictatorship or political instability and it may be conducive to more economic stability. Yet a coup may be recurrent, signalling that the country is fundamentally unstable due to, for instance, ethnic, religious or class cleavages. Thus, it is a healthy sign that military intervention is no longer frequent in Latin America, although presidents do get forced out of office by means of popular protest. But it was similarly shocking for many to observe a coup in Thailand in 2006 and in Fiji in 2006, despite the fact that both countries have had coups before. Pakistan remains a country with a strong military presence in politics. General Musharraf is typical of Pakistani politics. President and Chief of Staff of the Pakistan Army, he is the fourth Pakistani General to govern the country in the wake of a coup in 1999. A coup may be more or less bloody, it may succeed in creating political stability, or it may be the start of counter coups and anarchy. The latter holds especially for Sub-Saharan Africa.

One may count the number of *coup d'états* in order to get a global picture of the possibility of the military to enter into the role as agents of the political body (Table 4.8). The logic of military intervention is that once the threshold has been broken through once, there is little to stop the military returning to an intervention in one form or another. Chile had a long history of civil rule from 1932 before the Pinochet *putsh,* which led to authoritarian rule but also finally ended in a definite return to democracy.

One may differentiate between the military entrance into politics, military rule and military exits. The motivation that drives the military to attempt to play a political role has been debated: personal motives, reformist zeal, status quo preservation, revolutionary goals (Nordlinger, 1977; Finer, 2002). Although military take-overs have been made stating that the prevailing order was threatened, it is also true that there have occurred radical military coups, such as in Egypt in 1952, Iraq in 1958, Syria in 1963 and Libya in 1969. Few countries in Africa have not experienced military rule: Botswana, Senegal, Swaziland and Tunisia. The occurrence of a *putsch* reflects how the boundary lines between the political leaders and the military are institutionalised. Typical of Latin America and Africa is that the separation between politics and the military is weak. There, the military has not only

Table 4.8 Military coups

Civilisation	Coups	n
Arab	0.60	15
Western Europe	0.06	18
Eastern Europe	0.15	20
Other occidentals	0.00	5
South Asia	0.00	4
Africa Sub-Sahara	1.17	36
Muslim non-Arab	1.57	7
Latin America	1.14	22
Turkish	0.43	7
Asean	0.85	13
Pacific	0.00	2
Total	0.70	149
Eta squared		0.153

Source: Adapted from Banks (1996).

intervened in politics several times, but it has also attempted to preserve influence after relinquishing rule. Thus, the exit of military juntas is often based upon agreements that protect the military in various ways, including judicial examination of human rights crimes committed by the military when in power. Turkey is an example of a regime where the military establishment refuses to exit definitively, although refraining from all direct interventions in politics. Here, the tacit and indirect military involvement in the state has resulted from the so-called Kemalist tradition, i.e. the modernised leadership of Mustafa Kemal Atatürk (1881–1938), leading Turkey out of its Ottoman past and into a nation-state, using the army whenever necessary to guarantee political stability.

The communist model

Although it was known that communist states faced increasingly difficult problems, the system's collapse in several countries around 1989 came as a surprise, in particular its non-violent nature. One may argue that the communist state did not disappear due to political tensions expressed in the organisation of explicit resistance against the regime, because what made the difference were the ever-growing economic and ecological problems. The collapse of the communist regimes in Eastern Europe followed a combination of legitimacy deficit and economic inefficiency, the one factor reinforcing the other (Clark and Wildavsky, 1990). It was possible to mobilise citizen support for the communist ideals at an early stage and during the Second World War, but the more distant the accomplishment of the promises – especially economic ones – became, the less support there was for the party.

The communist state appeared for many years to be stable but not performing very well. Now it is known that besides poor performance with regard to policy outputs and policy outcomes there was a severe stability problem growing in force from around 1975. At that time the communist economies started to decline, first in Poland and then in the whole of Eastern Europe. An analysis of the special features of communist institutions would focus on how political institutions of the Leninist state (*soviets* = councils) became tied up with the economic institutions of the Stalinist planned economy. An immense concentration of political and economic power in a small elite, protected by the double hierarchy of both the Soviet state and the Communist Party, guaranteed repressive state stability for 80 years. The structure of the communist states is called "*parallelism*". Fainsod (1958) showed that state and party were built up as an isomorphism, meaning that complex structures could be mapped on to each other in such a way that for each part of one structure there is a corresponding part in the other structure, where "corresponding" means that the two parts play similar roles in their respective structures.

Yet communist regimes were not all alike. In some states there were participatory elements, which eased the harsh features typical of other states. The communist states in the Third World were different from those in what was called "the Second World". The separation between the party and the military was drawn differently. In some the party remained the power centre, whereas in others a left-wing military was decisive for the creation and continuation of a Marxist regime.

Institutional consolidation or decay

The process of institutionalisation received much attention during the 1980s in the wake of the new institutionalism (March and Olsen, 1989). One trend has been to focus in more detail on country-specific contexts of political institutions, resulting in numerous case studies enquiring into state- or nation-building. Yet, when asking what the differential impact of various special institutions could be, one should also employ the general inductive methods in comparative politics. One important hypothesis, reminiscent of Burke's philosophy of tradition and legacy, states that the length of time of state institutionalisation is a crucial factor, accounting for political or economic outcomes (Huntington, 1968; Olson, 1982).

Two models of institutional evolution have been launched. The first, the positive consolidation model, argues that the length of time of uninterrupted institution-building matters positively for the state, enhancing state stability and state performance. There is a starting point in time when a modernising political leadership is introduced, which also coincides with the overall process of social and economic transformation. The earlier in time the process of institutionalising a modern state starts, the more likely it is that it will be a stable democracy.

The second model of institutional sclerosis implies a less positive attitude towards institution-building, arguing that the longer the time span since the introduction of a set of modern state institutions, the more there will be of so-called institutional sclerosis. And institutional sclerosis could matter for the state, as it would enhance the power of special interest groups (trade unions, employers' associations) to engage in so-called rent-seeking, which may threaten economic performance.

The concepts of institutional consolidation and sclerosis do not single out the introduction of rule of law institutions as the starting point of the modern institutional state. What is referred to instead is the length in time for the consolidation of modern leadership, introducing bureaucracy as the model organisation of the state, opening the way for economic and social transformation away from *agraria* towards *industria*. Table 4.9 suggests two measures of institutional evolution.

One finding in the data reported in Table 4.9 about modern institution-building is that political modernisation pre-dates large-scale economic and social modernisation (i.e the transition from *agrarian* to *industria*) on all continents. The basic trust of the institutional models is to model the length of time since the introduction of a modern leadership as conducive to state maturity, meaning more of stability, rule of law and the provision of public services. The crucial difference in Table 4.9 is between Africa and Asia on

Table 4.9 Institutional consolidation

Civilisation	Scler 1	n	Modeeco 1	n
Arab	61.4	15	49.2	9
Western Europe	184.6	18	115.4	18
Eastern Europe	130.9	20	82.2	15
Other occidentals	173.2	5	102.4	5
South Asia	48.8	4	52.5	2
Africa Sub-Sahara	38.8	36	38.0	1
Muslim non-Arab	65.6	7	63.5	4
Latin America	112.0	22	59.9	10
Turkish	128.3	7	77.0	1
Asean	69.2	14	53.0	7
Pacific	59.0	2	54.0	1
Total	94.8	150	79.0	73
Eta squared	0.7		0.6	

Source: Adopted from Black (1966).

Note
Adapted from Sclerosis 1 = start of modernised leadership; Modeeco 1 = start of industrialisation.

the one hand and the remaining continents on the other, because only among the former do we find the very young states. The consolidation model predicts that states will be more stable and perform better, the longer the time for consolidation of institutions has lapsed – a warning about any hopes of early state improvements in Africa in particular.

However, the institutional sclerosis model outlined by Olson (1982) predicts that this is not necessarily so, as states that were created early, such as those in Latin America, could suffer from institutional decay, meaning red tape and bureaucratic inefficiency. If certain institutions matter for macropolitical outcomes such as stable rule of law, then do such institutions tend to last? The rise of neo-institutionalism during the past 20 years entails a clear reply to this question (Ostrom, 2005). Yet, there is one seminal idea in political thought which implies a word of warning against any form of institutional optimism, as it were. The theory of institutional decline or decay as an immanent process in all republics entails that values play a crucial role. Republicanism according to Machiavelli, Guicciardini, Harrington, Madison and Jefferson theorised the longevity of a republican state. Since most of the states of the world today are republics in their basic nature, there are perhaps some grains of truth in republicanism where, besides rules, motivation (*virtue*) also matters greatly in society.

Republicanism is actually highly applicable to all countries, as it targets the role of institutional integrity in shaping the life span of a political regime. This is a cultural factor which may be tapped by various indicators, i.e. what is today called "social capital" or what is referred to as state transparency or good governance (Transparency International, 2004). Pocock writes:

> It was the virtue, as it was the end, of man to be a political animal; the polity was the form in which human matter developed its proper virtue, and it was the function of virtue to impose form on *fortuna*.
>
> (Pocock, 1975: 184)

This Aristotelian language may perhaps be translated into the basic concern in modern political theory for active citizenship, transparency in institutional enforcement and due process of law. Yet states are under pressure from the forces of institutional decay, as political actors fail to live up to the demands of *civile vivere*: "But not only was it a fact of experience and history that such structures of virtue could become corrupt and disintegrate; it was, by a terrible paradox, inherent in the very nature of republics that this should be so" (Pocock, 1975: 185). When, to speak with Machiavelli, *fortuna* invades *virtu* as is bound to happen sooner or later given the nature of human incentives (corruption), then the survival of the republic is very much at stake (Table 4.10).

One need not accept the life-cycle span theory of republics to understand that institutional integrity poses a problem for any state, which cannot be

Table 4.10 Control of corruption in government in various civilisations around 2000

Civilisation	Trans 1996	n	Trans 2000	n	Trans 2004	n	Trans 2005	n
Arab	3.9	2	4.4	4	3.7	15	3.8	15
Western Europe	7.5	16	7.8	18	7.9	18	8.0	18
Eastern Europe	4.6	4	3.5	17	3.6	20	3.7	20
Other occidentals	8.5	5	8.3	5	8.2	5	7.8	5
South Asia	2.6	1	2.8	1	3.0	3	2.9	3
Africa Sub-Sahara	2.8	5	3.2	19	2.8	27	2.8	32
Muslim non-Arab	2.0	3	1.7	1	2.2	5	2.3	7
Latin America	3.5	8	3.9	11	3.4	22	3.5	22
Turkish	3.5	1	2.7	4	2.3	7	2.4	7
Asean	5.5	8	5.1	9	4.9	11	4.7	13
Pacific	2.7	1	2.0	1	2.6	2	2.4	2
Total	5.3	54	4.8	90	4.1	135	4.1	144

Source: Based on Transparency International (2005).

resolved within neo-institutionalism. The index of corruption taps respect for institutions.

The most drastic diminution of social capital occurs in countries where government is also involved in large-scale corruption, if not in straightforward crime. This occurs when a country goes into a prolonged civil war or falls into anarchy due to the existence of warlords (Bayart *et al.*, 1999). The lack of trust in society and the absence of transparence in government pose a major challenge to rebuilding the state in several parts of Africa, Asia and the Pacific (Roy, 2000; Clammer, 2004; Kpundeh and Levy, 2004). Good governance is linked with the basic categories of civilisation (Table 4.11).

Judicial institutions

Law is a major restriction upon power. It forces rulers to follow rules, enhancing predictability in the state. Constitutional law offers a number of

Table 4.11 Analysis of variance of corruption scores

Measures of association	Eta	Eta squared
Scler 1996	0.818	0.670
Scler 2000	0.815	0.665
Scler 2004	0.821	0.674
Scler 2005	0.807	0.651

Source: Author.

rules that restrain the exercise of power when these rules are really enforced. Thus, judicial institutions may enhance rule of law, but they must be real and not merely paper rules.

The most elementary legal institution that restrains the political elites as agents of the people, the principal, is the Ombudsman Office. This serves the small man or woman, offering a direct road to the testing of administrative decisions in relation to their compliance with law. It is a very inexpensive way to remind the power holders that they must abide by the principle of legality, meaning that each and every decision must comply with the law. A more extravagant form of judicial control of politics is the legal review. Under legal review, the courts (American system) or the constitutional court (Austrian-German system) have the right to test the constitutionality not only of administrative decisions but also of legislation, i.e. acts by the national assembly. Legal review, when it really works and the decisions of judges are respected by the executive, leads to the *judicialisation of politics*, meaning that judges or courts enter the political arena in competition with politicians or political parties. Finally, it may matter what basic legal system a country employs. There are two legal families that endorse rule of law, namely English Common Law and Continental European Civil Law. Which of these two promote rule of law the most, looking at evidence from as many countries as possible (Table 4.12)? Well, common law may not do better than civil law, because both systems have been adopted in Third World countries. It is the Ombudsman that is most decisive (see Table 4.13). Originating from the Nordic countries, the Ombudsman is today a global institution, enhancing the rule of law.

Table 4.12 Judicial institutions

	Civil law	Common law	Socialist law	Muslim law	Customary law	Total
Arab	0	0	0	14	1	15
Western Europe	16	2	0	0	0	18
Eastern Europe	0	0	20	0	0	20
Other occidentals	0	4	0	0	1	5
South Asia	0	1	0	0	3	4
Africa Sub-Sahara	4	7	0	2	22	35
Muslim non-Arab	0	1	1	3	1	6
Latin America	17	4	1	0	0	22
Turkish	1	0	6	0	0	7
Asean	1	6	3	0	2	12
Pacific	0	0	0	1	1	2
Total	39	25	31	20	31	146
Eta squared						0.582

Sources: Based on Rhyne (1978); CIA (1994).

Table 4.13 Legal institutions: legal review and Ombudsman institution

Civilisation	Legal review			Ombudsman: year of institutionalisation			
	No legal review	Legal review	Total	No.	Late	Early	Total
Arab	11	4	15	13	2	0	15
Western Europe	9	9	18	1	3	14	18
Eastern Europe	16	4	20	7	13	0	20
Other occidentals	3	2	5	0	0	5	5
South Asia	2	2	4	2	1	1	4
Africa Sub-Sahara	19	16	35	16	16	4	36
Muslim non-Arab	5	1	6	6	1	0	7
Latin America	8	14	22	7	13	2	22
Turkish	7	0	7	5	2	0	7
Asean	7	5	12	10	3	1	14
Pacific	1	1	2	0	0	2	2
Total	88	58	146	67	54	29	150
Eta squared			0.117				0.467

Sources: Based on Rhyne (1978); CIA (1994); Maddex (1996); International Ombudsman Institute (1999).

Relevance of institutions

Political institutions may be important for two reasons. One could be their intrinsic value, whereas the other would be their extrinsic value. Here, I focus on the latter, searching for any clues to the impact of political institutions on regime stability and rule of law. Table 4.14 contains the simple correlations.

A number of findings stand out here. First, institutional longevity is associated with rule of law, confirming the positive consolidation model. Older states may be expected to be characterised by more of regime duration than younger states. Second, Parliamentarianism performs better than presidentialism. A multi-party system, based on PR, is more conducive to rule of law than majoritarian election techniques. Third, the Ombudsman promotes rule of law strongly, whereas coups demote it. Some basic state institutional features are weakly related to rule of law. Federalism is hardly a guarantee of state stability, as the risk of secession or deadlock between central and provincial government can never be excluded. Bicameralism strengthens rule of law to some extent.

Interpreting these findings in terms of a principal–agent model, the population as the principal of the political body must have access to different and independent agents, competing somehow with each. This is why a

Table 4.14 Institutional relationships

	Frind 104	Sig	n
Scler 1	0.512**	0.000	150
Modeecol	0.546**	0.000	73
Derder/regime	−0.625**	0.000	149
Cha 2000	0.336**	0.000	148
ELS 02_1	−0.558**	0.000	143
Watts/federalism	0.181*	0.027	150
Coupsdet	−0.221**	0.007	149
Trans 2000	0.610**	0.000	90
Trans 2005	0.608**	0.000	144
Ombudsman	0.563**	0.000	150
Leg inst	0.261**	0.001	146
Legal families	−0.472**	0.000	146

Sources: Rule of law (Table 2.1); Institutional consolidation (Table 4.14); Political regime (Tables 4.5, 4.6, 4.7); Legislative institutions (Table 4.6); Election systems (Table 4.2); Federalism (Watts (1999)); military coups (Table 4.8); Control of corruption (Table 4.10); Legal institutions (Table 4.13); Legal families (Table 4.12).

Notes
** Correlation significant at the 0.01 level (2-tailed).
* Correlation significant at the 0.05 level (2-tailed).

multi-party system, bicameralism and the Ombudsman promote the rule of law.

Conclusion

Principal–agent theory, when applied to politics entails that the access to more than one agent presents an advantage to the principal. If political elites can be neatly divided into different and more or less exclusive groups, then collusion between them becomes very difficult. Moreover, if they can be forced to compete for the allegiance of the principal by means of a recurrent electoral contract, then that is so much the better for the principal in trying to restrain his/her agents. When politics is modelled as a sequential game with interaction between principal and agents, then access to several competing agents makes it easier to reveal the opportunism of the agents, whether in the form of moral hazard or adverse selection. Agents who control each other are also advantageous for the principal.

A number of findings support these principal–agent hypotheses, as the framing of political institutions matters greatly for the occurrence of rule of law. The positive contribution of open and pluralistic institutions stands out. Length of time of institution-building matters. We need to test models that combine various factors. The correlations between institutions and outcomes have the expected sign, but one should add other factors to

Table 4.15 Conditions for rule of law (Freedom House = dependent variable)

	B	Std error	Beta	t
(Constant)	4.061	1.102		3.686
Hdin 2001	4.742	1.206	0.318	3.930
Impe 7598	0.002	0.004	0.027	0.440
Musl 2000	−0.015	0.005	−0.170	−2.768
Els 02_1	−0.836	0.150	−0.341	−5.569
Elf 10	0.671	0.797	0.059	0.842
Ombudsman	0.910	0.247	0.247	3.686
Parlrule	0.876	0.395	0.140	2.216
Adj rsq	0.598			
n	133			

Source: Author.

Note
Rule of law (Table 2.1); Human development (Table 2.7); Openness of the economy (Table 3.13/11); Muslim population (Table 3.9/7); Election system (Table 4.2); Linguistic fragmentation (Table 3.8/6); Ombudsman (Table 4.13); Parliamentary rule (Table 4.5).

the institutional ones (e.g. social conditions). Rule of law would depend less upon economic factors and more upon institutional ones. Three institutions have a profound impact on rule of law, namely presidentialism (negative), the election system (PR positive) and the Ombudsman (positive). Either a state, which does not respect civil and political rights, installs the one party system in order to enhance the ruling regime; or one major political party, operating in a country, consolidates its power by restricting civil and political rights through presidentialism. Table 4.15 tests a regression model combining economic, cultural and institutional factors.

Rule of law has a substantial footing in institutions. The existence of the political regime of rule of law is strongly conditioned by the enforcement of institutions such as the electoral system, the executive: parliamentarianism/presidentialism, and the legal system: the Ombudsman Office. Yet rule of law is also conditioned by the general level of economic development (HDI) and culture, i.e. the spread of Islam.

5 Changing principal–agent institutions

Introduction

In a longitudinal approach to the state, the past has a marked influence upon the present. In some countries there is strong continuity with the basic parameters of government laid down early. In other countries, sharp breaks have occurred as with the occurrence of revolutionary events or processes. The distinction between evolutionary and revolutionary processes appears relevant when looking at the state from a longitudinal and dynamic perspective. It involves major institutional change as well as institutional consolidation.

The transformation process that countries in the former communist world face involves not just the transition to a rule of law, but there is also the reform of economic institutions towards enforcing the market economy. Both problems are institutional ones, meaning that they require a long-term commitment from the state to support new rules. This double institutional choice problem has been most acute for Eastern Europe. Several of these countries, removing communist dictatorship and introducing rule of law, seek to introduce and enforce the smooth functioning of a market economy. However, a few of the East European countries have not been successful (e.g. the Khanates, where rule of law is weak and the government's role in the economy large). Besides Eastern Europe, a number of countries attempt to make the transition to the market economy, whether they adhere to the planned economy model as in Eastern Europe or the state-capitalist model in many Third World countries.

Introducing the market economy

If affluence is conducive to rule of law, then the question of economic institutions becomes relevant for political change. Crucial in the transition towards a market economy is the time dimension – shock or slow transition. Should capitalist institutions be introduced quickly or slowly? Should the institutional framework for the economy be reformed comprehensively or in a marginal fashion? The separation between capitalism and socialism does not cover all economic system changes since 1990.

The pure socialist model – the model of a planned economy with almost all resources in public ownership implemented on a grand scale when the forced industrialisation process was initiated in 1929 in the Soviet Union – is no longer a viable option. Actually, a large number of countries have moved towards decentralised capitalism from the so-called state-capitalist model, i.e. economic systems that although recognising private ownership institutions acknowledge a major role for the state in the economy both in terms of ownership and regulation – economic nationalism. During the 1980s and 1990s several countries such as Argentina, Brazil, Venezuela, Mexico, Zaire, Kenya, Indonesia, South Korea and Taiwan began dismantling an extensive state involvement in the economy. How far this process of market reform will go depends not the least upon the development of the world economy, in particular the tension between a free trade regime and the temptation to resort to protectionism, involving the WTO, IMF and the WB. After the Asian crisis in 1996 to 1997, the legitimacy of economic nationalism is gone. Thus import substitution and export orientation is no longer accepted globally.

It has been claimed that there is more than only one socialist model (Lindblom, 1977). One may even speak of three socialist alternatives to decentralised capitalism. First, there is the existing welfare state model, which combines private ownership with large-scale public spending for allocative and redistributive purposes. Second, the market socialism model suggests that while ownership could remain, public resources could be allocated by means of market mechanisms (China). Third, there is the planner sovereignty model, where ownership would be basically private but allocative decisions would be concentrated to state planners, the practicality of which is small.

The search for more markets characterises not only the new states in Eastern Europe, but holds generally for Third World countries. The attempts to increase the scope of markets follow upon decades of state intervention policies. The main goal for Third World states is not so much economic system reform per se but much more the search for improved economic outcomes, i.e. a sustained process of economic growth raising the level of affluence considerably. Yet only markets deliver sustained economic growth.

Thus, we have a distinction between decentralised capitalism in the Adam Smith version and state *dirigiste* economies in the Friedrich List interpretation on the one hand, and affluence and poverty on the other. The crucial question is: Which economic system is the best guarantee of economic prosperity? The Third World states whether former communist systems or adherents of state-capitalism seek a route towards economic growth by means of institutional transformation towards more of markets and less of states. Thus, if level of affluence is necessary for the establishment of rule of law, then economic system transformation from state regulation to the market economy will tend to bring forward economic outcomes that help the political transition from authoritarian rule. Eastern Europe provides an ample number of cases of institutional change. Thus, the performance records of East European countries after 1989 are interesting from a dynamic perspective upon the state. It is government which defines and enforces the rules of the market economy. The neo-institutionalists argue that a successful implementation of transparent economic institutions underlining the force of incentives is a *sine qua non* for economic development. Yet, economic prosperity tends always to reflect economic forces in the first place, such as investments, low inflation and full employment. Is there an institutional effect in the data about East European economic development since the fall of the communist system?

Hayek stressed that economic prosperity is always generated in the market economy, as when he rejected the planned economy in the 1930s. However, the market can only operate well if it is supported institutionally by government. Markets deliver efficient outcomes when incentives are recognised in the legal system as well as when information is not distorted. Incentives and information underpin the price system of the market economy, which is conducive to economic efficiency. Governments may promote economic outcomes by either strengthening the market through institutional measures such as validating contracts, protecting private property, safeguarding the bourse mechanism against cheating or by taking care of market failures such as involuntary unemployment and under-investment due to "animal spirits". Neo-institutionalists favour a strong role of government and public administration in relation to the micro foundations of the market economy whereas macroeconomists see a large role for government in managing demand in the economy. The neo-institutionalist literature emphasises that governments may enhance the transparent implementation of the rules of the game, the selection of transaction cost minimising regulations as well as the free flow of correct information about economic activities.

The neo-institutionalist approach does not claim mono-causality for institutions. There is no denying that the factors in a neo-classical growth model are important. Yet neo-institutionalists argue that institutions matter besides economic aggregates such as investment, labour, education, capital and technology. And institutions are highly important in shaping outcomes, not merely a set of additional factors. The key hypotheses in relation to East European developments comprise the institutions that guarantee the market economy. The state is relevant in relation to the market in several ways, even when one takes a Hayekian approach to government – the guardian state. The institutions of the market economy tap not only the status of property rights and the extent of privatisation, but they also measure various aspects of the quality of the state machinery when it comes to law enforcement. What is at stake is the performance of the guardian state in all its aspects: political stability, capacity to tax, absence of corruption. Do these institutional factors matter for the variation in economic development in Eastern Europe after 1989?

The dependent variable is a simple indicator on GDP change between 1992 and 1999. All independent institutional variables hold that higher scores mean more advanced institution-building, the only exception being the variable property rights, where low scores mean high property rights protection. One would however expect positive correlations from all specific institutional variables with our dependent variable, except for property rights (see Table 5.1 for the findings).

The major finding here is that all institutional factors correlate positively with economic growth. As a matter of fact, the correlations for institutional variables are strong indeed, especially if one compares them with standard economic factors such as rate of inflation and contribution of manufacture. Economic development in Eastern Europe has a strong foundation in the enforcement of new institutions for the economy, where government plays a major role in the implementation of these rules of the market economy.

It would be interesting to see whether these surface interactions are really maintained when regression equations are tested. The finding in Table 5.2 is that the specific institutions matter greatly. In institutional analysis of economic growth, general economic factors tend to matter more than institutions. The specific main variables such as property rights protection, the working of government and administration and the operating of the legal system are more important in explaining GDP growth than the control variables relative to the political system, to economy regulation and the initial share of industry.

In brief, the regression analysis confirms what was formerly shown by the correlation analysis. The specific institutional variables – property rights protection, the clean working of government and administration, and the effective operation of the legal system – seem to be more important for explaining GDP growth than the control variables relative to the political system, to economy regulation and the initial share of industry.

The overall economic institutions indicator tapping the guardian state regroups the indicators with respect to the rules of the market economy – the institutions of capitalism according to Williamson (1985). The countries which achieve high scores for all three aspects get an overall score of three points, the

Table 5.1 GDP growth and institutions

Institutions	GDP growth 1992–1999
Property rights	−0.65
Government efficiency	0.68
Corruption	0.76
Regulatory quality	0.63
Rule of law	0.74
Political stability	0.51
Inflation 1992–1999	−0.37
Share of industry	0.37

Source: Author. Appendix 5.1.

Table 5.2 Regression analysis

OLS Regressions with GDP Growth 9299 as dependent variable							
	(a)	*(b)*	*(c)*	*(d)*	*(e)*	*(f)*	*(g)*
Constant	180.04***	187.9***	198.2***	104.48***	105.6***	76***	83.76***
t–stat	*6.773*	*9.395*	*9.617*	*15.046*	*17.39*	*3*	*4.05*
Property rights	−0.602***	−0.55***	−0.563***				
t–stat	*−3.733*	*−3.426*	*−3.61*				
Government efficiency				0.677***			
t–stat				*3.642*			
Corruption					0.749***		
t–stat					*4.835*		
Regulation quality						0.556***	
t–stat						*2.92*	
Rule Of Law							0.69***
t–stat							*4.54*
Political stability	0.339						
t–stat	*1.528*						
Democratic		−0.42**					
t–stat		*−2.62*					
Economic policy			−0.437**				
t–stat			*−2.8*				
Inflation 9299	−0.155			−0.003	−0.28	−0.04	
t–stat	*−0.707*			*−0.17*	*−0.18*	*−0.19*	
Share industry						0.201	0.126
t–stat						*1.16*	*0.83*
Number indep. var.	3	2	2	2	2	3	2
Number cases	20	20	20	25	25	25	26
R–square	0.629	0.586	0.603	0.46	0.581	0.439	0.554
Adjusted R–square	0.559	0.538	0.556	0.411	0.542	0.359	0.514

Source: Author.

Notes
*** = significant at a 1 per cent level of error.
** = significant at a 5 per cent level of error.
* = significant at a 10 per cent level of error.

Table 5.3 Institutionalisation of the rules of the market economy

Low	Medium	High
Belarus	Armenia	Croatia
Kazakhstan	Azerbaijan	Estonia
Kyrgyz Republic	Bulgaria	Hungary
Moldova	Czech Republic	Poland
Russia	Georgia	Slovakia
Ukraine	Lithuania	Slovenia
	Romania	
	Uzbekistan	

Source: Author.

countries which underperform everywhere score one, the other's score two. Table 5.3 shows how the East European countries score on this index.

The guardian state is weakly institutionalised in the CIS area including the Khanates. Here private property rights are not fully protected and contract validity is not entirely enforced. Corruption is rampant and public administration is not transparent. This is one extreme. The other extreme is the strong guardian state in a few Central European countries where there are now no remaining traces of the communist economy, the market economy prevailing to a high degree. Figure 5.1 offers strong confirmation

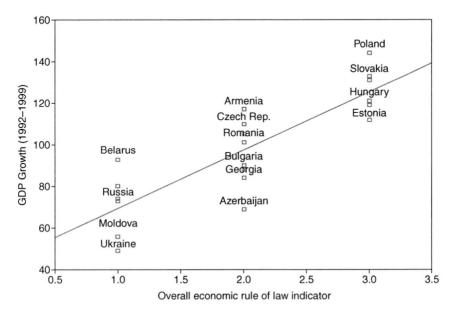

Figure 5.1 GDP growth 1992 to 1999 and economic institutions (source: Author).

of the role of government in providing the correct institutions for economic incentives to enhance economic prosperity. The Pearson correlation of 0.85 between GDP growth from 1992 to 1999 and market economic institutions is high and significant.

The issue of getting the institutions right is particularly crucial in the case of former communist countries, which began the building of economic institutions from almost zero at the beginning of the 1990s. Specific institutions and their enforcement, such as property rights, government efficiency, corruption, regulating quality as well as rule of law, have an impact on economic outcomes, such as GDP growth over time.

Third World state transformation

The consolidation of rule of law in Third World states – in Central Asia, Latin America or in Africa and Asia – hinges upon economic outcomes, rising affluence ameliorating mass poverty, the pacification of the military and the emergence of a multi-party system. All these three conditions are necessary individually, and taken together they are sufficient for the establishment of rule of law. The wave of democratisation initiated in 1990 has resulted in a roller-coaster process in several Third World countries where the threats to political stability are large. Regime transformation in the Third World may target rule of law, but the outcomes are often disappointing.

Whereas state transformation in Latin America has increased rule of law in several countries since 1990, state change in Sub-Saharan Africa has often resulted in anarchy or anomy. Scholars have offered widely different interpretations of the Third World state: (1) personal rulership and patrimonialism (Roth, 1968), (2) soft states (Myrdal, 1968), (3) overdeveloped states (Alavai, 1972), (4) bureaucratic bourgeois states (Shivji, 1976), (5) bureaucratic-authoritarian states (O'Donnell, 1973), (6) underdeveloped states (Medard, 1982), (7) strong states with weak regimes (Dominguez, 1987), (8) weak states in strong societies (Migdal, 1988), (9) predatory states (Lundahl, 1991) (10) prebendal states (Joseph, 1987, 1999) and the Arab state (Luciani, 1990). Whichever of these Third World state models fits the one state or the other is an open question. The need for accepting more of rule of law cannot be doubted, both in Africa and Asia (Leftwich, 1994, 2004). One may discuss whether parliamentarianism or presidentialism would promote rule of law in Third World states. Despite the legacy of the Westminster model of ruling in the many countries that entered the British Empire, the prevailing trend has been towards a presidential regime. The explanation is that presidentialism offers the possibility of the legitimisation of patrimonialism or clientelism – a legacy in many countries in Africa and Asia. The type of politics characteristic of democracy tends to be absent, i.e. the politics of bargaining between major social groups or the compromise between government and opposition as well as the acceptance of reciprocity between contenders for political power. Crucial for a rule of law regime is that the opposition is tolerated, if not accepted as legitimate, as, for example, in Botswana, Gambia, Mauritius, Senegal, Malaysia and Thailand.

Besides the Marxist regimes in the Third World (e.g. Ethiopia, Benin, Afghanistan, Cuba, North Korea), there have been personal dictatorships, one-party regimes and bureaucratic states. Marxist regimes tended to be authoritarian dictatorships embracing all kinds of social relationships, whereas personal dictatorship would be less penetrating but equally if not even more brutal. When the party and not the ruler is the main vehicle of political power, the regimen becomes less personalised and arbitrary, as party ideology substitutes for personal aggrandisement. Finally, the bureaucratic rule avoids the search for ideological blueprints, underlining the day-to-day administration of the mundane business of government. Personal dictatorships may be found during certain periods in Uganda, the Ivory Coast, Zaire, Madagascar and Paraguay. To the one-party regimes one would add Tanzania, Zimbabwe as well as Kenya and Malawi. The bureaucratic regime was to be found during certain times in, for example, Argentina, Brazil, Chile, Egypt, Taiwan and South Korea. An unstable state with massive corruption amounts to a *prebendal* state, to be found in Nigeria, Pakistan and Indonesia. Common to all these countries is that their regimes have suffered from political instability during longer or shorter periods.

The process of democratisation of the Marxist and socialist states of the Third World has not been a smooth one due to the ever-present dangers of military coups. In addition, there is the immense difficulty for these countries to adapt to the global market economy. These countries have had to engage in the so-called *structural adjustment policies* monitored by the World Bank and the International Monetary Fund. In some countries, these neo-liberal policies have worked, meaning favouring the introduction of a market economy with so-called capitalist institutions. But far from all countries have done well under *structural adjustment policies*, reducing public services in the country and making the state even more unstable. It depends greatly on the capacity of the country to benefit from globalisation and international markets. Many countries in Africa experienced a premature socialist experiment together with personal dictatorships: Nkrumah (Ghana), Senghor (Senegal), Sekou Toure (Guinea), Mengistu (Ethiopia) and Sassou-Nguesso (Congo-Brazzaville). Coping with dictatorship and socialism at the same time strained the state in many countries, opening up opportunities for anarchy. The list of African dictatorships is a long one, including right-wing dictators such as Houphouet-Boigny (Ivory Coast), Bokassa (Central African Republic), Eyadema (Togo), Kenyatta and Moi (Kenya), Banda (Malawi) and Mobutu (Zaire) as well as Doe (Liberia), Nguema (Equatorial Guinea) and Bongo (Gabon). In post-colonial Africa, the establishment of a modern state with a transparent bureaucracy governing the country with rule *by* law or, even better, rule *of* law has proved problematic, to say the least (Chazan *et al.*, 1999; Herbst, 2000; Schraeder, 2003; Hyden, 2005).

Institutional economics would predict that a state that is parasitic upon society will not promote economic development, which is a *sine qua non* for poverty alleviation. One speaks of the APC countries: the African–Caribbean–Pacific cluster of states which tends to be among the poorest in the world. They have suffered from state instability, as witnessed in numerous *coup d'états*, extensive corruption and sometimes the long-term presence of dictators. In the Caribbean, one encounters the terrible names of Trujillo (Dominican Republic), Batista (Cuba) and Duvalier (Francois and Jean-Claude) (Haiti).

African politics since independence has offered a never-ending succession of principal–agent games where the new rules have not been able to resist the temptation of looting. Many African politicians have attempted desperately to prolong their mandate and they leave politics with an impoverished country. Take as an example Madagascar under the 27-year-long rule of President Ratsiraka. One party rule presents an irresistible temptation to engage in the strategy of looting. Another telling example was the Nigerian dictator Abasha, an expert in corruption and money laundering. The same strategy – looting – has surfaced in the Khanates following the collapse of the Soviet economy and the one-party state, such as in Kazakhstan and Turkmenistan.

The negative implications of a low level of affluence in combination with few prospects for rapid economic growth reduce the probability of rule of law in Third World countries, even when they have transformed their economy. Nationalism in several Third World countries keeps fostering a military establishment that is often a lingering threat to democratic practices. The institutionalisation of a definitive border between politicians and military leaders has proven impossible in several Third World states, especially Sub-Saharan Africa. Finally, affluence and a low profile of the military is not enough to bring about rule of law, as the interesting case of super-rich Singapore testifies. As long as the largest political party is not willing to cede its hegemonic position, the type of opposition, competition, contestation and openness that characterises the rule of law regime will not be forthcoming, despite good governance. Yet some Third World countries such as South Korea and Taiwan have successfully adapted to the global market economy, while at the same time introducing more and more rule of law.

The principal–agent difficulties in the Third World state loom large. First, rules that restrain opportunism among politicians are either non-existent or weakly institutionalised. First, free and fair elections are not to be found, despite the increasing resort to international observers. Political competition is seen as a threat to the regime and not as a natural venue for power alteration. Second, agent opportunism is rampant, meaning that politicians in power do not hesitate to engage in looting at worst and reneging at best. Only better enforcement of institutions that restrain political agents can channel the incentives of Third World rulers to work more for the interests of their principals, the people.

Political stability

The World Bank has taken a much-needed initiative when funding a big research project on the modern state (www.govindicators.org). If state and market are the two chief coordination mechanisms in the world around the year 2000, then the latter has been more explored than the former. Thus, the economies of the countries of the world have been researched in great detail, which is also true of global or international markets. The World Bank project "Governance Matters V" takes a huge step towards filling many lacunae about the empirical knowledge of the states of the world. As the World Bank project focused on political stability or instability, it may be consulted when resolving a key puzzle in comparative politics theory, namely: How is constitutional democracy or rule of law related to general state firmness/weakness?

The concept of political instability covers both the failure of a state to stabilise democracy and the occurrence of anarchy, civil war and corruption in a dictatorship. One would wish to have tools that allow one to analyse the occurrence of democracy on the one hand and of political instability on the other. The World Bank data offer such tools. *Governance Matters V: Governance Indicators for 1996–2005* by Kaufmann *et al.* (2006) reports on the latest update of the worldwide governance indicators, covering some 210 countries and territories and measuring six dimensions of governance: voice and accountability, political stability in the absence of violence, government effectiveness, regulatory quality, rule of law and control of corruption. The scope of the study is all-encompassing, covering all units called "states", even when they are tiny in terms of population or merely semi-independent units. The depth of the inquiry is unprecedented, using a gigantic dataset about many features of government, collected from all available data sources in the world, including the rankings of many country experts. The immense effort in arriving at reliable information about modern government on a global scale appears from the list of research papers done for the project by D. Kaufmann.

Methodologically speaking, the governance project employs an inductive research strategy. Kaufmann, Kray and Mastruzzi present the newly updated estimates of six dimensions of governance covering some 210 countries and territories for five time periods: 1996, 1998, 2000, 2002 and 2004. These indicators are based on several hundred individual variables measuring perceptions of governance, drawn from 37 separate data sources constructed by 31 different organisations. The authors assign these individual measures of governance to categories capturing key dimensions of governance, and use an unobserved component model to construct six aggregate governance indicators in each of the four periods. In other words, they employ factor analyses of a large number of indicator scores to derive six dimensions of governance. These are: (1) voice and accountability (va); (2) political stability and absence of violence (ps); (3) government effectiveness (ge); (4) regulatory quality (rq); (5) rule of law (rl); and (6) control of corruption (cc).

Table 5.4 Cross-tabulation of governance dimensions

		Correlations					
		Cc 05	ge 05	ps 05	rl 05	rq 05	va 05
cc D5	Pearson correlation	1	0.950*	0.750*	0.949*	0.898*	0.745*
	sig. (2-tailed)		0.000	0.000	0.000	0.000	0.000
	n	204	204	203	204	203	204
ge 05	Pearson correlation	0.950*	1	0.732*	0.937*	0.958*	0.768*
	sig. (2-tailed)	0.000		0.000	0.000	0.000	0.000
	n	204	210	207	208	203	208
ps 05	Pearson correlation	0.750*	0.732*	1	0.814*	0.718*	0.705*
	sig. (2-tailecd)	0.000	0.000		0.000	0.000	0.000
	n	203	207	213	207	203	207
rl 05	Pearson correlation	0.949*	0.937*	0.814*	1	0.906*	0.775*
	sig. (2-tailed)	0.000	0.000	0.000		0.000	0.000
	n	204	208	207	208	203	208
rq 05	Pearson correlation	0.898*	0.958*	0.718*	0.906*	1	0.802*
	sig. (2-tailed)	0.000	0.000	0.000	0.000		0.000
	n	203	203	203	203	203	203
va 05	Pearson correlation	0.745*	0.768*	0.705*	0.775*	0.802*	1
	sig. (2-tailed)	0.000	0.000	0.000	0.000	0.000	
	n	204	208	207	208	203	208

Source: Kaufmann *et al.* (2005).

Note
* Correlation is significant at the 0.01 level (2-tailed).

As is well known in any inductive research design, such as advanced methods of factor analysis, the basic categories do not speak for themselves. They have to be interpreted in the light of theory. Consider the category named "Rule of Law" in the World Bank study. The World Bank list of indicators mixes two entirely different concepts: the enforcement of laws and regulation on the one hand (principle of legality), and the independence, neutrality and strength of the judiciary in protecting citizens (autonomy of courts) on the other. Countries may score high on the first concept but low on the second, such as rich Arab countries like Oman, UAE and Kuwait, or a South East Asian country like Singapore. The difficulty lies in the validity of the interpretation. The concept of rule of law covers more than the World

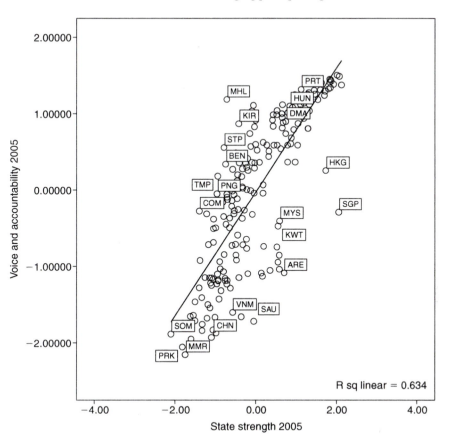

Figure 5.2 The two dimensions of political stability (source: Author).

Bank list of indicators in the extent to which agents have confidence in and abide by the rules of society, in particular the quality of contract enforcement, the police and the courts, as well as the likelihood of crime and violence.

Rule of law harbours the idea that governmental authority is to be legitimately exercised, i.e. only in accordance with written, publicly disclosed laws adopted and enforced in accordance with the established procedure and a constitution. The idea is a safeguard against arbitrary governance. In continental European legal thinking, rule of law is associated with the *Rechtsstaat.* According to Anglo-American thinking, the rule of law regime includes a clear separation of powers, legal certainty, the principle of legitimate expectation and equality of all before the law. I will not employ the indicator "rule of law" (rl) from the World Bank data in the analysis below, but concentrate upon the other five aspects of political stability/ instability, as it is not clear what this category stands for.

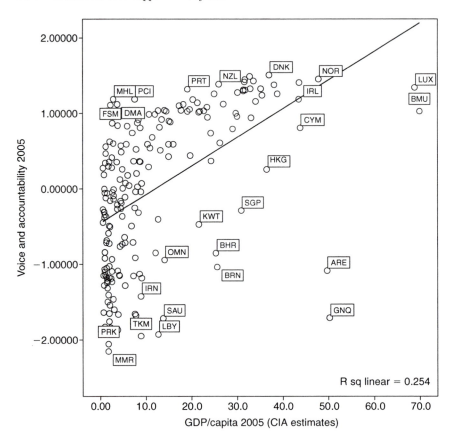

Figure 5.3 Affluence and voice and accountability.

When one captures a lot of information about a phenomenon such as the modern state, then it is unavoidable to embark upon a strategy to compress the data. When many indicators deliver scores that go together, one may try to find an underlying or latent concept that is manifested in the data. According to the World Bank study, governance has six such dimensions. Table 5.4 shows how they relate to each other for the year 2005.

There are two major findings from Table 5.4. First, it is the case that all six dimensions correlate with each other to a considerable degree. But, second, it also holds true that voice and accountability are less connected with all the other aspects of political stability. I will argue that *democracy* (voice and accountability) should be separated from *state strength or firmness* (government effectiveness + regulatory quality + control of corruption + absence of political violence). This distinction appears very promising when understanding political instability around the world. It is also in conformity with the analytical distinctions above.

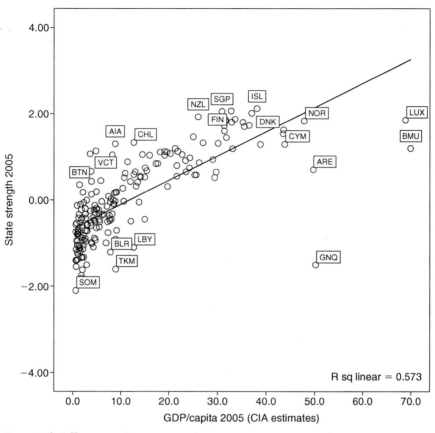

Figure 5.4 Affluence and state strength.

Political instability may of course occur in both democracies and dictatorships. Thus there may be massive corruption and low governmental effectiveness in both democracies and dictatorships. The opposite also holds. Thus both democracies and dictatorships may display state strength or firmness, meaning high government effectiveness, regulatory quality, control of corruption and absence of political violence. Yet there may be interaction between democracy and political stability, as revealed in probabilities. I will try to identify these probabilities by first looking at all the countries of the world. Figure 5.2 shows how voice and accountability relate to state strength.

It appears from Figure 5.2 that constitutional democracies are more likely to have strong states than dictatorships, but there are interesting exceptions with countries that score low on voice and accountability but high on state firmness. Figures 5.3 and 5.4 show that affluence has much less impact on voice and accountability than on state strength. Here we see that several super-affluent countries are not constitutional democracies. However, they need not lack state strength (see Figure 5.4).

Poor countries are likely to display state weakness or political instability, but there exist poor countries that score rather high on voice and accountability, i.e. democracy. It holds true in general that a democratic regime is more likely to go together with state strength than an authoritarian regime. A non-democratic regime would be likely to emerge when there is state weakness, but some authoritarian regimes display state firmness, especially when they have an affluent economy.

Conclusion

Principal–agent contracting lurks behind state reform. The principal would be interested in introducing rules which enhance the legitimacy of the agents as well as the efficiency of government. Institutions that promote legitimacy of agents and governmental efficiency would be most welcome from a principal–agent perspective. Legitimacy and efficiency are crucial links between state and society. When the state has a large degree of legitimacy, there is a special attitude among the citizens towards the public institutions, i.e. the institutions are bestowed with a special quality, meaning that the regime is accepted as *valid* in a moral sense. Efficient states deliver, but efficiency is neutral in relation to ends. State efficiency may be employed for the sake of humanitarian objectives or for so-called reasons of state. Both state legitimacy and state efficiency have dark sides, as aggressively nationalistic or religious regimes may meet with citizen legitimacy, or authoritarian regimes may employ massive amounts of repression to keep the state intact.

Institutional factors offering rule of law such as long-term institutionalisation or institutions that offer participation and power-sharing enhance state legitimacy. Leaders in general and political actors in particular may provide the state with temporary legitimation by invoking charisma or an authoritarian ideology at the stage of mass mobilisation.

Around the year 2000, state transformation focused more upon the institutions of liberalism, i.e. the market economy and rule of law (Fukuyama, 1993). There was convergence towards these two institutions for the economy and the polity, as the socialist economy failed in the Soviet Union and China. Central Europe has managed well in this major system transition. Rule of law and the market economy has also gained ground in Far Asia, as with South Korea and Taiwan. The same applies to South America. However, outcomes are mixed with regard to the poorest countries of the world, the Caribbean and Sub-Saharan Africa. Political instability has gained ground in Central Asia, Indonesia and the Pacific as well as Africa especially. When system transformation fails, anarchy or anomy is often the result. In such a situation, the modern warlord appears, often with infant soldiers, creating havoc for society. Finally, there is a set of stable authoritarian regimes which are nourished by good economic developments, such as the Gulf monarchies, Islamique Iran and communist China. Underneath state transformation there is the search for principal–agent interactions that benefit the population. Rule of law offers the best terms, because it gives protection against the most vicious agent strategy, namely looting. Only rules and their strict enforcement can prevent political agents from engaging in looting, enriching themselves and their families while impoverishing their countries.

Economic change introducing the institutions of the market economy also helps to solve principal–agent difficulties, as more rules restrain the opportunism of politicians, businesspeople and rulers. However, the introduction of the market economy does not guarantee that rule of law will be forthcoming. Only the institutions of a competitive polity – parliamentarianism, multi-party elections and judicial control – are strong enough to channel the incentives of agents towards respect for rule of law.

Appendix 5.1 List of the variables

Label of variable	Description	Sources
GDP Growth 9299	This variable measures the total growth of GDP at constant prices between 1992 and 1999.	IMF, World Economic Outlook, 2000
Property Rights	The results are based on a survey with a hundred companies. Year: 1999. The scale goes from 0 to 5 ; low values mean good property rights protection.	Worldbank, Worldbank Economic Survey, 2003
Government efficiency	This is a meta-indicator composed by several indicators, which measures the efficiency level of the state administration and of the government. Year: 2000. The scale goes from −2.5 to +2.5; high values mean good efficiency.	Kaufmann *et al.*, 2002
Corruption	This measures the level of corruption. High values correspond to a low level of corruption. It has the same features as Government Efficiency.	Kaufmann *et al.*, 2002
Regulatory quality	This measures the regulation burden relying on corporate companies. High values mean good regulation quality. It has the same features as Government Efficiency.	Kaufmann *et al.*, 2002
Rule Of law	This focuses on the operation of the legal system. High values mean efficient working of the legal system. It has the same features as Government Efficiency.	Kaufmann *et al.*, 2002
Politic stability	This considers political instability and violence. High values indicate a stable	Kaufmann *et al.*, 2002

(Continued)

Appendix 5.1 Continued

Label of variable	Description	Sources
	political environment. It has the same features as Government Efficiency.	
Democraticness	The scores are subjective measures given by the "rating committee" of Freedom House for the years 1999/2000, which go from 1 (good level of democracy) to 7 (low level of democracy).	Freedom House, 2001
Economic policy	This measures the economical liberalisation of a country. Low values indicate advanced economic liberalisation, and high values mean that a country has a low level of liberalisation. Otherwise, this indicator has the same features as "Democratic".	Freedom House, 2001
Inflation 9299	This measures the average inflation rate per year between 1992 and 1999.	IMF, 2000, database
Share of industry	Indicates the percentage industry contributed to GDP in 1990.	IMF, 2000: 115
Communism	This variable shows how many years the countries have been under a communist regime.	IMF, 2000: 115

6 Party system instability and volatility from the principal–agent perspective

Introduction

To understand the function of volatility in today's European democracies, one would need to employ the principal–agent model. Where democracy is exercised in the form of party government, it is especially essential for the electorate to monitor politicians. Electoral volatility may increase the responsiveness of the party system to the electorate and increase the accountability of politicians. Party system instability is persistently higher in the East European democracies than in Western Europe. System transition in Eastern Europe passes through the party system as new parties enter and try out their fortunes in the electoral arena. Political innovation in Western Europe also passes through the party system, as new movements challenge politics as the ordinary games of established parties. However, there are signs of decreasing volatility in the East, whereas volatility is on the rise in several West European democracies. There will be convergence between West and East European democracies, as both will have considerable volatility in the future. This is a positive for democratic vitality in Herbert Tingsten's conception. The level of party system fractionalisation is already the same over the regions of Europe. The principal–agent model would favour several agents as well as agent switches, i.e. a moderate level of party system instability.

The extension of the EU eastward on 1 May 2004 was just another sign that democracy is considered to be the only viable political system in today's world. East European democracy is like West European democracy based upon party government, meaning that political parties are the intermediaries between the people and government. Elections are done by means of the proportional technique, resulting in multi-party systems, from which are generated the governments of the new democracies. In a multi-party system democracy the electoral fortunes of political parties impact upon democratic stability and vitality. It is true that many or sharp changes in the size of political parties (*net volatility*) may harm the stability of the democratic system, but what needs to be discussed is whether or not democratic vitality, as conceived by Swedish political scientist Herbert Tingsten, may be stimulated by the electorate sending new signals to the parties by switching from one to another in elections. "Democratic vitality" stands for the interests of citizens in politics, policies and elections as well as the respect of the parties of rule of law institutions (Tingsten, 1965).

I wish to theorise net volatility in a new way by means of comparing the variation in party system stability between the old democracies in Western Europe and the new ones in Eastern Europe. One would like to know the developing trend in both parts of Europe: increasing or decreasing volatility? The conceptual framework of volatility (gross and net volatility) offers a neat method for analysing party system change (see e.g. Taagepera and Shugart, 1991; Mair, 1997; Karvonen and Kuhnle, 2001). Here I focus on net volatility (i.e. the aggregate changes in electoral support for the political parties in a country party system), and later add the number of parties to the picture of party system stability. The relationship between net and gross volatility is analysed in Ersson and Lane (1998: 29).

The concept of party system stability has no established definition, but one may say that a system of parties is stable to the extent that it can deliver in a predictable manner durable government based upon a firm allegiance between groups of citizens and their parties. A high level of voter volatility indicates that the traditional approach to voter alignments and party choice based on enduring cleavages – the frozen party system hypothesis – is not adequate. How, then, can we understand volatility, especially when it goes as high as 20 to 40 per cent? By developing the general principal–agent model in game theory for the purpose of understanding political parties and party system stability, we suggest drawing upon the new economics of information. In reality, political parties are agents of the principal, the electoral body, and they have their own interests besides working for the principal, representing him/her in the legislature and the executive.

One expression of party system instability is a high level of net volatility. How is the link between volatility, party system stability and democratic stability to be theorised?

Party system stability and democratic stability

Explaining party system volatility and instability is not an easy task, as both macro and micro models may account for it. Yet, the established theories of European party systems tend to take a negative view of volatility with respect to its impact on democratic stability.

In the classical Lipset–Rokkan approach to European politics party system stability was the main idea. The party system was conceived of as the key intermediation link between social cleavages and governments, society and state. It reflected society and it conditioned the polity. Countries were stable or unstable depending upon the party system, its configuration and historical legacy (Lipset and Rokkan, 1967). The stability of the democratic regime was linked with the existence of frozen cleavages meaning low volatility, which was looked upon as a *positive*.

The Sartori approach to the party system provided it with a powerful independent role in shaping political stability. Already, Duverger's simple model of two-partyism against multi-partyism implied that party systems that tend towards fractionalisation are conducive to political instability, a *negative* (Duverger, 1954). However, Sartori underlined that only polarised multi-partyism has a lethal impact upon political stability. As communism and fascism are no longer viable parties in Europe, Sartori's painstaking insight needs to be reinterpreted in relation to the present-day realities in Europe, such as the emergence of populist or nationalist parties. Thus, Sartori was correct in pointing out that some forms of multi-partyism are not healthy for a country (Sartori, 1976). But since polarisation is no longer a main feature of European democracies, excessive multi-partyism – party system fractionalisation as an expression of party system instability – would not necessarily hamper democratic stability and vitality.

A high degree of fractionalisation – too many parties – hinders the multi-party system from delivering durable and effective government which established party system theory entails. This proposition remains valid today even in the Lijphart approach to the party system (Lijphart, 1984), reversing Duverger's preferences between two-partyism and multi-partyism altogether. When the effective number of parties is high, transaction costs leading to government formation will rocket, and government coalitions, whether of majority or minority type, will be more difficult to maintain. As a matter of fact, Duverger's framework of party systems, two-partyism versus multi-partyism, is hardly an option in European democracy. Two-partyism is American democracy. In Europe, whether West, Central or East, social heterogeneity has always called for the employment of PR methods of election which sustain multi-partyism. Not even the two democracies, which do employ the majoritarian techniques, have two-partyism today, i.e. France and the UK. Yet, under the Taagepera interpretation, a high level of fractionalisation constitutes a *negative*, as party systems with a low score of effective number of parties function better.

In the Strom approach to party systems, multi-partyism in and of itself does not produce political instability. Several countries with a multi-party system display high scores on political stability, as they have stable minority governments (Strom, 1990). One may argue that the consolidation of democracy in Eastern Europe depends upon the arrival of moderate multi-partyism. With so many new parties being introduced in the wake of the fall of authoritarianism one would predict highly unstable party systems. Several parties cannot predict their size from one election to another and some may even be washed away. Can durable governments be formed upon such a chaotic foundation?

In the Pedersen approach to the party system it is not the number of parties or the system orientation of parties that is decisive. It is electoral change that shapes the party system. When volatility is high, the party system adapts to *new politics*, meaning that new parties come and go (*flash parties*), and old parties may crumble completely. The flash party is a typical Pedersen invention that captures some of the recent high volatility typical of several Western European countries where populism, xenophobism and the politics of discontent play a major role. Although Pedersen saw the immense force of electoral volatility for bringing about change in democratic polities, he also looked upon it as a *negative*, resulting in so-called *earthquake* elections (Pedersen, 1979).

In the Kirchheimer approach to the party system, political parties will take action against social changes affecting their traditional electoral niches. Thus, the bigger parties develop catch-all strategies to cope with changes in social stratification and secularisation. Smaller parties seek new issues on which to base a niche, thus fostering realignment in the electorate. Parties may also employ the Mair cartel strategy of joining up with other parties to enjoy the benefits of state financial support. The catch-all response as well as the cartel response by the politicians under party government constitute strategies to deal with increasing electoral volatility, but they do not enhance democratic vitality. In a sense, these strategies also take a negative view of increasing electoral volatility, because they look upon elections only from the perspective of the parties.

Party system stability, established party system theory argues, tends to enhance democratic stability. One may offer two interpretations of party system stability, linking the concept with democratic stability.

First, party system stability would entail that at least some of the major or pivotal parties face a high probability of long-term survival. If parties would come and go, emerge quickly and die suddenly, the entire political process leading up to government formation from the recording of election results would be impaired. If voters were to destroy the existing parties in every election and create new ones, democracy based upon party government would become entirely destabilised.

Second, if voters were to support 20 or 30 parties in an election, forming a workable government becomes an almost impossible task. Thus democratic consolidation is promoted when the voters form allegiances with a small number of parties that endure over several rounds of elections. Excessive party fragmentation is a negative for democratic stability at extremely high levels of (net) volatility.

Traditional party system theory thus assumes that volatility and fractionalisation are two key dimensions of party system stability, and both are related to the stability of a democratic regime. Yet, this approach bypasses the occurrence of opportunistic behaviour on the part of the political parties vis-à-vis the electorate. A moderate level of party system instability may actually improve democratic vitality, as volatility and party fractionalisation increase the possibilities for the voters to send signals to and monitor politicians/political parties – this is what principal–agent theory would suggest when applied to electoral politics.

Volatility and the vitality of democracy

Whatever philosophy of government one may adhere to, it is the case that politics is always a two-person game, i.e. an interaction between two sets of people, on the one hand the rulers and on the other those who are ruled. Even in theories, which present government with legitimacy derived from popular consent, it remains true that the rulers rule the population. Thus there arises the question as to the nature of this interaction between government and its people. The principal–agent approach solves this problem by suggesting that the persons in government constitute the agents of the population being the principal of the body politic. What would such a model of government as a series of principal–agent games unfolding over time entail for elections?

First, the agents act on behalf of the principal, meaning that the agents are somehow supposed to promote the interests of the principal. Thus, when applied to the politics setting, this implies that governments whatever their goals may be expected to maximise a utility function that includes the objectives of the population. By entailment, the principal–agent approach puts a major emphasis on the interests people bring into play in politics.

Second, when governments rule, expectations arise as to what governments will do. These expectations may be analysed as contracts between the agents and the principal, whether these agreements are explicit or implicit. These contracts contain the terms of reference for the interaction between the two groups, which may be more or less clear, transparent and detailed.

Third, any interaction between two persons involves a set of rules specifying what moves can be made or have to be made. Such norms would be part of the mutual understanding between two parties interacting, their expectations as it were. Such norms may be of various kinds, but as a minimum they would outline what the agents are supposed to do for the principal, how they are to be remunerated and what is to be done when expectations are not met, i.e. when disappointing outcomes occur.

It follows from the above that there are three essential components in the principal–agent approach (PA approach) when applied to government: (1) interests, (2) contracts and (3) rules. To analyse government according to the principal–agent framework involves clarifying the interests the players bring to the games of politics, the short-term expectations and mutual understandings that structure the interaction between rulers and the ruled as well as the long-term norms that define the outline of the various rounds of play. I shall assume the occurrence of opportunistic behaviour on the part of politicians, meaning that they tend to favour their own interests even with guile. If these assumptions are applied in the interpretation of electoral volatility and party systems, then party competition and electoral switches may be seen as tools to further the position of the principal, the population, under party governance.

If elections are looked upon as contracts between the population and the politicians/political parties, then the question arises as to how the principal can exercise some control over the agents it elects. Two mechanisms in the party system offer tools for the principal to monitor and make the agents respond to the wishes of the electorate: party competition and electoral volatility. Without these two mechanisms the politicians could neglect their principal and conduct any policy that enriches them at the expense of the population. In traditional party system theory only party competition was emphasised, as electoral volatility was seen as a threat to political stability. I would argue that electoral volatility bolsters the position of the principal and makes the agents even more anxious to work harder for the interests of the principal than for their own interests.

Thus, one should recognise the danger of committing the error of assuming that a low level of volatility is always better than a high level. Party systems cannot stay the same for ever. They need to adapt to *new politics*. Thus, an increase in volatility may signal party system adaptation. It is only excessive volatility that is a threat to party system stability. One may explain this important point by the employment of the principal–agent model.

Elections may be seen as the making of a contract between those governing and the governed. Due to the inter-temporal nature of elections, these contracts are both fuzzy and long term. This opens up the possibility of opportunism on the part of those making electoral promises. To check the tendencies towards reneging, the electorate has only one effective strategy, namely to vote for a different party in the next election. This punishment strategy is essential for democratic vitality. Thus, a rise in volatility should not be seen as a step towards instability and chaos, but rather to interpret it as a rational response with the electorate responding to the policy-making through their agents. As society becomes more complex and policy-making less transparent, the principal must dispose of some means to send effective messages to the agents, the politicians. Principal–agent theory applied to party system theory entails that multi-partysm and volatility would enhance democratic vitality.

The data

The new democracies in Eastern Europe have successfully operated a number of free and fair elections. Democratic consolidation would require a certain amount of stability in the party system in these countries. However, party system stability is not an obvious goal to be maximised without other considerations. The vitality of a democracy may need party system change in order to allow for alteration in power and the emergence of new parties. All the East European countries have multi-party systems of democracy, which calls for a comparison with West European democracies. How much more stable are the party systems in Western Europe when compared with Eastern Europe? One would expect quite substantial differences in volatility, as the party systems in Eastern Europe go through a process of consolidation whereas the party systems in Western Europe used to abide by the logic of a frozen party system. With respect to election systems in Central and Eastern Europe we rely on both published and unpublished sources (Lane and Ersson, 2007).

We employ two datasets in our analysis. The first one refers to 145 elections (cases) for the period from 1990 to 200 covering 38 countries. The second dataset is based on country-level data and thus contains 38 countries in this analysis of European democracy. Excluded are only the former Khanates (*Turkestan*, i.e. Kazakhstan, Kyrgyzstan, Tajikistan, Turkmenistan and Uzbekistan), where democracy has not yet stabilised in these new states created after the Soviet Union collapsed. For these 38 European countries we have collected information about the recent elections with regard to net volatility and the number of political parties. The analysis is based upon two indices, the Pedersen index on net volatility and the Laakso-Tagepeera index on the effective number of parties. We have checked how well our volatility scores tend to agree with scores reported in the literature. We have then relied on several published and unpublished sources where volatility scores are reported for party systems in Southern and Central and Eastern Europe (Lane and Ersson, 2007). As for the country dataset ($n = 38$) our volatility score correlates quite strongly with the average for the scores reported in the literature (r = 0.96; $n = 34$); a similar procedure for the election dataset ($n = 145$) arrives at a slightly lower correlation (r = 0.84; $n = 61$). Our conclusion is that our measure on net volatility is reasonably reliable.

We have grouped the countries according to the following regional divisions:

1 *Northern Europe*: Scandinavia, Iceland, Finland, the UK, Ireland, the Benelux countries, Austria and Germany.
2 *Southern Europe*: France, Spain, Portugal, Italy, Switzerland, Greece, Cyprus and Malta.
3 *Central Europe*: Poland, the Czech and Slovak Republics, Hungary and Slovenia.
4 *Eastern Europe*: Baltic States, Romania, Bulgaria, Bosnia, Croatia, Macedonia, Albania, Russia, Moldova, Ukraine and Turkey.

This classification ties in with standard images of European politics before the Iron Curtain went down with Yalta and Potsdam. It is believed that Northern Europe is more stable than Southern Europe, which is more stable than Central Europe, which again is more stable than Eastern Europe. Is this image true today?

Net volatility

A first picture of party system volatility is rendered in Table 6.1, covering all the countries and the four most recent elections. One may observe a huge difference between the most volatile party systems – scoring around 45 for some East European countries – and the least volatile party systems, scoring around 5 in some West European countries. The average rate of net volatility is a high 19 for all the elections reported upon here, where the rate has actually come down somewhat over the period.

Table 6.1 shows an extensive variation in net volatility. It is not only among East European countries that one finds very high scores (Albania, Bulgaria, Estonia, Latvia, Lithuania, Moldova, Ukraine and Russia). Some West European countries have also experienced earthquake elections (Italy, The Netherlands and France). One finds a few elections where there is hardly any volatility at all, such as for some elections in Malta, the UK, Greece, Cyprus

Table 6.1 Volatility in Europe in the 1990s and 2000s at four elections

Country	1	2	3	4	Mean	n	Std dev.
Albania	31.8	15.5	38.4	11.8	25.8	5	11.0
Austria	9.7	15.5	4.4	8.8	11.9	5	6.5
Belgium	13.4	9.6	12.6	14.1	12.4	4	2.0
Bosnia	25.4	23.5	17.8		22.2	3	4.0
Bulgaria	14.3	21.1	23.1	47.9	27.7	5	12.9
Croatia	30.1	9.5	23.5	14.5	19.4	4	9.2
Cyprus	8.4	7.5	6.2		7.4	3	1.1
Czech Republic	18.9	27.0	9.3	16.3	17.9	4	7.3
Denmark	13.3	10.8	11.9	13.3	11.4	5	2.3
Estonia	27.9	33.5	35.0		32.2	3	3.7
Finland	11.8	11.3	8.9	6.8	9.7	4	2.3
France	17.6	13.6	14.2		15.1	3	2.2
Germany	10.9	7.6	7.6	7.4	8.5	5	1.5
Greece	3.1	10.5	4.8	7.5	6.2	5	2.8
Hungary	26.1	31.4	18.1		25.2	3	6.7
Iceland	14.2	12.4	14.1	8.8	12.4	4	2.5
Ireland	15.5	9.7	11.2		12.1	3	3.0
Italy	19.3	37.3	13.7	26.8	24.3	4	10.2
Latvia	37.9	45.0	46.1		43.0	3	4.5
Lithuania	37.4	48.3	50.0		45.2	3	6.8
Luxembourg	5.6	10.4	10.6		8.9	3	2.8
Macedonia	39.4	37.3	25.3		34.0	3	7.6
Malta	2.6	4.2	4.0	0.6	2.9	4	1.7
Moldova	61.9	46.0	14.0		40.6	3	24.4
Netherlands	21.8	17.5	30.8	16.3	21.6	4	6.6

(Continued)

Table 6.1 Continued

Country	1	2	3	4	Mean	n	Std dev.
Norway	15.3	16.7	16.1	18.9	16.8	4	1.5
Poland	33.8	19.4	23.6	34.3	27.8	4	7.4
Portugal	9.6	20.3	2.5	8.8	10.8	5	6.5
Romania	33.2	16.8	34.7	12.1	24.2	4	11.5
Russia	51.2	49.7	23.9		41.6	3	15.3
Slovak Republic	20.0	13.7	21.5	28.6	22.0	4	6.1
Slovenia	25.3	24.4	18.7	22.2	22.6	4	3.0
Spain	11.2	6.1	10.7	10.3	9.6	4	2.3
Sweden	14.8	11.6	15.92	14.4	14.2	4	1.8
Switzerland	8.2	7.1	9.4	7.9	8.2	4	1.0
Turkey	16.5	22.7	22.6	44.0	26.5	4	12.0
Ukraine	53.5	16.5			35.0	2	26.2
United Kingdom	5.3	12.6	5.3	6.4	7.4	4	3.5
Total	21.5	19.8	17.9	16.3	19.0	145	12.6

Source: Author. See Appendix.

Note
The data matrix employed contains 145 elections.

and Austria. In general, net volatility stands at 20. Now, what explains most: country (space) or election (time)?

Looking at these country scores on net volatility one may establish first that the high standard deviance score refers mainly to one factor, namely *country* (see the analysis of variance in Table 6.2). This means that certain countries tend to have high or low volatility over several consecutive elections. The problem is to explain why there is this consistent country variation in party system volatility. Region plays a role in Table 6.2, which is interesting from our point of view. The regional analysis of net volatility is

Table 6.2 Volatility by space and time in Europe in the 1990s and 2000s

	Eta squared	Sig.
Country	0.716	0.00
Region	0.459	0.00
Election	0.022	0.53
Election year	0.094	0.57

Source: Author. See Appendix 6.1.

Notes
The data matrix employed contains 145 elections; Region: 1 = Northern Europe; 2 = Southern Europe; 3 = Central Europe; 4 = Eastern Europe. Election = 1st election, 2nd election, 3rd election, and 4th election.

done here by grouping the European democracies into four clusters: North-ern, Southern, Central and Eastern Europe, using the standard image of Europe before the Iron Curtain came down.

The high eta-squared scores for countries in Table 6.2 mean that the major differences in volatility between the European countries persist from one elec-tion to another. At the same time there is a regional effect in the data.

Table 6.3 shows the regional averages for three elections. The major differ-ences are those between Western Europe on the one hand and Central and Eastern Europe on the other. The latter two regions have more net volatility, especially Eastern Europe. Surprisingly, the average scores for Southern Europe are actually slightly lower than those for Northern Europe for two of three elections.

It is not surprising that Eastern Europe, especially Romania, Bulgaria, Russia, Turkey and Albania but also Latvia and Lithuania, has much higher volatility than Central Europe, given the differences in the consolidation of these democracies. Yet high volatility scores are to be found also in the other regions (e.g. Central Europe (Hungary, Poland), Northern Europe (the Netherlands) and Southern Europe (Italy)). The countries with very low scores on volatility include Malta, with extremely low numbers, Greece, Switzerland (Southern Europe) and Luxembourg, and the UK (Northern Europe).

The available evidence about the relationship between net and gross volatility may be expressed in a lawlike manner in the following way:

(1) Net volatility = Gross Volatility/2

The implication of (1) is that a net volatility number of roughly 15 indicates that roughly 30 per cent of the electorate voted for a different party. There are several countries in Western Europe with such a considerable gross volatility including Norway, Iceland, Belgium and Denmark. It is true that this level of net volatility is far different from a net volatility of almost 50. However, such a high score is only found in one election for a country like Lithuania and Moldova, meaning that most of the electorate shifted party from one election to another.

Table 6.3 Volatility in Europe in the 1990s and 2000s – four clusters

Region	1st election	2nd election	3rd election	Total
Northern Europe	12.6	12.1	12.5	12.2
Southern Europe	10.7	14.4	9.8	12.2
Central Europe	24.8	23.2	18.2	22.8
Eastern Europe	37.0	30.2	30.2	31.4

Source: Author. See Appendix.

Note
The data matrix employed contains 145 elections.

Some countries have experienced a sudden shift to a very high level of volatility: the earthquake election. We find such a one-shot dramatic increase in volatility in, for instance, Italy, the Netherlands and Poland, after which elections the situation stabilises. We would be inclined to predict that there will be more of these elections where the electorate repositions itself fundamentally because there are no longer any frozen party systems in Europe.

How, then, may we account for these immense country differences? What macro-level properties account for the fact that some countries hardly have any volatility while others have a volatility that ranges from a considerable 20 to an extreme 50? One plausible explanation would be to target another aspect of party system instability, namely the number of parties, since the more numerous the parties the more likely it is that voters will change from one to the other.

Party system fractionalisation

All democracies in Europe adhere to multi-partysm. The number of parties in the party system may be measured by the index of effective number of parties, which takes into account not merely number but also their electoral support. The average number of effective parties stands at five for all of Europe, which indicates quite a strong fractionalisation. However, the spread between the smallest effective number and the largest is truly large (see Table 6.4).

Table 6.4 indicates that the distinction between two-partysm and multi-partysm is no longer pertinent in relation to most recent elections in Europe. Yet a few countries have very fractionalised party systems (Belgium, France, Italy, Latvia, Russia and the Ukraine). In many European countries the real number of parties is above six, as the index on the effective number of parties reduces the level of fractionalisation by taking into account the size of electoral support. Thus a high level of fractionalisation at around eight to nine is to be found in several countries, whereas a low level occurs with countries that are close to but never at two-partysm, namely the UK, Portugal and Greece as well as Spain and Cyprus. Malta has the only real two-party system. Again we look at an analysis of variance to see which factor matters most: country, region (space) or election (time) (see Table 6.5).

It is again country that carries the coherence in the variation. Actually, region matters very little. This is surprising, since the standard image is that Northern Europe is less fractionalised than other parts of Europe. As we may note from Table 6.6, it is Southern Europe which scores lowest on the index of effective number of parties, but the differences between the four regions are not big. This is a surprising finding.

Thus, multi-partysm is entrenched to such an extent all over Europe that the variation in regional averages is only a minor one. However, we would still expect fractionalisation to be a major determinant of volatility although volatility would reflect region much more than the effective number of

Table 6.4 Effective number of parties in Europe in the 1990s and 2000s

Country	Effective number (mean)	Std deviation
Albania	4.3	3.5
Austria	3.5	0.4
Belgium	9.6	0.6
Bosnia	7.5	1.4
Bulgaria	4.2	1.0
Croatia	4.4	0.7
Cyprus	3.7	0.1
Czech Republic	5.5	1.2
Denmark	4.8	0.2
Estonia	6.1	0.7
Finland	5.8	0.1
France	6.2	0.8
Germany	3.9	0.3
Greece	2.7	0.2
Hungary	4.3	1.3
Iceland	4.0	0.3
Ireland	4.0	0.1
Italy	6.9	0.5
Latvia	7.8	1.6
Lithuania	6.2	0.9
Luxembourg	4.6	0.3
Macedonia	5.3	1.3
Malta	2.0	0.0
Moldova	4.2	1.4
Netherlands	5.5	0.5
Norway	5.3	0.6
Poland	6.2	2.5
Portugal	3.0	0.1
Romania	5.6	1.3
Russia	7.7	2.9
Slovak Republic	6.3	1.7
Slovenia	6.4	1.4
Spain	3.2	0.2
Sweden	4.4	0.4
Switzerland	6.4	0.8
Turkey	5.8	0.9
Ukraine	9.2	2.5
United Kingdom	3.3	0.2
Total	5.1	1.9

Source: Author.

Note
The data matrix employed contains 145 elections.

Table 6.5 Effective number of parties by space and time in Europe in the 1990s and 2000s

	Eta squared	Sig.
Country	0.718	0.00
Region	0.093	0.00
Election	0.034	0.30
Election year	0.098	0.52

Source: Author. See Appendix.

Notes
The data matrix employed contains 145 elections; Region: 1 = Northern Europe; 2 = Southern Europe; 3 = Central Europe; 4 = Eastern Europe. Election = 1st election, 2nd election, 3rd election and 4th election.

Table 6.6 Effective number of parties in Europe in the 1990s and 2000s: four clusters

Region	1st election	2nd election	3rd election	Total
Northern Europe	4.9	4.8	5.0	4.9
Southern Europe	4.4	4.6	4.5	4.3
Central Europe	7.3	5.3	4.5	5.8
Eastern Europe	6.7	5.5	5.0	5.7

Source: Author. See Appendix.

Note
The data matrix employed contains 145 elections.

parties. Let us first look at the interaction between volatility and fractionalisation before we try a regression model with a few relevant factors.

Volatility and fractionalisation

Net volatility and party fractionalisation are the central dimensions of a party system, both tapping party system stability. How do these two aspects of party system interact on the European scene? The more numerous the parties, the more potential there is for changing from one party to another. However, this holds for gross volatility but not necessarily for net volatility. Within net volatility massive voter changes may cancel each other out perfectly, meaning that the parties lose and gain the same number of voters. Yet, from a probabilistic point of view it is likely that party system fractionalisation feeds volatility. When the number of parties goes beyond five, then it is likely that some parties will experience large changes, especially if there is an earthquake election. Within new politics some parties are flash parties which rise and fall rapidly. Let me look at the interaction between the effective number of parties (party fractionalisation) and volatility (see Figure 6.1).

Here we move from an analysis of elections to a cross-country analysis of average scores on net volatility and the effective number of parties.

Figure 6.1 indicates a clear positive association between these two variables, but it is not strong. The size of the Pearson's correlation (r = 0.41; sig = 0.011) indicates that there is more to volatility than party system fractionalisation. One should look at the outliers in Figure 6.1: Belgium, Switzerland, Lithuania, Moldova, which all deviate from the linear trend shown in Figure 6.1. It is quite possible to have many parties but low volatility (Belgium) or high volatility but few parties (Moldova). However, the overall trend is that more parties invite higher net volatility.

What other factors could be added to party fractionalisation in an explanation of the substantial country variation in volatility in European demo-

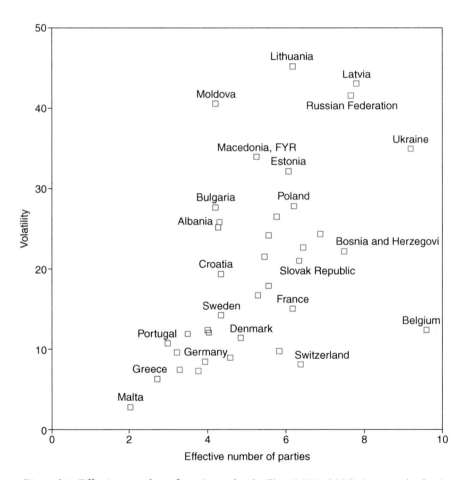

Figure 6.1 Effective number of parties and volatility (1990–2005) (source: Author).

Note
The data reported refer to country averages for the period 1990 to 2005; *n* = 38.

cracies today? We suggest that the remaining variation in volatility has to do with electoral and political institutions as well as the developmental stage, or the level of economic modernisation, and the historical heritage of Eastern Europe.

A regression model of volatility

The electoral system may be entered into the model accounting for volatility. Which properties of the electoral system are relevant, and how does one take into account changes in the electoral system introduced during this period mainly in some Central and Eastern European countries?

A simplified model of the electoral system captures on the one hand the kind of electoral formula employed (proportional (= 1) or non-proportional formula (= 0)) and on the other hand the use of an electoral threshold (no or low (= 0) versus a threshold on 2 per cent or higher (= 1)). Major changes in the electoral system have occurred only rarely: Albania 1992, Bulgaria 1991, Croatia 1995, Italy 1994, Macedonia 1998 and Ukraine 1998. For these countries we find no major impact of the change on the effective number and volatility of the party system. Therefore, the cross-country analysis employed below uses average scores for the electoral system variables for the countries where major changes have occurred. Admittedly, this is a simplification we have allowed ourselves in the analysis. The model we test for 38 European countries making use of average scores for the period 1990 to 2005 (roughly) includes the following factors:

(2) Volatility = f (effective number of parties, electoral system, contextual factors),

where the electoral formula and the electoral threshold tap the electoral system. The contextual factors covered are political institutions (parliamentary versus non-parliamentary system), socio-economic development (human development index for the year 2001) and historical legacy (as expressed by the degree of latitude). These contextual factors help capture both the North–South and the East–West differences among European polities.

The findings of the regression analyses are presented below in Table 6.7, which also contains the model (model 2) with the best empirical fit.

It is obvious that contextual factors have the largest impact on the variation in party system volatility. These variables certainly capture some of the differences, which go together with the development of democracy in Europe. Electoral formula, as we have operationalised it, has no impact, and electoral threshold has a certain impact. Higher thresholds are to be found in party systems with more volatility: the higher the threshold, the higher the score for electoral volatility. Thus, electoral system does not matter much for explaining the cross-country variation in electoral volatility. It is only the effective number of parties which displays the expected

Table 6.7 Volatility and its determinants: volatility is the dependent variable

Independent variables	Model 1		Model 2	
	B	t	B	t
Effective number of parties (EFFN)	1.9	3.0	1.89	3.21
Electoral system (ELSYS)	−1.52	−0.65		
Electoral Threshold (THRES)	4.78	1.94	5.57	2.51
Parliamentarism (PARL)	0.91	0.64		
Latitude (LAT)	45.23	3.40	46.00	3.54
Human development index (HDI)	−111.81	−6.54	−107.70	−7.04
(Constant)	79.84	5.39	76.62	5.47
Adjusted r^2	0.76		0.77	
n	38		38	

Source: Author. See Appendix.

Note
The data matrix employed contains 38 European countries.

effect on party system volatility when controlling for contextual factors. Since the level of socio-economic modernisation has the largest impact upon net volatility, one may expect volatility to come down in Eastern Europe, as has already happened in several countries in at least one election since the fall of the communist regime.

Conclusion

Party system stability separates the democracies in Western Europe from the democracies in Eastern Europe, volatility being much higher in the new democracies than in the old. The trend is however for volatility to decrease in Eastern Europe but to increase in several countries in Western Europe. However, the average scores for different parts of the new democratic Europe vary considerably. We specify a regression model of macro or net volatility with a high goodness of fit. Party fractionalisation is a factor accounting for volatility, but the context of politics plays a major role. Actually, the low level of economic modernisation in Eastern Europe explains more of party system instability than the fractionalisation of the party system. Therefore we may expect that the divergent pattern within Europe over time will decline, volatility decreasing in the East as these economies take off.

Democratic vitality, argued Tingsten already in the 1960s, is more important than democratic stability in today's Europe. There is no credible threat to constitutional democracy from anti-system parties, but the vitality of democracy is tested time and again in scandals and corruption cases. This can only be understood by applying the principal–agent approach from game theory to politics in the European democracies with their institutionalised party government. The principal–agent model implies that the population can only monitor and control their politicians/parties if its principal chooses several agents and is prepared to switch allegiance between them. This is the basic reason why growing volatility in Western Europe is a positive, fed by party system fractionalisation, which is not a negative. We must revise standard party system theory that puts too much value on democratic stability and too little on democratic vitality. Excessive volatility at 50 per cent would constitute a negative for democracy, but a moderate or slightly rising level of volatility would be conducive to the vitality of the democratic regime, especially under a principal–agent interpretation of democracy.

Appendix 6.1

Sources for party system data on net volatility and effective number of parties

Printed sources

Berglund, Sten, Joakim Ekman and Frank H. Aarebrot (eds) (2004) *The Handbook of Political Change in Eastern Europe*. Cheltenham: Edward Elgar.

Birch, Sarah (2003) *Electoral Systems and Political Transformation in Post-communist Europe*. Basingstoke: Palgrave Macmillan.

European Journal of Political Research (1992–2005) Political data yearbook.

Mackie, Tom and Richard Rose (1997) *A Decade of Election Results: Updating the International Almanac*. University of Strathclyde: Centre for the Study of Public Policy.

Rose, Richard and Neil Munro (2003) *Elections and Parties in new European Democracies*. Washington, DC: CQ Press.

Rose, Richard, Neil Munro and Tom Mackie (1998) *Elections in Central and Eastern Europe since 1990*. University of Strathclyde: Centre for the Study of Public Policy; Studies in Public Policy, 300.

General internet sources

Election resources on the internet; available at: http://electionresources.org/

ElectionGuide – Worldwide Coverage of National-level Elections; available at: www.electionguide.org

Office for Democratic Institutions and Human Rights – Elections; available at: www.osce.org/odihr-elections

Parties and elections in Europe; available at: www.parties-and-elections.de/index.html

Parties and elections; available at: www.cspp.strath.ac.uk

Project on Political Transformation and the Electoral Process in Post-Communist Europe; available at: www.essex.ac.uk/elections

Wikipedia: Elections by country; available at: http://en.wikipedia.org/wiki/List_of_election_results

Electoral authorities available on the internet (recent elections in 2004 and 2005)

Albanian election 2005; available at: www.cec.org.al/2004/eng/indexShqip.htm

Bulgarian election 2005; available at: www.2005izbori.org/results/index.html

Danish election 2005; available at: www.im.dk//imagesupload/dokument/valgpub1rev.pdf

German election 2005; available at: www.bundeswahlleiter.de/bundestagswahl2005/ergebnisse/bundesergebnisse/b_tabelle_99.html

Lithuanian election 2004; available at: www3.lrs.lt/rinkimai/index.eng.html

Norwegian election 2005; available at: http://odin.dep.no/krd/html/valgresultat2005/frameset.html

Polish election 2005; available at: www.wybory2005.pkw.gov.pl/index_EN.html

Portuguese election 2005; available at: http://eleicoes.cne.pt/raster/index.cfm? dia=20&mes=02&ano=2005&eleicao=ar

Romanian election 2004; available at: www.bec2004.ro/

Slovenian election 2004; available at: http://volitve.gov.si/dz2004/en/html/rez_si.htm

United Kingdom election 2005; available at: www.electoralcommission.org.uk/elections/generalelection2005.cfm

Variables employed in the regression analysis reported in Table 6.7

Variable description	Sources
Net volatility	Net changes for voter support for all the parties within a party system between two elections; the higher the score, the more volatility. See sources listed in this Appendix.
Effective number	Number of parties in a party system based on votes as of parties computed with the Laakso–Taagepera index. See sources listed in Lane and Ersson (2006).
Electoral system	PR-system = 1; non-PR-system = 0; if changes have occurred the value may be within the range from 0 to 1. See sources listed in Lane and Ersson (2007).

(Continued)

Continued

Variable description	Sources
Electoral threshold	A threshold on 2 per cent or higher = 1; a lower threshold = 0. See sources listed in Lane and Ersson (2006).
Parliamentarism	3 = parliamentarism; 2 = mixed system (semi-presidentialism); 1 = presidentialism. Based on various sources, such as Derbyshire and Derbyshire (1999); and Berglund *et al.* (2004).
Latitude	Distance from the equator in degrees – latitudes (geographic coordinates). CIA, *The World Factbook*; available at: www.odci.gov/cia/publications/factbook/.
Human development index	Human development index in 2001 as calculated by UNDP. UNDP, *Human Development Report*; available at: http://hdr.undp.org/.

Part III

Towards an evolutionary regime theory

Comparative politics is both cross-sectional and longitudinal in its scope. As human history shows, political regimes evolve. But which polity form is the most fit to be able to survive the longest? In this final part, I will dwell on the development of polity forms from an evolutionary perspective, attempting to explain why certain types of regime go under while others survive or prosper. Since known human civilisation a succession of political institutions may be observed. What drives the evolution of polities?

In an evolutionary perspective upon political regimes, there is no assumption about inertia or accumulated wisdom from the past, as with modern conservatism in the Burke interpretation (Stanlis, 2006). Revolutions are by no means fool hardy, since they may open the road towards a regime that is better than existing practices. Evolutionary politics would basically be a theory accounting for the historical variation of regimes. Weber's model of authority was an attempt to come to grips with dynamic aspects at the macro level of politics. Weber's paradigm mainly influenced the historical investigation of systems of rulership, ancient, medieval and modern (Eisenstadt, 1963; Bendix, 1978; Ertman, 2004). Most states today adhere to Weber's legal-rational type of authority, having different kinds of constitutions.

For a political regime to be successful, meaning viable and lasting, the governance of a country must be by means of a central power, securing external and internal stability, as well as enhancing local and regional administration. In an agrarian society, various solutions to the governance question stem from the variety of feudal arrangements. In an industrial or post-industrial society, the solution to the governance question tends to involve some form of legal-rational authority. First, I will discuss the relevance of the concept of survival fitness. Second, I will make a short evolutionary sketch of the development of political regimes. The survival capacity of a regime is a macro-political question, but its foundations are located in the principal–agent interaction between government and population.

7 Regime fitness

On the survival of politics

Introduction

Political regimes have always been the subject of intense debate among the population, because they affect human beings tremendously. They are as important as economic regimes, if not more important, since law and order may trump prosperity. Yet little is known about why political regimes succeed each other. Fukuyama ventured to suggest that democracy is the end-product of political evolution, arguing that the progression of human history as a struggle between ideologies is largely at an end, with the world settling upon liberal democracy following the end of the Cold War (Fukuyama, 1993). Democracy may score high on moral appeal, but one would like to understand the principal–agent mechanism which drives the search for democracy and results in a demand for regime change. Democracy is certainly not the sole polity today, and there are several types of democracies achieving rule of law. This chapter suggests a few central elements in the evolution of political regimes, which may help to explain why certain institutions have been successful while others have not. Polities clearly adapt to change, especially long-term economic change. If there is a concept such as political viability, what drives the evolution of political institutions on a macro scale? Political viability could be a new relevant concept, meaning that political systems survive if they can adapt to the environment. However, adaptation could mean several things which have to be pinned down.

Since the dawn of known civilisation around 5,000 years ago, mankind has witnessed a succession of political systems up until present-day democracy. What is the driving mechanism behind the succession of political regimes? If the struggle for survival is the core mechanism in the development of species according to evolutionary biology and the search for efficiency is behind the development of economic institutions according to evolutionary economics, then what drives the succession of political systems during the period of known human history? To consider how politics come and go, one may examine the history of the Middle East before the time of Jesus Christ – a constant flux of dynasties and regimes, new peoples, as well as conquest and defeats (Redford, 1992). To illuminate this question, I will conduct a short inquiry into the main alternatives for a polity, evaluating them against a few criteria of political viability.

The survival of a political regime is an interesting and relevant concept; yet not much research has been done using this biologically inspired conception. Political regimes do not last for ever, but are created, flourish and decay. How can one understand the basic mechanisms behind this political evolution? In political thought, one finds two rudiments of a theory of polity viability which are highly relevant for the concept of survival fitness of macro-political regimes, namely in Hobbes and Locke. For Hobbes it is governmental capacity which accounts for the survival of a polity, both the internal capacity of government to maintain law and order and the external capacity to fend off intruders. For Locke it is rights, their enactment and enforcement, which create long-term sustainability or evolutionary fitness in the form of governmental legitimacy. I will translate these two principles into government capacity, especially capability in warfare on the one hand and the respect for rule of law on the other.

Polity forms, fitness and evolutionary mechanisms

Human history is extremely short, as modern humans, classified as *Homo sapiens*, first began to appear 120,000 to 100,000 years ago, although life in its most elementary forms emerged much earlier. Schopf *et al.* (2002: 73–76) argue that the earliest life formations could be found in 3.5 billion-year-old fossilised algae microbes. The dinosaurs emerged "only" 200 million years ago as giant reptiles that dominated the terrestrial ecosystem for most of their time span. They became extinct 65 million years ago at the end of the Cretaceous period. Political science deals only with the evolution of political institutions during the period of known human civilisations.

The first fossils of *Homo sapiens* to be identified were found in 1868 in a 28,000-year-old rock shelter site near the village of Les Eyzies in southwestern France. Subsequently named the Cro-Magnon people, they were very similar in appearance to modern Europeans. The males were 5 feet 4 inches to 6 feet tall and their skeletons were lighter than the Neanderthals. *Homo sapiens* evolved from Africa and/or Southwest Asia, but it was not until 40,000 or 50,000 years ago that they began to appear in Europe and East Asia during a short temperate period in the midst of the last ice age.

The world population of modern *Homo sapiens* began to grow rapidly 40,000 to 50,000 years ago. Their movement into far northern areas coincided with the end of a long cold period that had begun about 75,000 years ago. Modern humans moved into Australia for the first time around 50,000 years ago or a little earlier. Australia was not connected to Southeast Asia by land, so it is probable that the first Australians arrived by boats or rafts. Around 30,000 to 35,000 years ago, human big game hunters moved into northeastern Siberia. As early as 30,000 years ago and no later than 11,000 years ago, they migrated into North America via the Bering Plain that appeared between Siberia and Alaska due to sea-level drop. Human population growth has continued to accelerate ever since. Now the world population is over six billion and intercontinental migration and gene flow are at higher levels than ever before. Yet, political institutions began to evolve at a much later stage, as we only have certain knowledge about the first kingdoms in the Middle East dating back at most 5,000 years.

One may identify a shortlist of the chief forms of political regimes drawing upon the brief period of time since individuals adhering to *Homo sapiens* established known political systems. This occurred in the Middle East in the river deltas of Euphrates and Tigris as well as in the Nile valley. Sumer formed the southern part of Mesopotamia from the time of settlement by the Sumerians until the time of Babylonia. Sumerian cuneiform script may pre-date any other form of writing, and dates to no later than about 3500 BC (Kramer, 1993). The Sumerians lived in city-states, having a central temple dedicated to the patron god of the city and ruled over by a king, who was linked with the city's religious rites. One can mention Eridu, Kish, Lagash, Uruk, Ur and Nippur. As these cities developed, they sought to assert primacy over each other, falling into a millennium of almost incessant warfare over water rights, trade routes and tribute from nomadic tribes.

As the early written evidence of the existence of political systems dates back to around 3,500 years BC, political evolution only spans some 5,000 years. What are the main driving forces behind polity evolution or the survival of the fit political institutions? When one examines the history of various kinds of polities (Finer, 1999a, b, c), one discovers that government or governing includes three dimensions:

1   Who is involved in ruling? Reply: monarchy (one), aristocracy (few) or democracy (many).
2   What is the size of the polity? Reply: city-state, principality, nation-state, empire or colony.
3   What is the link between the rulers and their servants? Reply: bureaucracy, kinship or bondage and vassalage.

Now what explains political evolution? Why has there been a succession of political regimes ever since the first known civilisations? One may look for the causes of polity evolution among two factors: economic on the one hand and political on the other. The traditional economic structure of society – agrarian, slave, hydraulic – has been singled out as a major polity determinant. The industrial society, or its postmodern successor, is said to be crucial for the democratic polity. It is, however, difficult to find convincing evidence for a tight one-to-one relationship between the economy and the polity. One may regard *polity capacity* as a derivative of economic resources to a large extent, since government needs access to a surplus generated in a flourishing economy. Yet polities often go under because they are conquered by other polities or are destroyed by more powerful neighbours. Besides foreign relations, one key political factor driving polity evolution has, I suggest, been the guarantee of rights in a wide sense. The search for rights not only accounts for the introduction of the bureaucratic state but it also explains the search for rule of law. Polity capacity and rights within a polity constitute two dimensions of polity evolution that are more or less independent of each other. Let us look more closely at them.

Capacity

In a linear conception of polity development one would primarily think of system capacity as an evolutionary mechanism. Political systems are supposed to deliver certain activities. The more capable they are in delivering these activities, the more developed they tend to be. In theories of empires, system capacity is a major consideration. This is called *"Leistungsfähigkeit"* in German. Somehow there would be a polity development towards more and more of system capacity. And polities will go under once they lose their capacity to deliver.

If one underlines military strength in an evolutionary conception of politics, then the capacity approach makes sense. The succession of polities would basically be explained by the change in military technology and its implications for political organisation. No doubt there is much to be said in favour of such a military interpretation of polity evolution. Political systems have gone under due to military defeats, and new political organisations have often displayed more military might than older ones.

A most telling example of military conquest destroying an old political system and introducing a new one is the Spanish *conquista* of America. The ease with which the conquistadores brought down the Aztecs and the Incas indicates that these empires were not viable, at least not from a global point of view. The succession of regimes in Central and South America, before the arrival of the *conquistadores*, indicates that political system viability depends on the neighbouring countries and their capacity to overrun another country (Williamson, 1992).

Capacity has two sides: internal capacity and external capacity. The external capacity of a political regime is maximised in major conquests such as those with the Mongol Empires and the Tamerlane Regime. However, since these empires had little internal capacity they did not last long. Both Genghis Khan and Tamerlane ruled over giant territories but their polities broke down shortly after their deaths.

External capacity

That war and the capacity to wage war is a major determinant of the survival of political regimes has always been emphasised in military history.

Conquest often meant the end of political regimes. What is not equally clear is whether a country that engaged in rapid foreign expansion also had the internal capacity necessary to maintain itself after conquest had been fulfilled. The Roman Empire is a good example of how external capacity works at first in favour of the regime and then begins to work against the regime in order to finally bring it down. The causes of the decline of the Roman Empire have been much discussed, but there is agreement upon the negative impact of the conduct of unending wars along the borders of the empire.

Conquest is the cause of the demise of the regime conquered, but it can also be the start of the demise of the conqueror. The twentieth century saw the rapid rise of three empires expanding through military conquest, but all three failed. The Third Reich and the Japanese Empire suffered quick defeats – unconditional surrender – whereas the Soviet Empire exhausted itself slowly but exorbitantly.

A lack of external capacity is a source of polity defeat, but so is an excessive external capacity that becomes the source of its own defeat. The Ottoman Empire displayed vigorous armed capacity in the first centuries of its existence, but exhausted itself to become "the sick man of Europe". However, external capacity need not translate into foreign expansion, as a regime may opt for viability through defensive capacity against hostile neighbours.

Internal capacity

One cannot explain the survival or death of political regimes only with war and military conquest. It is no doubt true that many political regimes have gone under due to military activities, either being taken over by another power or creating for themselves the conditions for their destruction by exorbitant military expansion. However, political regimes need more than external capacity to survive, meaning that internal capacity counts.

The internal capacity of a political regime is related to its capacity to govern a territory and a population. What counts is not merely the strength of the army. The administrative capacity of the regime is also at stake. The transition from feudal regimes to nation-states is an example of the quest for administrative strength with a political regime. Nation-states score high on internal capacity as they are based on the bureaucracy. The warlord regime today displays the same weaknesses as feudalism in history, namely the tendency towards anarchy.

Anarchy is a sign of the failure of a political regime. Civil war or general anomy indicates a lack of political viability and often leads to the demise of a political regime. Anarchy may result from foreign invasion, which somehow fails to establish a new regime, or it is the result of internal struggle in a country, which leads to armed conflict or civil war.

Nation-states score higher than feudal regimes on internal capacity. The small, compact nation-state has proved highly viable, but it is challenged by the growing interdependencies between countries that globalisation is conducive to. When it can no longer govern its territory fully, the remedy is regionalisation and the acceptance of international regimes. Besides, the nation-state is today challenged internally from the multicultural society. Few countries consist today of nations as compact groups of people with similar ethnic or religious creeds. And few nation-states can exercise control over their country or borders, meaning sovereignty. In the period of globalisation the viability of the nation-state is at stake.

Rights

Political systems may offer other things than might or security. They may provide their population with citizenship and citizens' rights. By guaranteeing rights, the regime also receives legitimacy and secures long-term viability. People would not want to live under a regime which provides them with few if any rights – this is the basic idea with regime survival as linked with the enforcement of citizen rights.

One can view the evolution of regimes in many countries as the slow but incessant search for a regime that provides for the rule of law. The victory of democracy in many countries may be interpreted as expressing this kind of political viability. Yet, democracy is the regime in only 50 per cent of the countries of the world. Does it mean that the other countries are less adaptable and will in time change their regimes, accepting democracy? The Fukuyama argument indicates this. But one must remember that regime viability has at least two sources, where several present-day authoritarian regimes score high in one of them, namely capacity.

The struggle for rights – especially human rights – has characterised much of the evolution of regimes, more so in the occidental world than in the Oriental world. In the constitutional history of Western countries, it was not enough that the nation-state displayed increasing capacity. People also demanded that it be responsive to citizens, enforcing a set of civil and political rights.

Regimes that are based upon the recognition and implementation of rights constitute rule of law political systems. They need not be democracies, as rule of law emerged before the advent of democracy and may be practised in countries that are not strictly speaking democracies (e.g. Singapore) today. In a rule of law polity, government is conducted *under* the laws, meaning that arbitrary government is excluded.

The development path of many nation-states has been towards an increasing recognition of rights, from the classical negative rights over the positive rights to the group rights or collective rights. Rule *by* law is not considered sufficient, although it is an advance in relation to arbitrary rule. Rule *of* law has a more specific sense than democracy. If democracy stands for party governance, then non-Western countries may hesitate to endorse it. Similarly, if democracy stands for contestation and competition, then again non-Western countries may hesitate to accept it. Rule of law entails legality, separation of powers and human rights.

Rule of law is not restricted to the internal affairs of the nation-state. It may also encompass the external affairs of the nation-state, to be monitored by regional or international regimes that evaluate the nation-states on the basis of a universal set of rights. Polity evolution has favoured the emergence of several regional or international regimes orientated towards the rule of law.

Efficacy and legitimacy of a political regime

Polity evolution involves the operation of the two mechanisms of system capacity as well as the establishment of rule of law. Political regimes may survive if they have the capacity to establish external and internal order – the survival mechanism identified by Hobbes. The Hobbes mechanism of survival – polity strength, state sovereignty, military power, law and order, safety – explains the downfall of many rulerships. But it is not the sole evolutionary mechanism.

Political regimes may go under because they do not respect the rights of citizens, as laid down in the idea of rule of law as well as in the doctrine of constitutional democracy. Rulerships may become insupportable, because they do not provide the population with a say in government or respect the rights of people – the survival mechanism launched by Locke. Political regimes may survive because they provide for a *Rechtsstaat*, according to the interpretation by Kant (1999). Rule of law is a powerful survival mechanism, especially when combined with democracy as conceived by Rousseau.

Thus, we arrive at two main evolutionary mechanisms that explain regime survival as well as the decay or death of regimes today, namely polity capacity and rule of law. If a regime provides for political stability as well as delivering public services and affluence like the oil monarchies in the Gulf, then its viability is not threatened by the lack of rule of law. Regimes which rely too much on repression may crumble quickly, however, due to the lack of rule of law and citizen participation, such as the communist regimes in Eastern Europe. Dictatorships are extremely vulnerable when they cannot deliver services or a decent level of existence to its population, as is the case in several countries in Africa and Asia. Democracies with a good performance record in terms of affluence and public services would be the most viable political regimes, given that they can handle external threats. Thus, we arrive at the hardly surprising conclusion that the United States of America is the regime that displays the highest fitness, combining rule of law with internal order as well as extreme military capability. However, small democracies also score high on regime fitness if they face no serious external threat. Regimes that are neither democracies nor able to secure internal stability will go under, for instance, Zaire under Mobuto.

Political regimes feed on legitimacy, which is a general belief among the population in the acceptability of the rulers. Legitimacy may have several

Table 7.1 Regime fitness: capacity and rights

		Capacity	
		Low	High
R I I G T S	Small Large	Zaire Weimar Republic	Saudia Arabia US

sources, where Weber identified three, namely tradition, religion and law. Charismatic authority with Weber is rulership based on a belief in the ultimate values of the regime, as with Muslim regimes based on Islam. In Muslim countries government is supposed to serve religious ends, such as the maintenance of Sharia Law. Legitimacy, however, is related to system capacity and the rule of law in shaping polity fitness. Even if a regime attempts to maximise charismatic authority based on religion or nationalism, it cannot survive if it fails to deliver or becomes too oppressive.

A theory of regime fitness would thus have two principal factors: capacity and rights, which today would correspond to political stability on the one hand and rule of law on the other. Thus, we are able to combine these two sources of regime survival (see Table 7.1).

From a principal–agent perspective, the population would – all other things being equal – want to have a political authority that is able to guarantee law and order as well as peace externally. A regime that achieves this in an efficient manner will persist. This is a necessary condition. In addition, the principal would want his/her political agents to represent his/her views in policy-making and legislation. A sufficient condition for regime persistence would then be to follow principal–agent theory that government is not only effective but also offers rights, i.e. rule of law. Political legitimacy derives from the belief that what the rulers do is acceptable as morally binding, which is likely to occur when there is rule of law.

Political efficiency and legitimacy may clash, as in revolutionary periods of politics. The tension between a repressive regime and revolutionary groups would at the end of the day lead to either one going under. Rule of law offers a possibility for peaceful political transition and social change.

Conclusion

Political regimes have changed time and again throughout the known history of human civilisations – polity innovations or *mutations*, as it were. Speculating about the driving forces behind polity change, one would want to have a theory about political system viability, or polity adaptability. Polities may fail to survive for two sets of reasons, one relating to capacity – internal or external – and another relating to rights. Polity capacity versus human rights are the two chief evolutionary mechanisms, I would suggest. The belief that only democracy is an evolutionary mechanism expresses not only a Western bias, but it is also out of touch with reality in Africa and Asia. What makes regimes go under in several parts of the world is not their lack of democraticness, but the fact that they cannot guarantee political stability.

Enquiring into regime fitness, one would wish to focus upon some of the main types of political regimes that have appeared during known human history. Here is a tentative list:

- The city-state versus Oriental despotism
- Feudalism: Western, Eastern and modern
- The nation-state and colonial empires
- Rule of law regimes versus authoritarian regimes
- Leagues, regional and international regimes.

Only the nation-state and the totalitarian regime are truly innovations. Despotism, feudalism, empires and leagues of states are to be found all through human history. I will argue that the Roman Republic at its peak with Cicero approached a rule of law regime, despite the omnipresence of slavery. Modern despotism is called totalitarianism – a failed mutation – and it will be analysed below with the Hitler and Stalin regimes as prototypes. Of course, the totalitarian regime brought the extent and arbitrariness of power to its extreme. They are marginal polities, as dictatorship tends to take the form of an authoritarian regime.

Various forms of feudal regimes occurred to a high extent in agricultural society, which was the prevailing form of social system up until the Industrial Revolution. Feudalism could be centripetal, resulting in despotic regimes as in the Romanov, Ottoman or Mughal empires, or feudalism could be centrifugal, leading to the regime of semi-independent principalities as in Germany. Industrial and urban society has a different mechanism of politics leading to the mobilisation of the population with a claim of the population to participate in legitimate government. Tocqueville has spelled out this dichotomy between agrarian politics on the one hand and urban or industrial politics on the other hand already in his two books *Democracy in the United States* from 1835 and 1840 respecively (Tocqueville, 1990): the aristocratic society versus the democratic society.

The city-state and Oriental despotism such as the Pharoahs and Persia belong to the Ancient era with a commercial economy based on slavery. Various forms of feudal regimes are the typical ways of governing an agrarian society. Feudalism encompasses both centralised regimes as well as a political system of decentralised principalities. The industrial society may be governed by democracy or dictatorship. The political evolutionary path has brought mankind to one successful regime, namely the rule of law polities in open socities. At the beginning of the twenty-first century, it has to be combined with international regimes, as the nation-state is no longer viable. All these polities that exist today have ancestors known throughout the history of human civilisation. I will discuss their advantages and disadvantages through an evolutionary account of the emergence of some such polities. Thus, I will provide an overview of the evolutionary mechanisms that operate behind polity transformation or polity mutations.

Political regimes rise and fall. Why? Is regime change a stochastic process where political regimes naturally die after a number of years? One could perhaps say that a political regime could not possibly live for more than about 200 to 300 years, as history teaches us. There have occurred many regime changes, as many countries have experienced the transition from one regime to another. Is there some evolutionary logic involved in regime change? Just as species evolve according to their Mendel-Darwin logic, and economic regimes change according to their transaction cost logic (North, 1990, 2005), so political regimes must come and go according to certain reasons. The first and most basic reason for regime change is violence. Politics is to a large extent a zero-sum game where the stronger prevails. War has been an ever-present aspect of social life. Governments have as their first task the promotion of external security. When political regimes fail in this task, then they succumb to foreign intruders or internal disorder. Yet, war and the capacity to engage in warfare or defend oneself against foreign threats is not the only reason for regime evolution. In addition, there are domestic ones that arise from the principal–agent considerations inherent in government, i.e. when rulers or politicians rule or govern a population, the people.

8 The concept of a polity

From the city-state to the empire

Introduction

In political evolution it is the regime which changes, or evolves, from one type to another. Thus, political evolution is about polity change and development. The main forms of polity that mankind has employed since the dawn of civilisation may be identified through an inspection of the history of polities. Thus, I will look for the mechanisms that account for polity evolution, from the Greek city-state to the modern nation-state. In order to gain an impression of the meanings of the word "polity", one may consult a few definitions from the literature. Wikipedia lists the following meanings for "polity":

1   The political organisation of a group. It covers not only a loosely organised society such as a tribe or community, but may also include any political group including a government or empire.
2   Religious political organisations, particularly Christian, such as subtypes of polities: hierarchical, presbyterial and congregational.
3   The rule by the many, who are neither wealthy nor poor, in the interests of the whole community – Aristotle's definition.

Here, I will focus on the first definition of "polity". The key concepts here are jurisdiction, organisation and authority. By "jurisdiction" is meant the territory of a polity, which may be minuscule as with the city-state or imperial as with the colonial systems. In a jurisdiction, the authority will be exercised by a group of people who may be recruited in a monarchical, aristocratic or democratic manner. Finally, the rulers of a polity whether a monarch, oligarchy or a demos will need an administration to effectuate governance, which may be either patrimonial, vassallic or bureaucratic. The aim of this chapter and the following ones is to exemplify these concepts and discuss their relevance for understanding the evolution of polities.

In Greek political philosophy, the pros and cons of two types of polities were much discussed, namely the city-state and the empire. Neither of these two types has much relevance today. One must reflect on their lack of viability or low survival fitness capacity.

The Greek heritage

Dictionaries presenting entries for "polity" link the concept with Aristotle. "Polity", like "politics", has a common source in Greek conceptions of the polis, or the city-state and its governance. Aristotle wrote two treatises on the city-state – *The Politics* and the *The Athenian Constitution*. The regimes discussed in relation to the city-state were monarchy, aristocracy or oligarchy and democracy, but the empire as a political regime was also examined in Greek political philosophy, especially with the great historians and in Hellenistic philosophies.

Aristotle: the "polis"

The Greek philosophy of the city-state along the lines outlined by Aristotle has played a major role in general Western political philosophy as well as within one special school, namely *republicanism*. Aristotle speaks of *politikê* or politics that is short for *politikê epistêmê* = "political science". Politics was for Aristotle a practical science, seeking to reform political systems towards more of human happiness. Aristotle compares the politician to a craftsman, as the framer and maintainer of the constitution. The political scientist must examine all existing constitutions, even the bad ones, and be knowledgeable about political change, i.e. the forces that undermine an existing regime. Important tasks for the politician derive from the role of lawgiver, i.e. to frame the appropriate constitution for the city-state comprising considerations about laws, customs and institutions. Once the constitution is in place, the politician needs to maintain it and to introduce reforms to prevent developments, which might subvert the polity. When things go wrong, only the lawgiver can deliver the necessary repairs.

The constitution is not merely a written document, but hands down the real rules of politics, constituting "the way of life" of the citizens. The citizens are that minority of the resident population who are adults with full political rights. Thus, the city-state is made up of households or economic classes (e.g. the rich and the poor), or demes (i.e. local political units). The moral education of citizens towards the goal of perfection and happiness is the aim of the city-state. The constitution outlines the governing body, which varies according to the goal served by the community. Aristotle distinguishes between six types of regime on the basis of the distinction between the correct and deviant implementation of the common goal. Hence there are six possible constitutional forms, according to his schema, which have recurred time and again in political thought (Table 8.1).

Aristotle's inquiry into the constitution, where he employed empirical observations, led him towards his recommendation of the *best* as well as

Table 8.1 Aristotles' typology (number and common good)

Number	Correct goals	Deviant goals
One ruler	Kingship	Tyranny
Few rulers	Aristocracy	Oligarchy
Many rulers	Polity	Democracy

the *second-best* regime. The dominant class in oligarchy is typically the wealthy, whereas in democracy it is the poor. Aristotle's best constitution – aristocracy – presupposes that each and every citizen possesses moral virtue and can and will carry it out in practice, so as to attain a life of excellence and complete happiness. The citizens will hold political office and possess private property. Yet there must be a common system of education for all the citizens, because they must share the same end. His second-best system takes the form of a polity in which citizens possess an inferior virtue within a *mixed constitution*, combining features of democracy, monarchy and aristocracy, so that no group of citizens is in a position to abuse its rights – further developed by Polybius (1970) in his interpretation of Roman republicanism as well as revived in Renaissance republicanism.

The communitarian theory of Aristotle was challenged by other currents in late Greek moral philosophy as well as within Roman political thought: epicurism and stoicism. Here, I will deal with the opposite concept of a polity, namely the empire. One finds a theory of the Persian Empire with Herodotus. By the sixth century a few cities had emerged as dominant in Greek affairs: Athens, Sparta, Corinth and Thebes, controlling the surrounding rural areas and smaller towns. A city-state was sovereign, although many cities were joined in formal or informal leagues under a high king such as the Peloponnesian League. The Greek cities were originally monarchies, as power rested with a small class of landowners who formed a warrior aristocracy on the basis of land ownership and use. The rise of a mercantile class during the seventh century BC led to class conflict in the cities. From 650 onwards, the aristocracies were overthrown and replaced by populist leaders called tyrants (*tyrranoi*). Yet the landed aristocracy in Sparta retained their power, as the constitution of Lycurgus (about 650) entrenched their power and gave Sparta a permanent militarist regime under a dual monarchy. In Athens, by contrast, the monarchy was abolished in 683, and the reforms of Solon established a semi-constitutional system of aristocratic government. When tyrant Pisistratids was overthrown, Cleisthenes established the world's first democracy (500), with power being held by an assembly of all the male citizens.

The Greek city-states proved efficient in rejecting the Persian onslaught, because they entered into a league combining their forces both at land and sea. However, they could not resist the Macedonian intrusion into Greek politics. Already, 150 years after the decisive Greek victories over the Persians, there was an empire in place, namely the Hellenistic Empire of Alexander the Great. And the history of the Ancient period thereafter up until the fall of the Roman Empire is the struggle for imperial power, where the city-states proved too small, lacking the capacity to stay independent. The viability of the city-state is thus linked with its capacity, especially its external capacity. Today, only a few city-states exist (e.g. Singapore). Why? Let me mention a few famous city-states in the twentieth century and how they were merged into other polities, first and foremost the nation-state.

Survival fitness of city-states

The medieval tradition of free cities, independent of their surrounding terrain, outlived the German Empire's demise in 1806. Yet, circumstances left several self-governing enclaves, in each case centred on a city such as Fiume, Danzig, Memel and Trieste as well as Tangier. None of them survived as a city-state, but each caused considerable conflict among nation-states.

The Adriatic port of Trieste, in the province of Venezia Giulia, was the chief port of Austria prior to the First World War. The population of the region was predominantly Italian. The Italian army conquered Venezia Giulia during the First World War, and it became part of Italy after the war. At the end of the Second World War in May 1945, Yugoslav troops captured the city. After the war, Trieste and the surrounding territory became the Free Territory of Trieste under United Nations protection during 1947 to 1954. In 1954, the city reverted to Italy, while the surroundings became part of the Yugoslavian republic of Slovenia.

The Adriatic port of Fiume on the Istrian peninsula was under Habsburg rule from 1466. Today, it is the Croatian city of Rijeka. Croats predominated in the city's population until the nineteenth century, when the Austro-Hungarian monarchy began to encourage Italian immigration to check the rise of Slavic nationalism. Italy signed a secret treaty with the Allies in 1915, in which Italy was promised the Habsburg lands on the Adriatic in return for active military support on the Allied side. Wilson believed the city should be given to the new Kingdom of Serbs, Croats and Slovenes. However, poet D'Annunzio organised a paramilitary force of demobilised soldiers – the Arditi. D'Annunzio remained dictator until December 1920 when the Italian government sent a battleship into Fiume. D'Annunzio surrendered, and Fiume was proclaimed a "free state" under a provisional government. In 1924 Mussolini negotiated the Treaty of Rome by which the Kingdom of Serbs, Croats and Slovenes ceded Fiume to Italy. After the Second World War the Italian population was evacuated and the city was handed over to Yugoslavia.

Danzig, or Gdansk on the Baltic Sea in West Prussia, had an overwhelmingly German population of about 400,000. The re-emergence of a

Polish nation after the First World War left large German minorities living in Polish territory. West Prussia became the Polish Corridor to the Baltic Sea, cutting East Prussia off from the rest of Germany. The League of Nations created Danzig as a free city, but it satisfied neither the Poles (who needed the city's port facilities) nor the German population. On 1 September 1939, Germany invaded Poland, and Danzig was temporarily restored to Germany. In December 1943 the city was occupied by the Red Army and the German population was soon to be expelled to Germany.

Memel was founded in 1252 by the Teutonic Knights on the Baltic Sea, a holdover of the Hanseatic League, isolated within Lithuanian territory. Memel was detached from Germany by the Treaty of Versailles and was governed by an Allied and Associated Powers Commission. In January 1923, Lithuania invaded Memel and expelled the French garrison. In 1924 the League of Nations acknowledged the *fait accompli*, and Memel was incorporated into Lithuania as a semi-autonomous district. In March 1939, Hitler sent German warships to Memel and Lithuania surrendered the city. After the war, the German population was expelled, since the city was returned to Lithuania as the city of Klaipeda.

Tangier was given special status when the Sultanate of Morocco was divided into French and Spanish zones under the Treaty of Fez in 1912. The Convention of 1923 made Tangier an international zone, governed by a legislative assembly of foreign representatives from Britain, France, Spain, Portugal, Italy, Belgium, Netherlands, Sweden and the United States. Executive power was vested in the Committee of Control composed *inter alia* of the consuls of the signatory powers. Mixed courts with French, Spanish, British and Belgian judges administered justice, and Arabs as well as Jews had their own court systems. Foreign powers operated a number of postal systems in the city, and Spain, France and Britain issued stamps for Tangier. After a period of effective Spanish control from 1940 to 1945 during the Second World War, Tangier was reunited with independent Morocco in 1956.

A few interesting examples of city-states are to be found in South East Asia. Hong Kong and Macao were not really states, and today they constitute special administrative regions (SAR) in China. Hong Kong achieved economic success while a British crown colony. As a special administrative region of China it enjoys considerable autonomy, but it cannot hold free and fair elections to its legislature and the governor is appointed by the central government in Beijing. The same applies to the old gambling town of Macao – a former Portuguese colony. How could Hong Kong and Singapore reach such economic success? As city-states with a big harbour they could concentrate on economic development through massive imports and exports in an economically dynamic region – *entrepôt stations*.

Singapore is the most successful city-state, comprising more than four million inhabitants in a tiny portion of territory cut out from the Malaysian peninsula. Although Singapore has free and fair elections within a parliamentary system of government, it does not rank in the top part of the standard indicators of democracy. This city-state has only one major political party, the National Party, and power has remained concentrated around a group with the family of Lee Kuan Yew for decades. This does not entail that Singapore does not have considerable rule of law, albeit its politics lacks contestation.

Herodotus: the empire

Herodotus' work, *The History*, tells the story of the war between the huge Persian Empire and the much smaller Greek city-states. In itself it is an exciting story, but the book is significant for its method of enquiry as well as for its scope, covering the entire Eastern Mediterranean world from the time of the Lydian Empire (*c.*672 BC) to the defeat of Xerxes in 479 BC, discussing the customs of the Egyptians, the Hittites, and most of the peoples withwhom the Greeks would have come into contact. This encyclopedia of the Ancient Mediterranean comprises the theme of the struggle between the East and the West. The East, represented by the Persian Empire, signifies tyranny and oppression, while the West, represented by the Greek city-states, stands for freedom. Thus it is said that the Persian Wars constitute the beginnings of Western civilisation and its vital connection with freedom. In Ionia on the Aegean coast of modern Turkey, the Greek cities were unable to maintain their independence, falling to the rule of the Persian Empire in the mid-sixth century. In 499 the Greeks rose in the Ionian Revolt, supported by Athens. Xerxes I sent a powerful force by land against Greece, after being delayed by the Spartan King Leonidas at Thermopile, and Xerxes captured Athens. Yet the Athenians under Themistocles defeated the Persian fleet at the Sea Battle of Salamis in 480. A year later the Greeks under the Spartan Pausanius defeated the Persian army at Plataea. However, the defeat of the Persian Empire was to be followed by developments which paved the way for the elimination of the independence of the city-states in the wake of the Hellenistic era.

Herodotus asked himself how the tiny Greek city-states could defeat a giant empire. He pointed at the inherent weakness of all empires, namely the extreme role that the ruler himself plays for good and bad as well as the lack of motivation among his troops, who are often forced to fight. The competence of his generals would be compromised at one stage or another through mistakes by the ruler or by court intrigues. Herodotus states, allowing first the emperor Xerxes to speak:

> Tell me, therefore, what thinkest thou? Will the Greeks lift a hand against us? Mine own judgement is, that even if all the Greeks and all the barbarians of the West were gathered together in one place,

they would not be able to abide by my onset, not being really of one mind.

Herodotus then provides the Greek view by letting Demartus speak the following:

> Brave are all the Greeks who dwell in any Dorian land; but what I am about to say does not concern all, but only the Lacedaemonians. First then, come what may, they will never accept thy terms, which would reduce Greece to slavery; and further, they are sure to join battle with thee, though all the rest of the Greeks should submit to thy will.
>
> (Herodotus, 1952: 232–233)

Freedom defeats tyranny, at least as long as there is Sparta, Herodotus teaches, and he reminds us of Demartus' conversation with Xerxes when the final moment of total defeat for the "barbarians" has come. However, soon after the victory of the Persians, the Greeks tumbled into a vicious civil war, which brought down the free city-states.

Thucydides: the notion of hegemony

The Persian wars opened up Athenian dominance of Greek affairs with Athens as the unchallenged master of the sea, and also the leading commercial power, although Corinth remained a serious rival. Athens enrolled all the island states and some mainland allies into an alliance, called the Delian League, as its treasury was kept on the sacred island of Delos. Pericles used the tribute paid by the members of the Delian League to build the Parthenon. By the mid-fifth century, the League had become the Athenian Empire, symbolised by the transfer of the League's treasury to the Parthenon in 454.

The other Greek states at first accepted Athenian leadership, but after the fall of the conservative politician Cimon in 461, Athens became an increasingly imperialist power. Some states, such as Naxos, tried in vain to secede from the League. Relations between Athens and Sparta deteriorated until war broke out in 458. The end of the Peloponnesian War left Sparta as the master of Greece, but Sparta then attempted to weaken her former ally Thebes, which led to a war againt Thebes, now allied with the old enemy, Athens. The Theban generals Epaminondas and Pelopidas won a decisive victory at Leuctra (371). Thucydides was an Athenian, famous for writing *The Peloponnesian War*, based on the realisation that war had come to be fought over a new concept in the Greek world, namely hegemony. What emerges from his analysis is a sharp warning against the destruction of war and the perils of searching for hegemony. For instance, Thucydides tells of how Athens behaved against one of its allies, the Melians, who refused to give in to the demand for imperial power:

and you will not think it dishourable to submit to the greatest city in Hellas, when it makes you the moderate offer of becoming its tributary ally, without ceasing to enjoy the country that belongs to you; nor when you have the choice given you between war and security, will you be so blinded as to choose the worse.

According to Thucydides the Melians responded: "We will not in a moment deprive of freedom a city that has been inhabited these seven hundred years.... Meanwhile we invite you to allow us to be friends to you and foes to nether party." This answer provoked a terrible response, as "Athenians put to death all the grown men whom they took, and sold the women and the children for slaves, and subsequently sent out five hundred colonists and inhabited the place themselves" (Thucydides, 1952: 507–508).

Emergence of the Hellenistic empires and *Pax Romana*

The Greeks tended to regard the Macedonians as barbarians, although they belonged to Greek language and culture by the fifth century. They played little part in Greek politics until after the Peleponnesian War. Theban dominance followed the end of Spartan supremacy, but Athens also recovered much of her former power. The supremacy of Thebes was short-lived, as in 346 the Thebans appealed to Philip II of Macedon to help them against the Phocians, pulling Macedon into Greek affairs. Philip established Macedonian dominance, but Athenian Demosthenes in a series of famous speeches (*philippics*) roused the Greek cities to resist. In 339 Thebes, Athens, Sparta and other Greek states formed an alliance to resist Philip. The Greek defeat at Chaeronea in 338 marked the end of the era of the Greek city-state as a powerful political unit, although in fact Athens and other cities survived as independent states until Roman times.

In 334 Alexander crossed into Asia and defeated the Persians. Alexander's empire broke up soon after his death, but his conquests permanently changed the Greek world, introducing the Hellenistic empires. Greeks travelled to settle in the new Greek cities Alexander founded, for instance, Alexandria in Egypt. The Hellenistic age, ushering in a period of new empires, suffocated the city-states until one city-state created one empire covering most of the Western world under the concept of *Pax Romana*. The Roman Empire is especially interesting from the point of view of survival fitness. A huge debate has raged concerning the causes of the decline and fall of the Roman Empire. It may be linked with the debate on the fundamental weaknesses of all ancient empires in the form of the theory of Oriental despotism, but Rome was as a matter of fact an early site for republicanism and the rule by law, although it degenerated into Oriental despotism under the emperors (Rostovtseff, 1988).

Rome and Pax Romana

The founding of Rome is uncertain. The Romans believed that their city was founded in the year 753 BC, but modern historians believe it was the year 625 BC. Kings governed early Rome, but after seven of them had ruled, the Romans took power over their own city and ruled themselves, focusing power in a council known as the "Senate", which ruled over them in the form of the "Roman Republic". The word "Republic" comes from the Latin "*res publica*" meaning "public matters" or "matters of state". The Senate appointed a consul, who ruled Rome like a king, but only for one year. There were clear definitions of offices and a transparent erection of counter-weighting powers between both the top positions such as the Consul, *Praetor*, *Quaestor*, Promagistrate, *Aedile*, *Tribune*, Censor, Governor and *Dictator* on the one hand but also between the Senate and the *People's Assembly* on the other.

Rome knew four social classes. The lowest class were the slaves with no rights at all. The next class were the *plebeians*. Although free people, they had little say at all. The second highest class were the *equestrians*, as they were given a horse to ride if called to fight for Rome. An equestrian was usually rich. Real power in Rome belonged to the highest class, called "*patricians*". The Roman Republic was a very successful government, lasting from 510 BC until 23 BC – almost 500 years. It was based on a republican concept of government, which continued to be an ideal long after the republic had been replaced by the empire with an emperor.

Roman republicanism was heavily institutionalised with a rule of law approach to government involving a concept of citizenship and the separation of powers. However, the period of civil war in the first century BC led to permanent dictatorship in the form of the emergence of an emperor, anticipated by Julius Caesar, a Roman politician and a successful general who conquered the vast territory of the Gauls. In the year 49 BC, Caesar crossed the small river between his province and Italy, *Rubicon*, and conquered Rome itself as lifetime dictator. He was murdered in the Senate in Rome in 43 BC, but Roman republicanism could not be saved. Cicero, the great defender of republicanism in a series of books, was simply put to death (Grimal, 1986; Cicero, 1998). Roman republicanism was revived in Italian city-states such as Florentine, Genoa and Venice, where institutions for representative government and the separation of powers became very much alive in the medieval and Renaissance period.

The Roman Empire started to suffer from the instability typical of despotic rule, as some of its emperors were not up to the task of governing *Pax Romana*. In the end, it was overrun by a long series of barbarian tribes from the North and East of Europe. The great migrations proved too much for the Romans to stem. Their armies were designed to defeat other armies, not entire folks or peoples. The collapse was complete when the Visigoth Odoacer sacked Rome itself in 476. What is generally referred to as "the Fall of Rome" bypasses the fact that the Eastern empire with its centre in Constantinople managed to cling on for almost another thousand years in the form of the Byzantine polity. It was eventually extinguished by the Turks in the year AD 1453, paving the way for the empire of the Ottomans.

The decline of the Roman Empire has given rise to a vivid debate about the strengths and weaknesses of the Roman polities, which may be restated in terms of survival and polity fitness. The immense growth of the power of the Roman republic derived from both its capacity and its republican ethos, institutionalised in the classic Roman constitution, which entailed elements of rule of law. The Roman Empire failed to maintain the institutional asset of the republic, as various emperors were engulfed in despotic rule. Similarly, the ethos of the republic was attenuated when Rome became the centre of the entire Western civilisation, its military forces no longer relying upon recruits from Rome but being increasingly dependent upon mercenaries and barbarians. Gibbon in his classic study (1776) linked the decline of the Roman Empire with: (1) the invasion of the barbarians, and (2) the growth of Christianity within the Empire. The other-worldly attitude of early Christianity hurt the Empire during the barbarian invasions, since it diverted men from bearing arms to serve the *public* state and encouraged them to concentrate on *private* salvation. Yet, the Gibbon argument has been questioned, as a Christian Roman empire could have resisted the onslaught of barbarians. Economic historians such as Weber and Rostovseff searched for the causes of this lack of survival capacity in the decline of the urban centres and the commercial economy, draining the taxation resources of the Empire (Rostovtseff, 1930–1933; Weber, 1998). The countryside with its agrarian economy became increasingly important, centred upon the huge manors where the slave workers became settled for life in the form of serfs. Such a fundamental change in the economic structure of the Roman Empire precipitated the arrival of the feudal agrarian polity in Western Europe.

Conclusion

Two polity types occurred frequently in the Ancient period with the Greeks and the Romans, namely the city-state and the empire. These polity types are less relevant today, because nation-states have replaced them to a large extent. What is almost entirely lacking today is one of the key features of ancient political systems, namely large-scale slavery as well as large-scale traffic in slave commerce. City-states hardly occur today, but they had a long period of flourishing in Italy from the fall of the Roman Empire up until the unification of Italy under Cavour and Garibaldi. The list of magnificent city-states includes the republics of Venice and Florence. Yet nation-states have proved to be much more viable than city-states. In some of the city-states representative institutions survived for a long time, Italian republicanism being one of the major sources of rule of law.

The regime type of ancient empire has occurred often and in many places, but each had a short time span. What explains this typical short-term survival pattern: sudden rise, temporary expansion and quick decline? Not only did the Greek city-state defeat the Persian Empire, but the empires defeated each other in constant wars. The theory of the ancient empires is called *oriental despotism*, and it covers numerous empires on other continents besides the Middle East and Europe, such as pre-Colombian America, China, South Asia and South East Asia as well as Africa.

9 The ancient empires

Oriental despotism or the patrimonial state

Introduction

One finds many examples of empires in the history of mankind, most of which were of short duration. A few managed to stay alive for a few centuries, for instance, the long-lived Ottoman Empire. Many empires went under only to be replaced by new ones – *dynasties*. In Central and South America a few empires emerged which have aroused much attention. Yet before them there were many other less well-known empires in this part of the world. Even though some empires flourished for some time, their inherent weaknesses proved destructive.

Let me look briefly at these ancient empires to see whether they fit the picture drawn by Wittfogel (1957). His analysis of oriental despotism entails that these polities could maintain themselves as long as they successfully regulated the chief means of their existence, i.e. access to water. However, what is typical of Oriental despotism wherever it occurs – in Asia with the Khmer Empire, in Angkor and the Chinese dynasties, as well as the Indian Empires in Central and South America – is the resort to Pharaonic styles of capital city construction. It remains to be investigated whether these monumental buildings always served the single purpose of the regulation of water demand and supply – the hydraulic hypothesis.

Wittfogel's theory should be contrasted with Weber's emphasis upon the inherent administrative weakness of patrimonial domination. Although Weber anticipated Wittfogel and his insistence upon the control of water as a major concern in Oriental despotism, he saw all forms of patrimonial rule, whether in the occident or in the Orient, as fundamentally inefficient. Let me start with Wittfogel and then bring up Weber, although Wittfogel was to some extent a pupil of Weber. The purpose of this chapter is to illustrate what Oriental despotism amounted to as well as to discuss whether its survival fitness depended upon the hydraulic mechanism of Wittfogel or the administrative inefficiency of the patrimonial polity with Weber.

Wittfogel

Many ancient empires have taken the polity shape of Oriental despotism, a concept already identified by Weber in his theory about authority. The label "Oriental despotism" covers rulerships to be found in the Americas, Egypt, Mesopotamia, China and India as well as Africa. Weber suggested that basic economic forces relating to the production of food were involved behind the façade of Oriental despotism. In his *General Economic History* (2003a), Weber anticipated Wittfogel's hydraulic hypothesis, stating:

> Irrigation and its regulation presupposed a systematic and organised husbandry out of which the large scale royal enterprise of the near east developed, as is shown most characteristically in the New Empire of Thebes. The military campaigns of the Assyrian and Babylonian kings, which they undertook with their masses of retainers going back to the men's house system, were primarily man hunts for the purpose of securing the human material for building canals and bringing stretches of the desert under tillage.

The patrimonial regime was nourished by public organisation of the economy as a giant household. Thus, the need for irrigation led to bureaucratic organisation. Weber continued:

> The king retained control of water regulations, but required for its exercise an organised bureaucracy. The agricultural and irrigation bureaucracies of Egypt and Mesopotamia, the foundation of which is thus economic, are the oldest officialdom in the world; it remains throughout its history an adjunct of the king's personal economic enterprise.
>
> (Weber, 2003a: 56–57)

Wittfogel, emphasising irrigation more than officialdom, developed the concept of a hydraulic regime in his *magnum opus: Oriental Despotism*. Wittfogel's scholarly interest in China began with his studies at Leipzig University in 1914, and in 1920 he joined the German Communist Party, continuing his studies in history, economics and psychology at several German universities. Wittfogel theorised early that the control of the water supply for irrigation was the basis of the "Asiatic mode of production" involving a powerful, exploitative bureaucracy with "hydraulic monopoly". In 1924 Wittfogel joined the Institute of Social Research in Frankfurt, suggesting the significance of water control in Asian agriculture for the establishment of a "hydraulic bureaucracy" ruling the country. Arrested in 1933 by the Nazis, Wittfogel left Germany for London in 1934. He later secured support from Columbia University to undertake research on China to substantiate the hydraulic hypothesis, which is relevant for a survival theory of regimes. The *"hydraulic hypothesis"* states that the development of the ancient empires had become blocked due to the need to irrigate vast surfaces for agriculture. Water control and distribution necessitated authoritarian centralisation and huge bureaucracies. Western Europe was free from such limitations. Wittfogel identified the centralised and bureaucratic empire as the one blocking element for Chinese science, technology and economic development. The theory of Oriental despotism appears to be appropriate mainly for regimes based on an agrarian economy with a large component of slavery. Within an agricultural society, rulers in the capital seek to monopolise power in order to collect economic rents from the peasants or agrarian labour. They can of course do so without operating vast irrigation schemes. New empires in the form of Western colonialism had an entirely different foundation, as they benefited from Western advances in warfare, industrialisation and state administration.

The theory of Oriental despotism is supposed to be applicable to all kinds of empires of the old agrarian style. But how valid is Wittfogel's hypothesis about the necessity of large-scale hydraulic management? Can the ancient empire be fully or chiefly attributed to the need for irrigation? In fact, water management in China was often small scale and local in execution. Similarly, Wittfogel's hydraulic theory does not explain the chronic backwardness of Eastern Europe, similar to Western Europe in its non-irrigated agriculture. If the hydraulic hypothesis must be supplemented by other factors than irrigation, then how can we account for the ancient empires? Finer (1997a, 1997b) states that they all suffered from the problem of *palace politics*, meaning that the central administration at the realm would from time to time be invaded by strange anomalies such as the dementia of the sultan (Ottomans), the intervention of eunuchs or the control of slave soldiers (Mamelukes) as well as the peculiar influence of the family clan of the Chinese emperor or Russian tsar.

Weber

Weber's well-known theory of authority is evolutionary in its intent. It focuses upon the alternative means or tools of administration that rulers have employed to get their decisions enforced in a jurisdiction, arguing that only a bureaucracy leads to stable, predictable and efficient implementation. Weber's theory is summarised in Table 9.1.

Weber wrote succinctly about the administrative problem in the patrimonial state: Perhaps it was the inherent weakness in patrimonial administration that made the ancient empires unstable? The focus on the centralised regulation of water in the theory of Oriental despotism should be balanced by the underlining of the general limits to the administrative capacity of the patrimonial state. Even when there was an abundant supply of water as in the Ottoman Empire, China and the tsarist dynasties, the regime proceeded inefficiently to handle the challenges from the environment.

Table 9.1 Evolution of authority from patrimonial to legal-rational authority

Rulers	*Servants*	*Population*
Patrimonial:		
1 Kings, emperors amirs, sultans	Personal ties	Submission Bondage
2 Feudalism	Vassalage	Serfage
Charismatic	Disciples	Faith
Bureaucratic	Civil Servants	Citizenship, rights

Irrigation and the supply of fresh water is only one of the chief aspects of the history of ancient empires, when they were situated in the tropical or arid zones of the globe.

Weber's analysis of the patrimonial state pin-points the personal nature of this administration. Thus, Pharaonic or Ptolemaian Egypt appears as the extreme case of a single powerful *oikos* or household, ruled patrimonially by one man. The Inca state resembles extreme patrimonialism. The political realm of a ruler comprised not only his manors (*patrimonium*) but also the political dependencies on which taxes could be levied (*imperium*). The power of Oriental sultans and Far Eastern rulers centred on great patrimonial domains: "In these latter cases the political realm as a whole is approximately identical with a huge princely manor" (Weber, 1978: 1013). He continues:

> Originally patrimonial administration was adapted to the satisfaction of purely personal, primarily private household needs of the master. The establishment of a "political" domination, that is, of one master's domination over other masters who are not subject to his patriarchal power implies an affiliation of authority relations which differ only in degree and content, not in structure.
>
> (Weber, 1978: 1013)

Oriental despotism is intimately linked with the existence of a palace administration of the realm, which tends to be based on personal ties between the rulers and their servants (*major domus*). These ties originate in the conception of the realm as a household (*oikos*). Only in high medieval feudalism did there emerge a balance of power between the king and his lords, governing the fiefs of the realm, meaning reciprocity under the law. As long as the central administration did not evolve into a formal bureaucracy based upon competence and technology, the governance of the realm remained amateurish and thus inefficient. Herein lies the lack of survival fitness of patrimonialism.

Let me now substantiate this contrast between Wittfogel's theory of the hydraulic mechanism of Oriental despotism with Weber's focus upon the inefficiency of patrimonial authority. I will conduct a few short overviews of some old empires in history to see what evidence they may offer for deciding in favour of Weber or Wittfogel, starting with the pre-Columbian empires, moving to the African scene and ending with China and Mughal India. If such a short overview of the immensely detailed history of these ancient empires can help establish a few salient features of them, then many of the simplifications below may be excusable.

The Aztecs

The known history of the Tenochcas starts in 1168 on an island in the middle of a lake north of the Valley of Mexico. In 1248 they arrived in the Valley of Mexico and in 1300 some Tenochcas settled on an island in the middle of the lake, called "Tenochtitlan" meaning the place of the Tenochcas. The Tenochcas made allies in the constant conflicts between the various peoples of the area. It was not until Itzacoatl (1428–1440) that they really began to build their huge city, Tenochtitlan, where they established their government and religious hierarchy. The need for an aqueduct system to bring water from the mainland became obvious as conquests throughout the Valley of Mexico and the southern regions of Vera Cruz, Guerrero and Puebla resulted in empire.

Tenochtitlan was one of the biggest metropolises in the world at the time. The economy of Tenochtitlan was founded upon the necessary condition for an ancient empire to thrive, namely that the urban population on the island secured the material support from surrounding rural areas. The city comprised a large number of priests and craftspeople. The economy included an extensive trade of both necessary and luxury items. Agriculture was managed through the *chinampa* method, practised widely throughout Mesoamerica, i.e. flat reeds were placed in the shallow areas of the lake, covered with soil and then cultivated. In this way, the Aztecs reclaimed much of the lake for agriculture. When the city was at its largest size, or between 100,000–300,000, perhaps half the population would leave the city in the morning to farm and return in the evening. Tenochtitlan's economy was hydraulic, according to Wittfogel.

Human sacrifice was an integral part of Aztec culture, as blood-letting occurred at religious functions. Such blood-letting was tied to rank: the higher one was in social or priestly rank, the more blood one had to sacrifice. According to the Aztecs, conflicting forces of creation and destruction determined the universe. Humans could influence this balance through sacrifice. If a human being was captured in war, then slavery was a pleasant option, for the purposes of Aztec warfare included the capture of live human sacrifices. Aztec laws were harsh, as many crimes, from adultery to stealing, were punished by death and other offences usually involved severe corporal punishment or mutilation. Slavery was common among the Aztecs. One became a slave by being captured in war, by committing certain crimes, such as theft, by voluntarily entering into slavery, or by being sold by one's parents.

The Spaniards in the *conquista* exploited a large group of subject peoples with no loyalty to Tenochtitlan. Aztec conquest was based on the payment of tribute. The Aztecs had nothing like a formal military strategy. At the very top of the hierarchy was the chief of men, dominating the religious ceremonies and serving as a military leader. Society comprised both commoners and nobility, which two groups were not separated by birth, as skills in warfare led to promotion to the nobility. Despite a half-century of successful growth and conquest, tribute peoples began to revolt in the conquered territories. The invasion of the Spaniards under Cortez in 1519 to 1522 resulted in the fall of the city of Tenochtitlan. The empire of the Aztecs was short and violent. It fell due to its own weaknesses in terms of military capacity. However, it is true that the Aztecs founded a hydraulic civilisation but achieved little in terms of a stable state (Jones and Philips, 2006).

The Mayas

The empire of the Mayas lasted longer than that of the Aztecs. Originating in the Yucatan, the Mayas emerged around AD 250 in present-day southern Mexico, Guatemala, northern Belize and western Honduras. The Maya adopted a hierarchical system of government with rulership by nobles and kings. This civilisation created kingdoms during the Classical period, AD 200–900. The Mayas started to decline around AD 900 when the southern Mayas abandoned their cities. The northern Mayas were integrated into the Toltecs by 1200, but some peripheral centres continued to thrive until the Spanish Conquest in the early sixteenth century. Their society consisted of many independent states, each with a rural farming community and large urban sites built around ceremonial centres (Longhena, 2006).

From the standard accounts of Maya civilisation, one cannot detect that the control of water was the crucial element in this empire. Where ground water was scarce, building sizeable underground reservoirs for the storage of rainwater was achieved. The Mayas were skilled at ceremonial architecture: temple-pyramids, palaces and observatories. They were experienced farmers, clearing large sections of tropical rain forest. They were also weavers and potters, and cleared routes through jungles and swamps to foster extensive trade networks with distant peoples. The temples and pyramids of the Maya are located within the jungles of Mexico and Guatemala, extending into the limestone shelf of the Yucatan peninsula. The Mayas created the one and only true writing system native to the Americas. Knowing mathematics, they invented calendars. They constructed vast cities across a jungle landscape with architectural perfection but little of large scale hydraulic installations. Their legacy in stone is very impressive, but the cause of the demise of the empire is not yet known. Compared with the Incas however, the Mayas lasted longer (Prescott, 1992).

The Incas

Archaeologists studying the Andes region have identified numerous cultures before the Incas, dating back to 9000 BC. The Inca Empire achieved total domination of this region as late as 1493, but already in 1534 the fall of the Inca Empire had occurred. Controlling access to water was essential in the Andes region. Most of the cut-off years in the Peruvian table of cultures mark either the end of a severe drought or the beginning of one. Thus, there were hydraulic features, as the flow of different cultures involved a shift in productive farming to or from the mountains. The Incas began to expand their influence in the twelfth century, ending up controlling more territory than any other people had done in South American history. They were a distinct people with a language of their own living in a highland centre, Cuzco. The empire consisted of over one million individuals, and stretched from Ecuador to northern Chile. In 1438 the Incas set out from their base in Cuzco on a conquest that, during the next 50 years, brought under their control the area of present-day Peru, Bolivia, northern Argentina, Chile and Ecuador (Jones, 2007).

The Incas ruled by proxy, as after conquering a people, they would incorporate local rulers into their imperial system, generously reward anyone who fought for them, and make alliances with those conquered people who cooperated. The empire was a confederation of tribes with a single people, the Incas, in control. A council of elders ruled each of these tribes independently. Each tribe gave its allegiance to the ruler, or "*Inca*". The "Inca" was divine, meaning a descendant of the sun god. The social structure of the Incas was inflexible, with the Inca at the top, who exercised absolute power in principle. Below the Inca was the royal family, which consisted of the Inca's immediate family, concubines, and all his children. This royal family was a ruling aristocracy, as the ruler, *Sapa Inca*, and his wives, the *Coyas*, had supreme control over the empire. The High Priest and the Army Commander in Chief were next, the Four *Apus*, the regional army commanders then the temple priest. Next architects, administrators and army generals. Next were artisans, musicians, army captains and the *quipucamayoc*, the Incan accountants. At the bottom were sorcerers, farmers, herding families and conscripts. The common people were all grouped in squads of ten.

Cusco had advanced hydraulic engineering, agricultural techniques, marvellous architecture, textiles, ceramics and ironworks. The Incas ruled by means of their dexterity in constructing and maintaining roads. One road ran almost the entire length of the South American Pacific coast. The roads took great engineering and architectural skill to build. On the coast, the roads were not surfaced and were marked only by tree trunks. The Incas paved their highland roads with flat stones and built stonewalls to prevent travellers from falling off the cliffs. Communication and transport was efficient and speedy, linking the mountain peoples and lowland desert dwellers with Cuzco. Agriculture was of crucial importance to the Incas, which called for water regulation. They carved up mountains into terraced farmlands, turning steep mountain sides into terraced farms. The Incas cultivated corn and potatoes, and raised llama and alpaca for food and for labour. Given that rain tends to fall in the Andes between December and May and that there could be years of drought, the Incas constructed complex canals to bring water to terraces and other patches of arable land. The inhabitants of the Andean region developed agricultural products such as varieties of corn and potatoes, as well as one or more varieties of squash, beans, peppers, peanuts and cassava (a starchy root), and quinoa, which is made into a cereal. Mountainous terrain limited the land that could be used for agriculture, but the Incas improved the terracing methods invented by pre-Inca civilisations. Terraces created more arable land and prevented the topsoil from washing away in heavy rains. They also made use of natural fertiliser, guano. In the highlands, farmers used the remains of slaughtered llamas as a fertiliser. The Incas were engineers. Conquered people had to pay a labour tax (*mita*) to the state. They built massive forts with stone slabs without mortar as well as terraced farmlands and roads through the mountains from Ecuador to Chile with tunnels and bridges as well as aqueducts to their cities. They had no writing system at all, but kept records on various coloured knotted cords, or *quipu*.

Despite its huge size, the Inca Empire proved easy for the Spanish *conquista* to defeat. Once Pizarro had captured the Incas, all was lost, reflecting the immense dependency of the empire upon hierarchy. The pre-Columbian empires in the Americas resemble the Egyptian Pharaonic or the Persian type of rulership (Achaemenid Dynasty), meaning excessive dependency upon the chief ruler. Let us turn to the African scene and the empires in Western Africa, where no doubt commerce and the trade in slaves played a bigger role than the control of irrigation (Bethell, 1984).

West African empires

Most empires emerging in West Africa were based on Islam. One exception is the kingdom of Aksum that emerged in the sixth century based on trade. It exported ivory, glass crystal, brass and copper items, and slaves. Aksum's port city on the Red Sea, Adulis, bustled with activity. Its agriculture and cattle breeding flourished. Aksum extended its rule to Nubia, across the Red Sea to Yemen, and then to the northern Ethiopian Highlands and along the coast to Cape Guardafui. From Aksum's beginnings in the third century, Christianity had become widespread, but at the peak of Christianity's success, Aksum began its decline. In the late 600s, Aksum's trade was diminished by the clash between Constantinople and the Sassanid Empire over trade on the Red Sea and Yemen. Islam then united Arabia and began its expansion (Iliffe, 1995).

Trade across the Sahara had existed for centuries. In the third century AD Berber nomads began using camels. The camel could plod steadily over much longer distances, covering as much as 60 miles in a day as well as up to ten days without water, twice as long as most pack animals. With the camel, nomads blazed new routes across the desert and trade increased. The two most important trade items were gold and salt. Gold came from a forest region south of the savannah between the Niger and Senegal rivers. Miners dug gold from shafts as deep as 100 feet or sifted it from fast-moving streams. Until about 1350, perhaps two-thirds of the world's supply of gold came from West Africa. Although rich in gold, West Africa's savannah and forests lacked salt, a material essential to human life. The Sahara contained deposits of salt. Arab and Berber traders crossed the desert with camel caravans loaded with salt. They also carried cloth, weapons and manufactured goods from ports on the Mediterranean. After a long journey, they reached the market towns of the savannah. Meanwhile, African traders brought gold north from the forest regions.

By the year 800, Ghana had become an empire. Because Ghana's king controlled trade and commanded a large army, he could demand taxes and gifts from the chiefs of surrounding lands. As long as the chiefs made their payments, the king left them in peace to rule their own people. Eventually, Ghana's rulers converted to Islam. By 1235 the kingdom of Mali had emerged, built to a large degree upon gold. As miners found new gold deposits further east, the most important trade routes began to shift eastward, which prompted the people of Mali to seize power. By 1300, Mali's kings had converted to Islam. Muslim Mandingo merchants were trading as far east as the city-states in Hausa land and beyond to Lake Chad. Islam was spreading with the trade of its merchants, and in the 1300s or 1400s the kings of Hausa land converted to Islam. One well-known Mali emperor was Muslim Mansa Musa (1312–1337). Musa's pilgrimage to Mecca included 500 slaves with gold staffs and 100 camels with 300 pounds of gold, it is claimed. Mali was literate, but only insofar as it employed Muslim scribes at the court of its kings. Mali reached its peak in fame and fortune when Timbuktu became the most important city of the empire. It attracted Muslim judges, doctors, religious leaders and scholars from far and wide to its mosques and universities. Then weak and incompetent kings inherited power, which always meant the start of decline in ancient empires.

The Songhai people lived along the middle of the Niger River, monopolising fishing and canoe transport. Trade had brought Islam to Songhai and its royalty had converted to the new religion. Mali control over the Songhai capital, Gao, had never been firm. A Songhai king led his people in rebellion, which disrupted Mali's trade on the Niger River. Mali's empire suffered as the Songhai sacked and occupied Timbuktu in 1433 to 1434. In some 30 years of military campaigns, the victorious Songhai king won the title *King of Kings*. He dominated trade routes and the great grain-producing region of the Niger River delta. In the mid-1400s the ruler of Benin, Ewuare, built up his military, and captives taken in battle were traded to the Portuguese. Benin's empire extended to about 190 miles (300 kilometres) in width by the early 1500s.

The Hausa were a group of people named after the language they spoke. The cities of the Hausa people first emerged between the years 1000 and 1200 in what is today northern Nigeria. From their capitals, Hausa rulers governed the farming villages outside the city walls, as the kings depended on the crops of the farmers and on a thriving trade in salt, grain and cotton cloth made by urban weavers. Because they were located on trade routes that linked other West African states with the Mediterranean, Kano and Katsina became major trading states. They profited greatly from supplying the needs of caravans. Kano was noted for its woven and dyed cloth and for its leather goods. Zazzau, the southernmost state, conducted a vigorous trade in enslaved persons. Zazzau's traders raided an area south of the city and sold their captives to traders in other Hausa states. These traders sold them to other North or West African societies in exchange for horses, harnesses and guns. The Hausa kept some enslaved workers to build and repair city walls and grow food for the cities. Like the Hausa, the Yoruba people spoke a common language. Originally the Yoruba-speaking people belonged to a number of small city-states in the forests on the southern edge of the savannah in what is today Benin and southwestern Nigeria. Most people farmed in these communities. Over time, some of these smaller communities joined together under strong leaders. This led to the formation of several localised Yoruba kingdoms. Ife and Oyo were the two largest Yoruba kingdoms. Ife, developed by 1100, was the most powerful Yoruba kingdom until the late 1600s, when Oyo became more prosperous. As large urban centres, both Ife and Oyo were surrounded by high walls. With fertile soil and ample rainfall, most rural farms in the surrounding areas produced surplus food which was sent to the cities. This enabled city dwellers to become traders and craftspeople (Johnson, 2001).

To the south and west of Ife, near the delta of the Niger River, lay the kingdom of Benin. The first kings of Benin date from the 1300s. Like the Yoruba kings, the *oba*, or ruler, of Benin based his right to rule on claims of descent from the first king of Ife. In the 1400s, Benin had emerged as a major West African state controlling an area that came to stretch from the Niger River delta in the east to what is today Lagos. Inside the city, broad streets were lined by neat rows of houses, and the huge palace contained many courtyards with works of art. Artists working for the *oba* created magnificent brass heads of the royal family and copper urines. In the 1480s, Portuguese trading ships began to sail into Benin's port at Gwatto. The Portuguese traded with Benin merchants for pepper, leopard skins, ivory and enslaved persons (Quigley, 2002; Bovril, 1995).

Relating these short stories of a few major West African empires to the hydraulic hypothesis of Wittfogel, one may establish that water did not play the single overwhelming role that he claims. Centralised power emerged for certain, but it was brittle, resting upon anything in the agricultural society, which led to the control of the capital of key resource such as trade in gold and slaves, as well as the control of the means of religion. Although the spread of Islam enhanced uniformity and the use of written language in government, the West Africans were patrimonial in character (Oliver, 1977).

One cannot speak of states with regard to these temporary empires with such short time spans. They succumbed due either to changes in trade or to internal power struggles. Thus, these West African empires were short-lived, focusing on trade and slavery. Whether they may be classified as hydraulic depends upon how one regards their link with the River Niger. At least it was hardly hydraulic in the same sense as the Angkor Empire with its systems of reservoirs, canals and moats, serving the practical purposes of irrigation. The geographical location of the Angkor Empire involved two extreme seasons, i.e. heavy rainfall during the monsoon and the dry period during the off-monsoon season. Numerous large reservoirs, dikes, moats and ponds helped significantly to prevent floods over farmland during the heavy rainfall in the monsoon and to conserve water storage for use during the dry season. The efficient and extensive irrigation system of the ancient Khmer enabled the empire to cultivate crops two to three times a year, which led to high productivity and strong economy of the Angkor Empire. Yet the formerly efficient irrigation and drainage system later became silted up due to less water and the rice crops dropped dramatically, thus weakening the productivity and strength of the Khmer civilisation. Let us move to China where several components of a state had been erected already during the Han dynasty, 200 years BC (Higham, 2002; Kwang-Ching and Ebrey, 1999).

China

Chinese history is normally approached from the angle of its dynasties. A dynasty is a time period under the rule of a specific family and, as a new dynasty came into power, it would have overthrown the existing dynasty. The first historical emperor of China was Qinshi Huangdi, or the Yellow Emperor of the Qin clan. His tomb has become the famous archaeological site at Xian, known for its hundreds of terracotta guards and horses. Chinese civilisation, as described in mythology, begins with Pangu or the creator of the universe, and consists of a succession of legendary sage-emperors. The first real prehistoric dynasty is said to be Xia, from about the twenty-first to the sixteenth century BC. Archaeologists have uncovered urban sites, bronze implements and tombs that point to the existence of Xia civilisation in the same locations cited in ancient Chinese historical texts. The Xia period marked an evolutionary stage between the late Neolithic cultures and the typical Chinese urban civilisation of the Shang dynasty.

Chinese civilisation extended gradually over most of China proper north of and including the Yangtze Valley under the Chou dynasty between 1027 and 256 BC. Given the primitive state of overland communications, the Chous delegated authority to vassals, who ruled a walled town and the territory surrounding it. The hierarchy of these feudal-like states was headed by hereditary lordship. As these vassals became autonomous with endless wars breaking out among them, there was a decline in the political authority of the Chou dynasty resulting in the emergence of the powerful peripheral states. By the late fifth century BC, Chou China was plunged into a condition of interstate anarchy, known as the *Period of Warring States* (403–221 BC). One timeless book has truly captured the logic of the anarchy that prevailed: *The Art of Warfare* by Sun-Tzu. In 221 BC the King of Ch'in proclaimed himself first emperor of the Ch'in Dynasty. The name *China* is derived from this dynasty. The first emperor restrained the vassals by means of an administratively centralised and culturally unified empire. The hereditary aristocracies were abolished and their territories divided into provinces, governed by bureaucrats appointed by the emperor. The Ch'in capital, near the present-day city of Xi'an, became the first seat of imperial China. A standardised system of written characters was adopted and made compulsory throughout the empire. To promote internal trade and economic integration, the Ch'in standardised weights and measures, coinage and axle widths. Private landholding was adopted. Yet the most well known of the ancient dynasties is the Han (AD 206) with its capital at Chang'an.

The Han Empire adopted Confucian ideals of government. Confucian scholars gained prominent status as the core of the civil service. Intellectual, literary and artistic endeavours revived and flourished. The Han period produced China's most famous historian, Sima Qian (145–187 BC), whose *Shiji* (Historial Records) provides a detailed chronicle from the time of a legendary Xia emperor to that of the Han emperor Wu Di (141–187 BC). After 200 years, Han rule was interrupted briefly (in AD 9–24) and then restored for another 200 years. Riddled with the corruption characteristic of the dynastic cycle, the Han Empire collapsed in AD 200. During Han, the Chinese armies annexed parts of northern Vietnam and northern Korea towards the end of the second century BC. Han control of peripheral regions was insecure, but a mutually beneficial "tributary system" emerged. Non-Chinese states were allowed to remain autonomous in exchange for symbolic acceptance of Han overlordship. Tributary ties were confirmed and strengthened through intermarriages at the ruling level and periodic exchanges of gifts and goods. Technological advances occurred, such as in paper and porcelain. The empire expanded westward as far as the rim of the Tarim Basin in modern Xinjiang, making possible caravan traffic across Central Asia to Antioch, Baghdad and Alexandria, i.e. the "silk route" used to export Chinese silk to the Roman Empire.

Staffing the administrative hierarchy inherited from the Ch'in, the Han emperors followed the Confucian principle of appointing men on the basis of merit rather than birth. Interestingly, a civil service examination system was initiated, as written examinations were adopted as a means of determining the best-qualified people. In the late second century BC an imperial university was established, in which prospective bureaucrats were trained in the five classics of the Confucian School. The Han Dynasty identified the classical elements of a state in China, creating a bureaucracy out of the Confucian literati. However, Han had two fundamental weaknesses, namely the internal turbulence generated from court politics surrounding the all-too-powerful emperor as well as the external turbulence originating in the open nature of Chinese territory, making invasions by other people easy.

The decline of the Han Dynasty resulted in such a long period of conflict among independent states that the more or less uniform Chinese culture almost died out. Starting in AD 384, however, the Northern Wei kingdom began reuniting the kingdoms into a single empire. Although they failed to do so, they managed to preserve Chinese culture during the fractious centuries of the Three Kingdoms, part of an era of disunity called the Six Dynasties. During The Three Kingdoms, Chinese scholarship and thought was challenged by a widespread growth of two religions, Neo-Taoism and Buddhism. When the Han government collapsed, Buddhism spread primarily among the common population. By the time of the rise of the Northern Wei, Buddhism had spread over the whole of China. Although Buddhists were occasionally persecuted, on the whole they were tolerated. Some emperors even converted to Buddhism. One can hardly use the hydraulic hypotheis to explain that the political system of China has hovered between stability and instability, anarchy and unity, peace and invasion. Thus, China was reunited under the rule of the Sui Dynasty (589–618). The Sui revived the centralised administrative system of the Han and reinstated competitive examinations for the selection of officials. Although Confucianism was officially endorsed, Taoism and Buddhism were also acknowledged in formulating a new ideology for the empire. Buddhism flourished, as did foreign religious groups such as Nestorian Christians. The Sung Dynasty started in 960. The founders of the Sung Dynasty built an effective centralised bureaucracy staffed with civilian scholar officials. Centrally appointed officials replaced regional military governors and their supporters. This system of civilian rule led to a greater concentration of power in the emperor and his palace bureaucracy than had been achieved in the previous dynasties. They did not split up the land into sections with more or less independent governors. They re-established Confucianism as the master philosophy and reunified most of China proper.

Under the Sung Dynasty, the development of cities began, not only for administrative purposes but also as centres of trade, industry and maritime commerce. The landed scholar officials lived in the provincial centres alongside the shopkeepers, artisans and merchants. A new group or mercantile class arose as printing and education spread and private trade grew, the economy linking the coastal provinces with the interior. Landholding and government employment were no longer the only means of gaining wealth and prestige. Culturally, the Sung refined many of the developments of the previous centuries, including historical writings, painting, calligraphy and hard-glazed porcelain. Sung intellectuals looked for answers to philosophical and political questions in the Confucian Classics. A renewed interest in the Confucian ideals and society of ancient times coincided with the decline of Buddhism, as Sung Neo-Confucian philosophers revived the ancient classical texts. The most influential was Zhu Xi (1130–1200), whose synthesis of Confucian thought and Buddhism and Taoism became the official imperial ideology from late Sung times to the late nineteenth century. As incorporated into the examination system, Zhu Xi's philosophy evolved into a rigid official creed, which stressed the one-sided obligations of obedience and compliance of subject to ruler, child to father, wife to husband, and younger brother to elder brother.

The Mongols, who conquered China during the thirteenth century, lost their power rapidly in the fourteenth century because they did not adopt the Chinese language and customs from the earlier dynasties. Heavy taxes led to peasantry revolts. In the Yangtze Valley, Chu Yu-chang, a former Buddhist monk, had turned from religion to become a rebel leader. He led a peasant army to power in the 1360s, founding a new dynasty – the Mings. The Ming Dynasty restored the Confucian ideal of bureaucracy and thrived on commerce and economic expansion. However, defending their borders weakened the Ming. A rebellion broke out in the Shanxxi province that led to a famine. After the rebels took Beijing, the Ming formed a union with the Manchus who had recently gained power over Manchuria. Once inside China the Manchus refused to leave. The Manchu Dynasty reached their zenith of power in the eighteenth century when they controlled Manchuria, Mongolia and Tibet. In addition, Chinese influence had reached Nepal, Burma, Korea and Vietnam. Later, China was weakened by the Taiping Rebellion of 1850 to 1864, led by Hung Hsiu-ch'uan, who failed the Confucian exam four times. The rebellion was the most deadly in Chinese history. During the last decades of the nineteenth century foreign governments gained control over parts of China. In the Boxer Rebellion, the Chinese nation tried to drive out the Europeans and the Americans, but they were defeated. The Manchu government was weak enough for the revolutionary leader, Dr Sun Yat-Sen, to succeed in toppling the last Chinese dynasty in 1911.

Some of the Chinese dynasties lasted for quite a long time. What accounts for the life span of a Chinese dynasty is either internal instability due to 1) palace politics around the emperor, or 2) peasant uproars in a province, or external instability due to invasion from the bordering peoples. From the time of the Han Dynasty, one may speak of a state in China, resting upon a Confucian bureaucracy – the literati. The mandarins developed perfection of the rules through mastery of the written Chinese language with all its complicated signs. However, this hardly developed a high level of knowledge about technology and law. In comparison with Mongol rule anywhere, several Chinese dynasties accomplished much in terms of stateness. Yet one can hardly claim that the fate of he Chinese dynasties fluctuated with their hydraulic or irrigation capacity (Ebrey, 1999).

Mughal India

Regimes in the Arab world as well as with the Mongols are completely despotic. The rulers – caliphs, khans and sultans – express the essence of oriental despotism (Spuler, 1969a, 1969b; Lapidus, 1989; Hourani, 1991). Let us look at the Mughal rule of India as an example (Richard, 1996). The empire of Tamerlane, perhaps the largest ever, adheres fully to the logic of Oriental despotism, conceived as "sultanismus" by Weber (1978). It displays how far the most extreme version of looting as a strategy may be taken (Marozzi, 2005). Tamerlane, establishing himself as a Tartar Muslim in Samarkand, was the undisputed and never beaten ruler of a dynamic and populous part of the world at that time. His rule was based on plunder or savage looting in order to pay for his huge army and incredible splendour at Samarkand, his capital. Tamerlane not merely defeated the adjacent empires but also ruined them, some forever, by burning their cities and transporting away everything of value, often slaughtering the population or selling them into slavery. As his successors lacked his ruthless drive or military genius, his Tartar Islamic regime proved a failure, more due to the amateur nature of Oriental administration than to lacking haudraulic capacity.

The Mongol empires were based on military power and nothing else. As soon as the great military leader was gone, it cracked completely. In reality, the huge empire of Kublai Khan was nothing but a loose federation among warlords. It thus shared the principal weakness of the feudal regime, namely the risk of felonies on the part of the vassals of the emperor, reneging on their promise of fidelity (Man, 2006). In Mughal India an effort was made to erect an administration that could support the excessive splendour of the lifestyle of the rulers without engaging in plunder abroad. However, at the end of the Mughal period in India, the emperor was only in control of the Red Fort in Dehli and its gardens (Dalrymple, 2006), when the British finished it after the sepoy mutiny in 1857, for which the emperor was not even responsible (Keay, 2004).

It was actually a descendant of Tamerlane, Babar, who initiated Mughal India, as he came to India in 1522 at the request of an Indian governor in his fight against the last head of the Delhi Sultanate. Babar founded the Mughal Empire in India, but Muslims had invaded India several times, including Tamerlane's terrible sack of New Dehli in 1399. It was Akbar the Great who promoted the glory of this Muslim empire. Akbar reigned from 1556 to 1605, and extended his empire as far to the west as Afghanistan, and as far south as the Godavari river. Akbar attempted to blend Islam with Hinduism, Christianity and Jainism, welcoming Jesuit missionaries from Goa to his court. He promoted Hindus to important military and civil positions, conferring honours upon them. Akbar's empire supported vibrant intellectual and cultural life. A large imperial library included books in Hindi, Persian, Greek, Kashmiri, English and Arabic. Akbar directed the creation of the *Hamzanama*, an artistic masterpiece that included 1,400 large paintings.

Under Akbar's son Jahangir (1605–1627), culture again flourished, as Mughal painting reached its zenith. His son Shah Jahan left behind an extraordinarily rich architectural legacy, which includes the *Taj Mahal* and the old city of Delhi, *Shahjahanabad*. But a war of succession broke out between his four sons with the winner Aurangzeb being a controversial figure. Admired by Muslim historians for enforcing the Sharia, he is among Hindus remembered as a Muslim fanatic and bigot. After Aurangzeb's death in 1707, many of his vassals established themselves as rulers – the *princely states* (Maharajas, Nababs). The Mughal Empire survived until 1857, but, after 1803, its rulers were merely pensioners of the East India Company (Eraly, 2003).

There is little evidence to support the hydraulic hypothesis from analyses of Mughal rule in India. What counted was the capacity of the rulers to capture the rents from agriculture as well as to mobilise soldiers for the ongoing war efforts. The Mughal empire was Islamic, although many of the subjects of the empire were Hindus, including higher officials. The Mughals used the *mansabdar* system to generate land revenue. The emperor would grant revenue rights to a *mansabdar* in exchange for promises of soldiers in wartime. The greater the size of the land the emperor granted, the greater the number of soldiers the *mansabdar* had to promise. The *mansab* was both revocable and non-hereditary, which gave the centre a fairly high degree of control over the *mansabdars*. Akbar issued a revenue schedule that the peasantry could tolerate, while providing resources for the state. Revenue demands ranged from one-third to one-half of the crop and were paid in cash. However, Akbar relied heavily on landholding *zamindars*. They used their considerable local knowledge and influence to collect revenue and to transfer it to the Treasury, yet keeping a portion in return for services rendered – Oriental tax farming. Within his administrative system, the warrior aristocracy (*mansabdars*) held ranks (*mansabs*) expressed in numbers of troops, and indicating pay, armed contingents and obligations. The warrior aristocracy was generally paid from revenues of non-hereditary and transferable *jagirs* (revenue villages), but the economic position of peasants and artisans deteriorated. Revenue officials failed to generate resources independent of dominant Hindu *zamindars* and village leaders, whose self-interest prevented them from handing over the full amount of revenue to the imperial Treasury. In their ever-greater dependence on land revenue, the Mughals weakened their regime (Habib, 1963; Moreland, 1999). Again, Weber's emphasis on the inherent tendencies towards administrative decline in despotic regimes is borne out.

Conclusion

Ancient empires emerged not only in Asia Minor, South Asia and the Far East but also in the Americas. They were founded upon the capacity of a centralised power to monopolise enough surplus from agriculture in order to sustain both consumption splendour and the great military efforts that characterise them. Only in China did a class of bureaucrats emerge with an ethos reminiscent of the modern state. Clearly the control of water played a key role in several of these regimes, but the hydraulic hypothesis cannot explain the rise and decay of all of them, as Wittfogel hinted.

The ancient empires had to fight endless wars to maintain themselves. Sooner or later this strategy would founder. Besides, there was the instability deriving from the heritage of the throne. Not all emperors could equal Ramses II in capacity, i.e. the throne would sometimes be left in the hands of seriously handicapped persons, with disastrous consequences. The ancient empires were in Weber's terminology patrimonial states, i.e. they relied upon administrative machinery with strong elements of personal loyalty such as kinship or slaves. To understand the inherent instability of Oriental despotism, one may turn to the history of the Ottoman Empire. How come it first displayed such grandeur only later to embark upon a long process of decline ending with its breakup and the creation of modern Turkey first and later a number of Arab states? One expert writes:

> Süleyman's death in 1566 is reckoned by modern historians to mark the commencement of the Ottoman Empire's long decline. Although its external expansion did not yet come to a halt, its internal condition began to show dangerous symptoms of decay. First and foremost these affected the ruling dynasty. From this time onwards, the house of Osman ceased, on the whole, to produce capable rulers; with few exceptions, the princes who thereafter ascended the throne were spineless weaklings, addicted to the pleasures of their harems and often pathologically degenerate.
>
> (Kissling, 1996: 32)

Kissling argues further that government as practised within the Sublime Porte degenerated into "palace politics", described as follows:

> The dynasty and the government fell more and more under the influence of palace cliques carrying on intrigues for their own particular ends under the protection of influential harem ladies; a period of "petticoat rule" was beginning. Effective power passed from the titular Sultan to court parasites, and corruption spread in all quarters. The old strictness in the enforcement of laws, which ensured the state's well-being gave way to laxity. The feudal system, which had been the mainstay of the military structure, became warped by grave abuses. The Janissary corps gradually lost its distinctive character and former efficiency, but was able to make and unmake Sultans like puppets.
>
> (Kissling, 1996: 32–33)

Oriental despotism entailed extreme hierarchy. When the top functioned badly, then the central or provincial administration could perhaps compensate for these irrationalities around the emperor. However, the institutions of the Ottoman Empire did not evolve sufficiently to compensate for palace politics. Although the sultan was the supreme monarch, he had a number of advisers and ministers. The most powerful of these were the viziers of the *Divan*, led by the Grand Vizier. The *Divan* was a council where the viziers met and debated the politics of the empire. It was the Grand *Vizier's* duty to inform the sultan of the opinion of the *Divan*. The sultan often took his viziers' advice into consideration, but he by no means had to obey the *Divan*. Like other Oriental despotic regimes, the Ottoman Empire did not manage to introduce an efficienct and tolerable system of taxation that could alleviate the debt burden that finally made this empire dependent upon Europe (Ternon, 2002). Also in Russia, we find oriental despotism at its height in tsarism (Heller, 1997) in combination with the harshest form of serfage. Russian serfage and American enslavement may be compared in terms of harshness and relationships between masters and bondsmen. The American enslavement of black people and the Russian subjection of serfs flourished to varying degrees until they were both legally abolished in the mid-nineteenth century (Kolchin, 1990).

10 Feudalism

Political, economical and modern

Introduction

Feudal polities are commonly regarded as bad regimes, inefficient and anarchical in nature. They are closely linked with medieval Europe, where it is often stated that the feudal polity reached its apogee in France, England, Spain and Germany. Besides Western Europe, only Japan is singled out as having had full feudalism or almost so. Only in Western Europe was the ideal-type of feudalism put into practice in the estates society. However, feudalism may be found outside Western Europe such as in Eastern Europe, the Middle East, India and China. Feudalism may be regarded as omnipresent in agrarian political systems, since it is true that feudalism appears as either a political or an economic phenomenon, or both. But it is not true that feudal polities were only conducive to anarchy. Weber made a few distinctions between different kinds of feudalism which are well worth reproducing here (Weber, 1978: 255–266, 1073–1077).

What, then, is the core of a feudal polity? This regime is fundamentally contested. On the one hand, feudalism paved the way for the constitutional monarchy and representative institutions. Thus it is positively evaluated for its contribution to the rule of law. On the other hand, feudalism is equated with anarchy and the rule of the sword or the knights. "Feudalism" is a word employed to label a government which is fragile due through the intrusion of private relations – fidelity between lord and vassal. Feudal regimes often degenerated into anarchy. It is here that the relevance of feudalism today resides, i.e. in the occurrence of the rule of warlords in Africa and Asia as well as that of *Caudillos* in Latin America.

Occidental and Oriental feudalism

Weber states that feudalism tends to emerge in all traditional political systems, but he argues that there were two basic prototypes, one in the West and another in the East. He calls Western feudalism the "feudalism of the fief" and Eastern feudalism the "feudalism of the benefice", where the first was conducive to the estates society ("*Ständestaat*") with its representative institutions (Parliament) – a forerunner to rule of law, whereas the second constituted a suitable element in Oriental despotism, favouring arbitrariness and servility. Typical of Western feudalism are the powerful vassals of the king or emperor controlling huge provinces, the so-called fiefs or principalities. There occurred the same kind of principalities in Eastern Europe and in Russia, but they did not result in stable representative institutions with the exception of Poland (*sejm*) and Hungary (*diet*). Mediaeval Russia comprised a vast network of hierarchically arranged principalities (*Knyazy*), with the great sovereign states (*Veliky Knyazy*) such as Kiev, Vladimir and Tver at the top. Each of these controlled or influenced lesser principalities, and these in turn held in fief sub-principalities. Feudalism focused upon the benefice was a system of remuneration, i.e. a position that had attached to it a source of income. The occupant of a benefice received its revenues for the performance of stipulated duties. Benefices could be bestowed for life, and a person could hold a plurality of benefices. Benefices were originally in the form of land donations. At the same time, feudalism was characterised economically by the manor system, which centred on the power of the lord to exercise authority over his serfs. In Western feudalism, there emerged reciprocity between the king and the great lords of the realm, resulting in Parliaments. In Eastern feudalism, the despotic nature of rulership was not challenged by the agrarian lords, who dominated their serfs or peasants more than in Western feudalism.

"Feudalism" and related terms should be used with considerable caution owing to the range of meanings associated with the term. It is important to remember that no medieval society ever described itself or its institutions and relationships as "feudal". It is often stated that feudalism mixed public and private relations, or substituted friendship and loyalty, always unpredictable, for impersonal obligation. However, this merely amounts to saying that feudalism did not stand for legal-rational authority (Brunner, 1992). I will argue against the established negative view of feudalism, first that this regime has many appearances ranging from anarchy to constitutional monarchy, and second that in all its multifaceted nature it represents the regime typical of agrarian society. The term "feudalism" is, among medieval historians, perhaps the most widely debated concept when interpreting occidental medieval society. There exist many definitions of feudalism and indeed some have said that the term does not signify anything at all.

Interestingly, Round and Maitland, in analysing medieval Britain, arrived at different conclusions as to the character of English society prior to the start of Norman rule in 1066. Round claimed a Norman import of feudalism, whereas Maitland stated that the fundamentals were already in place in Britain (Ullmann, 1974; Barlow, 1988). Ganshof (1984) defined feudalism with legal and military terms arguing that feudal relationships existed only among the medieval knights: a lord granted a fief to a vassal against which the vassal provided military service in return. Bloch (1994) approached feudalism as a type of society. Like Ganshof, he recognised that there was a hierarchal relationship between lords and vassals, but he saw a similar hierarchy in the manor obtaining between lords and peasants/serfs. While the vassal performed military service in exchange for the fief, the peasant/serf performed physical labour in return for protection. According to Bloch, all aspects of life were centred on "lordship": the principalities, a feudal church with benefices, a feudal court (Parliament) and the feudal economy.

Brown (1974) challenged the value of using the word at all, rejecting the label as an anachronistic construct. She noted that in the absence of any accepted definition, feudalism is a construct with no basis in medieval reality, an invention of modern historians read back into the historical record. Reynolds (1994) expanded upon Brown's original thesis. Yet historians are hesitant to give up the term "feudalism", whether defined by Ganshof or Bloch. One must distinguish clearly between the political regime of feudalism and the economic system of manorialism, as the legal framework for the interaction between lord and vassal was different from that defining the landlord and the serf. Economic feudalism is concentrated upon the management of the manor as a productive unit (Fourquin, 1976).

Political feudalism

Political feudalism is intimately connected with the society of the knights in armour on horseback, the cavaliers. Economic feudalism occurs with agricultural society and lordship, which delivered the means of setting up knights in the first place. Political feudalism is focused upon the governance of the realm with the division of the country into principalities: dukedoms, baronies, counties (*"Lehnswesen"* (Brunner, 1968; Hintze, 1968, 1975)).

Vassalage and principalities

Vassalage agreements similar to what would later develop into legalised medieval feudalism originated from the blending of ancient Roman and Germanic traditions. The Romans had a custom of patronage whereby a stronger patron would provide protection to a weaker client in exchange for gifts, political support and prestige. The Germans had a custom of equality among warriors, an elected leader who kept the majority of the wealth (land) and who distributed it to members of the group in return for loyalty. Feudalism had begun as a contract, the exchange of land tenure (fief) for military service. Over time, as lords could no longer provide new lands to their vassals or enforce their right to reassign lands, which had become "de facto" hereditary property, transaction costs of feudalism became increasingly heavy. The thirteenth century saw a transformation of Europe's economy from a mostly agrarian system to one that was increasingly money-based and commercial. Landownership was still an important source of income, but wealthy nobles wanted more liquid assets, whether for luxury goods or to provide for wars. A vassal was expected to deal with most local issues and could not always expect help from a distant king. As the nobles could be unwilling to cooperate in providing military service, by the end of the Middle Ages the kings first hired mercenaries and later created standing national armies.

In France, the Merovingins and the Carolingians had vassals, as did other leading men in the kingdom (Geary, 1988). This relationship did become more and more standardised over the next two centuries, but there were differences in function and practice in different locations. In the German kingdoms as well as in the Slavic kingdoms, the feudal relationship was more closely connected to the rise of serfdom that tied peasants to the land. In Britain, feudalism had a centripetal tendency, reinforcing the monarchy and not unsettling the free peasants, despite the power of the magnates as exemplified in the Magna Carta (1215).

Standing for voluntary or customary bonds in medieval society, and an order in which civil and military power is exercised under private contractual arrangements, "vassalage" covers the voluntary, personal undertakings binding lords and free men to protection in return for support. The fully fledged feudal society had an established order of estates (corporations), dividing the population into nobility, clergy, merchants and sometimes peasants/serfs depending on whether three or four estates were recognised. The principality was its political form of organisation, whereas the manor was its economic base. Principalities have existed in the agrarian civilisations of Africa, Asia and Europe. Today a principality is a monarchical feudatory remnant state, whose monarch is a prince or princess, or small sovereign states led by lesser royalty, for instance, grand duchies, whose monarch is a grand duke or duchess. No sovereign duchy currently exists, but Luxembourg is a surviving example of a sovereign grand duchy. Surviving principalities include Andorra, Liechtenstein, and Monaco, but notable principalities existed until the early twentieth century in various regions of France, Germany, Italy, Portugal and Spain. An ecclesiastical form of principality exists in the Roman Catholic Church in the form of a diocese led by a cardinal, the principal papal elector, because the church entities were originally principalities to be run in accordance with the principles of political feudalism.

Economic feudalism: manorialism

The feudal society comprised basically two social groupings: knights and serfs. The knights were the lords of the manor or manors. This established uniformity in the regions where the mouldboard plough was used. Thus an aristocratic class arose in Europe in the eighth, ninth and tenth centuries which drew economic support from manors by improving services or rents from peasants or serfs. Most country people lived on a manor, which consisted of a village, the lord's house or castle, a church and the surrounding farmland (Coulton, 1985). The lord of the manor governed the local community under his control by appointing officials who made sure that the villagers carried out their duties. The lord's main duty included being a knight and as such would provide arms whenever he was required. The medieval manors originated from: (1) the villa estates of the Romans; and (2) the German villages after the migrating tribes settled down. The Roman villa or agricultural estates were worked by groups of slaves, who lived together in a separate unit in the grounds. The Germanic villages comprised peasants huddled together for cooperative work on the land.

The villagers farmed the lord's land and payed rent to the lord in the form of produce. Criminals were tried before the lord for justice, as he had the power to fine those who broke the law. The villagers produced everything they would need themselves, though salt and iron were brought in from outside. The lord appointed many officials but the most important was the steward for the day-to-day running of the manor. Hunting became one of the main leisure pursuits. The steward organised the farm workers and kept records of the estate's money. Stewards were the best paid and most powerful of all the lord's officials. After the steward came the bailiff. The bailiff was a freeholder who owned his own land and it was his role to allot the jobs to the peasants while taking care of running repairs to buildings for which he would hire in skilled labourers such as carpenters and blacksmiths. Just like the steward the bailiff also had a right-hand man called the reeve, i.e. a peasant chosen by the villagers to check that everyone turned up for work on time and that no one stole any produce from the lord. Thus, social status was defined by obligations to the manor. The lord had a right to the produce from some part of the land. Certain strips of the best arable land were set aside for the lord (*demesne*), handled by the bailiff. The lord also received dues from the serfs: sheaves of grain and other dues in kind. These dues varied from manor to manor, fixed by custom. The lord received the best animal when the head of a family died, and he collected fees from the serfs for using his still, winepress, bake oven and other utilities. The manor court handled various infractions of customs and rules, assessing fines.

The peasants belonged to one of three groups: free men, serfs (*villains*) and cotters. Free men had certain fixed dues, which they had to pay or deliver. Serfs had the same dues, but also had to provide labour services to the lord on his land. Cotters were essentially squatters with no rights to arable land whatsoever. They worked for some sort of wage in kind. The church also played an important role in all this. The peasants had to pay tithes or harvest products to the church in order to maintain it. These tithes (one-tenth of total income) were collected by the parish priest or the lord's agent.

An ideal-type feudal polity?

Feudalism as a political regime has met with two different responses, one negative and one positive. The negative view looks upon feudalism as merely a transitory regime between the Roman Empire and the nation-state. It was bound to go under due to its anarchical features. In addition, it was a necessary response to the collapse of the commercial economy in the Mediterranean, which was replaced by an agriculturally based economy. As soon as commerce started to grow, the rulers could get enough monetary resources to pay officials to govern the provinces as well as recruit standing armies, thus undoing the need to rely upon the unruly lords and their capricious vassals.

The positive evaluation takes an entirely different look at the feudal society. It targets what in German is called the "*Ständestaat*", meaning the high medieval society with its firm institutions expressed in the corporations or the estates, having representation in Parliaments (*Reichstag, Cortes*). Thus, feudalism is one of the sources of Western rule of law and ultimately constitutional democracy (Hintze, 1991). Political feudalism was not as backward as economic feudalism, focusing on the manor and its villages of serfs. However, only advanced forms of feudalism contributed to the introduction of the rule by underlining the supremacy of the law and the reciprocity between the lord and his vassals. Weber states:

> The struggle of the feudal chief with his feudal administrative staff coincided in the Western World, though not in Japan, largely with his struggle against the power of corporately privileged groups. In modern times it everywhere issued in the ruler's victory, and that meant in bureaucratic administration.
>
> (Weber, 1978: 259)

Weber appears to bypass the victory of representative institutions in, for example, England and Sweden. In some countries, the estates transformed themselves into representative institutions, paving the way for constitutional monarchy. In other countries, absolutism destroyed the institutions of the estates society, but the idea of representative institutions was not forgotten. Representation could be introduced later on in response to the demand for rule of law. Actually, the struggle between royal absolutism and representative institutions evolved over a long period of time, from late medieval society to the great revolutions in the eighteenth century. Once the idea of social representation had been successfully conceived in both *imperium* and *sacerdotium*, it could not be destroyed but kept coming back. This is the positive heritage of feudalism, namely the growth of representative institutions in the medieval period (Marongiu, 1968; Wilkinson, 1972).

In Japan, the feudal society developed towards anarchy before the advent of the Togukawa shoguns, who centralised power beneath the powerless emperor. After 200 years of rule, the shogunate in Muromachi ran into resistance from the competing clans from the rest of the country, resulting in civil wars in Japan at the end of sixteenth century. Togukawa

Ieyasu, the founder of Togukawa shogunate, brought peace to Japan in this transitional period with civil wars where castles were built for protection by the lords, i.e. the *daimyos* and their vassals, i.e. the *samurais*. Ieyasu founded a shogunate in Edo, later Tokyo. Tokugawa kept the sociopolitical structure intact by, for instance, cutting off Japan from the rest of the world in 1639. In 1543 Portuguese traders landed on a small southwestern Japanese island, bringing gunpowder and guns. A few years later Spanish and Jesuit missionaries arrived. Tokugawa forbade all nationalities to enter Japan except for the Dutch to a small island Dejima near Nagasaki, a bunch of Chinese living in Nagasaki and a few messengers of the Korean king. For two and a half centuries these people were the only source of contact with the outside world. Yet in 1853 American Commander Perry arrived in Tokyo Bay. After a year, he visited once more, and this time he managed to draw up an agreement making Japan and his country allies. Similar treaties including trade were made with Russia, Great Britain and the Netherlands as well as France. Eventually, the feudal shogunate system was abolished in 1867 and power was handed back to the emperor in 1868. Feudalism in Japan did not result in major representative institutions (Duus, 1993).

Modern feudalism: the war lords

One might believe that feudalism is only an historical regime which failed to display survival fitness. Nothing could be more erroneous. Feudalism is still with us, although it is now the warriors with Kalashnikovs who display their power to control sizeable areas. Modern forms of feudalism occur in Africa and Asia, where war lords exercise control over huge territories. Modern feudalism can degenerate into banditism, meaning that in several countries petty war lords spread death and violence with their Kalashnikovs, often using children soldiers, as in Uganda. However, this is typical of anarchy or civil war, as was the case in Somalia and Congo. True war lords of a feudal nature are to be found in Afghanistan, where they still rule sizeable parts of the country. One may also find feudal links constituting an informal government in some parts of the world where tribal connections loom large, as in Pakistan or in Arabia. Perhaps one should also mention the Latin American phenomenon of *caudillos* as examples of neo-feudalism. The quick collapse of the Taliban regime is explainable only if one understands the penetration of war lords all over the Afghan territory. When the Northern Alliance together with the Americans appeared invincible, numerous War Lords simply shifted sides overnight. The dismal impact upon society of the rule of war lords may be observed in all its tragedy in the recent developments in West Africa. A number of countries were systematically destabilised by war lords, spreading disaster in Liberia, Sierra Leone and Cote Ivoire with repercussions for neighbouring states.

Conclusion

Feudalism as a political regime was employed systematically in many agricultural countries, recognising the powerful position of huge landowners with a strong capacity to put up troops for the ruler. It is a distinctly agrarian regime where the central power relies upon personal ties (vassalage) with the governors of the provinces instead of using a bureaucracy. Its inherent instability derives from the difficulties in pinning down the conditions of the personal tie as well as in monitoring the actual fulfilment of the contract between the suzerain and his main vassals in the principalities.

One may wish to distinguish between several types of feudal regimes depending upon a number of factors such as: (1) the degree of institutionalisation of representation: the *"ständestaat"* or the shogun · regime; (2) the power of the suzerain or the degree of subfeudalisation between lords and vassals; (3) the nature of compensation: the fief or the benefice. The nation-state emerged in the late medieval period as a response to the decay of the feudal regime. Vassalage could become too complex or too costly to enforce. Even feudal Britain experienced periods of anarchy (e.g. Roger de Mortimer) and civil war (e.g. War of the Roses). Vassalage, however, did not disappear as clientelism or patronage continued to exist in government in various forms. Sad to say, the worst forms of feudalism have reappeared in the postmodern period where some young states have proved ineffective in containing violence when the country has tumbled into anarchy. Thus, the *homo vassus* or the *samurai* has come back in the form of the modern war lords, spreading death and destruction in Afghanistan, and Central and Western Africa. In fact, feudalism offers a peculiar solution to the principal–agent problem of contracting with people to do governance tasks. It provides too much room for manoevre for the agent, as the principal has few instruments to hold him down to the terms of the contract and enforce it. It invited opportunism on the part of the agents, as enforcing fidelity or correcting felonies resulted in excessive transaction costs not only for the principal but also for the entire society.

The positive contribution of political feudalism lies in its endorsement of representative institutions, restraining the monarch or the emperor. Thus we find Parliaments not only in England but also in France, Spain, Germany, Poland, Hungary and the Scandinavian countries. Political representation is not forthcoming outside of Europe, as it violates the basic principles of Oriental despotism. One of its sources is political feudalism (estates of the realm, *Etats-Généraux, Cortes*), the other being Italian republicanism with assemblies of some sort governing some of its city-states.

11 The nation-state and colonial empires

Introduction

Since the Westphalia Peace, the modern state is the prevailing type of political regime. Its core is reliance upon bureaucracy, the territorial jurisdiction and the monopoly on the means of physical violence, whether the regime is monarchical or republican, unitary or federal, democratic or authoritarian. The emergence of the modern state in Western Europe took one form that needs to be examined closely, namely the nation-state. This came to be regarded as the natural form of a political community to such an extent that the entire remodelling of the world after the First World War in the various peace treaties was based on the Wilsonian ambition to create nation-states not only in Europe but also in the Middle East.

The basic idea of the nation-state is to limit the range of the state to one nation, i.e. a people with a community of hearts, as Rousseau argued. The viability of the nation-state is thus intimately linked with the evolution of nationalism as a political doctrine. Besides the nation-state, there were also other forms of political community (e.g. colonies). The process of colonisation went so far that Western powers controlled almost the entire globe at one time. From where did this extreme occidental superiority come?

Today, the nation-state is under pressure from multiculturalism (Parekh, 2006). The idea of a compact and homogeneous nation-state seems less appropriate today than before, as migration in combination with the increased relevance of culture and community has created heterogeneous societies everywhere. The process of globalisation makes the flux of people stronger, especially towards the affluent countries, but it also strengthens international organisation or regional coordination mechanisms such as the European Union. Could nation-states become obsolete during the twenty-first century?

West European nation-states

The evolution of the modern state in Western Europe followed two developmental lines. On the one hand, small compact republican city-states were achieved in Italy, comprising representative institutions. On the other hand, a set of nation-states emerged in countries such as England, France, Spain, Portugal, the Netherlands, Sweden and Denmark. The arrival of the nation-state as a new regime for governing a country proved decisive for regime evolution. It became the model *par preference* for other countries as well, spreading not only to Eastern Europe but also to Italy. The success of the doctrine of nationalism increased the viability of the nation-state as the triumphant regime form. Thus, empires were broken up in order to allow for the creation of nation-states, such as the Hapsburg regime. Before the nation-state could be exported to other parts of the world, the West European powers, as a result of the survival capacity of the modern state, put another kind of regime in place globally, namely colonialism.

From the feudal regime to the nation-state

Following the demise of feudalism in West European countries the king turned to bureaucracy in order to have a central administration under him that could control the resources of the realm and manage the provinces. Thus, the patrimonial character of the central administration (*curia Regis*) had to be institutionalised in a hierarchy of public offices, recruited among social strata that would be loyal to the king. In addition, the principalities had to be changed into provinces belonging to the royal domain, to be administered directly under the control of the central administration. This process of regime transition was successfully achieved in several West European states during the fifteenth and sixteenth centuries, but did not come about in Germany until the nineteenth century (Strayer, 1970; Ertman, 2004).

The survival fitness of the nation-state was derived from the establishment of certain rules enforced over a territory with a population speaking the same language and having a common sense of historical destiny – the antiquity of nations (Smith, A.D., 2004). The key institutions included the Chancery, the Treasury and the Judiciary:

- The *fisc*: the income and assets of the realm (royal demesnes) were clearly identified and subject to institutionalised handling; the introduction of permanent taxation.
- The creation of a central bureaucracy as well as regional and local officers. France: *baillis, senechaux*, later on *intendents, surintendents*; England: *sheriffs, itinerant justices*.
- The unification of courts and legal justice: common law, *parlaments, lits de justice*.
- The setting up of standing armies.
- The employment of the juristic fiction of the state or the crown.

To balance the growth of the power of the king and his central administration, representative institutions based upon the feudal estates society evolved in several countries: *Parliament, Riksdag, Cortes, Sejm, Diet*. However, they did not survive in continental European countries apart from Sweden when the kings claimed absolutist powers. Ertman (2004) differentiates between patrimonial absolutism (France, Spain), bureaucratic constitutionalism (England) as well as bureaucratic absolutism (Prussia). In regimes with patrimonial absolutism, various forms of appropriation, i.e. prebendalism and venality, invaded the bureaucracy (*merchandage*), including the sale of offices as well as their transfer in inheritance, and there was the widespread use of tax farming. According to Ertman, this occurred especially in France and Spain. Interestingly, the great French bureaucrats under the throne – Sully, Richelleu and Mazerin – not only exercised the new power of office but also enriched themselves immensely (Anderson 1979, 1996; Goubert, 1990; Carré, 1998; Bluche, 2003).

Italian republicanism

The governance of the city-states in Italy adhered to the modern concept of the state, although nationalism did not emerge until the nineteenth century when an Italian nation-state was created out of the efforts of one of the Italian principalities, namely Piedmont. The republican ideal nurtured by Florence and Venice played a major role in making limited government and power sharing attractive around the world. Larger republics, such as the Netherlands, Switzerland and the United States, creating an evolutionary line of development very different from Oriental despotism, could imitate the rule of law achieved by these small city-state republics. Italian political philosophers theorised the new entity – *stato* – and argued for the existence of objective interests with the state – the doctrine of state reasons (*ragione di stato*). Machiavelli separated church and state, stating that the prince can or should do everything in politics in order to protect his city-state. Yet the Italian city-states were hardly viable, as Napoleon quickly ended Venetian independence. Italian republicanism delivered representative institutions, which were to prove a high survival capacity, despite the fact that Italian city-states did not survive the emergence of nationalism in the nineteenth century (Finer, 1997c). Republicanism harbours a principal–agent model that counteracts the trend towards absolutism. The basic idea is that rulers must act to promote the welfare of the people. And republicanism claims that representation delivers agents who are prepared to do so, as in historical Siena, Florence, Venice and Genoa (Marino 2002).

The rise of bureaucracy

No other change in the central administration of the realm was more decisive for political evolution than the emergence of formal bureaucracies. They originated from within the patrimonial regime where offices had already been defined, such as *major domus, marechal, senechal, vezir, grand vezir*, but without firm rules about employment, remuneration and recruitment/firing, to be monitored and enforced. As Weber emphasised, the transition from patrimonial to bureaucratic administration was decisive for the emergence of the modern state. Eventually, bureaucracy could also be employed in the regional and local administration, replacing feudalism (vassalage, fief) as the tool of the governance of regions (Kantorowicz, 2000).

Bureaucracy was not absent from the Roman republic with its heavy underlining of *Res Publica* and its structure of offices. Although Roman jurisprudence focused upon private law, especially contract law, the state was conceived of as a legal person: SPQR (*senatus populusque romanus*). Yet, despite the endorsement of republican ideals, motivated by means of a Stoicist philosophical foundation, well expressed in the works and speeches of Cicero such as *On Duties*, the Romans did not develop constitutional law at any great length. Thus, *Corpus Juris Civilis*, established by Emperor Justinianus around AD 525, comprised few elements of constitutional law. However, the model of an efficient bureaucracy was handed down in the form of the Catholic Church during the medieval period – a most impressive institutional achievement, especially considering the decline of the papacy resulting, for instance, in two popes as well as the temporary movement of the siege to Avignon. Canon law evolved as a giant systematic effort to run the *ecclesia universalis* as a rational organisation (Berman, 1983).

Modern Western legal concepts go back nine centuries to the Papal Revolution, when the Western church established its political and legal unity in independence from emperors, kings and feudal lords. Out of this upheaval came the Western idea of integrated legal systems consciously developed over generations and centuries. Berman describes the main features of these systems of law, including the canon law of the church, the royal law of the major kingdoms, the urban law of the newly emerging cities, feudal law, manorial law and mercantile law. The coexistence and competition of these systems was an important source of the Western belief in the supremacy of law, but decisive for the creation of Western legal families was the emergence of canon law in the twelfth century – the so-called Gratian revolution after the lawyer Gratian of Bologna (Berman, 1983). Berman states:

> The canon law, the first modern Western legal system, was conceived in the Twelfth century as an integrated system of law moving forward in time. The Church itself was conceived for the first time as a legal structure, a law-state, and it formed itself into a complex bureaucracy with a professional court, a professional treasury, and a chancery.
>
> (Berman, 1983: 530)

The development of canon law comprised much more than the internal governance of the church, as jurisprudence became a topic taught at the new universities encompassing also secular law, feudal law, manorial law, commercial law and royal law.

It was highly convenient, and not wholly accidental, that a manuscript of Justinian's *Digest* turned up in a library in Florence in the 1080s, and it was surely not accidental that very soon a university was founded in Bologna – the first European university – to study that manuscript.

(Berman, 1983: 528–529)

Roman law offered the model to proceed with codifying various kinds of law, old and new, which were interpreted, glossed and systematised anew by means of a moving conception of the living law. In the form of canon law, the medieval church attempted formal organisation and rule by law (Southern, 1997).

The emergence of free cities, representative institutions, peasants and distant commercial trade during the high medieval times underlined the importance of legal relations, favouring the growth of jurisprudence as a discipline. One of its most astonishing achievements was the arrival during the Renaissance at the concept of the state – *stato* – as a legal or juristic person that is different from the acting persons in government and towards which they are to be held accountable.

Birth of the nation-state

To identify the origin in time of a state is not a straightforward task. Often one mentions the year of introduction of a so-called *modernised leadership*. However, this criterion is associated with the introduction of political forms involving mass participation. What we are looking for here is some kind of criterion that is neutral in relation to the modernisation process in the twentieth century. There are several states in the world today that have not experienced the coming of a mass political culture. The nation-state is most commonly dated to the Renaissance and the Reformation, but the ideology of nationalism belongs to the French Revolution and Romanticism. The nature of a nation-state is a profoundly contested issue, involving contrary theories of nationalism (Hobsbawm, 1990; Schulze, 1998). The major attempt to organise the world according to the equation state = nation were the peace treaties of 1919 to 1920 (Macmillan, 2003).

Let us start from the birth of the concept of the state. German historian Meinecke argued that the concept of the state is a product of the Renaissance. The word *stato* began to occur as a designator for the new kinds of political units that came forth in the late medieval ages, challenging the universalist notions at that time, both the ambitions of Catholicism and the structure of the feudal society with its emperor, kings and dukes (Meinecke, 1997).

Europe

During the early Renaissance a number of political units may be said to have been founded which have the properties that Weber singled out in his definition of the state: territorial borders with a defined population, a legal order and the monopoly on the use or threat of legitimate physical force – so-called "modern states". It is arbitrary to mention a certain year as the birth date, since the process of introducing the neutral administrative machine that is typical of the modern state was a lengthy one. A few rulers may be mentioned who fought successfully for the centralisation of power resources to the *stato*: Francis I in France (d. 1547), Henry VIII in England (d. 1547), Gustav I Vasa in Sweden (d. 1560), Kristian III in Denmark (d. 1559), Henry the Navigator in Portugal (d. 1460), and Ferdinand and Isabella of Spain (married 1469).

What differentiates these political units as states from other political entities at that time (e.g. the Holy German Roman Empire or the Ottoman Empire) is the orientation of power towards an objective and predictable *stato*, i.e. a system of administrative offices. Characteristic of the new states of the seventeenth century is the concentration of political power to an impersonal organisation, the actions of which cover the entire population of a sharply delineated state territory in a direct relation of authority. It is hardly an accident that the modern states in Europe were the most active in extending their powers over the globe. It took centuries to arrive at the concept of an impersonal and abstract state concept. In England one employed the fiction of the "King's Two Bodies" (Kantorowicz, 1997).

The new state model of the Renaissance spread during the centuries that followed to several other countries. We mention here only some crucial dates: the Netherlands in 1648, Switzerland in 1648, Greece in 1829, Belgium in 1830, Italy in 1861 and Norway in 1905. The First World War changed profoundly the existing states at the end of the nineteenth century. It resulted in the dissolution of the great empires in Europe – the Double Monarchy in Austria and Hungary, the Ottoman Empire as well as the Romanov Empire in Russia.

At Versailles in 1919 and the other cities (Sevres, Lausanne) the peace treaties spoke at length of nation-states. The vague principle that each nation should also constitute a state had grown in importance during the nineteenth century with the spread of nationalist ideology. In some parts of Europe it was very important to create a number of new compact nation-states: Romania in 1881, Bulgaria in 1908, Albania in 1912, Finland in 1917, Austria in 1918, Czechoslovakia in 1918, Hungary in 1918, Poland in 1918 as well as Ireland in 1921.

The state formation process may comprise quite heavy changes over a long period of time. To say whether a state has really ceased to exit or changed dramatically is only a matter of linguistic usage. The English state is a telling example of the difficulty in specifying state identity. In 1707 Great Britain was formed including Scotland and Wales. The creation of the British Empire meant that the sun never set in the British state around 1900. In 1921 the United Kingdom of Great Britain and Northern Ireland was formed.

The question of a German state is also telling. The old Holy German-Roman Empire was dissolved by Napoleon in 1806 leaving a number of different kinds of political entities on German soil, including the state of Prussia. In 1871 a German state was introduced as a result of the ambitions of Prussia defeating the Double Monarchy in Vienna. However, the existence of the German state became precarious in the next century after losing two World Wars. A similar period of reshaping the map of states set in after the Second World War. West Germany was created in 1949 as was East Germany, but in 1990 these two states were united into a new Germany.

How to classify the Russian state is an ambiguous task. Tsarist Russia – an example of Oriental despotism – kept expanding in various directions until it crumbled in 1917 to be replaced by the communist state, the Union of Socialist Soviet Republics in 1922. It gave up vast territory in the peace in Brest-Litovsk in 1917, which made it possible to form the three Baltic republics, Estonia, Lithuania and Latvia as well as Finland. Moreover, Poland declared itself an independent state, re-establishing control over territories given to Prussia, Russia and Austria in the three historical partitions of Poland.

The outcome of the Second World War meant an immense increase in the amount of territory somehow controlled by the USSR. However, in a spectacular course of events in 1991 the Soviet Union was dissolved and replaced by a whole set of new and independent states besides the loose confederation CIS, *inter alia* Russia, the Ukraine, Belorussia, Azerbaijan, Georgia, Moldavia, Armenia, and the earlier khanates of Central Asia: Uzbekistan, Kazakhstan, Turkmenistan, Tajikistan and Kirgizstan as well as, again, the Baltic republics which were annexed by the USSR in 1940.

To sum up, a few European states date back some hundred years, but several are less than a hundred years old. Hardly any state in Europe has persisted in the strong sense that its territory for the exercise of political authority has remained unchanged for hundreds of years. The many wars in Europe have destroyed states more or less drastically. The occidental state model was introduced rather early in time meaning that its efficiency could be employed by a few states – the Spanish, Portuguese, French, British and Dutch empires – to build up huge empires that had a profound influence on the creation of states on the other continents (Wolf, 1982; Hall, 1986). The superiority of the West European states rested not only upon their military might or their economic edge from entering capitalist modes of organisation, but also upon their administrative capacity in running the new "modern" state, meaning the use of bureaucracy.

Asia and Oceania

It is not easy to identify the exact time of creation of states in Asia. The typical mode of political rule in Asia used to be strong patrimonial rule. The strong reliance on personal rule – dynasties – may be found in both China and India as well as Asia Minor. However, there were also feudal structures in Japan and India.

The process of creating European-type states took the form of a fight for independence against the European empires, which dominated almost all of Asia around 1900. Only a few countries resisted the penetration of the British, French and Dutch empires, such as Persia or Iran formed in 1499, Afghanistan dating back to 1747 and Nepal dating back to 1768 as well as Thailand founded as far back as 1350. Both Japan and China have had ancient civilisations with traditional systems of political domination, but Japan moved towards the creation of a modern state in 1868, abolishing the Tokugawa shogun and restoring the powers of the emperor who moved from Kyoto to Tokyo. China developed differently, as it came under foreign influence and was torn apart by civil war between the nationalists and the communists up until 1949.

Rudyard Kipling called the struggle between the tsarist and British Empire on the giant chessboard of Central Asia "the great game". The numerous independent khanates between the Caspian and Aral Sea, dating back to the rule of Genghis Khan (d. 1227), fell one after another to Russia's southward advance, later entering the Soviet Empire. By the end of 1991 they re-emerged as unstable independent republics.

New states were formed after both the First and Second World Wars. When the Ottoman Empire was dissolved some of its parts came under British or French rule in 1920, whereas other parts became new states (Hourani, 1991). Thus, Egypt became independent in 1922, Turkey was formed in 1923, Iraq in 1932, Yemen in 1918 and Saudi Arabia in 1932. The countries that remained under foreign rule, partly in accordance with the League of Nations, managed to achieve independent status as states within a few decades: Jordan in 1946, Kuwait in 1961, Lebanon in 1944, Syria in 1946, Oman in 1951 as well as Bahrain and Qatar in 1971.

The violent dissolution of the French Empire in Indochina after the Second World War resulted in a number of new states in Asia. Here we mention the larger ones: Cambodia in 1953, Laos in 1954 and Vietnam in 1954. The definitive end came with the major defeat at Dien Bien-Phu in 1954. The breakup of the British Empire was not quite as violent, although the UK put up resistance when a number of new states declared their independence, despite often remaining with the Commonwealth. Here we find India and Pakistan, founded in 1947, Burma and Sri Lanka in 1948, Malaysia in 1957 and Singapore in 1965.

There were two more empires involved in Far East Asia, namely the Dutch domination of Indonesia and the Japanese annexation of Korea in 1910. The Netherlands, which had conquered the "spice islands" in 1602, established a colony there in 1816 and integrated the vast territory of thousands of islands in 1922. In 1949 Indonesia was founded as a republic or new state after violent resistance from the Dutch. The Japanese domination in Korea was ended in 1945 as a result of imperial Japan's defeat in the

Second World War, but the country was divided into two states in 1948, North and South Korea, followed by the Korean War of 1950 to 1953.

The European state was exported to Asia in two very different forms. On the one hand, some powerful states in Europe managed to subdue several of the Asian countries in the process of empire-building that began in the seventeenth century and was consolidated in the late nineteenth century. The weak political structures in these huge states in terms of territorial area proved no match for Great Britain, France and the Netherlands. On the other hand, in the fight for independence from colonial powers the actors seeking independence often had in mind the creation of states structured along the lines of the European state model. Thus, the dismantling of European imperialism led to the foundation of numerous compact modern states.

The expansion of European imperialism came at a time when oriental despotism had started to disintegrate. This is true of both the Ottoman Empire in Asia Minor and China in Far East Asia. China came under foreign domination after the period of its famous dynasties – Sung (960–1279), Ming (1368–1644) and Manchu Qing (1644–1911) – which brought China to the forefront of civilisation. It could not resist Japanese penetration in the 1890s and 1930s. The introduction of a republic in 1912 was followed by anarchy and civil war between the communists and the nationalists, which ended in the foundation of communist China in 1949 leaving Taiwan (Formosa) as a separate state, although not recognised by the international community.

Likewise India under the Mughal Dynasty could not resist British penetration, first from the late seventeenth century to 1858 in the form of the British East India Company. After the sepoy rebellion in 1857, India was ruled by means of a British Viceroy, collaborating with numerous semi-independent "princely states" or *maharajas*. When it became an independent sovereign state, India stayed within the British Commonwealth.

The states in the region of the Pacific and Oceania are not old. The British, Spanish and Dutch fleets conquered these vast and numerous islands. The penetration of Australia and New Zealand by Great Britain was much slower as these islands were sparsely populated. In 1901 Australia was recognised as an independent state, as the Commonwealth of Australia, whereas New Zealand was made a dominion of the British Empire in 1907. Another big area in the region of Oceania is Papua New Guinea. It was actually part of three European empires: Britain, Holland and Germany. It came under the League of Nations in 1921, ruled under Australian guardianship. In 1975 an independent state was formed. The various groups of islands in the Pacific Ocean are sparsely populated. They came under foreign rule in terms of European colonialism involving all the colonial countries, which divided the islands between them. The South Pacific became independent after the Second World War as a large number of tiny states, with the exception of French Polynesia and New Caledonia.

Colonial empires

The European colonial powers left an indelible mark upon their subjugated territories, the more so the stronger these countries were assimilated into the power structure of the mother state. Whereas France relied heavily on the Napoleonic state to govern their colonies by means of the prefectoral principles, the United Kingdom made various distinctions between different countries.

Colonial empires were established in the wake of the European discovery of the world. They took decades or even centuries to establish but had a short time span of operation before they were questioned. This regime raised a fundamental question of legitimacy. On what right could an empire be claimed? Once this right, derived from a claim to superiority or merely claimed as a camouflage for economic interests, was demolished, colonial rule could not be sustained.

The European empires were established under resistance from subjugated people and they were all dismantled following the Second World War, often after fierce fighting for independence. In those countries where there were massive European settlements did some form of Western rule remain, as with the dominions in the British Empire.

The various empires established after Vasco da Gama had found the direct sea route to India and Columbus had discovered the Americas differed substantially in terms of administrative structures. The most viable form was no doubt the British model of indirect rule in combination with considerable white settlements, which opened up the possibility for colonial autonomy. It is difficult to tell whether the colonial empires made economic sense in the long-term perspective. In any case, their lack of legitimacy proved fatal for survival fitness. The Spanish Empire in Latin America has been much analysed in order to find out whether it contained the seeds of what was to characterise the new states in Latin America once independence from Spain was secured, namely clientelism, red tape and *caudillos.*

To acquire a colony was hardly a difficult task for the European powers, given their superiority in terms of military capacity and warfare. More interesting is the question of how vast territories far away from the homeland could be governed. Let us look at Spanish rule and contrast it with British rule. A critical question in all forms of colonial administration was the treatment of the subjugated native population.

The Spanish Empire

The spread of the new state from Europe to the vast American continent from 1492 onward involved a lengthy process of development of various modes of political domination over the colonies founded there. The first steps in this process were the conquest by the European intruders of the native land of the Indians. The onslaught of the conquistadors crushed the major empires of the Aztecs, Mayas and Incas with an advanced non-European culture. As a matter of fact, the extinction of the native population was awful, from some 25 million people to only one million.

After the conquest sharp political subjugation was combined with economic exploitation. The *conquista* resulted not only in the subjugation of the original population but also in making them Catholics (Williamson, 1992). Whereas the native population was used in the mining areas in the Spanish territories, the Portuguese set up a slave economy in Brazil, importing many blacks from Africa. Besides British Honduras (Belize) in Central America and three small British (Guyana), French (French Guiana) and Dutch (Suriname) colonies, all were under Spanish or Portuguese authority in Latin America.

It was not until some two centuries later that the new populations of the colonies resurrected their autonomy against their European governments by declaring sovereign states in the wake of Spanish defeat in the Napoleonic wars. In the case of the Spanish possessions, the four separate vice-royalties of the late colonial period split further to produce 14 independent states by the 1880s, besides Portuguese Brazil that also revolted against the European powers. Once Spanish domination crumbled a number of new states were formed in Central America: Haiti in 1804, Mexico and Costa Rica in 1821, El Salvador in 1830, Guatemala, Nicaragua and Honduras in 1838, and the Dominican Republic in 1844. The same development took place in South America where Spanish rule and the Portuguese empire including Brazil was wiped out: Paraguay in 1811, Argentina in 1816, Chile in 1818, Brazil in 1822, Peru in 1824, Bolivia and Uruguay in 1825, and Colombia and Ecuador as well as Venezuela in 1830.

It should be pointed out that the borders between some of the states in Latin America have been changed as a result of wars in the nineteenth and twentieth centuries. Thus, for instance, Paraguay lost much of its territory to Brazil and Argentina in 1870. The same happened to Peru, losing territory to Chile in 1884. Some of the islands in the Caribbean remained under foreign rule up until after the Second World War. Jamaica was founded in 1962, as were the republics of Trinidad and Tobago. Cuba became independent in 1899 as a result of the Spanish–American war.

One theme in state theory is the hypothesis that the Spanish and Portuguese state was radically different from the English state. Whereas the English state was suspicious of the bureaucratic aspects of the state favouring a type of guardian state, the Latin American model emphasised state intervention and red tape (North, 1990). Thus the economic development problems in Latin America stemmed partly from the early introduction of a state that restrained rapid economic growth derived from unfettered market institutions – an Iberian legacy. However, one needs also to look at the way the independent Latin American states were assimilated into the world economy during the nineteenth century in their role as export-based economies trading raw materials against manufactured goods.

At the outset the Spanish crown wanted to restrain the conquistadors or *encomenderos*, limiting their capacity to exploit the new crown territories. Thus, the New Laws of 1542 deprived the *encomenderos* and their heirs of their rights to Native American goods and services. A colonial administrative apparatus and bureaucracy was put in place after the conquistadors. Spain created viceroyalties to govern its huge new territories, stretching from Mexico to the bottom of South America except Brazil: one viceroy in Mexico City to govern New Spain, one in Lima, Peru to govern western South America. Due to the growing size of Spain's American colonies, new viceroyalties were created for New Granada (1717) and Río de la Plata (1776). Thus, the *Virreinato de Peru* later lost jurisdiction to the separate viceroyalties of New Granada (now Colombia, Ecuador, Panama and Venezuela, the last-named previously in the vice-royalty of New Spain) in 1717 and the Río de la Plata (Argentina, Bolivia, Paraguay and Uruguay) in 1776. The vice-royalty ended with the independence of the republics of Chile (1818) and Peru (1821). Early on, the vice-royalty contained six *audiencias* or provincial administrations: Panama, Santa Fé de Bogotá (Colombia), Quito (Ecuador), Lima (Peru proper), Charcas (Bolivia, Paraguay, Argentina and Uruguay) and Chile. The *audiencias* were further subdivided into provinces or districts (*corregimientos*) and finally municipalities, which included a city or town, governed by town councils (*cabildos*), composed of the most prominent citizens, mostly *encomenderos* in the early years and later *hacendados*. The Council of the Indies was the main governing body, located in Spain. It was supposed to monitor the local colonial powers. The royal official (viceroy) in place had a host of responsibilities ranging from general administration (particularly tax collection and construction of public works) and internal and external defence to support of the church and protection of the native population. There were a number of other judicial, ecclesiastical and treasury officials, who also reported to the Council in Spain. The structure of royal officials, along with an official review called the *residencia*, was meant to secure governance by law.

The early administrative functions in relation to the indigenous population (protection and Christianisation) were trusted with the new state-appointed officials called *correqidores de indios*: governors of Indians. They were charged at the provincial level with the administration of justice, control of commercial relations between Native Americans and Spaniards, and the collection of the tribute tax. The *corregidores* (Spanish magistrates) were assisted by *curacas* (i.e. members of the native elite), employed as mediators between the native population and the Europeans. Yet the *correqidores* used their office to accumulate wealth and power, establishing mutual alliances with local and regional elites such as the *curacas*, native American functionaries, municipal officials, rural priests (*doctrineros*), landowners, merchants and miners. The Spanish crown put in place a colonial export economy through the development of a bureaucratic and interventionist state, characterised by a plethora of mercantilist rules that regulated the conduct of business and commerce. Thus, Spain left a mercantilist and export-oriented pattern and legacy of "development" that survived into modern times. Operating according to the mercantilist strictures of the times, the crown sought to maximise investment in valuable export production, such as silver from Potosi and later other mineral and agricultural commodities, while supplying the new colonial market with manufactured imports, so as to create a favourable balance of trade for the metropolis.

The British empire

Great flexibility in the administrative structure was typical of the British approach to conquered countries. Thus, widely different institutional arrangements emerged, reflecting both the different local circumstances and the various ambitions of the colonial office. One may differentiate between at least six different institutional arrangements: *Dominions, Colonies, Protectorates, Protected and Associated States, Mandated* and *Trust Territories.* Protectorates or mandates were from the outset supposed to be handed back to sovereignty of the indigenous society, whereas crown colonies were regarded as integral parts of the British state. At the same time, bureaucracy evolved slowly as the basic tool to govern the many different territories from London, resulting in the colonial office in Whitehall. Self-rule was combined with indirect rule, all depending upon the local circumstances (Ferguson, 2003).

In particular, the status as dominion implied the possibility of self-rule. Home rule was granted large territories with considerable white settler populations during the nineteenth century, but the formal internal and external independence of the dominion status was not fully accepted until 1931 in the so-called Statute of Westminster. Being entirely different, "condominium" referred to the rule of two foreign powers over a country, whereas "protectorate" or later "mandate" in terms of the League of Nations framework or trusteeship with the United Nations denoted that a foreign power had been given administrative powers over a country for some time. Compared with these formulas the status of a colony or crown colony implied a stronger tie with the mother country, the territory belonging to the crown or forming an integral part of the British Commonwealth. Whereas the population in the colonies were British citizens, the people that lived in protectorates were not. Civil servants who were recognised as enrolled in the British state ran the colony. However, colonies could be granted various degrees of internal autonomy, such as Southern Rhodesia in 1923 (Zimbabwe) or India in 1909. India was a crown colony ruled by a viceroy representing the British crown, whereas a colony used to be governed by a governor appointed by Westminster.

Today the British Commonwealth includes 53 independent states, 16 of which also accept Queen Elisabeth II as their sovereign. A weak cooperation mechanism exists between the many states that used to be part of the British Empire with the exception of Ireland. Sometimes states are suspended from the Commonwealth such as Fiji in 2006. It is true that many states that formed parts of the British Empire stuck to Westminster political institutions when their independence was accepted. However, we find that there is considerable institution variation, as by no means all of the approximately 90 countries that belonged to the empire now adhere to the Westminster model, interpreted as an ideal-type of government (Lijphart, 1984). Not only were there some federal states (Canada, Australia) but there were also presidential regimes (South Africa, Tanzania, Zambia, Zimbabwe, Kenya).

The logic of the British conquest and administration of such vast territories has been much debated. Was it based on the commercial power of Britain? Or did military advancedness derived from the early occurrence of the Industrial Revolution in England play a major role? The Whitehall bureaucracy has been mentioned in the famous expression of Lloyd George about the Colonial Office and its civil service being the *"steel frame"* of the British Empire. In reality, Britain did not employ many civil servants of their own to handle the colonial administration in the field. Instead, native people were enrolled in the local administration, which is also true of the armed forces that guaranteed order in the colonies. Thus, the British Empire consisted of various territories all over the world conquered or colonised by Britain from about 1600. The British Empire was at its largest at the end of the First World War, consisting of roughly 25 per cent of the world's population and area.

The early growth of the Empire was not laid down in any coordinated plan and it was held together and administered by whatever means seemed most expedient for a particular time and place. Private individuals or companies often provided the initial impetus for the exploration and subsequent exploitation of foreign lands, frequently in the face of government reluctance, but, increasingly, British governments were drawn upon to maintain them. By the time the British began colonising overseas, the Portuguese and Spaniards had already divided a considerable part of the Earth's land surface between them. The Empire grew quickly with the acquisitions in North America and India, as well as some marginal settlement in Africa, in the seventeenth and eighteenth centuries. The eighteenth and nineteenth centuries saw the largest expansion of the Empire as the British took many former French possessions began to settle in large numbers in Australia and later competed fiercely with other European powers for territory in Africa. At the same time, there was serious expansion in Asia, notably the acquisition of Singapore (1824), Hong Kong (1841) and Burma (1886), and the South Pacific, particularly the settlement of New Zealand with the famous Treaty of Waitangi (1840) between the Crown and some 540 Maori chiefs.

Trade, not Empire

Commercial interests, rather than territorial ambition, dictated the growth of the early Empire: England in the sixteenth century was a poor country, lacking the wealth of Portugal and Spain and, unlike the Spaniards and Portuguese, the English were neither missionaries nor colonists. This pattern began to change in the seventeenth century as the English realised the huge commercial potential of overseas acquisitions, starting with the lucrative exploitation of produce from the West Indies. Between 1768 and 1780 scientific naval expeditions commanded by Captain Cook explored the islands and coasts of the Pacific Ocean all the way from the entrance to the Arctic to the then unknown coasts of New Zealand and Australia. The British government started to annex these southern lands when the loss of the American colonies deprived it of a dumping ground for the convicts and debtors who had up until then been deported to North America. The best-known example of private initiative leading the way was the East India Company. An important exception was in the West Indies, where many Members of Parliament had commercial interests and so there was frequent government intervention. However, as the Empire grew, Britain tended towards imperialism, annexing countries for national prestige rather than for commercial gain.

Home rule

The concept of self-government for some of the colonies was first formulated in Lord Durham's Report on British North America (1839). Responsible government, meaning the acceptance by governors of the advice of local ministers, was granted to Upper Canada (Ontario) and Lower Canada (Quebec). This model was subsequently applied to the other Canadian provinces and to the Australian colonies, which attained responsible government by 1859, except for Western Australia (1890). New Zealand obtained responsible government in 1856 and the Cape colony in 1872, followed by Natal in 1893. Another form of self-government, the dominion status, was devised in the late nineteenth and early twentieth century at a series of colonial conferences or imperial conferences in 1907. Canada became a dominion in 1867, Australia in 1901, New Zealand in 1907 and South Africa in 1910. Dominion status was inexactly defined until the Statute of Westminster (1931) established it as synonymous with complete independence.

Indirect rule

The flexible framework of the British Empire included not only the recognition of forms of home rule and local representative institutions. In addition, there was the unscrupulous employment of so-called *indirect rule*. In India, this led to the fainted government of many *maharajas*. India on becoming a republic in 1950 consisted of more than 600 princely kingdoms each with its own *raja* (Hindu) or *nawab*/sultan (Muslim). The British directly ruled one-third of India; the rest was ruled by the above-mentioned princes under the considerable influence of British representatives in court. The word *maharaja* may be construed to be simply "king" (as in Jammu and Kashmir), in spite of its literal translation as "great king". Actually, a handful of these kingdoms were powerful and wealthy enough for their rulers to be called kings, but the remainder were minor principalities, towns or groups of villages. The title of Maharaja was not as common before the British conquered India, elevating many *rajas* to *maharajas*. In India, the British also introduced representative institutions, although with limited powers.

Indirect rule sometimes worked well, sometimes not so well. In Africa, for instance, it was extended from the north of Nigeria to the south of Nigeria, which was formally a protectorate from 1906, although it did not always work out smoothly. The task proved relatively easy in Yorubaland, where the governments and boundaries of traditional kingdoms were retained or, in some instances, revived. In the southeast, where Aro hegemony had been crushed, the search for acceptable local administrators met with frustration. As a result, the tasks of government were left initially in the hands of colonial officials, who antagonised many Igbos. Frederick Lugard as High Commissioner of the Protectorate of Northern Nigeria since 1900 made it work under effective British political control employing indirect rule. His objective was to conquer the entire region and to obtain recognition of the British protectorate by its indigenous rulers, especially the Fulani emirs of the Sokoto Caliphate. Lugard subdued local resistance, using armed force when diplomatic measures failed. If the emirs accepted British authority, abandoned the slave-trade and cooperated with British officials in modernising their administrations, the colonial power was willing to confirm them in office. The emirs would keep their titles, but they were to be responsible to British district officers, exercising authority. The British high commissioners could depose emirs and other officials if necessary. Under indirect rule, the emir officials were transformed into salaried district heads as agents of ultimate British authority, responsible for peacekeeping and tax collection. The old chain of command was merely capped with the British high commissioners.

Indirect rule involved saving administrators, as it required only a limited number of colonial officers scattered throughout the territory as overseers. Flexible in relation to local conditions, indirect rule meant that these overseers exercised discretion in advising the emirs and local officials, but all orders from the high commissioners were transmitted through the emir. Although the high commissioners possessed unlimited executive and legislative powers in the protectorate, the emirs and their local administrations, who were subject to British approval, undertook most of the activities of government. A dual system of law functioned, where the Islamic lawcourts continued to deal with matters affecting the personal status of Muslims, including land disputes, divorce, debt and slave emancipation. However, one consequence of indirect rule was that

Hausa–Fulani domination was not merely confirmed but in some instances imposed on diverse ethnic groups, some of them non-Muslim, in the so-called middle belt (Perham, 1960).

The revenues available to the colonial government limited the accomplishments of Lugard and his successors in economic development. One of Lugard's initial acts was to separate the general treasury of each emirate from the emir's privy purse. From taxes collected by local officials, first one-quarter and later one-half was taken to support services of the colonial regime, which were meagre due to the protectorate's lack of public resources. In the south, missionaries made up for the lack of government expenditure on services; in the north, Lugard and his successors limited the activities of missionaries in order to maintain Muslim domination. Consequently, educational and medical services in the north lagged behind those in the south.

Burke's problem

When the British Empire was at its peak in the 1920s it controlled a quarter of the population and area of the world. Now there are only a few British crown territories left (Gibraltar and some tiny islands in the Atlantic), as the Commonwealth organisation is a weak mechanism of collaboration between the United Kingdom and some of its former territories. Hong Kong was transferred back to Chinese sovereignty in 1997. Edward Burke in his speeches on New England raised the issue of whether British colonial rule could be combined with local independence and tax sovereignty. He argued that Parliament should not impose its domination upon the British colonies, as they were capable of governing themselves without claiming independence. As Parliament did not follow Burke's far-sighted colonial philosophy, as revealed also in his quest for proper administration of India, New England claimed that even under British colonial rule the question was either subjugation or independence (O'Brien, 2002; Stanlis, 2006). The British Empire differentiated between several forms of government: (1) Dominions (Canada, South Africa, Australia, New Zealand); (2) Protectorates (Lesotho, Zambia, Tanzania, Egypt, Malaysia), Mandates (Palestine, Jordan, Iraq) or Trusteeships; (3) Condominiums (Sudan, Swaziland); and (4) Colonies or Crown-colonies (Jamaica, Barbados, Nigeria, Sri Lanka, Falkland Islands, Bermuda, Hong Kong and Fiji).

The first fatal challenge to the Empire came from Ireland, where it may be argued that British penetration began when Henry II declared himself "Lord of Ireland" in 1171. After 750 years of English domination and many rebellions, most of Ireland became the Irish Free State in 1922, with dominion status. A new constitution adopted by the Free State in 1937 dropped the name Irish Free State and declared Ireland (Eire) to be a "sovereign independent state". The break was completed in 1949 when Eire became a republic outside the Commonwealth, though remained in a special relationship with Britain; Northern Ireland is still an integral part of the United Kingdom.

High commissioners, governors and the Colonial Office

Crown colonies as British sovereign territory would be administered by a governor, while the most significant possessions, confederations and the independent Commonwealth dominions would be headed by a governor-general. High commissioners were used in several ways for ruling a country. Thus, they were appointed to manage protectorates or groups of territories not fully under the sovereignty of the British crown. High commissioners were also charged with managing diplomatic relations with native rulers and their states. They might have under them several resident commissioners attached to each state, for instance, when a Commissioner-General would be appointed, who would have control over several high commissioners and governors. The Commissioner-General for South-East Asia had responsibility for Malaya, Singapore and British Borneo. The title of High Commissioner was also used for the administrators of mandates and trust territories, (e.g. British Mandate of Palestine).

The Colonial Office was established to administer its colonial possessions, including British North America. It set up forms of government and the church, appointed governors, approved local laws and made grants for particular purposes. It managed "imperial subjects" such as commerce and shipping, which gradually came under the exclusive control of the self-governing colonies. As colonial affairs expanded and became more important, a permanent under-secretary was appointed in 1825 to deal with the colonies. This marks the beginning of the Colonial Office, although a separate Secretary of State for the Colonies was not created until 1854, after the Crimean War began. Further reorganisation occurred as the range of powers claimed by the colonies expanded, and as relations with these colonies became diplomatic rather than administrative. A Dominion Division within the Colonial Office dealt with the self-governing colonies between 1907 and 1925, when it became the Secretary of State for Dominion Affairs. In 1947 this became the Commonwealth Relations Office, which in 1966 merged with the Colonial Office, later to be swallowed up by the Foreign Office.

African colonialism

No continent was as much penetrated in a rapacious manner by colonial forces as Africa. It started early in the sixteenth century, continued with the massive transportation of slaves from Africa to America and was completed with the division of the whole of Africa between the European powers of Great Britain, France, Germany, Portugal, Belgium and Italy in 1884 to 1885 (Berlin Conference). Only one country was not drawn into colonial domination, namely Liberia, founded in 1847 by liberated black slaves from the United States. Although British, French and Portuguese rule was different with regard to the technology of rule employed, they all had a profound impact on Africa. All hitherto existing civilisations in Africa were uprooted and the African economy was integrated with its colonial counterparts. The purpose of exploitation was obvious behind the rhetoric of humanitarianism (Davidson, 1994).

The major European powers were able to establish domination in vast territories due to efficient administration and the possibility of employing a superior military force. The road to liberation for the African population was the take-over of the colonial state established by the Europeans. It had a different structure in the British, French, Belgian and Portuguese territories. Great Britain relied on mixing immigration from the motherland with collaboration with the indigenous population. Thus in British areas there were large minorities of white people who were deeply involved in running the colonies within the framework set by Westminster. British rule took the form of *indirect rule.* The French model was different from the British model, as it relied on centralisation, meaning that the administration of the colonies would be carried by the traditional prefecture system employed in the French interior. Thus a small French population had to carry out orders from Paris about how to govern the indigenous population. Finally, the Portuguese model relied heavily on the employment of repression.

By the time of the Berlin Conference the map of Africa had been drawn up by the colonial powers. Little attention had been paid to Africa's complicated system of tribes and ethnic minorities. The territorial borders were drawn up by European rulers, often with the direct intention to weaken the Africans by creating internal dissensus between ethnic groups: *Divide et Impera!* Germany arrived late with a colony in Namibia (1884–1915).

While the German Empire in Africa crumbled during the First World War, the other three empires lasted much longer. The African independent states were created almost always after fierce resistance from Great Britain, France and Portugal. German protectorates included Burundi, Cameroon, Rwanda, Tanganyika and Togo, which were taken over by the British, the Belgians and the French. Belgium held on to Belgian Congo, whereas Italy was active first and foremost in Libya but also in Somalia and later on in Ethiopia. Whereas Spain only dominated Equatorial Guinea and Spanish Sahara, Portugal ruled vast territories such as Angola and Mozambique in addition to Guinea-Bissau and Sao Tome and Principe.

The British colonial system was formidable in terms of size, whether measured by area of territory or of population. In Africa the British protectorates included Egypt, Libya (1942–1951), Sudan, Botswana, Gambia, Ghana, Kenya, Lesotho, Malawi, Mauritius, Nigeria, Seychelles, Sierra Leone, South Africa, Swaziland, Uganda, Zambia and Zimbabwe. In some of these colonies there were substantial white minorities occupying key positions in the administration and the economy, in particular in Zambia, Zimbabwe and Tanzania, which Great Britain took over from the Germans. The situation in South Africa was radically different from the beginning, as there was a substantial white minority which had come long before the English, namely the Boers originating in the Netherlands and France.

The French Empire in Africa was not of quite the same size, but it covered a number of territories that later on became independent states. France had concentrated holdings in North and Western Africa besides the huge island of Madagascar: Algeria, Tunisia, Morocco, Benin, Burkina Faso, the Central African Republic, Chad, Comoros, Congo, Gabon, Guinea, the Ivory Coast, Mali, Mauritania and Niger.

How easy it was for the European states to conquer Africa is well illustrated in Belgian Congo, or what was to become the independent state of Zaire. King Leopold II of Belgium claimed this vast territory as his personal colony in the 1870s, which met international acceptance in 1895. It was not until 1907 that it was transformed from a personal possession into a Belgian colony. It has been much debated in terms of African history what caused this complete lack of capacity to resist European penetration. The European great powers did not have to risk huge resources and manpower when subjugating African rulers. As a matter of fact, only the Boers put up fierce resistance against the British. Somehow the time of the great African dynasties had been used up and the African societies were badly weakened by the slave trade.

Again, the path to overcome foreign rule was to take over the administration and set up states following the European model. The process of liberation became difficult as the European colonial powers clinged firmly to their colonies, resorting to violence when other means did not work. The Second World War made the difference, as after 1945 independence could be claimed as entailed in the general victory over fascist oppression and foreign rule. Several African colonies had contributed soldiers to the Allied campaign.

Yet all the European powers tried at first to stop the independence movement by the use of force, which resulted in civil wars in several African countries, in particular in the French and Portuguese colonies. The British Empire had already granted South Africa independence in 1909 by introducing the dominion of the Union of South Africa. In 1960 South Africa became a republic, declining membership in the Commonwealth. It controlled Namibia up until 1989. Already in 1922 the control of Egypt had been partially given up, which was followed in 1936 by a full recognition of Egypt's independence from Great Britain with the exception of the Suez Canal, which British troops left in 1956. That same year Sudan became an independent republic.

The real decline of British power occurred in the 1950s when its key colonies in central Africa demanded independence. Following a civil war in Kenya, the British government decided to set these territories free, at the same time offering the new states membership within the Commonwealth, which some accepted. Thus, we have Ghana in 1957 and in 1960 the large state of Nigeria in West Africa. Kenya was set free in 1963, and in 1964

Malawi, a former part of the Federation of Rhodesia and Nyasaland, became an independent state. Tanzania followed in 1964 by a merger of Tanganyika and the sultanate Zanzibar, as well as Zambia or Northern Rhodesia in 1964. It was not until 1980 that Southern Rhodesia or Zimbabwe became independent due to the unsuccessful Ian Smith declaration of independence in 1965 and the ensuing civil war.

The challenge to the French Empire in Africa was initiated in North Africa, where there were sizeable French minorities after the Second World War. There were 250,000 Europeans in Tunisia, more than one million in Algeria and roughly 300,000 in Morocco. Following a period of clashes France gave in and acknowledged the independence of Tunisia in 1956. Similarly, Morocco became a free state after a nationalist uproar and a guerrilla war. However, the fight for independence became very bitter, bloody and protracted in Algeria, which had been ruled directly from Paris as an integral part of France whereas Morocco and Tunisia had been protectorates. The independence of the Algerian state was not recognised until 1962.

The breakup of colonial domination took place according to the domino-effect model. It was practically impossible to prevent the many colonies in Africa from successfully claiming independence once European domination had been given up (e.g. in South East Asia and North Africa). Thus by 1960 several new states had been created in West Africa (e.g. Guinea in 1958, Togo in 1960 and Cameroon in 1960). Besides, in 1960 the free state of Madagascar was recognised. Whereas the Belgian Empire was abandoned after a short period of upheaval in 1959 to 1960, the Portuguese colonies had to fight a long war until the authoritarian regime in Portugal fell in 1974. Thus, in 1960 Congo (Zaire) was created as were Rwanda and Burundi in the former Belgian colonies in 1962. Guinea-Bissau had to wait until 1974, and Angola, Mozambique, Cap Verde and Sao Tomé waited until 1975 for independence to be recognised.

Towards an American empire?

Several European powers were involved in the colonialisation of North America: England, France, Holland, Spain and Sweden. The French territories were large up until the loss of Canada to England in 1763 and the sale of the Louisiana territory in 1803 to the United States. The first independent state in America was the United States of America, founded in 1776 with a constitution from 1787. The USA was small at that time compared to what it would be in 1898 when Hawaii had been added to all the other land territories annexed or bought from other states including Mexico during the nineteenth century. The status of the Canadian state reflects the fact that Canada has remained within the British Empire, or Commonwealth as it is now called. This means that Queen Elizabeth II is still the head of state. In 1867 the self-governing dominion of Canada was founded by an amalgamation of the English- and French-speaking parts.

One may perhaps speak of an empire with regard to the United States itself, penetrating the crumbling Spanish empire. Actually, the Monroe Declaration in 1823 expressed the imperialist ambitions of the newly founded state in relation to the American continent. At the end of the nineteenth century the United States went to war in order to capture land from Spain. The Philippines with its many islands and numerous populations remained under Spain up until 1898 when it was ceded to the USA. While during the Second World War it was occupied by Japan, it became an independent state in 1946. The Philippines had been discovered, so to speak, by Magellan in 1521 and came under Spanish domination already in 1565. Today it is often argued that the United States has put in place some form of empire, *Pax Americana*, based on its enormous military effort. Whether the US also seeks global hegemony is a highly contested issue. The period of the empires appears to be finally over. No country can successfully uphold a claim to empire at the beginning of the twenty-first century, not even the United States of America with its overwhelming dominance in terms of military power. Since colonialism is dead as an ideology, there is little room for the creation of empires. In addition, the idea of empire is at odds with the notion of international rule of law as a regime shared among sovereign nation-states.

The difficulties in sustaining empires were one cause of the demise of the Soviet Union, and the Americans may experience similar problems today (Johnson, 2007). Sooner or later, America will reap the global resentments it is now sowing (Johnson, 2002). Johnson (2006) analyses in detail how American hegemony works involving 500,000 soldiers and support staff at 725 permanent bases in 38 countries. In the key oil-producing regions of the Middle East and Central Asia, there are bases in Iraq, Saudi Arabia, Kuwait, Qatar, Bahrain, the United Arab Emirates, Oman, Egypt, Djibouti, Turkey, Kyrgyzstan, Afghanistan and Pakistan, plus secret bases in Israel. Johnson underlines the unintended consequences of American policies and the dangers faced by an over-extended empire that insists on projecting its military power to every corner of the globe and using American capital and markets to force global economic integration on its own terms. In the wake of the Cold War, the USA has expanded the commitments it made over the previous 40 years. Perhaps it is time for the American Empire to demobilise before its bills become too expensive even for the United States (Brzezinski, 2004).

It is often argued that US policy is dictated by imperial motives, targeting access to first and foremost oil. The proposed Trans-Afghan oil and gas pipelines run south from Turkmenistan, through Afghanistan, to Pakistan's port of Gwadar. In Eastern Europe, Camps Bondsteel and Monteith in Kosovo bestride the proposed Trans-Balkan pipeline, which would run from Georgia through Bulgaria to Albania's port of Vlora. Camp Sarafovo is in Burgas, home to Bulgaria's biggest oil refinery, and the camp at Constanta dominates the centre of Rumania's oil industry. In Colombia, several hundred US "advisers" are fighting not drug runners, but to protect occidental

Petroleum's oil and gas interests in Arauca province. Yet this is not the place to discuss alternative theories of American foreign policy (Kagan, 2004). What can be underlined is, however, that the Americans pay a grim price for their hegemonic policy towards the United Nations in the Iraq question. The costs to the United States for the unfortunate second war in Iraq serve to emphasise the necessity of a multilateral approach to global war and peace, as the period of empires is over, which the principal–agent model (PAM) entails.

The postcolonial state

When colonial regimes were demolished or replaced peacefully, there emerged what has come to be called the Third World State. Although these new regimes were modelled upon European models, the aspiration to create nation-states proved far too ambitious. Ethnic and religious heterogeneity has made the European notion of a nation-state barely applicable in a Third World context. What, then, is the nature of the Third World State? And is it viable? Several models of the Third World State have been suggested. They all target a certain lack of survival capacity, attempting to identify where the weakness of the state originates. I will discuss some of these models below.

Weak states, strong societies

Migdal has presented a model that captures the predicament of some Third World states (Migdal, 1988): weak states, strong societies. Migdal argues that the standard definition of the state, according to Weber's approach, resembles more of an image than a practice. In reality, the state is not autonomous to social forces, but it may actually be invaded by society, the economy and local power holders. This competition between state and society would explain some relative state failures after the occidental colonies were abolished. Migdal states:

> This structure of society, with its fragmentation of social control, has denied the state the ability to mobilize these clients politically. The altered priorities of state leaders (survival over social change), the style of state politics ("big shuffles", "dirty tricks", etc.), the structure of state organization (redundant agencies), the difficulties in implementing policy, the calculus of pressures on the implementor, the capture of the tentacles of the state – all these have derived from the fragmented structure of society.
>
> (Migdal, 2001: 93)

One may wish also to add that the combination of weak state and weak society occurs in Third World countries. I am referring to the countries where poverty is so overwhelming that society is not strong enough to capture anything, not even a weak government. These societies would be in countries ravaged by anarchy and civil war, where a weak state is engaged in a power struggle with war lords.

Speaking of strong states and strong societies, one may refer to very different models. On the one hand, there is the law enforcement state according to the US model, meaning a strong government which however does not infringe much upon the operation of markets. On the other hand, there is the redistributive state in continental Europe, which attempts to tackle welfare besides the market economy. Finally, one may wish to mention the Singapore model, where a strong state directs a strong economy – *state dirigisme*. In Fukuyama (2004), there is an emphasis upon the importance for political development that at least a law enforcement state be put in place. As several Third World countries have weak states that cannot uphold law and order, Fukuyama calls for world-wide support for state-building in these countries.

African prebendal state

Joseph analysed the problems of state-building in Nigeria as well as the seeming impossibility of consolidating a democracy in this the largest country in Africa, employing the Weberian concept of prebendalism (Joseph, 1987). When scholars speak about the prebendal state in Africa they use this term "prebendalism", which originates in medieval Europe, as priests were provided with an income of whatever kind (*prebend*) for their services, sometimes delivered by others. Prebendalism covers more than corruption, patronage or clientelism, as it also involves the trade in government offices, taxes and resources as well as the lack of a *quid pro quo* between income provided and the delivery of a service. Hyden has called the African state "the politics of affection", while Young talks about "over-consumption and underperformance". Diamond and Mbembe speaks about the economic advantage of controlling positions in the bureaucracy. The instability of the state in Sub-Saharan Africa has had a very negative impact upon economic and social development (Bayart, 1993; Bayart *et al.*, 1999; Herbst, 2000; Kpundeh and Levy, 2004).

Arab rentier state

Several authors have employed the idea of a rentier state or semi-rentier state in order to pin down the basic features of government in both the oil monarchies and Arab republics (Luciani, 1990). In addition, Gabon in Africa has been labelled a *"rentier state"* (Yates, 1996). The Arab rentier state in its full version or its semi-version is to be found not only in the countries with abundant oil resources but this model would also have affected the other Arab countries that lack oil, if this theory is correct. Two features count as evidence for the existence of a rentier state: (1) the feeble development of representative institutions; and (2) the large size of public services of various kinds.

The basic rationale behind the rentier state is actually the European medieval principle: no representation, no taxation, which is here turned around, meaning that when the rulers do not need access to resources with the help of taxation, they can also refrain from sharing power with a national assembly. The enormous windfall profits from oil exploration provide the rulers with what they need to pay for abundant public services.

Fully directly elected national representative institutions are missing entirely in Saudi Arabia, Qatar, the United Arab Emirates and Oman. The Kuwaiti Parliament was introduced in 1961, but has been suspended twice, in 1976 and 1986. The Parliaments in the Gulf states include appointed members by the ruler and deliver counsels (*Shura*). The other Arab countries have representative institutions but they serve to legitimate the regime and not to challenge government. The oil monarchies appear to be more stable than ever as the petrol revenues increase. However, the modernisation of the societies in the Gulf has resulted in the emergence of a civil society which wants to have a say in government. Thus, consultative institutions (*shura*) have been accepted, but they include more petitions, indirectly elected councils and tribal participation than an independent role for a legislative assembly. The rich Arab countries have a high capacity to provide public services to their populations, but the state is characterised by heavy patronage.

Asian cronyism state

Wade has characterised government in South East Asia as suffering from endemic cronyism (Wade, 2003). This occurrence of a blending of public and private would characterise both the newly rich and the poor countries in Far East Asia including Malaysia, the Philippines, Indonesia and Taiwan but also mainland China today. By "cronyism" is meant an interpenetration of the economic system with the political system and vice versa. It is a side effect of the developmental state in South East Asia, or the combination of the doctrine of economic nationalism with patronage and corruption. A long period of economic growth based upon export-led expansion through various forms of subsidies to domestic entrepreneurs together with infrastructural development has offered lots of opportunities for the economic and political elites to enrich themselves through collaboration in various ventures and through state contracts. "Cronyism" reflects not only the model of economic development but also the strong state tradition in South East Asia where a lack of constitutional tradition is typical of all countries. The Asian crisis in 1996 to 1997 set off numerous reform attempts to clarify the borders between economics and politics and seal markets off from state intervention and control. However, the economic explosion in mainland China has hardly made things better, as the institutions of the Chinese economy are far from transparently defined or enforced.

Conclusion

The common core of the problem of the Third World state – the "rentier state", the "overextended state", the "parasitical state", the "predatory state", the "lame leviathan", "the patrimonial state", the "prebendal state", the "crony state", the "kleptocratic state", the "inverted state", – is the occurrence of corruption in government and the bureaucracy. The the so-called transparency index capturing the occurrence of corruption indicates that there are considerable differences between the 11 civilisations identified in Table 4.8 (eta squared = 0.60 in Table 4.9). During the twenty-first century Third World countries will need to improve so-called good governance. The reduction of corruption is extremely difficult to accomplish however, as the demand for and supply of corruption is closely linked with poverty. If state-building takes the form of transparency in government as well as respect for rule by law and rule of law, then much will be accomplished, even if nation-states are not forthcoming due to ethnic and religious heterogeneity.

Corruption is one aspect of the general strategy of looting that besets principal–agent interaction. Its occurrence can only be limited by the use of institutions and their strict enforcement. Colonialism offers a strange principal–agent game where foreign powers supply political agents to a country, often with the argument that it promotes development. At its best, colonialism is a form of tutelage, where political agents are of the opinon that they know the "true" interests of the population. At its worst, colonialism reverses the principal–agent relationship, making the principal a target of exploitation for the agents.

The nation–state was introduced in many European countries in the form of the absolutist regime, which retained basic features of the feudal society – see *Lineages of the Absolutist State* (Anderson, 1979). The centralised monarchies of, for example, France, Spain and Denmark was a break with the pyramidal, parcellised sovereignty of the estates society, but in Eastern Europe army, bureaucracy, diplomacy and dynasty made up a feudal complex, its costs carried by subjugated peasants or serfs. The political order remained feudal, while society became more and more bourgeois and vulnerable to rural unrest. Despite representative institutions being suppressed, except in England and Sweden, royal absolutism proved unsustainable politics from the principal–agent perspective. The *Boyar Duma*, for example, was stopped by Peter the Great in 1721, but in 1905 an Imperial State *Duma* was promised with legislative and oversight powers.

12 Regionalisation of the state

Introduction

Regional organisations are mushrooming at the moment. Regionalism is on its way to becoming a new interdisciplinary field in the social and economic sciences. This chapter stresses real agency, as regional blocks may be created out of mere political symbolism. Regional organisation is attractive because it offers a flexible response to the challenges of globalisation. However, the uncertainty in regional organisation is real, as governments tend to postpone or renege on ambitious plans for regional organisation, not knowing what the constitutional implications are from far-reaching regionalisation. When a regional organisation engages in a common market project, the question of the ratio of benefits against costs becomes so highly relevant that constitutional decision-making is called for. A new structure for economic regulation must be designed and enforced, the consequences of which spill over into other state regulations. A regional block of states must devise and run a minimum of common institutions in order to qualify as an organisation. In a maximum approach, a regional organisation takes over public competences from the participating nation-states.

Regional organisation is currently very popular with government (http://en.wikipedia.org/wiki/Trade_blocks). The pace of regional organisation will probably pick up speed after the failure of the so-called Doha round with the WTO and its global approach. One can now speak of a set of regional blocks of states that engage in certain activities that were normally run by the nation-state. Most of these have promised more in the years to come, but it is a typical feature of these new regional organisations that they promise more than they can deliver.

From an institutional point of view, there is a variation in the modes of regional organisation that is worth an explanation that goes beyond the simple Balassa framework of regional organisation: from the free trade area to the monetary union (Balassa, 1982). Why do some regional blocks choose one mode of organisation and not another? Some forms of regional organisation replace ordinary state organisation, calling for constitutional recognition.

Regional organisation is intimately linked with the incentives of govern-ments. It is these interests that lead the governments of states into various modes of regional organisation. The economic interests behind regional blocks cannot de doubted, given the global emphasis on trade and trade lib-eralisation. It is when governments take further steps beyond free trade or preferential trade agreements that they have to clarify what interests they aim to pursue in terms of a specific organisation. Regional organisation comes with costs that have to be picked up by the participants, who also need to take into account the risks involved. When regional organisation replaces state organisation, the participant governments need to be well aware of the benefits and the costs.

Bilateral regulation of reciprocities between states may appear as extremely heavy transaction costs, but multilateral regulation may not always be possible due to conflicts among major sets of countries in the world. Thus, regional organisation offers a promising mode of handling the interdependencies among countries that the ongoing process of globalisation throws up. But once it is actually done, it may have constitutional implica-tions, and it certainly comes with a cost bill. Public organisation deals with competences, rights and duties. When regional organisations multiply, the pertinent question is: What competences do they handle?

Basic modes of regional organisation

There are several outlines of or schemes for modes of regional organisation to be found with the many regional blocks of states, but it is far from certain that there is a corresponding institutional reality. Although decisions may have been made about plans for regional organisation, the implementation of such schemes tends to be slow and open to many reversals. Yet it would be fruitful to survey the new political units with *regional blocks of states* in order to pin down what they are doing. In Africa, for instance, there is a large number of regional organisations, but not all of them are actually oper-ating ones, as some of these free trade areas or common markets in Africa remain promises or projects only. It is impossible to achieve much in terms of state coordination regionally when the governments involved are not in control of their own territories.

A regional organisation is *not* the same as a mere free trade agreement, although it may include that. One motive for setting up a regional organisa-tion is clearly economic, but a regional organisation would include more than a mere contract to liberalise trade among a set of states. Typical of a regional organisation is that it takes over certain government tasks from the nation-state. The crucial question is to pin down which these competences tend to be. There are many bilateral trade agreements and some of them do not imply that state competences are to be handed over to a regional organi-sation somehow. A regional organisation includes at least a discussion forum, where the governments of sovereign states meet on a regular basis to deliberate common problems. Regional organisations often devote considerable time to spectacular conferences, merely to show a façade of unity where there is division and conflict. Yet a regional block of states must devise and run a minimum of common institutions in order to qualify as an organisation. Setting up a continous scheme for rounds of talks between sovereign states requires some planning and information gathering that commits governments to collaboration and the coordination of efforts.

If the creation of a regional forum for continuous information sharing and debate on issues is the starting point of regionalisation, then one may distinguish between alternative modes of regional organisation depending on how the set of competences is identified:

1   Politics: A regional forum
2   Policies: Regional facilities
3   Economics I: Trading blocks or customs union
4   Economics II: Currency areas
5   Economics III: Common markets
6   Federation: Common defence

Working through the above list results in an increasingly complex coordination mechanism, at the end of the day requiring some form of constitutional recognition. Regional cooperation may be discussion and information sharing, the running of a common facility, or various forms of economic collaboration. A common market is the most demanding form of regional economic organisation, as it requires much in terms of public regulation as well as dispute settlement. A federation would entail that the regional organisation becomes a new state, replacing the existing ones, but no regional organisation has gone that far.

The regional forum

Governments are increasingly attracted by the idea of a forum, i.e. a regular meeting place for rounds of talks about common problems. This amounts to a minimum level of organisation, involving a small secretariat with the resources necessary to hold meetings once or twice a year and engage in information gathering. The secretariat may only possess some intelligence resources, such as collecting data, preparing reports and disseminating information, but its planning may have a large impact on future events.

The forum may look innocuous, but it could serve basic political interests such as clarifying defence and foreign policy issues among states in tension. One example comes readily to one's mind: the SAARC, covering Bangladesh, Bhutan, India, the Maldives, Nepal, Pakistan and Sri Lanka. Although created already in 1985, it has only put in place a free trade area from 2006 (SAFTA). How could such a regional organisation really work, given the Kashmir problem between Pakistan and India, as well as the internal turmoil within Nepal and Sri Lanka? War-torn Afghanistan has been accepted as a member, and unruly Iran has also expressed interest in joining. Could that really work? It depends on what the real objectives are in regional organisation. Promoting peace and avoiding war is no small ambition, especially if some of the governments involved have nuclear capacity.

In debating issues of conflict between states, governments may promote peace. Although a long round of regular meetings may not resolve the fundamental conflicts, at least military confrontation is avoided. The longer this period of unstable peace lasts, the more one may hope that the worst outcome can be avoided. Such purposes of debating thorny issues between states may comprise not only the question of war and peace but also migration, border controls, transnational crime and the spread of diseases. Many of the regional organisations today are merely fora, meaning that governments meet and sign letters or treaties of intention in various fields.

The forum model is also attractive when the goals of regional cooperation are mainly cultural ones. Governments may wish to identify a common culture or historical legacy for a number of states, despite all economic differences between them. Culture would deliver the cement of cohesion for a regional block, especially if economics creates divergence among the countries involved. Here, the regional efforts in the Muslim civilisation come to mind: the Arab League and the Organisation of Islamic Conference, focusing upon Islam and its cultural roots in the Arab civilisation.

Another example of regional organisation as the forum would be the Asean. The Asean regularly conducts dialogue meetings with other countries and an organization, known under the label of the *ASEAN dialogue partners* during the Asean Regional Forum (ARF). The ARF is an informal multilateral dialogue of 25 members concerned with security issues in the Asia-Pacific region. The ARF met for the first time in 1994. ARF includes: Asean, Australia, Canada, the People's Republic of China, the European Union, India, Japan, North Korea, South Korea, Mongolia, New Zealand, Pakistan, Papua New Guinea, Russia, East Timor and the United States. Bangladesh was added to ARF as the twenty-sixth member, dating from 28 July 2006.

An ideal-type example of a forum is APEC, covering the entire Pacific Ocean area with the exception of the small island states there. Asia-Pacific Economic Cooperation, or APEC, is a forum for facilitating economic growth, cooperation, trade and investment in the Asia-Pacific region. APEC operates on the basis of non-binding commitments, open dialogue and equal respect for the views of all participants. Unlike other multilateral trade bodies, APEC requires no treaty obligations of its participants. APEC has 21 members – referred to as "Member Economies" – which account for approximately 40 per cent of the world's population, approximately 56 per cent of world GDP and about 48 per cent of world trade. It also proudly represents the most economically dynamic region in the world, having generated nearly 70 per cent of global economic growth in its first ten years.

APEC's 21 Members are: Australia; Brunei Darussalam; Canada; Chile; the People's Republic of China; Hong Kong; Indonesia; Japan; Republic of Korea; Malaysia; Mexico; New Zealand; Papua New Guinea; Peru; The Republic of the Philippines; The Russian Federation; Singapore; Chinese Taipei; Thailand; United States of America; and Vietnam. APEC was established in 1989 to further enhance economic growth and prosperity for the region and to strengthen the Asia-Pacific community. APEC has worked to reduce tariffs and other trade barriers across the Asia-Pacific region, creating efficient domestic economies and dramatically increasing exports. APEC's vision covers the "Bogor Goals" of free and open trade and investment in the Asia-Pacific by 2010 for industrialised economies and 2020 for developing economies.

The forum may simply serve as a tension reduction mechanism between states, pushing issues further into the future without resolving much. Or the forum may set the framework for regional planning, having a huge impact on the member states' governments. It may be highly successful in setting the agenda for several governments, enhancing common plans towards, for instance, global warming and environmental degradation. The forum may also be a façade that creates an illusion of regional cooperation and understanding. Take the example of the Commonwealth of Independent States, which replace the Soviet Union. What has come out of this forum is the plan of the EurAsEC: in 1995, Russia and Belarus created a customs union, which Kazakhstan and Kyrgyzstan later joined. Belarus, Kazakhstan, Kyrgyzstan, Russia and Tajikistan signed the treaty creating the Eurasian Economic Community in 2001. One objective is to develop a full-scale customs union and common economic space and another includes harmonisation of customs tariffs. It is difficult to tell whether there are any real outcomes of the CIS or its offspring. The forum is politics, often high politics. But regional organisation may also be low politics, or the implementation of a set of common facilities serving educational, health or communication policies.

Regional facilities

The pooling of country resources to set up regional organisations within a public law framework is hardly new. It has been done in the past outside of the regional integration ideology that is now so strong in all parts of the world with the possible exception of Japan and China. Such regional facilities offer a springboard for further integration, underlining that economies of scale pay a major role in organisation. The basic theory of regional facilities is the so-called *club theory* (Cornes and Sandler, 1996).

The set of regional facilities is a broad one, including common airline, common university, common space exploration policy, common air navigation policy, common cultural institutions, and common sports and leisure activities. Both rich and poor regional organisations operate one or another regional facility. From a club theory point of view, the tiny states of the world would have most to gain from offering regionally based services. In the Pacific Ocean, the South Pacific states operate a number of common institutions, such as: (1) the Pacific Forum (12 member states plus Australia and New Zealand); (2) the University of South Pacific; (3) Air Pacific, Pacific Forum Line; and (4) Forum Fisheries Agency.

Economics I: FTAs and customs unions

A free trade area or preferential trade area is formed by one or more tax, tariff and trade agreement. A number of regionally based trade blocs have emerged recently to promote trade between member states through trade liberalisation measures. Several blocs also have political goals – notably the EU. Economic blocs include free trade areas and customs unions with preferential trade agreements somewhere in between.

A trading block may be anything from a loose FTA to a compact customs union with a common market attached to it. It exists to the extent that expressed ambitions by governments at regional meetings are really put into practice. Yet, the Wikipedia list is a mixture of various kinds of regional organisation. It is far from exhaustive and may even include some phoney organisations, meaning paper ones. One may distinguish between a number of regional organisations depending on how strongly they integrate the various country economies. Often regional organisations have ambitions but the implementation tends to be projected into the future.

Thus one may, for example, question the existence of the following trade blocs: AEC, COMESA and CSN. In 1996, the AEC held its first ministerial session and adopted a work programme designed to accelerate the integration process on the entire continent. The AEC Assembly of Heads of State and Government held its inaugural session in Harare, Zimbabwe in 1997. In 1978 in Lusaka, COMESA advocated the creation of a subregional economic community with a PTA, beginning with a subregional preferential trade area. The PTA was established to take advantage of a larger market size. The PTA Treaty envisaged its transformation into a common market and, in conformity with this, the Treaty establishing the Common Market for Eastern and Southern Africa, COMESA, was signed in 1993. CSN (Spanish: *Comunidad Sudamericana de Naciones*) is meant to be a continent-wide free trade zone uniting the two existing free trade organisations – Mercosur and the Andean Community – eliminating tariffs for *non-sensitive products* by 2014 and *sensitive products* by 2019. The headquarters of this new organisation will be in Lima while the South American Bank will be in Brasilia. Although there are trade pacts that endorse the above regional organisations, most of it still comes in the form of plans and ambitions. One real trading bloc with a strong regional organisation is the OECS in the Caribbean region, where some of its member states are also included in CARICOM.

Economic incentives count for much when setting up a regional organisation. It is first and foremost trade that looms large in regionalisation, as fundamental trade theory promises considerable benefits if trade is liberalised. Countries that attempt to capture the benefits from trade liberalisation constitute themselves as trading blocs, whether it is a FTA or a customs union or something in between. A number of countries set up a secretariat in order to implement free trade agreements: FTAs or PTAs. Such a secretariat would define rules and interpret them with regard to the FTA or a preferential trade agreement. But it would not need any special institutions such as a judiciary: police and court. All countries have some kind of bilateral trade agreement, but they do not require any special institutions for their enforcement. When a group of states with more than five or ten member states come together under one trade regime, then things may be different, calling for a common mechanism of some sort, handling a set of rules and resolving problems in the implementation of these rules. Managing a free trade area involves so-called facilitation measures. The difference between an FTA and a customs union is blurred when countries operate a preferential trade agreement.

A Free Trade Area is a region in which obstacles to unrestricted trade have been reduced to a minimum. The Free Trade Area is a result of a Free Trade Agreement (a form of trade pact) between two or more countries. A Preferential Trade Area gives preferential access to certain products from certain countries by reducing tariffs, although not abolishing them completely. A Preferential Trade Area involves the EU and the ACP countries. A PTA is established through trade pact. A Free Trade Area is a designated group of countries that have agreed to eliminate tariffs, quotas and preferences on most (if not all) goods between them. Countries choose this kind of economic integration if their economical structures are complementary. If they are competitive, they will choose customs union. Unlike a customs union, members of a Free Trade Area do not have the same policies with respect to non-members, meaning different quotas and customs. To avoid evasion (through re-exportation) the countries use Rules of Origin, where there is a requirement for the minimum extent of local material inputs and local work on the goods (http://en.wikipedia.org/wiki/Free_trade_area).

The logic of Free Trade Areas/Agreements entails that they are *cascadable*. If some countries sign an agreement to form Free Trade Areas and choose to negotiate (either as a trade bloc or as a forum of individual members of their FTA) another Free Trade Agreement with some external country (or countries), then the new FTA will consist of the old FTA plus the new country (or countries). Cumulation occurs between different FTAs restricted only by the so-called Rules of Origin. Sometimes different FTAs supplement each other, but in other cases there may be no cross-cumulation between the FTAs.

The aim of a Free Trade Area is to reduce barriers to easy exchange so that trade can grow as a result of specialisation, division of labour, and most importantly via (the theory and practice of) comparative advantage. The theory of comparative advantage argues that in an unrestricted marketplace (in equilibrium) each source of production will tend to specialise in that activity where it has comparative (rather than absolute) advantage. The theory argues that the net result will be an increase in income and ultimately wealth and well-being for everyone in the Free Trade Area. However, the theory refers only to aggregate wealth and says nothing about the distribution of wealth. In fact there may be significant losers, in particular among the recently protected industries with a comparative disadvantage. The proponent of free trade can, however, retort that the gains of the gainers exceed the losses of the losers.

A customs union is a Free Trade Area with a set of common external tariffs. The participant countries set up a common external trade policy, but in some cases they use different import quotas. Common competition policy is also helpful to avoid competition deficiency. Purposes for establishing a customs union normally include increasing economic efficiency and establishing closer political and cultural ties between the member countries. Customs union is established through trade pact.

A customs union needs some administrative capacity tied to it. Thus, the common framework of tariffs and quotas needs to have surveillance. However, there is hardly any need for common political institutions, as these trade tasks can be handled through delegation to an agency at arm's length from the different governments.

Economics II: monetary unions

A monetary union may be a mere currency union (e.g. the Latin Monetary Union in the 1800s), which does not involve a single market, or it may be an economic union with a common market. The EMU is established through a currency-related trade pact and offers a monetary union but it does not cover the entire single market of the EU. The largest real economic and monetary union at present is the Eurozone. The Eurozone consists of the European Union member states that have completed the third stage of the EMU by adopting the euro. Some non-EU members have also adopted the euro, but they are not part of this EMU.

Monetary unions arise whenever two or more countries use one and the same currency. Thus, there have been several currency unions without common markets: The euro is used by 12 European Union member states and is also used in Monaco, San Marino and the Vatican City which are licensed to issue and use the euro. Monetary unions may be set up by *fiat*, for instance a regional block of states creating a central bank or an emission institute to enhance regional integration. Andorra, Kosovo and Montenegro all use the euro as legal tender although they are not part of the Eurozone. The CFA franc BEAC (Central Africa) is used by Cameroon, the Central African Republic, Chad, the Republic of Congo, Equatorial Guinea and Gabon and is issued by the *Communauté Économique et Monétaire de l'Afrique Centrale* (CEMAC), i.e. the Economic and Monetary Community of Central

Africa. The CFA franc BCEAO (West Africa) is used by Benin, Burkina Faso, Côte d'Ivoire, Guinea-Bissau, Mali, Niger, Senegal and Togo and is issued by the Union Économique et Monétaire Ouest Africaine (UEMOA), i.e. the West African Economic and Monetary Union. The CFP franc is used by French Polynesia, New Caledonia, and Wallis and Futuna and is issued by the Institut d'émission d'outre-mer (IEOM), i.e. the Overseas Issuing Institute. Moreover, the United States dollar is used in Palau, Micronesia, the Marshall Islands, Panama, Ecuador, El Salvador, East Timor, the British Virgin Islands and the Turks and Caicos Islands. The Australian dollar is used by Australia, Kiribati, Nauru and Tuvalu. The New Zealand dollar is used by New Zealand, Niue, the Cook Islands, Tokelau and the Pitcairn Islands. The South African rand is legal tender in South Africa, Swaziland, Lesotho and Namibia through the Common Monetary Area. The Russian ruble is used in Russia and the Georgian autonomous (self-declared independent) republics of Abkhazia and South Ossetia. The Palestinian territories under the control of the Palestinian National Authority use the new Israeli shekel (as does Israel). In the countries of Brunei and Singapore, the Brunei dollar and the Singapore dollar are legal tender in both countries.

Actually, a monetary union does not need a common central bank or a common facility issuing legal tender. It is enough that one country merely adopts the currency of another country. Sometimes countries use two currencies, the national official one and a shadow foreign currency. Yet, it is true that when countries formally set up a monetary union, they construct some money-issuing authority. Thus, for instance, the Organisation of East Carribean States supports a central bank as most OECS member-states are participants in the Eastern Caribbean Central Bank (ECCB) monetary authority. The regional central bank oversees financial and banking integrity for the Organisation of Eastern Caribbean States economic bloc of states to maintain the financial integrity of the Eastern Caribbean dollar (EC$). The British Virgin Islands do not use the Eastern Caribbean dollar as their de facto native currency. The East Caribbean dollar is used by Anguilla, Antigua and Barbuda, Dominica, Grenada, Montserrat, Saint Kitts and Nevis, Saint Lucia, and Saint Vincent and the Grenadines.

The basic theory of monetary unions is the *optimal currency area* (Calvo *et al.*, 2004). Yet it is not clear what the Mundell implications are for an area of states. If an optimal currency area requires labour mobility, then it leads to a common market. De facto currency areas seem to arise more from the collapse of the local currency than from explicit macro-economic considerations about how an area will react to so-called shocks, i.e. unanticipated economic adjustments that cause high unemployment.

Economics III: the common market

A common market means a quantitative leap in comparison with the FTA and customs union. Here, common institutions must be set up in order to handle the administration of the rules of the regional group. A common market can only be erected if it handles all questions relating to product acceptance and product comparability. This will require court action in settling disputes. A currency area will need a central bank being responsible for the supply of common currency as well as setting the interest rates in the area, but the organisational requirements of a common market go much further.

The common market requires far-reaching economic regulation in order to define how goods, services, capital and labour can move across borders. A typical sign of a common market is the regional passport that abolishes border controls. If the market is big, then economic regulation would need considerable regulatory resources besides a judicial organisation that can settle ensuing disputes. There may be such a sizeable need for administrative capacity to handle a common market that this replaces the nation-state. Regulatory tasks will have to be transferred to a regional organisation of some sort.

A single market poses a huge organisational challenge. The rules of economic activity will have to be defined for a number of states having different regulatory traditions. Various strategies may be employed. Harmonisation: different rules will be made similar; mutual recognition: each state accepts the rules of another state reciprocally; new legislation: a body of new regulation is created.

It is well known that harmonisation takes time, as its transaction costs are heavy. Mutual recognition is quicker, but it may not cover all aspects of the new common market. Finally, legislation requires new institutions such as a legislative body as well as a judicial body. How much new regional organisation is required depends on the size of the single market, but even small common markets like CARICOM and OECS have had to set up new public bodies in order to deal with the implications of a common market.

One of the typical problems encountered in setting up a common market is the creation of a common passport. It is easy to promise but harder to arrive at in reality. The free movement of persons implies a common passport, but migration is a sensitive state issue. It is when regional organisation takes on such a scale that the nation-state is mirrored in new bodies – legislative, executive and judicial – that regionalism becomes a substitute for the nation-state. It is the creation of a common market that calls for a structure of new political bodies and new agencies.

Take the case of CARICOM with its CSME (Caricom Single Market Economy). The Caribbean Community and Common Market (CARICOM) was established by Barbados, Jamaica, Guyana, and Trinidad and Tobago in 1973, replacing the 1965 to 1972 Caribbean Free Trade Association (CARIFTA), organised to provide a link between the English-speaking countries of the Caribbean following the dissolution of the West Indies Federation. A revised Treaty to establish the Caribbean community including the CARICOM Single Market and Economy (CSME) was signed in 2001.

CARICOM now has 15 small states as members, operating a large number of common facilities such as the Caribbean Disaster Emergency Response Agency (CDERA), Caribbean Meteorological Institute (CMI), Caribbean Food Corporation (CFC), Caribbean Environment Health Institute (CEHI), Caribbean Agriculture Research and Development Institute (CARDI), Caribbean Regional Centre for the Education and Training of Animal Health and Veterinary Public Health Assistants (REPAHA), Assembly of Caribbean Community Parliamentarians (ACCP), Caribbean Centre for Development Administration (CARICAD), Caribbean Food and Nutrition Institute (CFNI), Caribbean Examinations Council (CXC), Caribbean Development Bank (CDB), University of Guyana (UG) and University of the West Indies (UWI). CARICOM also uses economies of scale in diplomatic missions, one ambassador serving all 15 small states in Brussels and Geneva, for instance. The partners to a regional group may of course use private organisations too, setting up joint stock companies in the economy. However, economic organisation is mainly oriented towards facilitating trade and may go so far as the setting up of a community, i.e. a single market.

Regional organisation promises benefits but it also incurs costs. Thus, the participating governments must consider the ratio: benefits/costs. If this ratio is larger than 1, they may decide to go ahead. Benefits and costs involve both short-run and long-run considerations. Economic benefits and costs will be given close attention, but so-called intangible benefits and costs may also be involved.

The regional regimes: will they replace the state?

The new and spreading phenomenon of regional organisation harbours an interesting variety in public organisation. There are now so many regional organisations, at least on paper. One may expect that some of them will achieve a more firm structure in the decade to come. Countries may be members of several regional organisations, especially when it is only a matter of trading blocs. Regional organisation replaces the state to some extent when a common market is set up. Monetary unions require a central tender-issuing authority when it is not a case of simply using another country's money. The next decade will show which regional organisations are durable and whether some of them really achieve a community, i.e. a common market with the four freedoms: goods, services, capital and labour.

The nation as a foundation for legitimacy no longer has the same relevance as it did during the twentieth century, when the principle of the nation-state was at its zenith of attention and recognition. Nationalism as a basis for regime legitimacy is hardly as viable as it used to be, especially when societies become increasingly multicultural.

In state-building efforts in the Third World, nationalism is confronted with the political mobilisation of minorities as well as the ongoing relevance of tribal relationships. The building of a nation-state is an ideal based in

European history, originating in the replacement of the feudal regime with a modern polity. State-building in many parts of the Third World cannot take the nation as its starting point because nations do not exist in tribal societies. Whereas state-building is still a major occupation in several Third World countries (Fukuyama, 2004), there is at the same time a strong process towards the rationalisation of the state, as with the European Union.

State-building requires methods that are not easily transported to countries such as Somalia, Congo or Afghanistan. The formation of proper public institutions, such as an honest police force, uncorrupted courts, functioning schools and medical services and a strong civil service, is fraught with difficulties. The ability to create operational states has suddenly risen to the top of the world agenda. State-building has become a crucial matter of global security.

The regionalisation of states in Europe, Far East Asia and Latin America amounts to the creation of coordination tools which more strengthen than weaken the existing participating states. Regional groups of states may assure for themselves internal peace with the group, meaning that several kinds of military conflict have been outlawed. Regionalisation also strengthens the economic foundation of the participating states by expanding their economies, underlining further division of labour and export capacity.

When governments agree to create regional mechanisms, then the cement behind cooperation may be geographical position, historical legacy or culture besides economic interdependency. The size of a regional group is often not foreclosed, as new potential entrants arrive and claim membership. The "natural size" of the EU or the Asean is impossible to identify. In addition, the recent ambition to create an all-South American group, namely the plans of bringing together South America's two trading blocs, Mercosur and the Andean Group, testify to the dynamic nature of rationalisation. It is obvious that geographical proximity plays a major role as a foundation for regional coordination, as proximity in space is often connected with economic or political interdependency. However, culture also matters, as with the Arab League and the Moslem Conference.

More than half of the states of the world are members of one or another regional group, although some of these regional groups overlap in membership. Future developments may involve that some of these groups are combined into even bigger groups or that new members enter the existing groups. Thus, the EU now includes 27 states and may go up to 30 member states. There is much talk about one regional integration group for the entire South and Central Americas. In relation to the Asean, one speaks of ten plus three as if China, South Korea and Japan were already members.

States may of course be grouped into regional blocs in different ways. Such regional blocs may simply be abstract constructions for the purpose of presenting data. Here, however, we require *agency* or *governance*. Thus, a regional coordination mechanism is a regional group of states engaged in some form of coordination, i.e. common decision-making or more. One relevant question raised in the literature concerning the Europeanisation of the nation-state is how far regional integration can proceed without abolishing the autonomy of existing member states. However, most regional groups of states are not fully integrated. The regional groups differ widely in background characteristics, which may lead to the division of the globe into separate areas with more or less affluence and more or less democracy.

Yet these regional mechanisms in no case replace the nation-states. Some of these mechanisms offer merely opportunities for discussion, but others do engage in decision-making, resulting in the setting up of rules of various kinds offering a form of public organisation above the nation-states. These regional coordination mechanisms tend to concentrate on politics – peace and economics – and trade. They may be considered as examples of what German institutional economists called *"Ordnungspolitik"*, meaning that government defines and enforces a comprehensive set of rules for mainly economic activity. When such institutions are needed for handling the interdependencies between a set of countries, then a regional coordination mechanism may be a transaction cost-saving device.

Regional coordination offers a mechanism for states to handle reciprocities. International organisation is of course another mechanism that may offer governance of globalisation. One may pose the question of whether regionalisation or multilateralism is most effective in handling state interdependencies as well as externalities of an economic or environmental nature. Perhaps the evolution of events in the twenty-first century will involve both regionalisation and more international organisation. Reducing the number of players in the form of regional groups would after all always be helpful to international state coordination.

Although international organisations have increased in size and relevance during the post-Second World War period, they restrict or regulate the operations of the states, but they do not replace them. The foundations of the IGOs are the states of the world, which auto-limit themselves through the making of treaties setting up international coordination bodies. Globalisation creates a strong need for more international coordination to govern the global economy, the global environment and to maintain peace. However, global governance follows from respect for state sovereignty, as the international community disposes of few instruments of sanction against states that renege.

Yet, international organisation will not replace the states of the world. Instead, states will find it advantageous to support global governance in specific forms and under specified conditions. Certain global issues – climate change, the ozone layer protection, and the protection of open access resources, famine and poverty – require global governance if mankind is to resolve these problems. States will delegate power and resources to the system of IGOs to attack these issues using a multilateral approach. However, states will not be submerged into powerful regional or international organisations that take the place of states. To effectuate global governance, states will need to coordinate their responses to a set of global challenges. They may employ multilateral mechanisms, as these organisations are transaction cost-saving. Yet, states will remain the key political actors on the globe protecting their distinctive feature, namely sovereignty.

Conclusion

Regionalism may support the rule of law. Regional organisation promotes peace and stability among member states, even when there are historical animosities between them. Yet not all regional organisations include human rights among their objectives. Regionalism is an amorphous phenomenon, as it mixes ambition or intention with reality or results in a most confusing manner. Compact regional organisations are to be found in only a few regions such as Europe (EU) and – possibly – the Caribbean (Caricom) and the Gulf states (GCC) (Bulmer-Thomas, 2001; Ravenhill, 2001; Beeson, 2006; Fawole and Ukeje, 2005). When one examines the Caricom and the OECS as well as the Gulf Cooperation Council more closely, these regional blocs do not give the appearance of compact organisation, as the EU does. Only the EU is such a compact regional bloc that the economics of regional integration has constitutional implications for the structuring of principal–agent relationships. Besides the national agents, there are now powerful regional agents of the peoples of Europe.

Conclusion

Evolutionary advantage of rule of law regimes

In evolutionary economics, the selection mechanism in the development of economic institutions is the minimisation of costs, including especially transaction costs (North, 1990). This powerful theoretical argument may be employed in understanding the emergence of a variety of property rights as well as the inefficiency of the command economy.

In the evolution of political regimes, there is no one single force that accounts for the rise and decline of alternative political arrangements. Instead, one must acknowledge at least three forces:

1   *War*: The classic concern in political science about developing the most efficient strategy to ward off external threat. It is a trivial truth that war has brought down many regimes, from the early history of Mesopotamia dating back to 3000 BC to the recent events in Iraq, where a Western invasion destroyed a dictatorship or totalitarian regime. War works both ways. Actual war or the threat of war may enhance survival capacity, but offensive wars or long periods of aggressive wars in foreign countries may spell disaster for the regime, as Swedish King Charles XII, Napoleon and Hitler experienced, being entirely destroyed when entering the endless Russian steppes.
2   *Administrative efficiency*: This is the chief evolutionary mechanism of Weber, claiming that bureaucracy is the only long-lasting effective mechanism for ruling a country. Weber's analysis of the growth of a bureaucratic structure out of patrimonial authority is still as valid today as when it was launched around 1900. However, to Weber it was the sole evolutionary mechanism, or the main one besides war, of course.
3   *Representative institutions*: Here we have a most important evolutionary mechanism that lies behind the victory of democracy since the great revolutions in the late nineteenth century. It is not enough to have an efficient and loyal bureaucracy according to the Weberian approach, because the masters of the bureaucracy must be the representatives of the governed population. When the people set their own laws, only then are they free, as Rousseau paradoxically stated the case.

Military capacity, bureaucracy and representation are the three chief survival mechanisms that enhance regime fitness, I suggest. I will not deal at any length with military strategy or tactics, or its development since Sun Tsu. I will merely point out that military capacity alone as with the Mongol or Turkish conquerors in the thirteenth and fourteenth centuries cannot maintain a stable regime. What of lasting value did Genghis Khan or Tamurlane create?

The evolution of the Ottoman Regime has been analysed at great length in a search to find the causes of the long-run decline of the empire. It is agreed among scholars that the basic institutions of the Ottoman Regime operated less and less well, despite a few attempts at reorganising them. Following Weber's theory of institutional evolution there has been a concentration upon the malfunctioning of the military as well as the central and regional administration. However, the story of the Ottoman government lends more support to Finer's theory about palace politics destroying rationality in government (Finer, 1997a). From the fundamental instability in the harem surrounding the sultan came the waves of turbulence that so harmed governance.

The constitutional democracy overcomes the instability in leadership turnover through the operation of representative institutions, first and foremost Parliament. Through the orderly succession of leaders selected, appointed and dismissed in terms of transparent rules, the fundamental instability of authoritarian regimes is avoided. Non-democracies may score high on administrative stability, succeeding in putting in place an efficient bureaucracy. But the turbulence from designating leaders in dictatorships will not go away, even when there is a bureaucracy.

Can stable authoritarian regimes survive?

The survival fitness of a dictatorship depends upon its capacity only. It needs to be able to maintain itself, protecting its regime, which hinges upon its capacity to provide its citizens with safety and well-being. When an authoritarian regime is successful in protecting external and internal security as well as allocating a considerable economic surplus to its population, then it can survive for a long period. This is the basic lesson from the Arab world as well as from South East Asia and mainland China.

When representative institutions are lacking or remain feeble, then legitimacy may be bolstered by culture. Two versions of culture as a foundation for regime legitimacy come to mind at the beginning of the twenty-first century:

1   *Islam*: In several Arab and non-Arab Muslim countries, authoritarian rule is legitimated by an appeal to the protection of religion. Thus, the Koran and Sharia Law are considered as the constitution of the country or as essential parts of this supreme law. Often, the ruling family

attempts to legitimate its hold on power by this appeal to religion, confusing traditional authority with charismatic authority. Thus, the King of Morocco considers himself also as a descendant of the prophet Mohammed via his cousin Ali, meaning he can claim the title of caliph, or leader of the believers.

2   *Buddhism-Confucianism*: In South East Asia the combination of affluence with a lack of democracy is legitimated with a reference to so-called *Asian values*. In particular, Singapore's long-time leader Lee Kuan Yew developed this ideology to motivate the firm grip on power by governments in the Asean area. He embraced a form of Confucianism that entailed the following "I do not believe democracy necessarily leads to development. I believe a country needs to develop its discipline more than democracy" (Lee, 2000: 342).

The authoritarian regime may survive if it succeeds in maintaining political stability and offering a decent level of affluence to its population. The employment of religion may also help buffer a regime, but authoritarian regimes come under pressure sooner or later due to their lack of rule of law and free representative institutions. Oil and religion no doubt compensate for this lack in the Gulf monarchies.

States are viable today when they either provide for political stability or for rule of law, or both. These two selection mechanisms – stability and rights – put pressure upon governments in many countries. When the democratic regime is consolidated, meaning stable constitutional democracy, then it appears as the most fit regime mankind has come up with. However, there are authoritarian regimes which operate without major problems of political instability. And as democracy is far from stable in several countries of the world there is the dismal condition of anarchy in certain areas, as no stable state is forthcoming where war lords limit the range of operation of legitimate government. The micro foundations of regime stability are be found in the principal–agent interaction between politicians or rulers on the one hand and the population on the other. If it is true that people support government in order to have internal and external peace, then it is also true that the population wants to make sure that the agents it supports deliver what they promise and observe the rights of the principal.

The population as the principal of the political body provides government with considerable resources, demanding a *quid pro quo*: internal stability and external peace. This is the theme of Hobbes and his analysis of the principal–agent contract as the basis of government. However, there arises the Juvenil problem: *Sed quis custodiet ipsos custos?* The population would want to introduce rules that constrain its agents. The creation of political institutions that constrain politicians is facilitated by exogenous conditions such as affluence, modernisation, independent peasantry, early statehood, openness of the economy, low religious and ethnic fragmentation, as well as Protestantism. Rule of law institutions offer the most effective protection against opportunism with the agents. They enhance a system of checks and balances under which agents compete with each other, some agents controlling other agents, and the principal has a choice between alternative agents who can be removed within a specific time limit.

Politics as principal–agent contracting

Starting from the idea of a contract between government and the population, one would ask: If politics is based upon a contract, then what is the nature of this contract? Between who? For how long? Moreover, one would also be inclined to ask: If there is a political contract, then what is its content and how can its fulfilment be monitored? The notion of political evaluation entails that outcomes can be measured and government be held responsible for them. Thus, one would ask: If a political contract is monitored, then how can it be verified (meaning dissolved) when one of the parties to the contract is dissatisfied? This question leads to the final one: What are the stakes in a political contract, meaning what are politicians supposed to deliver against how large a remuneration? One would need a method of investigating these key questions about government, a model of government. Principal–agent theory offers such a tool of enquiry with its two key insights: moral hazard and adverse selection. Political contracts are opaque and very difficult to verify. Political contracts are not strategy proof. Political contracts allocate the risk to the population in a democracy but put a disproportionate risk with the agent in a dictatorship. Political institutions derive most of their sense from balancing the principal and the agent in carrying out political contracts, avoiding agent dominance or leaderless populism.

The application of the principal–agent model to politics raises a few difficult questions about the nature of the principal. For purposes of simplification, in public administration and public management the principal is assumed to be one person or a homogeneous group of people contracting in an unambiguous way with a set of agents, given an objectives function. But who is the principal in political games? One may draw upon the insights from historical institutionalism and comparative politics when debating some thorny problems in the principal–agent perspective upon political interaction. The nature of the principal becomes critical when political decisions concern taxation, warfare and directing the armed forces.

In economics, the principal–agent model (PAM) has been put to good use, illuminating several central problems of interaction in the provision of goods and services (Laffont, 2003). In a political science, some key problems in public administration and public management have been modelled with the principal–agent perspective in mind (Lane, 2005). Yet, in a most general formulation, the principal–agent model would cover the central problems in politics, namely how political leaders interact with the population.

Although the principal–agent perspective upon public regulation unravels in a clear way the risk of policy drift, the regulators pursuing their own goals instead of those of the principal (i.e. the government), it is only one application of the model (Weingast *et al.*, 2006). The same is true of the questions concerning shirking and informational rents that, the principal–agent model suggests, are omnipresent in bureaucracies and new public management (Laffont and Martimort, 2001). Besides displacement of objectives and economic inefficiencies, what insights does the principal–agent model harbour about politics? The stylised facts of PAM helps when interpreting regime evolution, the population (principal) searching for rules that restrain the rulers/politicians (agents).

Starting from the perspective of historical institutionalism and comparative politics, one may apply the principal–agent model to the evolution of political institutions, such as representation and elections, as well as to some very central political issues, such as taxation and conscription, meaning the draft army. Thus far, the main applications of the model have been micro-based, meaning that it attempts to explain the behaviour of individuals through contracts and incentives. In this book, I suggest the fruitfulness of applying the PAM in macro political settings. Thus, the contracts to be made are between social groups or classes. One interesting theoretical development is to consider the implications of two principals, as the classical principal–agent model deals with only one principal – one or more agents.

Acknowledging the fruitfulness of PAM for policy execution and implementation, I still wish to venture to state that it could deliver even more insights into politics. Let me deal with a few of the key issues in politics such as taxation, representation and war in order to explore what PAM may illuminate when these topics are approached from a comparative institutional perspective with a historical twist. The emphasis in principal–agent theory is on the selection and remuneration of agents, choosing among alternative arrangements in order to minimise the risk of policy drift or efficiency losses. However, let us raise the even more fundamental question: Who is the principal?

Under PAM, one assumes that the principal is simply around, looking for agents to get his/her job done. Assuming two or more principals complicates PAM immediately, as one would have to clarify which principal prevails. Much political fighting concerns exactly the power struggle between various principals, such as a national assembly against a president, or a government against a popular plebiscite. What I wish to raise here is the question of the nature of the principal and the implications of the resolution of that question for the choice of contracts with agents. Establishing who the principals are in a political system has strong implications for the choice of agents and the contracts with them.

Government cannot operate without resources. Government may be looked upon as a set of persons mobilising resources to be paid for by the population in the political body. Who is the principal and who are the agents? The basic difference between the patrimonial state and the modern state is the arrival of a transparent and unambiguous principal–agent perspective upon taxation. Historically, the patrimonial concept of governments proceeds from the view that the governors have some sort of residual claim upon the resources of the country, especially land (Weber, 1978). Taken to its extreme, the ruler or his family or tribe (king, sultan, emperor, emir) is the owner of last resort to all resources. In the modern state, all resources of government belong to the juristic concept of the state, to be accounted for by the governors in relation to the principal (Jellinek, 1901; Kelsen, 2005).

In the patrimonial state, the ruler(s) disposes of their own resources – the demesne, i.e. huge landholdings from which they derive the benefices necessary for paying their servants. In extreme cases, a patriarchical or sultanistic ruler may lay claim to all resources of the country, to be distributed by him/her according to need (Weber, 1978). In reality, the resources of the country tend to be divided among the higher social strata, including the ruler's clan and the landlords as well as their families or tribes. It is an open question whether small peasants may survive as independent farmers in a patrimonial approach to government. They run the risk of being reduced to serfs, falling into dependency to either the royal family or the great lords of the realm. In Russia, the slow but steady increase in serfdom indicates that royal absolutism offered no safe protection for the peasants against a powerful social class of nobility.

The demesne can deliver a substantial amount of resources, either in goods or in cash, if well managed and preserved. As these resources belonged to the royal family, there was a strong tendency for them to be used as favours or methods of payment for services. In a feudal polity, this tendency may go so far as to diminish the real amount of resources that the royal family controls to a minimum for their survival, the country being divided into semi-independent fiefs (Mitteis, 1953; Brunner, 1992). In the occidental scene, the Catholic Church that developed its own management of its vast landholdings and benefices – canon law – presented another major claim on resources, with large success (Berman, 1983).

Besides the variety of benefices that the rulers controlled more or less, the idea of taxes or levies also played a major role in the patrimonial state. Thus, the ruler could impose payments of various kinds upon the population. When the ruler needed additional resources, he/she could either try to manage the demesne better or attempt to impose new levies. Out of the first effort came the management philosophy of the *fisc*, meaning the institutionalisation of the royal household, to be handled by the chancery and chancellor of the exchequer, or Treasury. Out of the second endeavour came the call for representation and participation in tax decisions by those concerned. Whatever resources the king commanded as his own, benefices, fiefs or rents, they could with some ingenuity be transformed into the possessions of the realm – the theory of the king's two bodies (Kantorowicz, 1997). This interpretation changed the nature of kingship, from the king as a principal to the king as servant, i.e. agent.

The formula of taxation and representation holds empirically for many countries, as one may observe in a call for participation among various social strata in the population when new levies were to be introduced. Theoretically, one may interpret this *quid pro quo* as principal–agent interaction. The real strength of various social groups determined of course at the end of the day how much participation there would be and by whom. The most interesting experiment involving taxation and representation is, from the perspective of principal–agent theory, the estates society in the high medieval period (Duby, 1993, 1997). In several countries, there arose representative institutions for co-decision-making involving the corporations of the medieval society, being three or four depending upon the situation of the peasantry.

The representative idea fits well with the principal–agent perspective, as the purpose of these bodies – assemblies, Parliaments, councils, *Reichstag* – was to provide advice and support to the governors. These bodies – national or provincial – could also take on judicial tasks, sorting out conflicts between feudal vassals or between the king and his lords. Once the idea of representation was accepted, it was possible to develop it into a regular event, linking it, for instance, with the perennial questions of taxation and warfare.

Regalia

The principal–agent transformation of traditional or charismatic rulership into legal-rational domination always proceeded through two steps. First, the ruler had to be looked upon as an agent in the service of the realm. This implied that the ruler could not be seen as the principal in the interaction between governors and governed. All forms of patrimonialism had to be rejected. Second, once the ruler was seen as merely an agent for the governance of the realm, some restrictions had to be put in place in order to define his/her autonomy.

The concept of regalia was based on an attempt to clarify how the king could be looked upon as both a sovereign and an agent of the country (Bluche, 1993). These rights – *droits regaliens* – included levies, taxes and duties, justice, pardon and vengeance, money and debt, making war, conducting the army, and summoning the assemblies. From the principal–agent perspective, war and the use of the army became of critical importance, not only due to the fiscal implications of such enterprises, but also with regard to the risk that the army could be employed towards internal "enemies".

The conduct of warfare is a major endeavour in all human civilisations, as societies need to defend themselves against intruders from the outside. The governors would normally have to draw upon the support of the population in order to mount sufficient resources to defeat a foreign intrusion or be successful in waging a campaign abroad. Thus, there arises the question of who decides about such major operations: The governors as agents or the population as principal?

The significance of war in structuring the principal–agent interaction goes beyond its implications for taxation. Wars are normally very costly. Thus, once the governors decide to embark on warfare or are forced to do so, they need to extract resources. War goes together with the imposition of costs upon the population. Thus it may wish to have a say in matters relating to the waging of war and the drawing up of a defence policy.

It comes as no surprise that the concept of war as a common endeavour, to be decided through a meeting among the notables of the country, became firmly entrenched in the occidental medieval society, the estates society. The king would normally summon a meeting where he outlined both the plan for war and at the same time asked for the right to impose a new levy. As wars carry wide-ranging costs, the estates often combined *consilium* with *auxilium*. The king had little choice but to accept the demand for regular meetings, or Parliaments, as he disposed of too small troops by himself, having virtually no regular army at his disposal.

Changing military technology impacts upon the equation of war and representation. When the king became less dependent upon the nobility for soldiers, he could reduce the importance of sounding out the opinion of the estates of the realm. Mercenaries could be used, but they came with a heavy cost, to be covered by either loans or levies. If peasant armies were mobilised, then the peasants could claim advantages such as representation or secure land rights. The great experiment with representative bodies in the high medieval period was in several countries undone by royal absolutism, proclaiming that the ruler had divine agency. However, in several countries the idea of representation survived, only to be reinforced by the notion of the *demos* as the principal.

The development towards a conscript army would, according to the logic of this analysis, promote democracy, supporting the claims of ordinary citizens to have a say over the waging of wars. The democratisation of war with Napoleon Bonaparte coincided perfectly with the transformation of *l'ancien régime* into a mass polity. A few empires – Romanov, Habsburg and Ching – managed to delay the introduction of the principle one soldier–one vote, but they could not avoid the introduction of a mass polity. As military technology developed more and more effective tools of destruction and control, the problem of how to make the agents of war accountable became increasingly acute.

It is stated in the economic theory of the state that the purpose of government is to provide protection for a country. The monopoly on physical violence that characterises the state responds to a basic need in the community, namely for peace and safety. It is, with the terminology of economics, a public good. The "Lord Protector" can only fulfil this need if he has access to a police force and an army. This raises the corollary: *"Sed quis custodiet ipsos custos?"*

The police forces and the military forces – army, navy and air force – must be seen as agents, taking on tasks assigned to them by a principal. But who is this principal? In the modern period, two interpretations have been offered. According to the first, the principal of the military and the police forces is the democratic citizenry, who has to watch over how these forces of repression are employed. According to the second, these agents have a mandate from the nation, as interpreted by an authority with a legitimacy that goes beyond the democratic forces of the country.

Given the potential impact of the military and police forces upon society, it is small wonder that the question of their principal is given so much attention. These forces could be used against so-called "internal enemies", and not merely against foreign intruders or simple breakers of the order (eg. thieves). In authoritarian regimes, one often notices special care in making sure that the government has a set of loyal troops, no matter what. These forces would then follow orders from government, although they could go against the population. In processes of democratisation, keen interest is focused on control over the armed forces and the police. A democratic regime would favour strict popular control over these forces as well as ordinary recruitment from all strata of society.

Two or more agents?

Standard principal–agent theory implies strongly that the access to several agents helps the principal in writing contracts to his/her advantage. Competition among agents makes opportunistic behaviour less advantageous or promising. If one starts from democratic theory, acknowledging only one ultimate principal, the *demos*, modern polities tend to operate under more than one agent, having missions derived legitimately from the population. This occurs within the presidential regime, where the president confronts a national assembly, both having independent legitimacy. It may also occur to a certain extent in the parliamentary regime when Parliament instructs its own agents to investigate the government with, for instance, the Ombudsman Office. In referendum democracy, there is the tension between legislation in Parliament and the people's initiative that contests the former. When judges or courts have the right to legal review, then they may also be considered as principals.

One may perhaps wish to argue that the principal of modern government is the state. Thus, presidents, parliamentarians and judges act as agents of the abstract legal person that we refer to as the "state". This approach is, however, not allowed for the simple reason that the principal–agent model looks upon politics as interaction, i.e. strategic or tactical behaviour, and only people can engage in behaviour. In authoritarian argument, an abstract entity is often considered as the ultimate principal: the nation, the class or the people. But it is not a matter of real persons, as political power is vested with a group acting as the real principal in the name of these abstract entities. Speaking of several agents, one must enumerate them as persons or groups in action. The regime of a polity puts restrictions upon the agents who may act legitimately. The following list would be minimal: executive agents, presidents or premiers, national assemblies, the judges in the highest courts as well as the people under referendum democracy.

Political theory suggests how mechanisms can be conceived that make these agents oppose each other, cancelling out the risks of power abuse such that political system goals like freedom, justice and equality be promoted.

Conclusion

The principal–agent perspective upon politics goes far deeper than hitherto realised. The stylised facts that PAM has been used to explain include policy implementation and public regulation. The time has come to discuss some critical issues in politics under the principal–agent interpretation, such as who is the principal of the political body of a country. Before one looks for the agents who can do the job in politics, one would wish to identify the principal of the public sector. When one looks at the brief history of mankind, then one may establish a concept of the principal as the population only emerge later.

Theorising the interaction between principals and agents, it makes a difference how the principal is perceived. Several kinds of candidates may be mentioned for the identification of the principal: the king or emperor, the nobility, the *demos*, the estates, the nation, the state, the class, the race and so on. The basic point is that theorising the agents depends upon conceptualising the principal, as the possession of the role as principal matters for how the agents will be contracted. The three key issues in principal–agent contracting involve taxation, the waging of war and control over the security forces. As long as these competences are regarded as regalia, principal–agent contracting will be resolved within a special set of arrangements. When the *demos* is looked upon as the principal, then a quite different set of contracts will be up for consideration.

Constitutional democracies tend to score high on the measuring rod of survival fitness. They emerged through a combination of representation institutions with bureaucracy. Today they score high on both capacity and rights, especially when they occur in a post-industrial society. During the inter-war years, democracies went under in a large number of cases. Constitutional democracy has been coronated as the victorious regime by Fukuyama (1993), only later to discover that many countries struggle to create a stable state, let alone a consolidated democracy (2004). Only some 50 countries have stable democracies. Another 50 states may be described as consolidating democracies, or perhaps sometimes as unstable democracies. It should be emphasised that there also exist a fairly large number of non-democratic regimes, of which some are much more stable than others.

One may speak of two major concerns in policy developments today. First, there is the spread of constitutional democracy to more and more countries in the hope that they can eventually consolidate this regime. Second, there is the attempt to stabilise a regime in countries, even if it does not endorse constitutional democracy. Thus, various authoritarian regimes, milder or harsher, display a considerable survival capacity, despite their neglect of human rights. These regimes, whether benevolent or strong, authoritarian ones, will eventually have to make the transition towards rule of law, which is at least what the principal–agent model would predict. The unfit regimes are to be found in countries where there is civil war, excessive oppression or anarchy. The survival capacity of the constitutional democracy comes from its positive contribution to structuring principal–agent interaction.

The relevance of PAM for politics is not restricted to micro politics like, for instance, elections in democratic countries, but also covers macro politics such as the evolution of regimes. The principal would wish to introduce rules that restrain his/her agents when making decisions, laws and budgets/taxes. Such rules may be forthcoming either domestically or internationally. When one considers the atrocities committed by the Mongol Genghis Khan and Tartar Tamerlane as well as the genocides of the twentieth century (e.g. in the Nazi concentration camps (Owen, 2006) and Japan in Nanking (Chang, 1998)), then one can fully understand the connection made already by Kant between rule of law internally in a country and rule of law internationally. Kant's "Idea for a Universal History from a Cosmopolitan Point of View" from 1784 offers a masterpiece analysis of the moral imperative to extend rule of law from the domestic scene to the international context. The drive for rule of law can only be explained positively by means of the principal–agent perspective upon politics.

Bibliography

Abukhalil, A. (2004) *The Battle for Saudi Arabia.* New York: Seven Stories Press.

Adelman, I. and Morris, C.T. (1967) *Society, Politics and Economic Development: A Quantitative Approach.* Baltimore, MD: Johns Hopkins University Press.

Agh, A. (1998) *The Politics of Central Europe.* London: Sage.

Alavai, H. (1972) "The state in post-colonial societies: Pakistan and Bangladesh", *New Left Review*, 74: 59–81.

Alesina, A. and Spolaore, E. (2003) *The Size of Nations.* Cambridge: MIT Press.

Alesina, A., Devleeschauwer, A., Easterly, W., Kurlat, S. and Wacziarg, R. (2003) "Fractionalization", *Journal of Economic Growth*, 8: 155–194.

Allardt, E. and Rokkan, S. (eds) (1970) *Mass Politics: Studies in Political Sociology.* New York: Free Press.

Almond, G.A., Bingham Powell, G., Strom, S. and Dalton, R. (2003) *Comparative Politics: A Theoretical Framework.* New York: Pearson.

Althusius, J. (1964) *The Politics of Johannes Althusius*, trans. F.S. Carney. London: Eyre & Spottiswood.

Anderson, B. (2006) *Imagined Communities.* London: Verso.

Anderson, J. (ed.) (1986) *The Rise of the Modern State.* Atlantic Highlands, NJ: Humanities Press.

Anderson, P. (1979) *Lineages of the Absolutist State.* London: Verso.

Anderson, P. (1996) *Passages from Antiquity to Feudalism.* London: Verso.

Anderson, R.E., Simeon, D., Gerhard, P. and Stijn, C. (1997) "Privatization and restructuring in Central and Eastern Europe", *Private Sector* (World Bank) Note No. 123.

Aristotle (1981) *The Politics.* Harmondsworth: Penguin.

Atlas statistique: *Chiffres du monde* (yearly). Paris: Encyclopaedia Universalis.

Bagehot, W. ([1867] 1993) *The English Constitution.* London: Fontana.

Balassa, B. (1982) *The Theory of Economic Integration.* Westport, CT: Greenwood Press.

Balassa, B. (1991) *Economic Policies in the Pacific Area Developing Countries.* London: Macmillan.

Banks, Arthur S. (1996) *Cross-national Time-series Data Archive.* Binghampton, NY: Center for Social Analysis, State University of New York at Binghampton.

Barber, R. (2003) *The Black Prince.* Phoenix: Sutton Publishing.

Bardhan, P. (ed.) (1991) *The Economic Theory of Agrarian Institutions.* Oxford: Clarendon Press.

Barlow, F. (1988) *The Feudal Kingdom of England, 1042–1216.* London: Longman.

Barrett, D.B. (ed.) (1982) *World Christian Encyclopaedia: A Comparative Study of Churches and Religions in the Modern World AD 1900–2000.* Nairobi: Oxford University Press.

Barrett, D.B., Kurian, G.T. and Johnson, T.M. (2001) *World Christian Encyclopedia: A Comparative Survey of Churches and Religions in the Modern World.* Oxford: Oxford University Press.

Barzel, Y. (2002) *A Theory of the State.* Cambridge: Cambridge University Press.

Bates, R.H. (1981) *Markets and States in Tropical Africa.* Berkeley: University of California Press.

Bates, R.H. (1989) *Beyond the Miracle of the Market.* New York: Cambridge University Press.

Baxter, C. *et al.* (1993) *Government and Politics in South Asia.* Boulder, CO: Westview Press.

Bayart, J.-F. (1993) *The State in Africa: The Politics of the Belly.* London: Longman.

Bayart, J.-F. *et al.* (1999) *Criminalisation of the State in Africa.* Oxford: James Currey Publishers.

Bebler, A. and Seroka, J. (eds) (1990) *Contemporary Political Systems: Classifications and Typologies.* Boulder, Co: Lynne Rienner.

Beeson, M. (2006) *Regionalism and Globalization in East Asia: Politics, Security and Economic Development.* Basingstoke: Palgrave Macmillan.

Bell, D. (1996) *The Cultural Contradictions of Capitalism.* New York: Basic Books.

Bendix, R. (1978) *Kings or People: Power and the Mandate to Rule.* Berkeley: University of California Press.

Berg-Schlosser, D. (1990) "Typologies of third world political systems", in A. Bebler and J. Seroka (eds), pp. 173–201.

Berman, H.J. (1983) *Law and Revolution: The Formation of the Western Legal Tradition.* Cambridge, MA: Harvard University Press.

Bethell, L. (ed.) (1984) *The Cambridge History of Latin America: Colonial Latin America.* Cambridge: Cambridge University Press.

Black, C.E. (1966) *The Dynamics of Modernization: A Study in Comparative History.* New York: Harper & Row.

Bloch, M. (1994) *La Société féodale.* Paris: Albin Michel.

Blondel, J. (1990) *Comparative Government: An Introduction.* Hemel Hempstead: Philip Allan.

Bluche, F. (1993) *L'Ancien Régime – Institutions et Société.* Paris: Editions de Fallois.

Bluche, F. (2003) *Richelieu.* Paris: Perrin.

Blum, J. (1966) *Lord and Peasant in Russia from the Ninth to the Nineteenth Century.* New York: Atheneum.

Bogdanor, V. (ed.) (1988) *Constitutions in Democratic Politics.* Aldershot: Gower.

Borcherding, T.E. (1977) *Budgets and Bureaucrats: The Sources of Government Growth.* Durham, NC: Duke University Press.

Bovill, E.W. (1995) *The Golden Trade of the Moors: West African Kingdoms in the Fourteenth Century.* Princeton: Marcus Wiener.

Braudel, F. (1993) *Civilization and Capitalism, 3: The Perspective of the World.* New York: Fontana.

Brown, E.A.R. (1974) "The tyranny of a construct: feudalism and historians of Medieval Europe", *American Historical Review*, 79: 1063–1088.

Brownlie, I. (2003) *Principles of Public International Law.* Oxford: Oxford University Press.

Brunetti, A. and Weder, B. (1997) *Investment and Institutional Uncertainty*. Washington, DC: Worldbank (Technical Paper No. 4).

Brunetti, A., Kisunko G. and Weder, B. (1997) *Institutions in Transition*. Washington, DC: Worldbank (WP 1809).

Brunner, O. (1968) "Feudalism: the history of a concept", in F. Cheyette (ed.), *Lordship and Community in Medieval Europe*. New York: Holt, Rinehart & Winston, pp. 32–56.

Brunner, O. (1992) *Land and Lordship: Structures of Governance in Mediaeval Austria*. Philadelphia: University of Pennsylvania Press.

Bryce, J. (1921–1922) *Modern Democracies*. London: Macmillan.

Brzezinski, Z. (2004) *The Choice: Global Domination or Global Leadership*. New York: Basic Books.

Bulmer-Thomas, V. (2001) *Regional Integration in Latin America and the Caribbean: The Political Economy of Open Regionalism*. London: University of London.

Byres, T.J. (ed.) (1983) *Sharecropping and Sharecroppers*. London: Frank Cass.

Calhoun, J.C. (1953) *A Disquisition on Government*. Indianapolis: Bobbs-Merrill.

Calvert, R.L., McCubbins, M.D. and Weingast, B.R. (1989) "A theory of political control and agency discretion", *American Journal of Political Science*, 33(3): 588–611.

Calvo, G.A., Obstfeld, M. and Dornbusch, R. (eds) (2004) *Money, Capital Mobility, and Trade: Essays in Honor of Robert A. Mundell*. Boston, MA: MIT Press.

Cameron, D.R. (1978) "The expansion of the public economy: a comparative analysis", *American Political Science Review*, 72: 1243–1261.

Campbell, D.E. (2006) *Incentives: Motivation and the Economics of Information*. Cambridge: Cambridge University Press.

Cardoso, F.H. and Faletto, E. (1979) *Dependency and Development in Latin America*. Berkeley: University of California Press.

Carré, H. (1998) *Sully*. Paris: Payot.

Castles, F.G. (ed.) (1982) *The Impact of Parties: Politics and Policies in Democratic Capitalist States*. London: Sage.

Castles, F.G. (2004) *The Future of the Welfare State: Crisis Myths and Crisis Realities*. Oxford: Oxford University Press.

Chang, I. (1998) *The Rape of Nanking: The Forgotten Holocaust of World*. Harmondsworth: Penguin, new edn.

Chang, J. and Halliday, J. (2006) *Mao: The Unknown Story*. London: Vintage.

Chazan, N., Mortimer, R., Ravenhill, J. and Rothchild, D. (1999) *Politics and Society in Contemporary Africa*. Boulder, CO: Lynne Rienner.

Chehabi, H.E. and Linz, J.J. (eds) (1998) *Sultanistic Regimes*. Baltimore, MD: The Johns Hopkins University Press.

CIA (1994) *The World Factbook 1994–95*. Washington, DC: Brassey's.

CIA (2007) *The World Factbook;* available at: www.cia.gov/cia/publications/factbook/index.html

Cicero, Tullius and M. Powell, J. (ed.) (1998) *The Republic and the Laws*. Oxford: Oxford University Press.

Cipolla, C.M. (1965) *The Economic History of World Population*. Harmondsworth: Penguin.

Cipolla, C.M. (2003) *Historia Economica de La Poblacion Mundial*. Barcelona: Critica.

Clammer, P. (2004) *Central Asia*. London: Lonely Planet.

Clark, J. and Wildavsky, A. (1990) *The Collapse of Communism: Poland as a Cautionary Tale*. San Francisco: ICS Press.

Cohen, R. (1997) *Global Diasporas: An Introduction*. London: Routledge.

Cole, J. (2002) *Sacred Space and Holy War: The Politics, Culture and History of Shi'ite Islam*. London: I.B. Tauris.

Colomer, J.M. (ed.) (2004) *The Handbook of Electoral System Choice*. Basingstoke: Palgrave Macmillan.

Compact Edition of the Oxford English Dictionary (1970) Oxford: Oxford University Press.

Constant, B. (1988) "Principles of politics applicable to all representative governments", in B. Fontana (ed.), *Political Writings*. Cambridge: Cambridge University Press.

Cornes, R. and Sandler, T. (1996) *Theory of Externalities, Public Goods, and Club Goods*. Cambridge: Cambridge University Press.

Coulton, G.G. (1985) *Medieval Village, Manor, and Monastery*. London: Peter Smith.

Cutright, P. (1963) "National political development: measurement and analysis", *American Sociological Review*, 32: 562–578.

Dahl, R.A. (1956) *A Preface to Democratic Theory*. Chicago, IL: University of Chicago Press.

Dahl, R.A. (1971) *Polyarchy: Participation and Opposition*. New Haven, CT: Yale University Press.

Dahl, R.A. (1989) *Democracy and its Critics*. New Haven, CT: Yale University Press.

Dahl, R.A. and Tufte, E.R. (1973) *Size and Democracy*. Stanford, CA: Stanford University Press.

Dalrymple, W. (2006) *The Last Mugal*. London: Bloomsbury.

Danziger, D. and Gillingham, J. (2003) *The Year of Magna Carta*. London: Coronet Books.

Davidson, B. (1994a) *Africa in History*. London: Weidenfeld & Nicolson.

Davidson, B. (1994b) *Modern Africa: A Social and Political History*. London: Longman.

de Montesquieu, C. (1748, 1989) *The Spirit of the Laws*. Cambridge: Cambridge University Press.

DeFronzo, J. (1991) *Revolutions and Revolutionary Movements*. Boulder, CO: Westview Press.

Derbyshire, J.D. and Derbyshire, I. (1999) *Political Systems of the World* (3rd edn). Oxford: Helicon.

Deutsch, K.W. (1963) *The Nerves of Government: Models of Political Communication and Control*. New York: Free Press.

Deutsch, K.W. (1980) *Politics and Government: How People Decide their Fate*. Boston, MA: Houghton Mifflin.

Di Palma, G. (1990) *To Craft Democracies: An Essay on Democratic Transitions*. Berkeley: University of California Press.

Diamond, L. (1999) *Developing Democracy: Toward Consolidation*. Baltimore, MD: The Johns Hopkins University Press.

Diamond, L. and Linz, J.J. (1995) *Politics in Developing Countries*. Boulder, CO: Lynne Rienner.

Diamond, L. and Plattner, M.F. (1995) *Economic Reform and Democracy*. Baltimore, MD: The Johns Hopkins University Press.

Dicey, A.V. (1885, 1982) Introduction to *The Study of the Law of the Constitution*, ed. Roger E. Michener. Indianapolis, MN: Liberty Fund Inc.

Djankov, S. and Murrel, P. (2000) *The Determinants of Enterprise Restructuring in Transition: An Assessment of the Evidence*. Washington, DC: Worldbank.

Dogan, M. and Kasarda, J. (1988a) *Mega-cities I–II.* London: Sage.

Dogan, M. and Kasarda, J. (1988b) "Introduction: How giant cities will multiply and grow", in *The Metropolis Era*, Vol. 2: *Mega-cities.* London: Sage, pp. 12–29.

Dominguez, J.I. (1987) "Political change: Central America, South America, the Caribbean", in M. Weiner and S.P. Huntington (eds), *Understanding Political Development.* Boston, MA: Little, Brown, pp. 65–99.

Donnelley, J. (1989) *Universal Human Rights in Theory and Practice.* Ithaca, NY: Cornell University Press.

Downs, A. (1957) *An Economic Theory of Democracy.* New York: Harper & Brothers.

Downs, A. (1965) *An Economic Theory of Democracy.* London: Longman.

Drewry, G. (1989) *The New Select Committees: A Study of the 1979 Reforms.* Oxford: Clarendon Press.

Dreyer, J.T. (1993) *China's Political System: Modernization and Tradition.* London: Macmillan.

Duby, G. (1993) *Seigneurs et Paysans: Hommes et structures du Moyen Age.* Paris: Flammarion.

Duby, G. (1997) *Art et société au Moyen Age.* Paris: Seuil.

Dunleavy, P. and O'Leary, B. (1987) *Theories of the State: The Politics of Liberal Democracy.* Basingstoke: Macmillan.

Duus, P. (1993) *Feudalism in Japan.* New York: McGraw-Hill.

Duverger, M. (1954) *Political Parties: Their Organization and Activity in the Modern State.* London: Methuen.

Duverger, M. (1992) *Les Partis politiques.* Paris: Poche.

Easton, D. (1965) *A Systems Analysis of Political Life.* New York: Wiley.

Ebenstein A.O. (2001) *Friedrich Hayek: A Biography.* New York: St Martin's Press.

Ebrey, P.B. (1999) *The Cambridge Illustrated History of China.* Cambridge: Cambridge University Press.

Eckstein, H. (1966) *Division and Cohesion in Democracy: A Study of Norway.* Princeton, NJ: Princeton University Press.

Eckstein, H. and Gurr, T.R. (1975) *Patterns of Authority: A Structural Basis for Political Inquiry.* New York: Wiley.

Eisenstadt, S.N. (1963) *The Political Systems of Empires.* New York: Free Press.

EIU (1965) *Shorter Oxford Economic Atlas.* Oxford: Oxford University Press.

Elazar, D.J. (1968) "Federalism", in D. Sills (ed.), *An International Encyclopedia of the Social Sciences*, vol. 5. New York: Collier-Macmillan, pp. 353–367.

Elazar, D.J. (1987) *Exploring Federalism.* Tuscaloosa: University of Alabama Press.

Elazar, D.J. (ed.) (1991) *Federal Systems of the World: A Handbook on Federal, Confederal and Autonomy Arrangements.* Harlow: Longman.

Elster, J. (ed.) (1998) *Deliberative Democracy* (Cambridge Studies in the Theory of Democracy). Cambridge: Cambridge University Press.

Ember R.C., Ember, M. and Skoggard, I. (eds) (2004) *Encyclopedia of Diasporas: Immigrant and Refugee Cultures Around the World: Overviews and Topics.* vol. 1. Amsterdam: Kluwer.

Enayat, H. (2005) *Modern Islamic Political Thought.* London: I.B. Tauris.

Encyclopaedia Britannica (2000) *Britannica World Data.* Chicago, IL: Encyclopaedia Britannica.

Encyclopedia Britannica (yearly) *Book of the Year: World Data.* Chicago: Encyclopaedia Britannica.

Eraly, A. (2003) *The Mughal Throne: The Saga of India's Great Emperors.* London: Butler & Tanner.

Ersson, S. and Lane, J.-E. (1998) "Electoral instability and party change in Western Europe", in P. Pennings and J.-E. Lane (eds), *Comparing Party System Change.* London: Routledge, pp. 23–39.

Ertman, Th. (2004) *Birth of the Leviathan.* Cambridge: Cambridge University Press.

Esping-Andersen, G. (1990) *The Three Worlds of Welfare Capitalism.* Cambridge: Polity Press.

Esping-Andersen, G. (1999) *Social Foundations of Postindustrial Economies.* Oxford: Oxford University Press.

Europa Yearbook (yearly) London: Europa Publications.

Evans, P.B., Rueschmeyer, D. and Skocpol, T. (eds) (1985) *Bringing the State Back In.* Cambridge: Cambridge University Press.

Fainsod, M. (1958) *Smolensk under Soviet Rule.* New York: Vintage.

Fawole, W.A. and Ukeje, C. (eds) (2005) *The Crisis of the State and Regionalism in West Africa: Identity, Citizenship and Conflict.* Dakar: Council for the Development of Social Research in Africa.

Ferdinand, P. (1991) *Communist Regimes in Comparative Perspective.* Hemel Hempstead: Harvester-Wheatsheaf.

Ferguson, N. (2003) *Empire: How Britain Made the Modern World.* Harmondsworth: Penguin.

Ferguson, N. (2006) *The War of the World.* Hasmondsworth: Allen Lane and Penguin.

Finer, H. (1932) *Theory and Practice of Modern Government.* London: Methuen.

Finer, S.E. (1970) *Comparative Government.* London: Allen Lane.

Finer, S.E. (1999a) *The History of Government I: Ancient Monarchies and Empires.* Oxford: Oxford University Press.

Finer, S.E. (1999b) *The History of Government II: The Intermediate Ages.* Oxford: Oxford University Press.

Finer, S.E. (1999c) *The History of Government III: Empires, Monarchies and the Modern State.* Oxford: Oxford University Press.

Finer, S.E. (2002) *The Man on Horseback: The Role of the Military in Politics.* Somerset, NJ: Transaction Publishers.

Fischer Welt Almanach (yearly, 1959–) Frankfurt am Main: Fischer Taschenbuchverlag.

Fortes, M. and Evans-Pritchard, E.E. (eds) (1940) *African Political Systems.* Oxford: Oxford University Press.

Fourquin, G. (1976) *Lordship and Feudalism in the Middle Ages.* London: Allen & Unwin.

Frank, A.G. (1967) *Capitalism and Underdevelopment in Latin America: Historical Studies of Chile and Brazil.* New York: Monthly Review Press.

Freedom House (ed.) (1992) *Freedom in the World: Political Rights and Civil Liberties, 1991–1992.* New York: Freedom House.

Freedom House (2001) *Nations in Transit 2001;* data available at www. freedomhouse.org/research/nattransit.htm (Version: september 2002).

Freedom House (2006) *Freedom in the World Historical Rankings;* data available at www.freedomhouse.org/.

Friedrich, C. (1950) *Constitutional Government and Democracy: Theory and Practice in Europe and America.* Boston, MA: Ginn.

Friedrich, C. (1963) *Man and his Government: An Empirical Theory of Politics.* New York: McGraw-Hill.

Fukuyama, F. (1993) *The End of History and the Last Man.* Harmondsworth: Penguin.

Fukuyama, F. (2004) *State-building: Governance and World Order in the 21st Century.* Ithacan, NY: Cornell University Press.

Furubotn, E.G. and Richter, R. (2005) *Institutions and Economic Theory.* Cambridge: Cambridge University Press.

Ganshof, F-L. (1982) *Qu'est-ce que la féodalité?* Paris: Tallandier.

Gastil, R.D. (ed.) (1987) *Freedom in the World: Political Rights.* New York: Greenwood Press.

Gastil, R.D. (1990) "The comparative survey of freedom: experiences and suggestions", *Studies in Comparative International Development*, 25: 25–50.

Geary, P.J. (1988) *Naissance de la France: Le monde mérovingien.* Paris: Flammarion.

Gibbons, E. (2000) *The History of the Decline and Fall of the Roman Empire.* Harmondsworth: Penguin.

Goldstone, J.A. (1991) *Revolution and Rebellion in the Early Modern World.* Berkeley: University of California Press.

Goldstone, J.A., Gurr, T.R. and Moshiri, F. (eds) (1991) *Revolutions of the Late Twentieth Century.* Boulder, CO: Westview Press.

Goodin, R.E. (1996) *The Theory of Institutional Design.* Cambridge: Cambridge University Press.

Gosarevski, S., Hughes, H. and Windybank, S. (2004) "Is Papua New Guinea viable", *Pacific Economic Bulletin*, 19(1): 134–148.

Goubert, P. (1990) *Mazarin.* Paris: Fayard.

Gregory, P.R. and Stuart, R.C. (1989) *Comparative Economic Systems.* Boston, MA: Houghton Mifflin.

Grigorian D.A. and Martinez, A. (2000) *Industrial Growth and Quality of Institutions: What do (Transition) Economies have to Gain From the Rule of Law?* Washington: World Bank.

Grimal, P. (1986) *Cicéron.* Paris: Fayard.

Gurr, T.R. (1990) *Polity II: Political Structures and Regime Change, 1800–1986 {Computer file}.* Boulder, CO: Center for Comparative Politics.

Gurr, T.R. (1993) "Why minorities rebel: a global analysis of communal mobilization and conflict since 1945", *International Political Science Review*, 14: 161–201.

Gwartney, J. and Lawson, R. with Easterley, W. (2006) *Economic Freedom of the World.* Vancouver: Fraser Institute; data available from www.freetheworld.com/release.html.

Habib, I. (1963) *The Agrarian System of Mughal India.* Oxford: Oxford University Press.

Hagopian, F. and Mainwaring, S. (eds) (2005) *The Third Wave of Democratization in Latin America: Advances and Setback.* Cambridge: Cambridge University Press.

Hall, J.A. (1986) *Powers and Liberties: The Causes and Consequences of the Rise of the West.* Harmondsworth: Penguin.

Hall, K. and Benn, D. (eds) (2005) *Caribbean Imperatives. Regional Governance and Integrated Development.* Kingston: Ian Randle.

Hamilton, A., Madison, J. and Jay, J. ([1787–1788] 1961) *The Federalist Papers.* New York: New American Library.

Havrylyshin, O. and Van Rooden, R. (2000) *Institutions Matter in Transition, but so do Policies.* Washington, DC: IMF Working Paper.

Havrylyshin, O., Izvorski, I. and Van Rooden, R. (1998) *Recovery and Growth in Transition Economies 1990–97: A Stylised Regression Analysis.* Washington, DC: IMF (WP 98/141).

Hayek, F.A. (1944) *The Road to Serfdom.* London: Routledge.

Hayek, F.A. (1996) *Individualism and Economic Order.* Chicago, IL: University of Chicago Press.

Heady, F. (1979) *Public Administration: A Comparative Perspective.* New York: Dekker.

Heidenheimer, A.J., Heclo, H. and Adams, C.T. (1990) *Comparative Public Policy: The Politics of Social Choice in America, Europe, and Japan.* New York: St Martin's Press.

Held, D. (ed.) (1987) *Models of Democracy.* Cambridge: Polity Press.

Held, D. (ed.) (1991) *Political Theory Today.* Cambridge: Polity Press.

Held, D. *et al.* (eds) (1983) *States and Societies.* Oxford: Blackwell.

Heller, M. (1997) *Histoire de la Russie et de son Empire.* Paris: Flammarion.

Herbst, J. (2000) *States and Power in Africa: Comparative Lessons in Authority and Control.* Princeton, NJ: Princeton University Press.

Herodotus (1952) *Great Books of the Western World*, ed. R.M. Hutchins. Chicago, IL: Encyclopaedia Britannica.

Hill, M. (2004) *The Public Policy Process.* Upper Saddle River, NJ: Pearson Education.

Hintze, O. (1968) "The nature of feudalism", in F. Cheyette (ed.), *Lordship and Community in Medieval Europe.* New York: Holt, Reinhart & Winston, pp. 22–31.

Hintze, O. (1975) "The Preconditions of Representative Government in the Context of World History", in F. Gilbert (ed.), *The Historical Essays of Otto Hintze.* New York: Oxford University Press, pp. 302–353.

Hintze, O. (1991) *Feodalité, capitalisme et état moderne.* Paris: éditions de la maison des sciences de l'homme.

Hobsbawm, E.J. (1990) *Nations and Nationalism since 1780: Program, Myth, Reality.* Cambridge: Cambridge University Press.

Horowitz, D.L. (1985) *Ethnic Groups in Conflict.* Berkeley: University of California Press.

Hourani, A. (1991) *A History of the Arabic People.* London: Faber & Faber.

Hughes, H. and Gosarevski, S. (2004) "Does size matter? Tuvalu and Nauru compared", *Policy,* winter: 16–20.

Huntington, S.P. (1968) *Political Order in Changing Societies.* New Haven, CT: Yale University Press.

Huntington, S.P. (1991) *The Third Wave: Democratization in the Late Twentieth Century.* Norman: University of Oklahoma Press.

Huntington, S.P. (1993) "The clash of civilizations?", *Foreign Affairs,* 72(3): 22–48.

Huntington, S.P. (1997) *The Clash of Civilisations.* New York: Simon & Schuster.

Huntington, S.P. (2005) *Who Are We?: America's Great Debate.* New York: Free Press.

Huntington, S.P. and Dominguez, J.I. (1975) "Political development", in F-1. Greenstein, and N.W. Polsby (eds), *Handbook of Political Science.* Vol 3: *Macropolitical Theory.* Reading, MA: Addison-Wesley, pp. 1–114.

Hyden, G. (2005) *African Politics in Comparative Perspective.* Cambridge: Cambridge University Press.

Hyden, G. and Bratton, M. (eds) (1992) *Governance and Politics in Africa.* Boulder, CO: Lynne Rienner.

IDEA (1997) *Voter Turnout from 1945 to 1997: A Global Report on Political Participation.* Stockholm: IDEA.

IDEA (2002) *Electoral Systems Design;* data available at www.idea.int/esd/world.cfm.

Iliffe, J. (1995) *Les Africains: Histoire d'un Continent.* Paris: Flammarion.

ILO (1991) *Yearbook of Labour Statistics.* Geneva: ILO.

IMF (2000) *World Economic Outlook – Working Paper and Data Base;* available at www.imf.org/external/pubs/ft/weo/2000/02 (Version February 2003).

IMF (2006) *The World Economic Outlook* (WEO) database September 2006; available at: www.imf.org/.

International Ombudsman Institute (1999) *International Ombudsman Institute Directory of World-Wide Ombudsman Offices.* Edmonton: International Ombudsman Institute.

Ionescu, G. (1988) "The Theory of Liberal Constitutionalism" in Bogdanor (ed.), pp. 33–52.

Jackson, D.W. and Neal Tate, C. (eds) (1992) *Comparative Judicial Review and Public Policy.* Westport, CT: Greenwood Press.

Jellinek, G. (1966; 1901) *Allgemeine Staatslehre.* Bad Homburg: Verlag Max Gehlen.

Jennings, I. (1951) *Cabinet.* Cambridge: Cambridge University Press.

Jennings, I. (1961) *Parliament.* Cambridge: Cambridge University Press.

Johnson, C. (2002) *Blowback.* New York: Time Warner Paperbacks.

Johnson, C. (2006) *The Sorrows of Empire: Militarism, Secrecy and the End of the Republic.* London: Verso Books.

Johnson, C. (2007) *Nemesis: The Last Days of the American Republic.* London: Metropolitan Books.

Johnson, S. (2001) *The History of the Yorubas.* Lagos, Nigeria: CSS Bookshop.

Jones, D.M. (2007) *The Illustrated Encyclopedia of Incas: The History, Legends, Myths and Culture of the Ancient Native peoples of the Andes.* London: Lorenz Books.

Jones, D.M. and Charles Phillips (2006) *The Aztec and Maya World: Everyday Life, Society and Culture in Ancient Central America and Mexico.* London: Lorenz Books.

Joseph, R.A. (1987) *Democracy and Prebendal Politics in Nigeria: The Rise and Fall of the Second Republic.* Cambridge: Cambridge University Press.

Joseph, R.A. (1999) *State, Conflict and Democracy in Africa.* Boulder, CO: Lynne Rienner.

Kagan, R. (2004) *Paradise and Power: America and Europe in the New World Order.* New York: Atlantic Books.

Kalyvas, S.N. (2006) *The Logic of Violence in Civil War.* Cambridge: Cambridge University Press.

Kant, E. (1999) *Métaphysique des mœurs.* Paris: Flammarion.

Kant, E., Lafitte, J. and Baraquin, N. (2006) *Idée d'une histoire universelle au point de vue cosmopolitique: Réponse à la question.* Paris: Fernand Nathan.

Kant, I. (1991) *Kant: Political Writings,* ed. H. Reiss. Cambridge: Cambridge University Press.

Kantorowicz, E.H. (1997) *The King's Two Bodies: A Study in Mediaeval Political Theology.* Princeton, NJ: Princeton University Press.

Kantorowicz, E.H. (2000) *Œuvres.* Paris: Gallimard.

Karvonen, L. and Kuhnle, S. (eds) (2001) *Party Systems and Voter Alignments Revisited.* London: Routledge.

Kaufmann D., Kraay, A. and Zoido–Labaton, P. (2002) *Governance Matters II: Updated Indicators for 2001–02.* Washington, DC: World Bank.

Kaufmann, D., Kraay, A. and Mastruzzi, M. (2005) *Government Matters IV: Governance Indicators for 1986–2004;* data available at www.worldbank.org/wbi/governance/data.

Keay, J. (2004) *India: A History.* London: Harper Perennial.

Kelsen, H. (2005) *General Theory of Law and State*. Somerset, NJ: Transaction Books.

Keman, H. (ed.) (2005) *Comparative Politics: New Directions in Theory and Method*. Amsterdam: VU University Press.

Kennedy, P. (1987) *The Rise and Fall of the Great Powers*. New York: Random House.

Kennedy, P. (1993) *Preparing for the Twenty-first Century*. New York: HarperCollins.

Keohane, R.O. (1984) *After Hegemony: Cooperation and Discord in the World Political Economy*. Princeton, NJ: Princeton University Press.

Kesselman, M., Joseph, W., Krieger, J., Abrahamian, E. and DeBardeleben, J. (2003) *Introduction to Comparative Politics with Map*. New York: Houghton Mifflin.

Kirchheimer, O. (1966) "The transformation of the Western European Party systems", in J. LaPalombara and M. Weiner (eds), *Political Parties and Political Development*. Princeton, NJ: Princeton University Press, pp. 177–200.

Kissling, H.J. (1996) *The Last Great Muslim Empires*. Princeton, NJ: Markus Wiener.

Kolchin, P. (1990) *Unfree Labor: American Slavery and Russian Serfdom*. Cambridge, MA: Belknap Press.

Kornai, J. (1990) *The Road to a Free Economy*. London: Norton Press.

Kpundeh, S. and Levy, B. (2004) *Building State Capacity in Africa: New Approaches, Emerging Lessons*. Washington, DC: World Bank.

Kramer, S.N. (1993) *L'Histoire commence à Sumer*. Paris: Flammarion.

Krasner, S. (1982) *International Regimes*. Ithaca, NY: Cornell University Press.

Kuhn, T. (1962) *The Structure of Scientific Revolutions*. Chicago, IL: University of Chicago Press.

Kuhnle, S. and Kildal, N. (2005) *Normative Foundations of the Welfare State: The Nordic Experience*. London: Routledge.

Kymlicka, W. (1996) *Multicultural Citizenship*. Oxford: Clarendon Press.

Kymlicka, W. (2001) *Politics in the Vernacular: Nationalism, Multiculturalism and Citizenship*. Oxford: Oxford University Press.

Kymlicka, W. and Norman, W. (2000) *Citizenship in Diverse Societies*. Oxford: Oxford University Press.

Laffont, J.-J. (ed.) (2003) *The Principal–Agent Model: The Economic Theory of Incentives*. Cheltenham: Edward Elgar.

Laffont, J.-J. and Martimort, D. (2001) *The Theory of Incentives: The Principal–Agent Model*. Princeton, NJ: Princeton University Press.

Lane, J.-E. (2005) *Public Administration and Public Management: The Principal–Agent Perspective*. London: Routledge.

Lane, J.-E. and Ersson, S. (2001) *Government and the Economy: A Global Perspective*. London: Continuum.

Lane, J.-E. and Ersson, S. (2005) *Culture and Politics*. Aldershot: Ashgate.

Lane, J.-E. and Ersson, S. (2007) "Party system instability in Europe: persistent differences in volatility between West and East?", *Democratization*, 14(1): 92–110.

Lapidus, I.M. (1989) *A History of Islamic Societies*. Cambridge: Cambridge University Press.

Lee, K.Y. (2000) *From Third World to First*. New York: HarperCollins.

Leftwich, A. (1994) "States of underdevelopment: the Third World state in theoretical perspective", *Journal of Theoretical Politics*, 6(1): 55–74.

Leftwich, A. (2004) "Theorising the state", in P. Burnell and V. Randal (eds), *Politics in the Developing World*. Oxford: Oxford University Press.

Lerner, D. (1958) *The Passing of Traditional Society: Modernizing the Middle East*. New York: Free Press.

Levy, M. (1952) *The Structure of Society*. Princeton, NJ: Princeton University Press.

Lewis, B. (2000) *The Middle East*. London: Phoenix Press.

Lijphart, A. (1974) "Consociational democracy", in K. McRae (ed.), *Consociational Democracy: Political Accommodation in Segmented Societies*. Toronto: McClelland and Stewart, pp. 70–89.

Lijphart, A. (1975) *The Politics of Accommodation: Pluralism and Democracy in the Netherlands*. Berkeley: University of California Press.

Lijphart, A. (1977) *Democracy in Plural Societies: A Comparative Exploration*. New Haven: Yale University Press.

Lijphart, A. (1984) *Democracies: Patterns of Majoritarian and Consensus Government in Twenty-one Countries*. New Haven: Yale University Press.

Lijphart, A. (1991a) "Constitutional choices for new democracies", *Journal of Democracy*, 2(1): 72–84.

Lijphart, A. (1991b) "Double-checking the evidence", *Journal of Democracy*, 2(3): 42–48.

Lijphart, A. (1994) *Electoral Systems and Party Systems: A Study of Twenty-seven Democracies, 1945–1990*. Oxford: Oxford University Press.

Lijphart, A. (1999) *Patterns of Democracies*. New Haven, CT: Yale University Press.

Lim, T. (2005) *Doing Comparative Politics: An Introduction to Approaches and Issues*. Boulder, CO: Lynne Rienner.

Lindblom, C.E. (1977) *Politics and Markets: The World's Political-Economic Systems*. New York: Basic Books.

Lindblom, C.E. (2002) *The Market System: What It Is, How It Works and What to Make of It*. New Haven, CT: Yale University Press.

Lindblom, C.E. and Woodhouse, E.J. (1994) *The Policy Making Process*. Upper Saddle River, NJ: Pearson.

Linz, J.J. (1975) "Totalitarian and authoritarian regimes", in F.I. Greenstein and N.W. Polsby (eds), *Handbook of Political Science*. Vol. 3: *Macropolitical Theory*. Reading, MA: Addison-Wesley, pp. 175–411.

Linz, J.L. (2000) *Totalitarian and Authoritarian Regimes*. Boulder, CO: Lynne Rienner.

Linz, J.J. (2006) *Robert Michels, Political Sociology and the Future of Democracy*. Somerset, NJ: Transaction Publishers.

Linz, J.J. and Stepan, A. (1996) *Problems of Democratic Transition and Consolidation: Southern Europe, South America and Post-communist Europe*. Baltimore, MD: The Johns Hopkins University Press.

Linz, J.J. and Valenzuela, A. (1994) *The Failure of Presidential Democracy: Comparative Perspectives*. Baltimore, MD: Johns Hopkins University Press.

Lipset, S.M. (1960) *Political Man*. New York: Doubleday.

Lipset, S.M. and Rokkan, S. (eds) (1967) *Party Systems and Voter Alignments: Cross-national Perspectives*. New York: Free Press.

Lively, J. (1975) *Democracy*. Oxford: Blackwell.

Loewenstein, K. (1965) *Political Power and the Governmental Process*. Chicago, IL: University of Chicago Press.

Longhena, M. (2006) *Ancient Mexico: History and Culture of the Maya, Aztecs and Other Pre-Columbian Populations*. Vercelli: White Star.

Luciani, G. (ed.) (1990) *The Arab State*. London: Routledge.

Ludden, D. (ed.) (2005) *Agricultural Production and South Asian History*. New Delhi: Oxford University Press.

Lundahl, M. (1991) *Peasants and Poverty: A Study of Haiti.* London: Croom Helm.

Lybeck, J.A. and Henrekson, M. (1988) *Explaining the Growth of Government.* Amsterdam, New York: North-Holland.

Macho-Stadler, I., Perez-Castrillo, J.D. and Watt, R. (2001) *An Introduction to the Economics of Information: Incentives and Contracts.* Oxford: Oxford University Press.

McDowell, D. (1996) *A Modern History of The Kurds.* London, New York: I.B. Tauris.

Macmillan, M. (2003) *Peacemakers: The Paris Peace Conference of 1919 and Its Attempt to End War.* London: John Murray.

MacPherson, S. and Midgley, J. (1987) *Comparative Social Policy and the Third World.* Brighton: Wheatsheaf.

McRae, K. (ed.) (1974) *Consociational Democracy: Political Accommodation in Segmented Societies.* Toronto: McClelland & Stewart.

Maddex, R.L. (1996) *Constitutions of the World.* London: Routledge.

Madison, J., Hamilton, A. and Jay, J. (1961) *Federalist Papers.* London: Everyman's Library.

Mahoney, J. and Rueschemeyer, D. (2003) *Comparative Historical Analysis in the Social Sciences.* Cambridge: Cambridge University Press.

Mainwaring, S. and Shugart, M.S. (eds) (1997) *Presidentialism and Democracy in Latin America.* Cambridge: Cambridge University Press.

Mair, P. (1997) *Party System Change: Approaches and Interpretations.* Oxford: Oxford University Press.

Man, J. (2006) *Kublai Khan, The Mongol King Who Remade China.* London: Bantam Press.

Mansbridge, J.J. (1983) *Beyond Adversary Democracy.* Chicago, IL: Chicago University Press.

March, J.G. and Olsen, J.P. (1989) *Rediscovering Institutions: The Organizational Basis of Politics.* New York: Free Press.

Marino, J.A. (ed.) (2002) *Early Modern Italy: 1550–1796.* Oxford: Oxford University Press.

Marongiu, A. (1968) *Medieval Parliaments: A Comparative Study.* London: Eyre & Spottiswoode.

Marozzi, J. (1995) *Tamerlane – Sword of Islam, Conqueror of the World.* New York: Harper Perennial.

Marshall, M.G. (2005) *Major Episodes of Political Violence 1946–2004*; data available at http://members.aol.com/CSPmgm/warlist.htm.

Marshall, M.G., Jaggers, K. and Gurr, T.R. (2005) *Polity IV Project*; data available at www.cidcm.umd.edu/polity.

Medard, J-F. (1982) "The underdeveloped state in tropical Africa: political clientelism or neo-patrimonialism", in C. Clapham (ed.), *Private Patronage and Public Power.* London: Pinter.

Meinecke, F. ([1908] 1962) *Weltbürgertum und Nationalstaat.* Munich: Oldenbourg.

Meinecke, F. (1997) *Machiavellism: The Doctrine of Raison D'Etat and Its Place in Modern History.* Somerset, NJ: Transaction Books.

Merrill, S. III and Grofman, B. (2005) *A Unified Theory of Party Competition: A Cross-national Analysis Integrating Spatial and Behavioral Factors.* Cambridge: Cambridge University Press.

Migdal, J.S. (1988) *Strong Societies and Weak States.* Princeton, NJ: Princeton University Press.

Migdal, J.S. (2001) *State in Society.* Cambridge: Cambridge University Press.

Milgrom, P. and Roberts, J. (1992) *Economics, Organization and Management.* Englewood Cliffs, NJ: Prentice-Hall.

Mill, J.S. (1869, 1991) *Considerations on Representative Government.* London: Prometheus Books.

Mills, C.W. (1999) *The Power Elite.* Oxford: Oxford University Press.

Mitteis, H. (1953) *Der Staat des hohen Mittelalters.* Weimar: Hermann Böhlaus Nachfolger.

Moe, T.M. (1984) "The new economics of organization", *American Journal of Political Science*, 28(4): 739–777.

Montesquieu, C. de (1989) *The Spirit of the Laws.* Cambridge: Cambridge University Press.

Monthias, J.M. (1976) *The Structure of Economic Systems.* New Haven, CT: Yale University Press.

Moore, B. (1968) *Social Origins of Dictatorship and Democracy: Lord and Peasant in the Making of the Modern World.* Boston, MA: Beacon Press.

Moreland, W.H. (1999) *From Akbar to Aurangzeb: A Study of Indian Economic History.* Delhi: A K Fine Art Press.

Morris, M.D. (1979) *Measuring the Conditions of the World's Poor: The Physical Quality of Life Index.* New York: Pergamon Press.

Mortimer, I. (2003) *The Greatest Traitor.* London: Pimlico.

Musallam, A.A. (2005) *From Secularism to Jihad: Sayyid Qutb and the Foundations of Radical Islamism.* New York: Greenwood Press.

Myrdal, G. (1968) *Asian Drama I-III.* New York: Pantheon.

Newton, K. and van Deth, J. (2005) *Foundations of Comparative Politics.* Cambridge: Cambridge University Press.

Nordlinger, E.A. (1977) *Soldiers in Politics: Military Coups and Governments.* Englewood Cliffs, NJ: Prentice-Hall.

North, D.C. (1990) *Institutions, Institutional Change and Economic Performance.* Cambridge: Cambridge University Press.

North, D.C. (2005) *Understanding the Process of Economic Change.* Princeton, NJ: Princeton University Press.

O'Brien, C.C. (2002) *Edmund Burke.* London: Vintage.

O'Donnell, G. (1973) *Modernization and Bureaucratic-authoritarianism: Studies in South American Politics.* Berkeley, CA: Institute of International Studies.

O'Donnell, G. (1988) *Bureaucratic Authoritariansim: Argentina 1966–1973 in Comparative Perspective.* Berkeley: University of California Press.

O'Donnell, G. and Schmitter, P. (1986) *Transitions from Authoritarian Rule: Prospects for Democracy.* Baltimore, MD: The Johns Hopkins University Press.

Okey, R. (1987) *Eastern Europe, 1740–1985: Feudalism to Communism.* Minneapolis: University of Minnesota Press.

Oliver, O. (ed.) (1977) *The Cambridge History of Africa: From c.1050–c.1600.* Cambridge: Cambridge University Press.

Olson, M. (1963) "Rapid growth as a destabilizing force", *Journal of Economic History*, 23: 529–552.

Olson, M. (1965) *The Logic of Collective Action.* Cambridge, MA: Harvard University Press.

Olson, M. (1982) *The Rise and Decline of Nations: Economic Growth, Stagflation and Social Rigidities.* New Haven, CT: Yale University Press.

Olson, M. (2001) *Power and Prosperity: Outgrowing Communist and Capitalist Dictatorships.* New York: Basic Books.

Oomen, B. (2005) *Chiefs in South Africa: Law, Culture, and Power in the Post-Apartheid Era.* Basingstoke: Palgrave Macmillan.

Ostrom, E. (2005) *Understanding Institutional Diversity.* Princeton, NJ: Princeton University Press.

Ostrom, V. (1987) *The Political Theory of a Compound Republic: Designing the American Experience.* Lincoln: University of Nebraska Press.

Owen, J. (2006) *Nuremberg Evil on Trial.* London: Headline Publishing Group.

Page, E. (1991) *Localism and Centralism in Europe: The Political and Legal Bases of Local Self-government.* Oxford: Oxford University Press.

Page, E. (1992) *Political Authority and Bureaucratic Power: A Comparative Analysis.* Englewood Cliffs, NJ: Prentice-Hall.

Parekh, B. (2006) *Rethinking Multiculturalism: Cultural Diversity and Political Theory.* Basingstoke: Palgrave.

Parsons, W. (1995) *Public Policy: An Introduction to the Theory and Practice of Policy Analysis.* Cheltenham: Edward Elgar.

Pateman, C. (1970) *Participation and Democratic Theory.* Cambridge: Cambridge University Press.

Pedersen, M. (1979) "The dynamics of European party systems: changing patterns of electoral volatility", *European Journal of Political Research*, 7(1): 1–26.

Perham, Margery. (1960) *Lugard. Volume 2: The Years of Authority 1898–1945.* London: Collins.

Peters, B.G. (1987) *The Politics of Bureaucracy: A Comparative Perspective.* New York: Longman.

Pfeffermann, G.P. and Kisunko, G. (1999) *Perceived Obstacles to Doing Business: Worldwide Survey Results.* Washington, DC: World Bank.

Pierson, D. and Castles, F.G. (2006) *The Welfare State Reader.* Cambridge: Polity Press.

Pistor, K. (2001) "Law as determinant for equity market development. The experience of transition economies", in P. Murrel (ed.), *Assessing the Value of Law in Transition Economies.* Ann Arbor: University of Michigan Press, pp. 249–287.

Plato (1985) *The Republic.* Harmondsworth: Penguin.

Pocock, J.G.A. (1975) *The Machiavellian Moment.* Princeton, NJ: Princeton University Press.

Poggi, G. (1978) *The Development of the Modern State.* London: Hutchinson.

Poggi, G. (1990) *The State: Its Nature, Development and Prospects.* Cambridge: Polity Press.

Polybius (1970) *Histoires.* Paris: Broché.

Posner, R.A. (1993) *The Problems of Jurisprudence.* Cambridge, MA: Harvard University Press.

Posner, R.A. (1998) "Creating a legal framework for economic development", *The World Bank Research Observer*, 13(1): 1–11.

Posner, R.A. (2004) *Frontiers of Legal Theory.* Boston, MA: Harvard University Press.

Powell, W.W. and Dimaggio, P. (1991) *The New Institutionalism in Organizational Analysis.* Chicago, IL: Unversity of Chicago Press.

Prebisch, R. (1971) *Change and Development: Latin America's Great Task* (International Economic and Development Series). New York: Praeger Publishers.

Prescott, W.H. (1992) *Aztèques et Incas: Grandeur et décadence de deux empires fabuleux.* Paris: Pygmalion – Gérard Watelet.

Przeworski, A. (1991) *Democracy and the Market: Political and Economic Reforms in Eastern Europe and Latin America.* Cambridge: Cambridge University Press.

Quigley, M. (2002) *Ancient West African Kingdoms: Ghana, Mali, and Songhai.* London: Heinemann.

Raiser, M., Di Tommaso, M.L. and Weeks, M. (2000) *The Measurement and Determinants of Institutional Change: Evidence from Transition Economies.* London: EBRD Working Paper.

Randall, V. (ed.) (1987) *Political Parties in the Third World.* London: Sage.

Rasmusen, E. (2001) *Readings in Games and Information.* Oxford: Blackwell.

Rasmusen, E. (2006) *Games and Information: An Introduction to Game Theory.* Oxford: Blackwell.

Ravenhill, J. (2001) *APEC and the Construction of Pacific Rim Regionalism.* Cambridge: Cambridge University Press.

Redford, D.B. (1992) *Egypt, Canaan and Israel in Ancient Times.* Princeton, NJ: Princeton University Press.

Reynolds, S. (1994) *Fiefs and Vassals: The Medieval Evidence Reinterpreted.* Oxford: Clarendon Press.

Rhyne, Charles S. (1978) *Law and Judicial Systems of Nations.* Washington, DC: World Peace Through Law Center.

Richard, J.F. (1996) *The Mughal Empire*, Vol. I, Part 5 of the *New Cambridge History of India.* Cambridge: Cambridge University Press.

Ricketts, M. (2003) *The Economics of Business Enterprise: An Introduction to Economic Organisation and the Theory of the Firm.* Cheltenham: Edward Elgar.

Riker, W.H. (1962) *The Theory of Political Coalitions.* New Haven: Yale University Press.

Riker, W.H. (1975) "Federalism", in F.-I. Greenstein and N.W. Polsby (eds), *The Handbook of Political Science*, Vol. 5. Reading, MA: Addison-Wesley.

Riker, W.H. (1982) *Liberalism Against Populism.* San Francisco: Freeman.

Rokkan, S. and Urwin, D. (1983) *Economy, Territory, Identity: Politics of West European Peripheries.* London: Sage.

Rokkan, S. *et al.* (1970) *Citizens, Elections, Parties: Approaches to the Comparative Study of the Process of Development.* Oslo: Universitetsforlaget.

Roller, E. (2005) *The Performance of Democracies: Political Institutions and Public Policy.* Oxford: Oxford University Press.

Rose, R. (1984) *Understanding Big Government: The Programme Approach.* London: Sage.

Rose, R. (1989) *Ordinary People in Public Policy: A Behavioural Analysis.* London: Sage.

Rostovtseff, M.I. (1930–1933) *A History of the Ancient World.* Oxford: Clarendon Press.

Rostovtseff, M.I. (1988) *Histoire economique et sociale de l'Empire romain.* Paris: Robert Laffont.

Roth, G. (1968) "Personal rulership, patrimonialism and empire-building in the new states", *World Politics*, 20: 195–206.

Rousseau, J.J. (1985) *The Social Contract.* Cambridge: Cambridge University Press.

Rowat, C.L. (1988) *Public Administration in Developed Democracies.* New York: Marcel Dekker.

Roy, O. (2000) *The New Central Asia: Creation of Nations.* London: I.B. Tauris.

Russett, B.R., Singer, J.M. and Small, M. (1968) "National political units in the twentieth century", *American Political Science Review*, 62: 930–951.

Rustow, D.A. (1967) *A World of Nations: Problems of Political Modernization.* Washington, DC: Brookings.

Sanders, D. (1981) *Patterns of Political Instability.* London: Macmillan.

Sandler, T. and Tschirhart, J.T. (1980) "The economic theory of clubs: an evaluative survey", *Journal of Economic Literature*, 18(4): 1481–1521.

Sartori, G. (1976) *Parties and Party Systems*, Vol. 1. Cambridge: Cambridge University Press.

Sartori, G. (1987) *The Theory of Democracy Revisited I-II.* Chatham, NJ: Chatham House.

Schmitter, P.C. (1983) "Democratic theory and neo-corporatist practice", *Social Research*, 50: 885–928.

Schopf, J.W. *et al.* (2002) "Laser-Raman imagery of Earth's earliest fossils", *Nature*, 416: 73–76.

Schraeder, P.J. (2003) *African Politics and Society: A Mosaic in Transformation.* Belmont, CA: Wadsworth.

Schulze, H. (1998) *States, Nations and Nationalism: From the Middle Ages to the Present.* London: Blackwell.

Schumpeter, J.A. (1944) *Capitalism, Socialism and Democracy.* London: Allen & Unwin.

Schumpeter, J.A. (1989) *Essays: On Entrepreneurs, Innovations, Business Cycles and the Evolution of Capitalism.* Somerset, NJ: Transaction Publishers.

Schumpeter, J.A. (1994) *Capitalism, Socialism and Democracy.* London: Routledge.

Seward, D. (1995) *The Wars of the Roses.* London: Robinson.

Shaw, M.N. (2003) *International Law.* Cambridge: Cambridge University Press.

Sheffer, G. (2006) *Diaspora Politics: At Home Abroad.* Cambridge: Cambridge University Press.

Shugart, M.S. and Carey, J.M. (1992) *Presidents and Assemblies: Constitutional Design and Electoral Dynamics.* Cambridge: Cambridge University Press.

Shugart, M.S. and Wattenberg, M.P. (eds) (2003) *Mixed-member Electoral Systems: The Best of Both Worlds?* Oxford: Oxford University Press.

Shivji, I. (1976) *Class Struggle in Tanzania.* New York: Monthly Review Press.

Skidmore, T.E. and Smith, P.H. (1984) *Modern Latin America.* New York: Oxford University Press.

Skocpol, T. (1979) *States and Social Revolutions.* Cambridge: Cambridge University Press.

Smith, A.D. (1993) *National Identity.* Lincoln: University of Nevada Press.

Smith, A.D. (1998) *Nationalism and Modernism.* London: Routledge.

Smith, A.D. (2004) *The Antiquity of Nations.* Cambridge: Polity Press.

Smith, P.H. (2004) *Democracy in Latin America: Political Change in Comparative Perspective.* Oxford: Oxford University Press.

Southern, R.W. (1997) *L'Eglise et la société dans l'Occident médiéval.* Paris: Flammarion.

Spuler, B. (1969a) *The Age of the Caliphs: History of the Muslim World.* Princeton, NJ: Markus Wiener.

Spuler, B. (1969b) *The Mongol Period: History of the Muslim World.* Princeton, NJ: Markus Wiener.

Stanlis, P.J. (ed.) (2006) *Edmund Burke: Selected Writings and Speeches*. Edison, NJ: Transaction Publishers.

Statesman's Yearbook (yearly) London: Macmillan.

Steinmo, S., Thelen, K.A. and Longstreth, F. (eds) (1992) *Structuring Politics: Historical Institutionalism in Comparative Analysis*. Cambridge: Cambridge University Press.

Strayer, J.R. (1970) *On the Medieval Origins of the Modern State*. Princeton, NJ: Princeton University Press.

Strom, K. (1990) *Minority Government and Majority Rule*. Cambridge: Cambridge University Press.

Sun-Tzu (2000) "The art of warfare", in C. Carr (ed.), *The Book of War*. New York: Modern Library Paperback Edition.

Taagepera, R. and Shugart, M.S. (1991) *Seats and Votes: Effects and Determinants of Electoral Systems*. New Haven, CT: Yale University Press.

Taylor, C.L. (1983) *World Handbook of Political and Social Indicators* (3rd edn). New Haven, CT: Yale University Press.

Ternon, Y. (2002) *Empire Ottoman: Le decline, la chute, l'effacement*. Paris: Editions Michel de Maule.

The Oxford English Dictionary (1987) Oxford: Oxford University Press.

Thompson, J. (1989) *Theories of Ethnicity: A Critical Appraisal*. New York: Greenwood Press.

Thompson, M., Ellis, R. and Wildavsky, A. (1990) *Cultural Theory*. Boulder, CO: Westview Press.

Thucydides (1952) *Great Books of the Western World*, ed. R.M. Hutchins. Chicago, IL: Encyclopaedia Britannica.

Tilly, C. (ed.) (1975) *The Formation of National States in Western Europe*. Princeton, NJ: Princeton University Press.

Tingsten, H. (1965) *The Problems of Democracy*. Totowa, NJ: Bedminster Press.

Tocqueville, A. (1988) *The Ancient Regime*. London: Dent.

Tocqueville, A. (1990) *Democracy in America I–II*. New York: Vintage.

Todd, E. (1983) *La troisième planète: structures familiales et systèmes idéologiques*. Paris: Seuil.

Todd, E. (1985) *The Explanation of Ideology: Family Structures and Social Systems*. Oxford: Blackwell.

Transparency International (2005) *TI Corruptions Perception Index;* data available at www.transparency.org/policy_research/surveys_indices/global/cpi.

Trevino, A.J. (ed.) (2001) *Talcott Parsons Today: His Theory and Legacy in Contemporary Sociology*. London: Rowman & Littlefield.

Tsebelis, G. (1991) *Nested Games: Rational Choice in Comparative Politics*. Berkeley: University of California Press.

Tsebelis, G. (2002) *Veto Players: How Political Institutions Work*. Princeton, NJ: Princeton University Press.

Tsebelis, G. and Money, J. (1997) *Bicameralism*. Cambridge: Cambridge University Press.

Ullmann, W. (1974) *Principles of Government and Politics in the Middle Ages*. New York: Barnes & Noble.

UNDP (1990-) *Human Development Report* (yearly). New York: Oxford University Press.

UNDP (1999) *Human Development Report For Central and Eastern Europe and the CIS*. New York: UNDP.

UNDP (2006) *Human Development Report;* data available at http://hdr.undp.org/hdr2006/statistics/.

United Nations (2006) available at www.un.org/members/growth.shtml.

US Census Bureau (2006) *International Data Base*; data available at www.census.gov/ipc/www/idbsprd.html.

Vile, M.J.C. (1998) *Constitutionalism and the Separation of Powers.* Indianapolis, MN: Liberty Fund.

Vincent, A. (1987) *Theories of the State.* Oxford: Blackwell.

Wade, R. (2003) *Governing the Market: Economic Theory and the Role of Government in East Asian Industrialization.* Princeton, NJ: Princeton University Press.

Watts, R.L. (1999) *Comparing Federal Systems in the 1990s* (2nd edn). Montreal: McGill-Queens University Press.

Weber, M. (1978) *Economy and Society: An Outline of Interpretive Sociology I–II.* Berkeley: University of California Press.

Weber, M. (1993) *The Sociology of Religion.* London: Beacon Press.

Weber, M. (1998) *The Agrarian Sociology of Ancient Civilizations.* London: Verso.

Weber, M. (2001) *Economie et société dans l'Antiquité.* Paris: La Decouverte.

Weber, M. (2003a) *General Economic History.* New York: Dover Publications.

Weber, M. (2003b) *The Protestant Ethic and the Spirit of Capitalism.* New York: Dover Publications.

Weingast, B.R. and Wittman, D. (eds) (2006) *The Oxford Handbook of Political Economy.* Oxford: Oxford University Press.

Wesson, R. (ed.) (1987) *Democracy: A Worldwide Survey.* New York: Praeger.

WIDER (2005) *World Income Inequality Database V 2.0a June 2005*; data available at www.wider.unu.edu/wiid/wiid.htm.

Wildavsky, A. (1979) *Speaking Truth to Power: The Art and Craft of Policy Analysis.* Boston, MA: Little, Brown.

Wildavsky, A. (1986) *Budgeting: A Comparative Theory of the Budgetary Process.* New Brunswick: Transaction Publishers.

Wildavsky, A. (2006) *Budgeting and Governing.* Vancouver: University of British Columbia Press.

Wilensky, H. (1975) *The Welfare State and Equality.* Berkeley: University of California Press.

Wilkinson, B. (1972) *The Creation of Medieval Parliaments.* New York: Wiley.

Williamson, E. (1992) *The Penguin History of Latin America.* Harmondworth: Penguin.

Williamson, O. (1985) *The Economic Institutions of Capitalism.* New York: Free Press.

Wittfogel, K. (1957) *Oriental Despotism.* New Haven, CT: Yale University Press.

Wolf, E.R. (1982) *Europe and the People Without History.* Berkeley: University of California Press.

Worger, W.H. and Clark, N.L. (2003) *South Africa: The Rise and Fall of Apartheid (SSH).* London: Longman.

World Bank (2000) *World Development Indicators 2000.* Washington, DC: World Bank (CD-ROM).

World Bank (2003) *World Bank Environment Survey*; available at http://info.worldbank.org/governance/wbes (Version: February 2003).

World Bank (2005) *Global Development Finance*, Washington, DC: World Bank; available at: www.worldbank.org/.

Woytinsky, W.S. and Woytinsky, E.S. (1953) *World Population and Production: Trends and Outlook.* New York: Twentieth Century Fund.

Yates, D.A. (1996) *The Rentier State in Africa: Oil Rent Dependency and Neo-colonialism in the Republic of Gabon.* Trenton, NJ: Africa Research & Publications.

Index